The Masks of Proteus

The Masks of Proteus: Canadian Reflections on the State

Philip Resnick

McGill-Queen's University Press
Montreal & Kingston • London • Buffalo

© McGill-Queen's University Press 1990
ISBN 0-7735-0731-0

Legal deposit first quarter 1990
Bibliothèque nationale du Québec

Printed in Canada on acid-free paper

This book has been published
with the help of a grant from the
Social Science Federation of Canada,
using funds provided by the
Social Sciences and Humanities
Research Council of Canada.

Canadian Cataloguing in Publication Data

Resnick, Philip, 1944–
The masks of Proteus

Includes bibliographical references.
ISBN 0-7735-0731-0

1. State, The
2. Canada–Politics and government.
I. Title.

JC325.R38 1990   320.1   C89-090358-1

To the memory of
C.B. Macpherson,
model scholar
and teacher to
a generation of
Canadian students

Of Proteus it is said
that chained in his noon-day sleep
he would from serpent to leopard to burning fire
change in an eye's twinkle
until reluctantly resuming his true shape,
divulging future he dived into the sea.
To theorists who call the state Leviathan,
dirt-caked Behemoth or Minotaur
may I imprudently suggest another metaphor?
Changing and unchanged,
master of the hidden symbolism
of half a universe,
is it not Proteus who beckons
through a century's carnage
delivering his secrets
to those who track him to his lair?

Contents

Acknowledgments xi
Introduction 3

PART ONE POLITICAL THEORY

1 Democracy and Its Philosophical Rivals:
Theories of the State 13

2 Jacobin Strains in Canada 38

3 "Dominion" and "Province," "Government" and "State" 54

4 Montesquieu Revisited 71

5 Burke or Rousseau? Parliament or People? 88

PART TWO POLITICAL ECONOMY AND SOCIOLOGY

6 Functions of the Modern State 109

7 The Limits of a Royal Commission 132

8 "Organized Capitalism" and the Canadian State 153

9 From Semi-periphery to Perimeter of the Core:
Canada in the Capitalist World Economy 179

PART THREE NATIONALISM, FEDERALISM, SOCIALISM

10 English Canada and Quebec: State v. Nation 207

11   Federalism and Socialism: A Reconsideration   221

12   Democracy, Socialism, and the State   245

Notes   265
Index   321

Acknowledgments

The author has incurred a number of debts.

To several institutions. The University of British Columbia granted me a sabbatical year 1987-8 and a Killam Faculty Research Fellowship that allowed me to complete this study. The Département de science politique at the Université de Montréal and its chair, Denis Monière, provided a very convivial environment during that same year, 1987-8, which I spent at that institution. A number of universities – Alberta, British Columbia, Concordia, Laval, McGill, Montréal, Ottawa, Queen's, and York – and organizations – l'Association d'économie politique, the Canadian Political Science Association, the International Political Science Association, and the Karl Polanyi Institute – provided venues where many of the chapters of this book were first presented.

To several publications which have allowed me to use, with permission, material – some of it here substantially revised – that had already been published: chapter 4, in *Canadian Journal of Political Science*, 20 no. 1 (March 1987), 97-115; chapter 6, in Ali Kazancigil, ed., *The State in Global Perspective*, Aldershot: U N E S C O/Gower, 1986, 155-82; chapter 7, in *Canadian Journal of Political Science*, 20 no. 2 (June 1987), 379-401; and chapter 11, in *Praxis International*, 5 no. 1 (1985), 400-20.

To a good number of friends and colleagues who, over the past few years, have provided comments, help, or suggestions, including André Bélanger, Alan Cairns, Duncan Cameron, Frank Cunningham, Daniel Drache, Graciela Ducatenzeiler, Philippe Faucher, Terry Heinrichs, James Mallory, Harvey Mitchell, Larry Pratt, John Richards, Garth Stevenson, and Reg Whitaker. In addition, Stephen Eggleston, my research assistant for three months in the summer of 1987 under the Challenge 87 program, did yeoman's labour in researching many of the references that would find their way into chapters 3, 5, and 9.

To Philip Cercone, for his very supportive role as an editor through the various stages of the manuscript, and to John Parry, for his assistance in copy-editing.

To Nancy Mina and Petula Muller for retyping portions of the manuscript.

To the Aid to Publishing Program of the Social Science Federation of Canada both for a grant and for the comments of its anonymous reviewers.

Most of all, to Mahie, Amos, and Jonah for putting up with the many months that went into the completion of the book, the change of cities, and the disruption of familiar routines.

The Masks of Proteus

Introduction

The theme of this volume is the protean character of state power. In reflecting over the past decade on the nature of the modern state, I have gradually concluded that no single, overarching theory can capture it in all its dimensions. Political theory has its contribution to make, as does a historically rooted sociology, or a broadly gauged political economy perspective. Yet no single approach can account for the very different features of state power across the twentieth century or for the multiple aspects of state power within any one society.

The grand constructs of the social sciences, regardless of their ideological underpinnings, are of only limited assistance. Whether we think of state power in terms of the friend–enemy distinction of Carl Schmitt, the arch-realist constitutional writer of Weimar and the early Nazi period,[1] or of the plurality of institutions and structures dear to liberal writers, or as a variant of Marx and Engels's executive committee of the ruling class, the dangers are great of lapsing into Procrustean-type argument. Not everything in politics, domestic or international, entails the designation of some as enemies and our striving for their elimination. Nor are structures of power always plural, always open to multitudinous influences and countervailing pressures. Nor is it necessarily the case that political rule and economic domination automatically overlap or that there is not a great measure of autonomy to the way in which political rulers, in capitalist or non-capitalist societies, go about their business.

Alternative approaches – for example, attempts at meta-theory that would draw many factors together in explaining the development of the state in general, or in specific societies – have their own difficulties. They may seek to pack a great deal of information, drawn from a variety of disciplines, within a single volume or collection of volumes. The result, however, may be too cumbersome for the reader to assimilate and ultimately fail to provide a grand synthesis of all that has come before.[2]

Still another tack would be to make the state itself the independent variable for sociological or historical inquiry.[3] Not only are there problems, however, flowing from the different ways in which the state can come to be defined from one century or half-continent to the next, but there is the additional problem of delineating the relationship between state and social forces. What are the boundaries between civil society and the state, and do the determining relations all flow in one direction?

In thinking about the voluminous literature that has been published on the modern state over the past two decades, the international colloquia and congresses,[4] I have been all too aware of the methodological pitfalls awaiting the would-be theorist. Nonetheless, I have also been conscious of a renewed interest in the state as a theme in political science and related disciplines, from the neo-Marxist writings of the late 1960s and since associated with Ralph Miliband, Nicos Poulantzas, Perry Anderson, Claus Offe, or Bob Jessop[5] to the more mainstream contributions of J.R. Strayer, Charles Tilly, Gianfranco Poggi, Reinhard Bendix, or Eric Nordlinger[6] to the neo-conservative critique of the welfare state and of the state *tout court* that was with us in the 1980s.[7]

The "state" provides an organizing theme around which an often-diffuse discipline, increasingly splintered into sub-fields of national and sub-national politics, comparative politics, political theory, public policy, political economy, or international relations, can find a minimum of coherence. At a deeper level, the state has acquired a new salience in all twentieth century societies, measured in terms of its economic or social activities, its claims to legitimacy, or its attempts to enforce its sovereignty in a world in which the number of sovereign nation-states has grown by leaps and bounds. Here is a development that captures the attention of analysts with diverse theoretical interests and approaches, whether they set out to examine the advanced capitalist countries, the countries of state socialism, or that whole range of polities making up the Third World.[8]

The author of a book-length study on the state may choose to apply a variety of approaches to the subject. A fundamental question will remain. Is there a single theme on which the reader can focus, one that expresses the author's central argument? What I propose by way of an answer is to add a new metaphor to the long list going back to the prince, Leviathan, or the social contract. The one I have chosen is that of Proteus, the god-figure in Greek mythology, known for his frequent changes in shape and appearance. Like Proteus, the state wears many masks – coercive and consensual, centralized and decentralized, democratic and anti-democratic, economic and social, sovereign and dependent. One can hardly hope to capture all its shifting and elusive shapes. Still, the very diversity of its manifestations rivets our attention. Why not, then, make a virtue of necessity and, eschewing the search for some grand theory, adopt as one's objective the tracking of Proteus in some of his multiple guises?

What follows are twelve chapters, linked by the common theme of the state, grouped according to themes: political theory or political discourse-type arguments (chapters 1–5), political economy/political sociology (chapters 6–9), and evocations of nationalism, federalism, and socialism (chapters 10–12). There are many cross-references back and forth, though no single chapter can lay claim to capturing more than a facet of the subject.

At the same time, my purpose in this book has been to address the theme of the state in a way that brings the discussion more directly home to Canada. My concerns with political theory, political economy, or political sociology are balanced by equal, if not greater concern with the specific state in which I happen to live – Canada – and I have not set out to write a book that would interest only the academically oriented student of politics. I do hope the latter will pay it some attention, but the book is aimed, at least as much, at a more diverse public, for which democratic citizenship requires close and careful thinking about the nature of politics in this and other twentieth-century societies.

The author has his normative biases. His inclinations lie to the left of the political spectrum, despite the ascendancy of neo-conservative arguments in the 1980s. Still, his views on socialism have evolved considerably over the past decade, from neo-Marxism to something a good deal closer to market socialism, and much influenced by radical democratic principles. This is reflected in a number of the chapters.

The prime focus of the book, none the less, is on the state. I would be the last to believe that authors on the left have any particular monopoly of virtue on this subject. As a result, there is in this volume a willingness to grapple with a wide variety of authors and approaches, regardless of ideological character, that may shed light on the Canadian and modern state. True to the theme of Proteus, I advance no single position throughout the volume and have made a quite conscious attempt to be as open-minded as possible in developing my arguments. If I have one commitment, it is to the value of conceptual playfulness in intellectual debate.

Let me, then, provide some guidance for the reader by setting out the themes of the twelve chapters that follow.

Chapter 1 tries to come to terms with views on the state that can be gleaned from classical political philosophy. I divide the corpus of Western political writings into five main categories, which I call the aristocratic, the republican, the philosophy of order, the liberal, and the democratic. While my own views tend strongly toward a democratic theory of the state, I argue the need for would-be defenders of a democratic public sphere to take seriously views emanating from proponents of the four other state paradigms.

Chapter 2 attempts to use one of the more powerful examples of state-building in the modern world, the Jacobin experience during the French Revolution, to illuminate certain aspects of state-building in Canada. My thesis is that, notwithstanding a counter-revolutionary tradition in Canada, there are some interesting parallels between those who sought to build a strong, centralized Canadian state – from Macdonald to Trudeau – and the Jacobin experience.

Chapter 3 sets out to examine the changing terminology of Canadian politics. Where once "dominion" held pride of place in official publications or academic writing, the term has virtually disappeared today. In its place, "government" and "state" have come to the fore. Underlying this transformation has been the increased importance of the state at both the federal and provincial levels.

Chapter 4 goes back to Montesquieu and the celebrated chapter on the English constitution in book x i of his *Spirit of the Laws*, suggesting that this may well constitute a fruitful source of analysis for the Canadian constitution. I argue that Montesquieu's doctrine is made up of two components, the theory of the mixed constitution – monarchy, aristocracy, and democracy – which goes back to the ancients; and the notion of a separation of powers – executive, legislative, and judicial – which strongly influenced the Americans and French at the time of their revolutions. Each component has been present in Canada, the first from 1867 down to the Second World War, and the second, increasingly, over the past decade(s).

Chapter 5 similarly goes back to political theory in trying to argue about Canada. The focus here is on Burke and Rousseau, who held diametrically opposed views on the nature of representation. While Burke's notion of the representative acting independently of his constituents is part and parcel of the notion of parliamentary sovereignty that has prevailed in Canada, there have occasionally been

Rousseauean impulses at work, speaking more directly to the notion of popular sovereignty. I outline some of these and conclude by arguing that we need more Rousseauean-type thinking about democracy in this country.

Chapter 6 attempts to make sense of some of the literature on the modern state, neo-Marxist and non-Marxist, and to speak more directly to the economic and social activities of the state and to the functions of sovereignty and legitimacy. In the second part of this chapter, I briefly address the nature of five major twentieth-century states, namely France, Germany, Great Britain, the United States, and the Soviet Union.

Chapter 7 addresses the image of the state that emerges from the opening chapter of the Macdonald Commission Report and from five of the research volumes prepared for this commission. While there are several individual contributions of note contained in the volumes under review, my overall conclusion is that both the commission and its researchers fall far short of providing us with a convincing analysis of the Canadian state.

Chapter 8 makes use of a construct – "organized capitalism," which originated with the Austro-Marxist theorist Rudolf Hilferding – in trying to chart the economic role of the Canadian state over the past century. My thesis, in a nutshell, is that the logic for state growth, at least until recently, can be related to the need to help organize capitalist development and to tendencies toward greater concentration within international and Canadian capitalism. It is my contention that "organized capitalism" may allow us to synthesize a number of diverse approaches to and interpretations of Canadian state development that have been offered hitherto by economic historians, political scientists, and others.

Chapter 9 takes as its point of departure the theoretical constructs of Immanuel Wallerstein regarding centre, semi-periphery, and periphery in the capitalist world economy. I argue that Canada, in fact, has moved from what could be called a semi-peripheral position earlier to one that lies on the perimeter of the core. The chapter gives a number of arguments – economic and political – for such a classification and in the process says something about the nature of sovereignty in the contemporary state-system.

In Chapter 10, the focus of attention is the rather different relationships between state and nation that have existed in English Canada and in Quebec. In English Canada, state precedes nation, so that even today the sense of nationalism is relatively weaker within English-Canadian civil society. Conversely, in Quebec the sense of nation precedes the existence of any French-Canadian/Quebec state and has continued to be deeply rooted in civil society. Some of the conflict between English Canada and Quebec can be illuminated by the rather different roles that state and nation have played within each society.

Chapter 11 looks at the problematic relationship between socialism and federalism from the nineteenth century on. There was a strong centralizing component to socialist theory going back to the Jacobins, hostile to anything threatening the unity of the post-revolutionary state. Yet the reality of nationality conflict forced socialists of the Marxist-Leninist variety to come to terms with federalism when they came to power and has forced Western socialists and social democrats to temper their views on federalism over time. Canadian socialists, too, after a much more negative view in the 1930s, have come to accept the underlying premises of a federal-type state and should, in my opinion, no longer identify socialism automatically with centralized state power.

In chapter 12 I explore three different types of left argument in the twentieth century – social democratic, Marxist-Leninist, and what I call the alternative left – and the diverging positions each has taken on questions of democracy, socialism, and the state. I underline some of the shortcomings of each and, after a short excursus into classical political thought, suggest the need for rather different approaches if socialism is to retain any real appeal in the late twentieth century.

Such then are the chapters that make up this volume. The author makes no claims to be comprehensive or all-inclusive – many possible themes have been omitted, and a lot more could have been said about the subjects treated. What I have sought to do is to open up certain subjects for investigation. Is it helpful to bring Montesquieu or Jacobinism to bear in thinking about the Canadian state? Are Burke and Rousseau useful references in focusing on the roots of notions of sovereignty in this country? Is the view of nation and state one and the same in Quebec and English Canada? Has the pattern of Canadian state development been one of "organized capitalism" for much of the twentieth century, and have we in the recent period acceded to a position within the world capitalist system that can be termed "perimeter of the core"? How might we begin to develop more democratic political institutions in the late twentieth century, and what might be required to make socialism more relevant to our concerns?

In exploring these questions, the volume sets out to advance our reflections on an institution – the state – that in Canada as elsewhere, has come to occupy a central place. No apology need be offered for having chosen so grandiose a topic. Canadian political science can only gain from broadening its horizons and bringing a large comparative perspective to bear on its inquiries. It will be for the reader to determine whether this work succeeds in the objective it has set itself – uncovering some of the many masks Proteus has come to wear in this century. Nothing, however, would please the author more than to see wide-ranging debate about the theme addressed here, not only within the rarefied circles of Canadian political science, but within the Canadian polity at large.

PART ONE

Political Theory

CHAPTER ONE

Democracy and Its Philosophical Rivals: Theories of the State

In trying to come to terms with the nature of the modern state, we can gain much by going back to political theory. What images or paradigms of the state do we find in the works of the great theorists and philosophers? How might we classify them, the better to see the choices that we ourselves, in the late twentieth century, may face?

At the risk of over-simplification, I would like to suggest a five-fold typology of political theories of the state: (1) aristocratic, (2) republican, (3) the philosophy of order, (4) liberal, and (5) democratic. These do not necessarily exist in airtight compartments, but are often jumbled together, as in aristocratic republicanism, or coexist in political thinkers whose work cannot be pigeon-holed – for example, Machiavelli, Montesquieu, Hegel. However, this exercise in classification may be helpful if, in the spirit of Weberian ideal types, it allows us better to glean values underlying the larger corpus of Western writing and better to understand how these rival approaches differ. In the process, if I may confess to a hidden agenda, we may find reasons to ground a democratic theory of the state – the one to which, normatively, this author strongly subscribes – in a way that incorporates at least some of the principles these other alternatives suggest.

Let us take each of these approaches in turn.

An aristocratic theory of the state is one that assumes that there is a small group of people that, by reason of birth or training, is especially fit for the business of rule.

Plato is a prime example of this approach, arguing that, even more than the art of the physician or the captain of a ship, that of a would-be ruler of men is highly specialized in character and should be entrusted only to those with the necessary knowledge and quality of character, namely, philosopher-kings. His three-class myth of the gold, silver, and bronze in the Republic; his theory of justice, with each class doing that for which it is most fit; and the elaborate pedagogical program he outlines for the education of his ruling class all bespeak a view that a specialized elité is of the essence to the good state.[1]

If some elements in the Republic, such as communism of property for the ruling class, are not compatible with the landed estates we associate with aristocratic rule, in the Laws Plato is perfectly pre-pared to bring landed property back in. Plato's version in the Repub-lic further differs from that of traditional aristocracy, since there is potentially a meritocratic component to recruitment into his ruling class and demotion out of it. I emphasize potentially, since he fails to provide any fool-proof mechanism by which this promotion or demotion is to occur. But unlike the Woods who, in their treatment of Plato, tend to equate aristocratic with the land-owning class of classical Marxism,[2] I propose to use the term more broadly. There is in Plato both a meritocratic component, as in the Republic, and a more traditionally grounded argument in terms of property in land, as in the Laws, for an aristocratic type of state.

Aristotle, too, fits under this rubric. In the Politics, he calls a popu-lation royal that would "produce a breed of outstanding virtue fit-ting it for leadership in the state," and "aristocratic" one that is "governed by those whose virtue equips them to be leaders in the holding of offices in the state."[3] From his negative comments about the members of the banausic (mechanical) classes and his depreca-tory view of the undisciplined lives that democracy tends to foster to his praise for the leisured life and the training in virtue that ought to characterize it,[4] his writing is imbued with an aristocratic ethos. If he disdains Plato's meritocratic and communistic extremes, and has at least grudging praise for the less egalitarian, more agrarian-based democratic models, his philosophy is of and for the well-raised aris-tocrat who alone has the quality of great-souledness (megapsychia) that attaches to political, no less than to philosophical, undertak-ings.

Cicero is best seen as an aristocratic republican, offering a defence of the institutions of the late Roman Republic, even while defending the privileges and powers of the senatorial caste of which he was an eminent member. He excoriates the advocates of agrarian laws in words that defenders of aristocratic privilege through the ages would echo: "Those who wish to become popular and, for this motive, propose agrarian laws to expel the legitimate owners from their land, or insistently demand the remission of debts at the expense of creditors, sap the foundation of the state ... What sort of equity would entail taking away from its owner a field which had belonged to his family for many years or even centuries, to hand it over to some intruder?"[5] He makes of aristocracy one of the three elements, along with monarchy and popular power, in his ideal constitution, associating it with the principle of authority, without which the best of states would perish.[6] For all his lip-service to the libertas associated with the republic, Cicero has little but disdain for the common people and for their poverty, which, for him, is synonymous with evil.[7]

An aristocratic spirit can be found pervading much of early modern political thought, from Machiavelli to James Harrington, from Montesquieu to Edmund Burke. For these and many other writers the best of states is one that gives due weight to the interests of this class. Thus Machiavelli, in his *Discourses*, reproduces the Ciceronian attack on agrarian laws: "The Roman plebs were not content with having made their position secure in regard to the nobles by the creation of tribunes, which necessity constrained them to demand; but, having acquired them, at once began to quarrel with the nobles out of ambition, and to demand also a share in the distribution of honours and of property than which man esteems nothing more highly."[8]

James Harrington, in his *Oceana*, insists on the stabilizing role of a nobility: "For where there is not a nobility to bolt out the people, they are slothful, regardless of the world and the public interest of liberty, as even that of Rome had been without her gentry; wherefore let the people embrace the gentry, in peace as the light of their eyes, and in war as the trophy of their arms."[9]

For Montesquieu, aristocracy introduces a moderating element into the state, requiring appropriate recognition: "Il y a toujours dans un Etat des gens distingués par la naissance, les richesses, ou les honneurs; mais s'ils n'y avaient qu'une voix comme les autres, la liberté commune serait leur esclavage. La part qu'ils ont à la législation doit donc être proportionée aux autres avantages qu'ils ont dans l'Etat."[10] And for Burke, "Prescription is the most solid of all titles, not only to property but, which is to secure that property, to government."[11]

Long after the French Revolution, an aristocratic view of the state carries on. This is most evident in the legitimism of counter-revolutionary writers like Bonald, de Maistre, or Chateaubriand in France, in the dominant political credos of Prussia, Austro-Hungary, or tsarist Russia, and in the lingering aristocratic bias of English-speaking conservatism as well.[12]

Yet there are two other forms, meritocratic rather than hereditary in character, that the aristocratic principle can take in the modern world. One is élitist theory, associated with twentieth-century writers like Mosca, Pareto, and Michels and, if we go back a little, with the philosophical views of Social Darwinism or Nietzsche.

The essence of such theories is that some – by dint of their own efforts, or natural superiority, or hierarchial position – are either fit to rule or destined to rule over others: "In all societies ... two classes of people appear – a class that rules and a class that is ruled. The first class, always the less numerous, performs all political functions, monopolizes power and enjoys the advantages that power brings ... All ruling classes tend to become hereditary in fact if not in law ... Everywhere those who have reached the top rungs on the social ladder have set up defences for themselves and their children against those who also wished to climb."[13] Democracy is for Nietzsche a hopeless dream – an expression of the "herd instinct" at its worst – inevitably giving way either to the triumph of mediocrity or to the ascendancy of some dominant élite (or Übermensch).

Elitist theory can range from a fairly conservative notion of those groups who ought, by reason of background or training, to fill important positions in the state (Mosca), to revisionist liberal interpretations that look to the masses in modern states to choose, in periodic elections, between competing political élites to rule over them (Schumpeter[14]), to radical versions as in fascism, that look to charismatic individuals or self-selected groups to provide the impulse and direction ostensibly lacking in Western societies in their period of alleged decline.

A second version of meritocracy is associated with the Leninist theory of the vanguard party. Revolution, according to the Lenin of *What Is to Be Done?*, cannot, at least in a backward and policed society like tsarist Russia's, be carried out spontaneously by the broad masses of the working people. Rather, it requires a small group of politically trained cadre, steeped in Marxism and revolutionary theory, committed to a long-term rather than a day-to-day perspective, to bring revolutionary ideas to the working class and prepare the overthrow of a reactionary regime. The vanguard theory of the party, which underlies all successful examples of Marxist-Leninist revolution in this century, is implicitly aristocratic in character. Only some, by dint of their special efforts or proven commitment, are worthy of membership in the party of the working class. Within the party, democratic centralism prevails, with the emphasis usually lying on the authoritative transmission of decisions from the higher levels to the lower, from a leadership endowed with superior knowledge and understanding of the needs of the broad strata of society to party members, and thence to the masses. The party-state, at least as it has developed hitherto, bears more analogies to Plato's *Republic* of philosopher-kings than to the "self-governing producers" Marx sketched in *The Civil War in France*.[15]

Republican theory tends to look to some balance or mixture in the state, as between social classes or political institutions.

Classical republicanism, as in Polybius and Cicero, speaks the language of the mixed constitution: "We must regard as the best constitution a combination of all these three varieties (i.e. kingship, aristocracy, democracy)."[16] "The best form of political constitution is one where the three sorts of government, royal, aristocratic, and popular, are rationally mixed."[17] Consuls require supply from the Senate and must in turn give an account of the administration to the people. Treaties negotiated by the Senate must be ratified by the people, while the tribunes have the power to block much that the Senate might do. The people, in turn, depend upon the Senate for contracts and for judgments, while they are subject to consular authority when they find themselves as soldiers in the field. "When one part having grown out of proportion to the other aims at supremacy and tends to become too predominant, it is evident that, as for the reasons above given, none of the three is absolute."[18] There is nothing inherently democratic about such republicanism, though its advocates are quick to wrap themselves in a mantle of civic virtue and champion forms of citizen participation within such a framework.

Machiavelli, for example, shares with Cicero and Polybius a commitment to the mixed constitution: "The blending of these estates made a perfect commonwealth."[19] He is also quick to praise that "love of country" that for the Romans "weighed more than any other consideration."[20] He sees greater danger to liberty from the tyranny of a single prince than from the actions of the people[21] and stresses the creative tension that flowed from the conflict between plebs and Senate: "In every republic there are two different dispositions, that of the populace and that of the upper class ... all legislation favourable to liberty is brought about by the clash between them."[22]

Yet that same Machiavelli is not prepared to sacrifice unduly at the altar of popular sovereignty – "A multitude without a head is useless."[23] Nor does he have any illusion about the very different types of political discourse to be found "in piazza" and "in palazzo,"[24] investing a good deal more in the latter than in the former. Well might Friedrich Meinecke write: "[Machiavelli] was far from believing, with closed eyes, in the natural and incorruptible virtue of the republican; moreover, he conceived of the republic from the top down, from the point of view of the governors rather than the popular masses."[25] This position, I believe, is a good deal closer to the historical essence of republicanism than the emphasis on civic participation that leads contemporary theorists of the republican tradition like Pocock to overlook its strongly anti-democratic biases.[26]

From this vantage point, Harrington, Montesquieu, and even Madison can be seen as exemplars of a classically republican tradition: "Let a commonwealth be equal or unequal, it must consist, as hath been shown by reason and all experience of the three general orders, that is to say, of the senate debating and proposing, of the people resolving and of the magistracy executing."[27] writes Harrington in his *Oceana*. Making clear his own anti-democratic sentiments, he adds for good measure: "Athens, as hath been shown, was plainly lost through the want of a good aristocracy; but a sufficiency of an aristocracy goes demonstrably upon the hand of a nobility or gentry, for that the politics can be mastered without study, or that the people can have leisure to study, is a vain imagination."[28]

Montesquieu, for his part, created the modern formula of the separation of powers. As I argue in chapter 4, this development in turn is closely linked to the classical republican doctrine of the mixed constitution. True liberty lies where the legislative, executive, and judicial are separated from each other, where neither a single ruler, nor the nobility, nor the people controls by itself the three compartments of state. The implications of this doctrine for revolutions like the American and French are obvious. Yet Montesquieu is unambiguous about his anti-democratic sentiments: "Il y avait un grand vice dans la plupart des anciennes républiques: c'est que le peuple avait droit d'y prendre des résolutions actives, et qui demandent quelque exécution, chose dont il est entièrement incapable."[29] "La démocratie et l'aristocratie ne sont point des Etats libres par leur nature. La liberté politique ne se trouve que dans les gouvernements modérés."[30]

Madison in the *Federalist Papers* looks to checks and balances as the crowning attribute of republican government: "In the compound republic of America, the power surrendered by the people is first divided between two distinct governments, and then the portion allotted to each subdivided among distinct and separate departments ... The different governments will control each other, at the same time that each will be controlled by itself."[31]

While he is more prepared than his republican forbears formally to trace all forms of governmental authority back to the people,[32] Madison is no less hostile to any direct expression of the popular will. Pure democracies, like those of the ancient world, "consisting of a small number of citizens who assemble and administer the government in person ... have ever been spectacles of turbulence and contention; have ever been found incompatible with personal security or the rights of property, and have in general been as short in their lives as they have been violent in their deaths."[33] It is to a well-ordered republic, with an indirectly elected Senate and president, an appointed judiciary, and checks and balances within and between federal and state governments that Madison looks for protection against "the abuses of liberty"[34] or "rage for an equal division of property"[35] that threaten the United States more surely than the abuses of power characteristic of despotically run states. Madison, in short, is less than an effusive democrat.

For the philosophers of order, the state is the incarnation of a supreme temporal or moral authority, which forces potentially recalcitrant citizens or subjects to obey its higher commands.

Exponents of such a philosophy can range from believers in realpolitik ("the state can do no wrong") to theorists of sovereignty, from Christian divines looking to the city of god to philosophers of history mapping the Weltgeist and its unfolding here on earth. The names I will include here are those of Thucydides, St Augustine, Machiavelli, Jean Bodin, Thomas Hobbes, Hegel, and Carl Schmitt.

For Thucydides, writing his *History of the Peloponnesian War* at the end of the fifth century B C, war unleashes forms of human behaviour that might not be seen in more normal periods. Civil strife rages through the smaller city-states variously allied to Athens or to Sparta, while the actors in that conflict often speak their thoughts with a bluntness that might otherwise be hidden from sight.

One such example is the famous dialogue at Melos between the invading Athenians and the inhabitants of a small island of would-be neutrals of Spartan descent. There are few more chilling renditions of the doctrine that "might makes right," and that political rule – both in international relations and within the state – is ultimately a matter not of morality and justice but of power in the raw. Here are the words that Thucydides, accurately or inaccurately, puts into the mouths of the Athenian envoys. "You know as well as we know that right, as the world goes, is only in question between equals in power, while the strong do what they can and the weak suffer what they must."[36] "The question (before you is one) of self-preservation, and of not resisting those who are far stronger than you in author-ity."[37] "Of the gods we believe, and of men we know, that by a necessary law of their nature they rule wherever they can."[38] No nonsense about aristocratic entitlements, no fussing about republi-can constraints in a theory of the state that makes the power of the strong and the obedience of the weak the well-spring of all authority.

More surprising to some may be the expression of identical senti-ments by St Augustine in *The City of God*, written at the beginning of the fifth century A D. Throughout this work he contrasts the imper-fect city of men with the perfect city of god. In the former, it is fallen man, sinful man, who dominates; in the latter, we have the after-world of redeemed man. In the former there is a libido dominandi – a lust for power – that characterizes human beings, necessitating in its turn the hard and heavy hand of temporal authority. As one of Augustine's more knowledgable commentators writes: "The basic task of the state is the absolutely crucial function of preserving 'the peace of Babylon', maintaining enough external peace and order among sinful, quarrelsome, jealous lustful men so that they will not completely destroy one another – so that they can obtain by their united efforts 'the things which are helpful in this life.' "[39]

Augustine has no illusion regarding the less than moral grounding of the temporal state: "And so justice removed, what are kingdoms but great robber bands? And what are robber bands but small king-doms? ... Kingdoms (are characterized) not by the removal of covet-ousness but by the addition of impunity."[40] Like Thucydides' Athenian envoys, Augustine's temporal rulers speak the language of force in ordering the lives of their subjects. The latter, at least within a Christian state, have but one temporal duty – to obey.

Machiavelli's amorality/immorality is legendary, and the mirror he held up to princes subordinates means to the end of achieving and retaining power. It matters little whether Machiavelli's version of statecraft was ultimately born of the love of country that dominates the final chapter of his *Prince* or emerges from his *History of Florence*. What is clear is his praise for those who use force or cunning to build states and impose their authority: "All armed prophets have con-quered and unarmed prophets have come to grief."[41] "The fact is that a man who wants to act virtuously in every way necessarily comes to grief among so many who are not virtuous."[42] "It is far better to be feared than loved if you cannot be both."[43] "One must be a fox to recognize traps, and a lion to frighten off wolves."[44]

His *Prince* yields little to Augustine in its bleak reading of human nature – half-beast, half-man; half-law, half-force – but there is no heavenly city to wipe away the muck of our earthly passage. His

Prince a steady bed-companion of Richelieu and Napoleon, Machiavelli has become a synonym for reason of state in its purest form. The republicanism of his *Discourses* in no way diminishes this side of his legacy.

Bodin coins the term *sovereignty* – "the most high, absolute and perpetual power over the citizens and subjects of a commonwealth" – to emphasize the need for a single source of power in a France bedevilled by religious conflict. "Tout aussi que le navire n'est plus que bois sans forme de vaisseau ... aussi sans puissance souveraine qui unit tous les membres et parties d'icelle, et tous les ménages et collèges en un corps, la République n'est plus."[45] He categorically rejects the notion of a mixed constitution – "attendu que les marques de soveraineté sont indivisibles" – arguing that these have never existed and cannot be imagined.[46] Even as the father commands complete obedience within his family, up to and including the power of life and death over his offspring, so the sovereign is in no way subject to the command of others and can lay down the law to his subjects. If there are some constraints on Bodin's monarch (for it is monarchy that he upholds over its rivals) – for example, divine law and property holdings – his powers are extensive, including those of legislation, of peace and war, of naming the principal officers of state, of pardon, and of final resort.[47] The emphasis in his writings is on the quasi-absolute authority of the sovereign and on the obligation of a citizen "to be a frank subject of another's sovereignty."[48]

Bodin's absolutism and Hobbes's are not worlds apart in their consequences, though the epistemological underpinnings of Hobbes's theory are more sophisticated and modern. There is a striking mechanism to Hobbes's reading of human nature in book 1 of *Leviathan* and a new note of individualism in the description of the human passions. From these, he proceeds to a discussion of a putative state of nature. As Hobbes's readers know, the relentless competitiveness and invasiveness of men – the war of all against all that characterizes the state of nature – roots out all industry and culture, leading to continual fear and danger of violent death, and ultimately serves to justify the attempt to attain some lasting peace.[49]

That peace can be achieved only when all willingly surrender their strength and power "upon one man or one assembly," namely, a sovereign.[50] As in Bodin, this sovereign prescribes all rules for civil society and has the right of judicature, of making peace and war, of choosing ministers and counsellors, and of decreeing which opinions and doctrines shall hold reign.[51] Not for Hobbes any "mixt government,"[52] nor for him any excessive liberty for the subject inspired by Greek or Latin authors.[53] If he allows certain lapses from the doctrine of absolute obedience – for example, the need of the sovereign to extend effective protection to those under his jurisdiction – his dominant refrain is celebration of the state as the highest form of authority "under the immortal god."[54] Without the order that this mortal god, the state, imposes, men will fall victims to their own covetousness and pride and lapse into a state of civil war not unlike the one that England of the 1640s was to know. Human nature itself dictates the need for strong authority.

Hegel's is a more complex and less single-mindedly political philosophy than Hobbes's. And there are aspects of Hegel's political doctrine, such as his prescient distinction between civil society and state and his phenomenology of human emancipation that open the door to potentially liberal or revolutionary theories.

Yet there is also in the *Philosophy of Right* and the *Philosophy of History* a tendency to fetishize the state and identify it with the inner workings of the world-spirit itself: "All the value that man possesses, his spiritual reality, he possesses only through the state."[55] "Man must therefore venerate the state as a secular deity and observe that if it is difficult to comprehend nature, it is infinitely harder to understand the state."[56] "The state must be treated as a great architectonic structure, as a hieroglyph of the reason which reveals itself in actuality."[57] "War is the state of affairs which deals in earnest with the vanity of temporal goods and concerns ... by its agency ... the ethical health of peoples is preserved."[58]

If Hegel is not simply the state philosopher of Prussia, he none the less sees in the higher ethical life of the state an explanation and justification of the historical process, one in which war and conflict, domination and destruction, play a leading part. As Meinecke notes, "Since Hegel's time, Germans have tended to allow the problem of power an ever-larger place in their conception of the world."[59] This aspect of Hegel cannot simply be wished away.[60]

Finally, reference may be made to a twentieth century theorist, Carl Schmitt, whose support for Hitler during the first years of Nazi rule earns him the label "theorist of the Reich,"[61] but whose writings of the 1920s, such as *Political Theology, The Crisis of Parliamentary Democracy*, and *The Concept of the Political*,[62] were highly original works in the philosophy-of-order vein. Schmitt was strongly influenced by Hobbes, Machiavelli, and other "realistic" writers in his view of human nature: "True political theory postulates man as a corrupt being, that is to say as a dangerous, dynamic and perfectly problematic being."[63] At the heart of the political, and therefore of the state, for Schmitt, lies the ability to distinguish between friend and foe. While liberalism blurs this distinction, lulling itself with the religion of progress, the valorization of commerce, and a faith in parliamentary institutions,[64] the more acute theorists and practitioners of twentieth century statecraft, from Sorel to Lenin, like their sixteenth and seventeenth century predecessors, correctly recognized the importance of the direct use of force against their political enemies. The function of the state is to not be agnostic when faced with threats to its authority, in the economic, religious, or civil spheres. Rather, it is to act decisively, using emergency powers to the hilt. Hence Schmitt's unsentimental defence of sovereignty: "Sovereign is he who is in a position to decide on the state of exception."[65] And hence, too, his enunciation of a *doctrine* whose roots are steeped in the tradition of reason of state.[66]

Liberal theorists of the state emphasize the representative and limited character of state authority and the existence of a significant sphere of individual liberty – political, economic, and religious – for the citizens.

A large number of writers from the seventeenth century on could be encompassed under the above definition. Let me single out Locke, Montesquieu, Madison, Burke, Hegel, Constant, and J.S. Mill.

Central to Locke's explanation of individuals uniting into a commonwealth and putting themselves under government is "the mutual preservation of their lives, liberties, and estates which I call by the name 'Property.' "[67] Such a purpose is best realized not through some Hobbesian sovereign but through a more limited type of government, with a legislature "made up of representatives chosen for that time by the people"[68] and an executive who "is to be considered as the image, phantom, or representative of the commonwealth ... and thus (with) no will, no power, but that of the law."[69]

There are elements in Locke's *Second Treatise* – majority consent, the appeal to heaven – that, by certain interpretations, open the door to a more democratic type of theory.[70] Yet Locke's single-minded emphasis on the importance of property, in both its narrow and broad senses; his seeming exclusion of servants and labourers from any active sense of citizenship, viz. the notions of tacit consent;[71] his careful distinction between democracy and commonwealth;[72] and his attack on Spartacus and the type of levelling of property a successful slave rebellion in Italy during the first century B C would have entailed[73] speak to something a good deal less than democratic. Whether one sees in Locke an example of possessive individualism, or a defender of agrarian capitalism, or even an "unintended" bourgeois theorist of individual appropriation,[74] one gains little from over-emphasizing the "democratic" character of his liberalism.

What stands out, rather, in the *Two Treatises on Government* and in his *Letter on Toleration*, as in other writings, is consistent opposition to what we might call patriarchal or absolutist government, belief in the representative and therefore responsible character of government to those – essentially property-holders – who contract together to form civil society, and defence of a measure of liberty of conscience, speech, and the like, which are key attributes in an emerging liberal theory.

Montesquieu, whom I have already discussed under the headings of aristocratic and republican theory, also fits under my liberal rubric. He strongly defends the notion of representation in terms that pitch it against a more directly democratic conception of the state: "Le grand avantage des représentants c'est qu'ils sont capables de discuter les affaires. Le peuple n'y est point de tout propre; ce qui forme un des grands inconvénients de la démocratie."[75] He too holds liberty to be an important value, to be contrasted with the fear that is the very essence of despotism: "Il pourra arriver que la constitution sera libre, et que le citoyen ne le sera point ... Il n'y a que la disposition des lois et même des lois fondamentales, qui forme la liberté dans son rapport avec la constitution."[76] And he praises commerce and its civilizing role, in chapters that seem to anticipate the paeans to economic liberty that Adam Smith and others were soon to pen.[77]

This is not to reduce Montesquieu to a pure liberal. He can be acerbic in his denunciation of luxury and wealth, i.e. economic liberalism, in the name of a higher republican virtue: "Les politiques grecs, qui vivaient dans le gouvernement populaire, ne reconnaissaient d'autre force qui pût les soutenir que celle de la vertu. Ceux d'aujourd'hui ne nous parlent que de manufactures, de commerce, de finance, de richesse et de luxe même."[78] The origins of his separation-of-powers doctrine reside in earlier theories of the mixed constitution that had nothing to do with liberalism. And there are more than passing indications of an aristocratic/monarchical sympathy.[79] But he has his liberal edge as well.

Burke is another writer in whom liberal and illiberal sentiments overlap. His reverence for the state, in passages of his *Reflections on the Revolution in France*, seems to approach that of an aristocratic critic of the commercial classes: "The state ought not to be considered as nothing better than a partnership agreement in the trade of pepper and coffee, calico or tobacco, or some other such low concern, to be taken up for a little temporary interest, and to be dissolved by the fancy of the parties. It is to be looked on with some other reverence."[80]

Yet in writings like *Thoughts and Details on Scarcity* and in his letters and speeches, he becomes the oracle of the limited state: "The state ought to confine itself to what regards the state or the creatures of that state; namely the exterior establishment of its religion, its magistracy; its revenue; its military force ... in a word, to everything that is truly and properly public. Any kind of regulation 'against free trade in provisions' is 'senseless, barbarous, and wicked.' The danger 'is in governments intermeddling too much.' "[81]

Burke's theory of representation is the epitome of an élitist liberalism in which members of Parliament, not their constituents, become the repositories of a true philosophy of state: "When leaders choose to make themselves bidders at an auction of popularity, their talents in the construction of the state will be of no use. They will become flatterers, instead of legislators, the instruments, not the guides of the people."[82] "Parliament is not a *congress* of ambassadors from different and hostile interests, which interests each must maintain as an agent and advocate, against other agents and advocates; but Parliament is a *deliberative* assembly of *one* nation with *one* interest that of the whole."[83]

Just as he shuns "the tyranny of the multitude,"[84] or a Jacobinism which he identifies with "a contempt of property ... that has led to all the other evils which have ruined France," so Burke finds, in the time-honoured principles of a less than democratic British constitution, the essence of his own sometime liberal credo: "The distinguishing part of our Constitution is its liberty ... To preserve that liberty inviolate seems the particular duty and proper trust of a member of the House of Commons. But the liberty, the only liberty I mean, is a liberty connected with order ... No experience has taught us that in any other course or method than that of an *hereditary crown* our liberties can be regularly perpetuated and preserved sacred as our *hereditary right*."[86] (For discussion of the influence that Burke's theory of representation has had on Canadian political culture in particular, see chapter 5.)

For Madison (and Hamilton), representation is the very essence of a republican system of government: "The two great points of difference between a democracy and a republic are: first the delegation of the government in the latter to a small number of citizens by the rest; secondly, the greater number of citizens and greater sphere of country over which the latter may be extended."[87] True, the representatives are not likely to be drawn from all classes of society, since "landholders, merchants, and men of the learned professions" are certain to dominate.[88] But these will be forced to compromise with one another and "curry the favour of the people"; moreover, the interests of the former are held to be compatible with those of the less-propertied sections of society, such as mechanics.

Madison and Hamilton's concept of representation certainly is bourgeois and to it is joined a quite explicit defence of property in their larger scheme. They excoriate a rage "for an equal division of property,"[89] speak of the need to protect it "against those irregular and high-handed combinations which sometimes interrupt the ordinary course of justice,"[90] and identify it as a leading principle, along with liberty, in republican government.[91] The spirit of their liberalism has little to do with equality of condition.

It does, however, emphasize limited government and individual rights. Thus Madison argues against "bills of attainder, *ex post facto* laws, and laws impairing the obligation of contract" as "contrary to the first principles of the social contract," defending their exclusion by the Philadelphia convention as a "constitutional bulwark in favour of personal security and private rights."[92] He emphasizes the need "to guard one part of the society against the injustice of the other part,"[93] i.e. civil and religious rights, which a federal republican form of government can best secure. And Hamilton looks to an independent judiciary to safeguard both the constitution and the rights of individuals.[94]

Although I have included Hegel under the philosophers of order, it is also necessary to recognize a more liberal element in his thought. Hegel was one of the first to speak of civil society as a distinct moment lying between the family and the state. Work and property are situated there, reflecting Hegel's attempt to incorporate the insights of classical political economy – Smith, Say, and Ricardo – into his larger philosophy.[95] "What Hegel made the times aware of with the phrase 'civil society' was nothing less than the result of the modern revolution; the emergence of a depoliticized society through the shift of society's focal point towards economics."[96] If Hegel's "civil society" includes institutions like the judiciary and the police (or public authority) that we hardly associate with the term, it also points to a sphere of private activity separate from and in contradistinction to that carried out in the public sphere. In this sense, it captures the essence of the liberal transformation of European society which created an economic and contractual sphere lying outside state control, and suggests a more enduring contrast, on which could build today's critics of an excessive state role (liberals, but also conservatives and non-statist socialists – eastern European dissidents no less than Latin American victims of authoritarianism).[97]

Other features of Hegel's philosophy blend into liberal theory. He makes law the defining characteristic of both the duties of the state and the rights of the citizen.[98] He seems to echo Montesquieu in the celebration of constitutional government: "Despotism means any state of affairs where law has disappeared and where the particular will as such, whether of a monarch or a mob, counts as law or rather takes the place of law; while it is precisely in legal, constitutional government that sovereignty is to be found as the moment of ideality – the ideality of the particular spheres and functions."[99] He too looks to deputies – the estates and their assembly – as one part of the constitution, along with an aristocratic house and the crown.[100] And like other eighteenth and nineteenth century liberals, he spurns a more participatory vision of politics: "Another presupposition of the idea that all should participate in the business of the state is that everyone is at home in this business, a ridiculous notion."[101]

Benjamin Constant's distinction between the liberty of the ancients and the liberty of the moderns is particularly insightful on the contrast between liberalism and classical notions of democracy. The ancient citizen, Constant argues, was fully sovereign when it came to questions of peace and war or public deliberation; in his personal life he was circumscribed in all his movements.[102] By comparison, the modern citizen, for example in Great Britain or the United States, is fully free in his or her private life but can partake of sovereignty only momentarily and in a very limited way: "His personal influence is an imperceptible element in the social will which gives government its direction."[103]

Part of this transformation Constant attributes to the size of modern states; part to the spirit of commerce, which unlike war, inspires in people "un vif amour pour l'indépendance individuelle." Whatever the reasons, the goal of the moderns is not the active exercise of political rights so much as the security of private activities against interference by the state. There is little to be gained in transporting ancient theories of collective sovereignty à la Rousseau into the modern world. Instead, one must make do with a representative system, "an organization by means of which a nation discharges onto several individuals what it cannot or will not do itself ... it is the power of proxy handed over to a certain number of men by the mass of the people who want their interests to be defended and lack the time to always do so themselves."[104] If Constant has certain fears of citizens becoming absorbed only by the pursuit of individual interest, he none the less looks to individual rights and the political and economic independence of citizens as the underpinning of a liberal-type state.

Nor would John Stuart Mill have differed with him on this score. Mill extols individual liberty against the despotism of custom and belief: "Unless opinions favourable to democracy and aristocracy, to property and to equality, to cooperation and to competition, to luxury and to abstinence ... are expressed with equal freedom ... there is no chance of both elements obtaining their due; one scale is sure to go up and the other down."[105] A state, in the end, is worth little more than the worth of the citizens who make it up: "A state which dwarfs its men, in order that they may be more docile instruments in its hands even for beneficial purposes will find that with small men no great thing can really be accomplished."[106] Liberty of speech and of opinion must be maximized, while "the absorption of all the principal ability of the country into the governing body is fatal."[107]

Mill's ideal government is representative in character. Not all peoples, alas, are equally suitable to sustain it, but those that have sufficient craving for personal independence will develop "a government strictly limited in its powers and attributions, required to hold its hands from over-meddling."[108] Mill looks to the reform of the franchise to make of Parliament a body more broadly representative of the population of the day, especially the working class. Yet the reservations he adds suggest that as late as the mid-nineteenth century, liberalism had still not made its peace with democracy.

Mill is quite concerned about "the danger of class legislation" stemming from democracy,[109] and seeks ways of heading off the Demos's worst intentions. One such technique is a commission of legislation, a small body of officials appointed for five years at a time, who alone could draft the legislation for consideration by Parliament.[110] A second would see those receiving parish relief (the mid-nineteenth century equivalent of welfare recipients) excluded from the franchise.[111] A third, which, from Mill's point of view, would maintain a better class balance than one person – one vote, lay in the provision for plural votes for certain categories of the population: "An employer of labour is on the average more intelligent than a labourer ... A foreman is generally more intelligent than an ordinary labourer ... A banker, merchant, or manufacturer is likely to be more intelligent than a tradesman ... The liberal professions imply, of course, a still higher degree of instruction."[112]

While Mill is more than a laissez-faire liberal (cf. all the exceptions to laissez-faire he outlines in his *Principles of Political Economy*)[113] and here and there shows real sympathy for what one might term political participation ("the ideally best form of government is that in which ... every citizen [is] at least occasionally called on to take an actual part in the government by the personal discharge of some public function, local or general"),[114] his instincts push him far more toward maximization of individual liberty than of that popular sovereignty that we associate with democracy.

Democratic theorists of the state emphasize economic and political equality, significant citizen participation in the political sphere, and popular sovereignty as the source of state authority.

The roots of democratic theory in the Western world go back to the Greeks. The model that we tend to summon up is that of Athens in the fifth and fourth centuries B C, with political power being vested in the ecclesia, or assembly, which all adult (male) citizens had the right to attend, and the boule, or council, whose membership was rotating and based on 500 individuals chosen by lot, 50 from each of the ten tribes, on an annual basis. The formula "archein kai archesthai" – ruling and being ruled in turn – seems to capture the underlying spirit very well.

For the critics of democracy, which includes almost all the political writers of antiquity from Plato and Aristotle to Cicero and Seneca, it was a system that tended to favour the poor over the leisured few, the ignorant over the enlightened, the unskilled over those with a special aptitude for the royal art of politics. Demagoguery, class division, and ultimately tyranny were its bitter fruits.

Yet democracy had its defenders, even if we are often forced to piece together their positions from the work of its opponents. The Pericles of Thucydides' funeral oration, for example, makes much of the participatory quality of citizenship in his city-state and of Athen's role as a model for all of Greece: "Our ordinary citizens ... are fair judges of public matters; for unlike any other nation, [we] regard him who takes no part in these duties not as unambitious but as useless."[115]

Protagoras, in the Platonic dialogue that bears his name, delivers one of the more eloquent defences of the inherent universality of political skills against the Socratic defenders of politics as specialized knowledge:

Hermes asked Zeus how he should impart justice and reverence among men: "Should he distribute them as the arts are distributed, that is to say, to a favoured few only ... or shall I give them to all?" "To all," said Zeus, "I should like them all to have a share; for cities cannot exist, if a few only share in the virtues, as in the arts." And this is the reason, Socrates, why the

Athenians and mankind in general, when the question relates to carpenter-
ing or any other mechanical art, allow but a few to share in their delibera-
tions ... But when they meet to deliberate about political virtue ... they are
patient of any man who speaks of them ... because they think that every
man ought to share in this sort of virtue, and that states could not exist if
this were otherwise.[116]

There is no need, of course, in invoking Athenian direct democracy, to make light of the very real limitations it must have in our
eyes. The exclusion of women from citizenship is the most obvious;
the institution of slavery – true of all the ancient world – another; the
imperialism Athens pursued in the aftermath of the Persian Wars yet
another. Nonetheless, there are good reasons why the Athenian
model has been invoked time and time again by those who aspire to
a more publicly rooted, face to face vision of community than is
realized in the modern nation-state.

The Greek concept of democracy is ultimately caught up with the
notion of equality. There are at least three different words that the
Greeks used to describe this concept – each, I think, highly relevant
to our concerns.

Isonomía is the term Herodotus[117] uses to describe a democratic
regime and can be translated literally as equality through the law or
equality before the law.[118] This can be contrasted with oligarchical
and aristocratic regimes, which excluded the many from the very
definition of citizenship, while providing quite different privileges
and powers to the few.

Isegoría is a term referring to the right to speak in the assembly. It
originates some time early in the fifth century B C[119] and speaks to
the formal right given to all Athenian citizens, not only to attend
meetings of the ecclesia and, with time, to receive payment for that
attendance but also to make their views known. Historical evidence
would suggest that this remained something of a pious wish, since
only a small minority of those attending the assemblies ever
spoke.[120] But as an aspiration to significant equality in citizen participation, it is well worth our noting.

Isomoiría is a term referring to equal division of the earth. It is used
by Solon in one of his political poems when he tells us that he did
not proceed, as some were insisting, to redivide the land of Attica
equally.[121] It can be seen, however, as the motivating inspiration for
the indebted and the landless – not only in sixth-century B C Athens
but, say, in the Rome of the second century B C – who sought
through agrarian laws more egalitarian distribution of the economic
wealth on which to ground the polis or res publica.

My argument is that a democratic theory of the state (or public sphere) must speak to all three of these elements. First, it recognizes the equality of legal rights or citizenship, disdaining special privileges or powers for some, whether based on heredity, wealth, and social or political position. Second, it recognizes further the need for citizens to be able to participate in some ongoing manner in political affairs. That such a condition can be fully satisfied through the casting of a ballot in elections every four or five years, when competing political parties present their programs to a largely atomized electorate, is highly dubious. "The right to speak in the assembly" suggests the need for some more active exercise of citizenship than voting alone allows. Third, and no less important, it sees equality of condition (or something approaching this) as the prerequisite for the practice of democratic citizenship. Whether this entails absolute equality or simply a good deal more equality than characterizes the present distribution of wealth and ownership over the means of production in, say, capitalist societies is open to discussion. But to separate the concept of democracy from its egalitarian moorings is to lose sight of its historical derivation.

When we turn to political theory, there is a dearth of major writers who can be classified as democratic, at least until the eighteenth century. Most theorists and philosophers have been men of leisure or privileged observers of power, writing on the political universe from the vantage point of aristocrat, courtier, or gentleman rather than from that of the overwhelming majority of the population. If there is a democratic type of political theorizing to the Hellenistic period, the Roman Empire, the Middle Ages, the Protestant Reformation, or to movements like the Levellers and the Diggers in mid-seventeenth century England, this seldom finds expression in a political treatise. We can detect an aspiration to greater equality in the distribution of earthly goods among the Anabaptists or Diggers – "No man shall have any more land than he can labour himself or have others to labour with him"[122] – and abhorrence of monarchical and aristocratic privilege on the part of radical soldiers and artisans during the English Civil War – "The poorest he that is in England hath a life to live, as the greatest he ... every man that is to live under a government ought first by his own consent to put himself under that government"[123] – without thereby arguing that we have a worked-out democratic theory of the state.

There are two figures, however, one of the eighteenth century, one of the nineteenth, who are more helpful in this regard – Rousseau and Marx. Let me say a little about each.

Rousseau's vision of democracy is rich in a number of regards. He is the first of the moderns to ground the notion of sovereignty directly in the people and to make it something inalienable.[124] He is the first to see in equality the natural condition of mankind and associate the rise of civilized society with an unequal appropriation of property and the usurpations of the rich: "Le premier qui ayant enclos un terrain, s'avisa de dire, *ceci est à moi*, et trouva des gens aussi simples pour le croire, fut le vrai fondateur de la société civile ... Telle fut, ou dut être l'origine de la Société et des Loix, qui donnèrent de nouvelles entraves au foible et de nouvelles forces au riche."[125] He abhors the inequality he sees in Europe and advocates a division of wealth in which "all will have something and no one too much."[126]

Rousseau's egalitarianism leads him in the *Social Contract* to celebrate the small-scale community and to transplant into an agrarian setting the democratic ethos of an earlier day. The conditions he sets down for the realization of democracy are the following: i) a small state in which the people can be easily assembled and each citizen knows the other; ii) a great simplicity of manners; iii) a great deal of equality in rank and fortune; iv) little luxury, which corrupts both rich and poor and saps the foundations of the state.[127]

He lashes out against representation, which entails the alienation of sovereignty and the general will into the hands of a small number of elected representatives: "The English people thinks itself free; it is so only during the election of members of parliament ... as soon as they are elected it is a slave, it is nothing."[128] He contrasts this feudal innovation with the direct democracy of the Greeks. He pictures a peasant society where citizens regulate the affairs of state wisely under an oak, or in annual assemblies, where they decide whether to maintain their existing form of government and those charged with its administration.[129] And later, in his projected constitution for Corsica, he once more upholds the virtues of small-scale agrarian democracy, freed from the corruption of large cities and commerce, and involving a fairly egalitarian distribution of property.[130]

Now the agrarian part of Rousseau's vision (much like Jefferson's) is a little hard to take seriously in the late twentieth century. But some of the other elements – popular sovereignty, direct participation, economic equality – loomed large indeed during the French Revolution and continue to characterize democratic theories of the state to this day (cf. chapter 5). When the sans-culottes erupted into the National Assembly shouting "Descend representatives of the people – the sovereign is here," they were evoking a model of sectional democracy with deeply Rousseauean overtones.[131] When Sylvain Maréchal blurts out, "Begone abhorrent distinction between governors and governed," one conjures up the classical formula "archein kai archesthai" (ruling and being ruled in turn) in a new guise. And from Gracchus Babeuf's *Manifesto of the Equals* – "The sun shines for everyone" – to twentieth-century critiques of the power of multinationals or oligarchical landowners, something of the spirit of Rousseau is still alive.[132]

Marx is a theorist less of democracy than of class conflict. That his is a radically egalitarian vision, in which private property and class division will have been transcended, is what sets his theory of communism off from what had come before. From the critique of alienation and private property in the *Economic and Philosophical Manuscripts* to the call to proletarian revolution in the *Communist Manifesto* to the castigation of the fetishism of commodities in Volume I of *Capital*, Marx's writings in this regard are of one piece.

The early Marx is prepared to speak the language of radical democracy – against Hegel: "Democracy is the solution to the *riddle* of every constitution. In it we find the constitution founded on its true ground: *real human beings and real people* ... In democracy the formal principle is identical with the substantive principle."[133] And it would appear, judging by the early texts, that, as in Rousseau, there is a critique of representation that anticipated a more participatory notion of democracy. "The separation of the political state from civil society takes the form of a separation of the deputies from their electors. Society simply deputes elements of itself to become its political existence."[134]

But in Marx, that vision is only rarely fleshed out. Instead, as in the *Manifesto*, one finds an argument pointing to the abolition of all forms of politics with the ending of class domination,[135] something that Engels will later call "the withering away of the state." One finds in the *Critique of the Gotha Programme* the formula "revolutionary dictatorship of the proletariat" to describe the transitional stage between capitalism and communism, something that does not much sound like Athenian isegoría. It is only in *The Civil War in France*, in his famous defence of the Paris Commune, that Marx once again sounds a strongly participatory note, in both the political and the economic arenas:

The communal *régime* once established in Paris and the secondary centres, the old centralised Government would in the provinces, too, have to give way to the self-government of the producers ... The merely repressive organs of the old governmental power were to be amputated, its legitimate functions restored to the responsible agents of society. Instead of deciding once in three or six years which member of the ruling class was to misrepresent the people in Parliament, universal suffrage was to serve the people, constituted in the Communes, ... to put the right man in the right place.[136]

Marx's critique of parliamentarism here recalls Rousseau's excoriation of the English, while his notion of "the self-government of the producers" seems to open the door to a worker- or producer-controlled economy run on decentralized and highly democratic lines. Isomoiría here takes a highly modern form, alongside the isegoría in the communes and the isonomía of universal citizenship in a fully democratized society.

The Russian Revolution, as we know, for all its celebration of the soviets, or workers' councils, as the embodiment of revolutionary forms of democracy against the bourgeois parliamentary ones in the West, did not succeed in introducing lasting participatory features into the Soviet system. Democratic centralism, with the emphasis on the centralism, and vanguard party control over all important political, economic, and social institutions made a mockery of the more democratic components in the Marxian vision (cf. chapter 12). They also, for the next seventy-five years, gave Western liberals and conservatives, who were now making their peace with universal suffrage and capitalist democracy, a much easier run for their money. Democracy came to be redefined by the so-called revisionist liberal theorists as a strictly political choice between competing parties in successive elections, with the question of equality removed.[137]

A plethora of theorists in the immediate post–Second World War period, moreover, warned about the dangers of excessive political participation, justifying the barriers between representative élites and mass electorate: "The average voter does not act, but reacts. The majority remains passive ... not because they cannot learn about politics but because they are not interested in it. It is nobody's fault in particular, and it is time we stopped seeking scapegoats."[138] "A high rate of mass behaviour may be expected when both elites and non-elites lack social insulation; that is, when elites are accessible to direct intervention by non-elites, and when non-elites are available for direct mobilization by elites."[139] "A State which has 'cured' apathy is likely to be a State in which too many people have fallen into the error of believing in the efficiency of political solutions for the problems of ordinary lives."[140]

Still, something of the classical tradition of democracy remained alive, surfacing in radical moments such as the student revolts of the 1960s, or in new phenomena like feminism, the Greens, or the anti-nuclear movement. And, in the process, participatory democratic theory has enjoyed something of a revival, both in the West and elsewhere.

One could cite the works of Carole Pateman or C.B. Macpherson, which did much to reintroduce participatory democracy as a theme in contemporary Western political theory: "For a democratic polity to exist it is necessary for a participatory society to exist, i.e. a society where all political systems have been democratised and socialisation through participation can take place in all areas."[141] Macpherson, for his part, outlines a pyramidal model of democracy as an alternative to the "competing élite" model: "One would start with direct democracy at the neighbourhood or factory level – actual face to face discussion and decision by consensus or majority, and election of delegates who would make up a council at the next, more inclusive level, say a city borough or ward or township. The delegates would have to be sufficiently instructed by and accountable to those who elected them to make decisions at the council level reasonably democratic. So it would go on up to the top level."[142] And his discussion properly notes some of the preconditions – a stronger sense of community, reduction in the present level of social and economic inequality – that would be needed before any such model could be made to work.[143]

There have been similar arguments advanced by a variety of writers – Benjamin Barber, Jurgen Habermas, David Held, John Keane, and Charles Taylor, to name but five[144] – all positing a democratic public sphere, i.e. an open, communicative society, characterized by face-to-face structures and significant economic and political democracy. For example, Habermas writes, "By 'the public sphere' we mean first of all the realm of our social life in which something approaching public opinion can be formed. Access is guaranteed to all citizens ... citizens behave as a public body when they confer in an unrestrained fashion ... about matters of general interest."[145] And Charles Taylor writes: "It would be truly liberating to ... open the road to projects ... which lie in the direction of decentralization and self-management. This might restore to contemporary society a credible horizon of hope."[146] With this position I strongly concur, as indeed with the efforts of would-be reformers in eastern Europe who have looked at ways to democratize their societies.[147]

Yet here we must be realistic. This chapter, like the larger volume of which it is a part, is after all about what de Gaulle once called "le monstre froid parmi les monstres froids," namely the state. The wholesale transcendence of capitalism is not on the agenda in Western societies, any more than is the replacement of the world's one party–dominated Marxist-Leninist régimes by self-managed institutions. We can dream our democratic reveries, but as Marx himself once soberly noted, "The tradition of the dead generations weighs like a nightmare on the brain of the living."[148] And an important part of that nightmare – or better, legacy – is contained within the four other paradigms of the state I have identified in this chapter – aristocratic, republican, philosophy of order, and liberal. This, therefore, brings me to my concluding argument.

If we are serious about realizing a democratic public sphere, we cannot simply reject root and branch what the four other theories of the state advocate. At first glance, there is little common ground between an aristocratic theory of the state and a democratic, between the republicanism of the separation of powers and the communitarianism of direct democracy, between a Hobbesian-type sovereign and popular sovereignty, between the essentially private liberties of liberalism (and the capitalism with which it has been closely associated), and the more public liberties and greater egalitarianism of democratic theory.

Yet I want to argue that advocates of a democratic theory of the state must not see their goals in all-or-nothing terms. Any possible transformation in a democratic direction must be carried out within the existing political systems in the world. Some significant dilution of the democratic vision is, therefore, called for.

From the aristocratic theorists we can learn about the importance of leadership – even in the most participatory of democratic movements. What Thucydides tells us about Pericles – "What was nominally a democracy became in his hands government by the first citizen"[149] – is a truth we cannot ignore. We may not wish to abdicate power to an all-knowing lawgiver or charismatic ruler, of whom this century has see all too many. Still, we must recognize that some are more gifted in political leadership than others, that leaders will inevitably give to popular sovereignty a particular direction. The crucial thing is that there be genuinely participatory political structures, operating from the bottom up, and greater equality of condition in the society we seek.

From republicanism comes the importance of separation of powers. Democratic theory must take seriously the business of constitutions, institutional separation, federal arrangements, and the like, even if these make it more difficult to carry out the unmediated popular will in certain circumstances (cf. chapter 11). In Soviet-type societies as well, there must be greater separation between party and government, greater judicial independence, if perestroïka is to have some lasting effect and the crimes of Stalin are not to be a recurring phenomenon.

From the theorists of order comes a sobering reminder that democratic dreams alone may not always allow for effective decision-making, especially in times of crisis. We must not expect too much good from human nature, for without some overriding order we may end up, not with a model public sphere, but with the chaos of a Lebanon, i.e. a Hobbesian state of nature. There is no need to embrace Augustine's libido dominandi or Schmitt's friend – foe distinction to recognize that the imperative to order will be at work even in model democratic states. This places limits on how far we can take our participatory ideals.

From liberalism, we must first accept the inevitability of representation, given the size and scale of modern nation-states. At best, we may be able to combine more directly democratic forms of politics with representative ones – we will not be able simply to substitute participatory for representative structures across whole societies. Another lesson of liberalism regards the importance of individual rights side by side with the collective/communitarian ones that democratic theory posits. Where the exact balance ought to be between collective and individual rights is no easy matter to decide. We can neither go back to the ancient city with its civic religion and exclusively public liberty, as Constant reminds us, nor can we rest content with an absolutist "individual liberty" position, as others, in the tradition of Mill, tend to argue. Somewhere between these two, democratic theorists must stake out a defensible position.

What may be left, when we think about these modifications, is a more realistic democratic agenda than the one pursued by the sans-culottes or Robespierre, by Rousseau or Marx, or by many twentieth-century advocates of participatory democracy. We must seek to put more democracy into state structures, east, west, and south, rather than anticipate their aufhebung or total abolition. Democratic theory has important truths to teach its rivals, regarding equality, community, and participation, without which there can be no morally satisfactory basis for citizenship in the modern state. But there will be no democratic new Jerusalems without careful attention being paid, in turn, to the non-democratic theories of the state bequeathed us by the political philosophers.

CHAPTER TWO

Jacobin Strains in Canada

In this chapter, I wish to examine ideological features of the state tradition in Canada. For many decades, Canadian social scientists and historians, in contrasting Canadian with American development, have emphasized the significantly stronger state tradition on this side of the border. A number, moreover, have associated this with the more conservative set of values that characterized Canada and with the organic Toryism that found its way into our political culture: "Man and his society are organic formations which have birth, growth and decay ... The good of the individual is not conceivable apart for the good of the whole, determined by a 'natural' elite consulting a sacred tradition."[1] "Canadian conservatives have something British about them ... It is not simply their emphasis on loyalty to the crown and to the British connection, but a touch of the authentic tory aura – traditionalism, elitism, the strong state and so on."[2]

I have no quarrel with this argument so far as it goes, though there were clearly material reasons that were at least as important as ideological ones in determining the use of the state in a new, thinly populated society. The developmental role of the state in relation to transportation (the Lachine Canal, the Grand Trunk, the Canadian Pacific Railway) or to manufacturing (the National Policy) is too well known to need repeating. So, too, the economic role of the twentieth-century state, be it at the provincial level ("Hydros" and the other crown corporations) or at the federal (the Canadian National Railways, the Canadian Broadcasting Corporation, Air Canada, Atomic Energy of Canada, Petro-Canada), has been the object of analysis by a good number of writers, pointing to a "staple" base for state activity, its "defensive" role vis-à-vis the United States, its accumulation function with respect to capitalist interests, and so on.[3] With much of this I am also in agreement, although I provide a somewhat different interpretation of state development in chapter 8.

Still, something is amiss when ideological and economic explanations for state activity seem so far removed from one another. On the one hand, we are led to believe that there is an organic Tory streak, passed on, no doubt, through the United Empire Loyalists, with their disdain for American republicanism and democracy. On the other hand, we have economic constraints that differentiate us from the United States, leading Canadians to accept a somewhat larger role for the state than seems the case south of the border. In what way the first has shaped the second or been shaped by it is left unresolved.

It seems to me that there is a connection between Toryism and the use of the state, particularly at the central level, and that ideological factors – for example, the absence of a revolutionary tradition, the relative weakness of democratic values, a subservience to things British and imperialist – go hand in hand with the economic needs of a staples-based, capital-short, semi-peripheral political economy like Canada's. What results is an amalgam of Tory ideology and a strong centralizing impulse, the grounding of a potentially powerful state structure on counter-revolutionary premises, something I am tempted to call Tory Jacobinism.

This term may strike the reader as slightly perverse. Were not the French Jacobins, Robespierre, St-Just, and their followers, the most committed revolutionaries during the years 1789–94 and therefore anathema to all that Toryism stood for? Were they not behind the revolutionary journées, the execution of the king and the Girondins, the "excesses" against which Edmund Burke had thundered in 1791 and after?: "We are at war with a principle and an example – That *example* has shown ... that it is possible to subvert the whole frame and order of the best constructed states, by corrupting the common people with the spoil of the superior classes."[4] Were not the Jacobins, moreover, arch-believers in popular sovereignty and the rights of man, in the revolutionary overthrow of "legitimate" institutions, in fairly radical notions of equality? What possible link, then, could one make between their political philosophy and that of British Conservatives or their colonial offspring?

Certainly, George-Etienne Cartier would not have subscribed to St-Just's famous dictum that "the wretched are the power of the earth," nor Macdonald to Marat's phrase about the "despotism of liberty" or to Robespierre's Cult of Supreme Reason. If there is a historical analogy to be made, it has been often argued, it is more fittingly between Jacobinism and later revolutionary doctrines like

Marxism and Leninism than counter-revolutionary ones like Toryism. For Marx and Trotsky and Lenin meditated positively upon the Jacobin experience,[5] while their adversaries on the right saw in it the incarnation of all evil.

In speaking of Tory Jacobinism as one example of the Jacobin strain in Canada, I am trying to focus on possible elements of similarity between founding a new state under revolutionary circumstances in the Old World and doing so under counter-revolutionary circumstances in the New. In a similar vein, a number of contemporary Latin American writers have coined terms like "creole Leviathan"[6] to describe authoritarian state structures in the southern hemisphere, or have talked about Junker-type roads to industrialization for countries like Argentina.[7]

There are two features of French Jacobinism I would single out as of particular pertinence to our discussion: insistence on a strong centralized state, the republic "one and indivisible," with a concomitant condemnation of regionalist tendencies, secessions, and opposition to the capital; and construction of a state system "from above," particularly in the period of the Jacobin dictatorship, 1793-4.

The Jacobins from 1792 on were strong centralizers. They opposed the more moderate party known as the Girondins, who "advocated a federation on the American mould, made up of provincial units that would be free to take any decisions at the local level and would be dependent on the capital solely for matters of national import."[8] In the words of St-Just: "Federalism does not only mean a divided government, but a divided people."[9] The Jacobins, accordingly, "favoured a Paris-centred federalism instead, so that 'a single impulse would spread to all the *départements* of the Republic, and the shock wave, issuing forth from the Convention ... would jolt everyone at the same instance and in the same direction.' "[10]

Further, the Jacobins, while strongly Rousseauean in their conception of the general will and of popular sovereignty, had little difficulty substituting their own interpretation of the general will for that of the people in the critical situation of 1793-4. Faced with external threats from all sides and internal insurrection, the Jacobins reacted with an iron fist, imposing a revolutionary order on society from above: "At the political level, war required a strong government ... Democracy, as the members of the militant [Paris] sections conceived and practiced it, entered into contradiction with both the political conceptions and practices of the Jacobins."[11] The state structure was remade, the sans-culottes were gradually squeezed out of the political process, while in the name of efficiency, "the State interfered everywhere and claimed to exert its sway over individuals and institutions."[12] Authority had replaced liberty in the practice of the Jacobin dictatorship.

The pre-revolutionary regime had known its own cult of the state. One recalls Louis x i v's "L'état c'est moi," or de Tocqueville's discussion in his *The Ancien Regime and the Coming of the French Revolution*. Nor was it only in France that conservatives revelled in the mystique of authority. For Burke: "The state ought not to be considered as nothing better than a partnership agreement in a trade of pepper and coffee ... or some other such low concern, to be taken up for a little temporary interest, and to be dissolved by the fancy of the parties."[13] The same passion for the state underlay the political thought of the later Hegel or Treitschke and the practice of such autocratic regimes as Prussia/Imperial Germany or Russia. To be sure, tradition and dynastic legitimacy, not revolution and popular sovereignty, were their hallmark: "Here my grandfather put the royal crown on his head by his own right, definitely stressing once again that it was granted to him by God's Grace alone and not by parliaments, popular assemblies, and popular decision."[14] The dictates of economic development, no less than warfare, led such regimes to an ever-more centralized conception of authority.

Turning to the Canadian scene, we discover, toutes proportions gardées, that it is Tories whose vision of the state has centralizing characteristics that recall the Jacobins. Here is John A. Macdonald speaking on the Quebec resolutions in 1864:

Now as regards the comparative advantage of a Legislative and a Federal Union, I have never hesitated to state my own opinion. I have again and again stated in the House that, if practicable, I thought a Legislative Union would be preferable ... We have adopted a different system [from the Americans]. We have strengthened the General Government. We have given the General Legislature all the subjects of legislation. We have conferred on them, not only specifically and in detail, all the powers which are incident to sovereignty, but we have expressly declared that all subjects of general interest not distinctly and exclusively conferred upon the local governments and local legislatures shall be conferred upon the General Government and Legislature.[15]

The whole thrust behind the British North America Act was to avoid the errors of the American constitution, with its doctrine of states' rights, introducing instead, beneath the veneer of the imperial tie, a highly centralized state structure. It was also highly anti-democratic in flavour: "We must strengthen the General Government ... Thus we shall have a strong and lasting government under which we can work out constitutional liberty as opposed to democracy."[16] No wonder liberal nationalists like A.A. Dorion denounced Macdonald's handiwork as "the most conservative measure ever laid before Parliament"[17] and that provinces like New Brunswick and Nova Scotia reacted angrily to what they saw as central Canadian domination.

Let us compare French Jacobinism and Canadian Toryism a little more closely with respect to three issues: external threats to national sovereignty, the ideological foundations of patriotism, and economic constraints on political power.

For the revolutionary government of 1792 on, external threats were clear enough. Dynastic Europe, trembling in horror at the spectacle of a deposed and executed monarch, at doctrines that might spill beyond France's borders, sparking revolution far and wide, pressed the attack. Prussia, Austria-Hungary, Spain, and England were at war with France, with parts of the east, the south (Toulon), and the west (Vendée) of France under foreign occupation or in revolt. With the survival of the revolution hanging by a thread, the impulse of the regime was ruthlessly centralizing: "Federalism and superstition speak Breton; the emigration and hatred for the Republic speak German; the counter-revolution speaks Italian and fanaticism speaks Basque. Let us smash these instruments of fanaticism and error."[18]

For the counter-revolutionary Tories of 1864-7, the threat to Canada came from a triumphant United States, fresh from victory in the Civil War and estranged from England by the latter's equivocal role with respect to the defeated Confederacy. The Fenian Raids into Canada and abrogation of the Reciprocity Treaty by the Americans in 1866 seemed to confirm the danger. When coupled with earlier memories of an aggressive United States (the War of 1812), this fear of annexation was to provide a strong strategic impetus for centralized government: "If we are true to Canada - if we do not desire to become part and parcel of this people [the United States], we cannot overlook the greatest revolution of our times ... I said this in this House, during the session of the 1861, that the first gun fired at Fort Sumner had 'a message for us'; I was unheeded then; I repeat now that every one of the 2700 great guns in the field, and every one of the 4600 guns afloat, whenever it opens its mouth, repeats the solemn warning of England ... prepare, prepare, prepare."[19]

As for the ideological foundations of patriotism, the Jacobins saw the unity of the republic as springing from the unity of the French people, which had been forged in grandiose events from the fall of the Bastille to the Battle of Valmy. Patriotism was rooted in the principles of liberty, equality, and fraternity that the revolution had developed: "There is something terrible about the sacred love for one's country; it is so exclusive that it immolates everything without pity, without fear, without human respect for the public good."[20] The crucible of patriotism burnt with a sacred flame, giving France a mission against all the powers of Europe: "One does not make revolutions by halves. It seems to me that you are destined to change the face of the governments of Europe; you will not be able to rest until she is free; her liberty will guarantee your own."[21]

That very mission, however, ensured that the democratic principles incarnated in the constitution of 1793 would remain still-born, that centralization and governmental efficiency, not direct democracy or popular sovereignty, would win the day: 'Dictatorship was established "from above"; it was bourgeois ... It was inflexible and at times inhuman. The authorities used it as an expedient justified by military and economic imperatives.'[22] With the "republic in danger" would come a new scale of values by which members of the Committee of Public Safety would judge each other and their fellows: "One does not count patriots; one weighs them ... On the scales of justice, one patriot must outweigh a hundred thousand aristocrats."[23] Only the revolutionary few could imbue the state with the requisite virtues and save the people from their own weaknesses, by use of terror if necessary.

For Canadian Tories, the sense of patrie was a good deal more muted than for the Jacobins. To being with, their patriotism was but a second-hand reflection of that of another country, England. Further, there was a bi-national reality to Canada that could not be effaced, much as certain Tories might have wished.[24] Also, the absence of fervour, what Claude Bissell has called "a tendency to equate the exuberant and the expansive with the empty and the vulgar,"[25] which is the corollary of a counter-revolutionary tradition, militated against the type of patriotism just described.

Yet Canadian Tories had their own sense of historical mission that made of England and, therefore, of Canada, the elect nation, much as the Jacobins had made of France. Quoth Bishop John Strachan in 1838: "Three centuries have elapsed since England was considered the true seat of Christianity, She arose from the slumber of ages and shook off the mass of heavy corruptions which had accumulated in darkness, and stood forth dauntlessly in her purity, the witness of God amidst a world lying in wickedness."[26] For Macdonald, in the final year of his life: "Under the broad folds of the Union Jack, we enjoy the same ample liberty to govern ourselves as we please, and at the same time we participate in the advantages which flow from association with the mightiest Empire the world has ever seen ... In our relations with the outside world, we enjoy the prestige inspired by the consciousness of the fact that behind us towers the majesty of England."[27]

For J.H. Coyne, in his "Memorial to the U.E.L." of 1898, the Loyalists had been the cream of the population of the thirteen colonies, characterized by their "devotion to law and order, British institutions and the unity of the Empire." From them had been inherited "the principles of religion, patriotism, law and order" of the people of Canada.[28] If Canada was not quite "God's new Israel,"[29] in the way that American preachers had interpreted the destiny of their new country, the trials and tribulations that had surrounded the birth of the northern colonies, the British Empire to which Canada was now linked, seemed in their own way to mark out its special role.

In France, revolutionary patriotism and the experience of war led the Jacobins to look to a strong dictatorial state; in Canada, the conservative ethos of a colonial ruling class, its pessimistic view of human nature, led it to posit a state with notably hierarchical features. Bishop Strachan had argued: "The present age has demonstrated that no great and decided amelioration of the lower classes of society can be reasonably expected ... labour is the lot of man, and no system of policy can render it unnecessary, or relieve the greater portions of mankind from suffering many privations."[30] The state that was established in the 1860s, with its pseudo-monarchial trappings, would "strengthen the position of the Crown in the British North American provinces,"[31] represent "classes and property ... as well as numbers,"[32] and ensure that the people as such would remain at the receiving end of a politics fashioned from above. The more centralized the state, the further removed from local grievances and petty factions, the greater the possibility of instilling the respect for authority and traditional values without which the demos might be unleashed upon the land.

Tories, to be sure, did not subscribe to Jacobin ideas of virtue or to the extreme methods used by the Jacobins to bring these about. Tory Jacobins, however, would look to a strong, potentially repressive state to shepherd the people toward a virtuous conduct they could never achieve by themselves. In the words of Burke: "If [the] people came to turn their liberty into a cloak for maliciousness, and to seek a privilege of exemption, not from power, but from the rules of morality and virtuous discipline, then I would join my hand to make them feel the force which a few united in a good cause have over a multitude of the profligate and ferocious."[33]

Economic constraints, the third factor leading to centralization, require particular scrutiny. For the Jacobins, faced with war on numerous fronts, with food shortages in the cities, with an inflated, almost worthless currency, pressures to turn to the state were over-whelming. It is not as though the Jacobins had ceased to believe in the value of private property.[34] Rather, grain requisition against hoarders, price and wage controls (maximum général), a food com-mission, and "revolutionary taxes" and "loans"[35] were the instru-ments which the Jacobins, well before twentieth-century societies caught up in war, were to devise in an emergency situation. This led the state in its economic role beyond the boundaries that liberal theory and the emerging doctrine of laissez-faire in particular would accept: "The government must not only be revolutionary against the aristocracy. It must also be so against those who rob the soldier, who corrupt the army through their insolence, and who by their squan-dering of public goods would return the people to slavery."[36]

This is not to imply that the Canadian Tory version of the state was one and the same with the Jacobin. The Tory version, however, was also strongly interventionist, reflecting the economic situation of British North America on the periphery of empire and the need to use state power as an instrument for infrastructural development. Canada was about to embark upon a road that Alexander Ger-schenkron has defined as "derived industrialization," where one economy "is closely tied up with the economy of some other larger and more advanced country or countries."[37] A significant compo-nent of public input, through cash subsidies, land grants, monopoly clauses, protection, and the like, would be required to make this work. As Gerschenkron has argued "The development of a back-ward country may, by the very virtue of its backwardness, tend to differ fundamentally from that of an advanced country."[38] The Tory instinct to look to the central government to foster economic growth (through public support for private capital) was a peculiarly Cana-dian response to the challenges of capital shortage and industrial take-off. Railway building and the opening of the west required an administrative and economic centralization that, in more extreme form, the state of siege had forced upon Jacobin France.

There were to be further reinforcements of state power under Tory governments, during the First World War and, again, in the 1930s. Canadian participation in the war was to bring the same dramatic increase in state activity as had occurred in Jacobin France, and for very similar reasons – military considerations. The defence of the mother country, the prime mover for Canadian Tories, loomed just as large as "la patrie en danger" had for the Jacobins, with analogous results. "Canada is very proud that her sons have upheld so worthily the splendid tradition of our great pioneer races,"[39] wrote Robert Borden to Earl Grey after the battle of Ypres, with a pride that recalled the French after Valmy. "The time has come *when the authority of the state should be invoked* to provide reinforcements necessary to maintain the gallant men at the front"[40] (my emphasis), Borden told Parliament in May, 1917, prior to the introduction of the Military Service Bill – conscription.

The War Measures Act was passed, new sources of taxation were developed (the income tax), a War Purchasing Commission was established, wage controls were introduced, and the general powers of the central government were expanded between 1914 and 1918: "The War-time experience with the regulation and direction of enterprise was an important factor in bringing on the wide extension of government control which economic and social chaos seemed to make desirable."[41] Just as in Britain, "the State loomed much larger in the inter-war economy than it normally had in peacetime conditions in the nineteenth century."[42] A permanent "displacement effect" upward in state expenditures had occurred.[43]

In the mid-1930s, the Conservative government of R.B. Bennett, its policies of imperial preference and of work camps in disrepute, thought it had found in a more powerful central government the key to saving the capitalist system and its own fortunes. Borrowing heavily from Franklin Roosevelt's New Deal policies, Bennett in January 1935 introduced his own mini-version with an Employment and Social Insurance Act, a Dominion Trade and Industry Act, and a number of other measures. His radio addresses of that month provided an extraordinary rationale for an expanded social role for the state:

Reform means Government intervention. It means Government control and regulation. It means the end of laissez-faire ... I summon the power of the State to its support.

... Government will have a new function to perform in the economic system. It will be a permanent guide and regulator, with the rights and power of correction, with the duty and responsibility of maintaining hereafter in our whole industrial and capitalist system, a better and more equitable distribution of its benefits; so that wealth may come more readily to the rescue of poverty ... [and] capitalism will be in fact your servant and not your master.[44]

The Jacobins had argued nothing very different 140 years earlier: "A State is close to ruin indeed whenever it offers the spectacle of extreme indigence alongside extreme affluence. Let Europe learn that you [the Convention] will no longer tolerate any unhappy man or oppressor on French territory."[45]

My argument, then, is that at three crucial junctures – the 1860s, the 1910s, and the 1930s – Canadian Tories found themselves advocates of a strong central government. This is not to make of them the sole architects of such a state – much of this in the twentieth century has occurred under Liberal, rather than Conservative auspices. But the centralizing motif of Tory policy, whether for infrastructural reasons or for reasons of patriotism (British-linked) or capitalist crisis, has, at critical moments, given a Jacobin-type stamp to Canadian politics, as opposed to the provincially oriented, Girondin current that has flowed at other times.

To be a Jacobin was to be a centralizer. To be a Canadian Tory was to be an adherent of strong central government of a British stripe and to defend it against the adherents of powerful provincial governments. This is not to argue that Tories like Macdonald were not prepared to make their peace with federalism in a way that French Jacobins never could: "The people of Lower Canada, being a minority with a different language, nationality, and religion from the majority,"[46] there was no alternative. But Macdonald's own instincts, like those of his fellow Conservatives, were strongly centralizing. As Peter Smith has argued:

In many ways it could be said that John A. Macdonald obtained most of what Alexander Hamilton wanted in 1787. This included a strong central government that would not only possess the political offices that would mute political discontent and provide political stability but would, at the same time, vastly enhance public credit and provide the capital to underwrite commercial expansion across the continent. The localist attachments in Canadian political culture, particularly in French Canada and amongst English Canadian Reformers, would have to be satisfied with the greatly inferior provincial governments that were given.[47]

Now the practice of Canadian federalism, as we know, was to prove a good deal more decentralizing over time than the letter and the spirit of the Confederation Debates and the B N A Act might have suggested. Tory ideology, with its strongly counter-revolutionary values, its attachment to the symbolism of privilege and crown, was to gradually lose its hold over English-Canadian opinion in the twentieth century. Nor as a grounding for English-Canadian nationalism was it to survive easily the bloodletting of the First

World War. Whatever impulse it might once have given to the legitimacy of the central government could no longer hold much sway in
the more American-influenced political economy and culture that
were to follow.

The concept of Jacobinism need not be discarded so quickly. Not only
Tories could be centralizers; for their own good reasons, so could
Liberals and socialists. It might be well, therefore, to say something
about these twentieth-century variants of Jacobinism in Canada.

The Liberal party, in particular that of Wilfrid Laurier (leader
1887–1919) and William Lyon Mackenzie King (1919–48), owed its
success in no small degree to its willingness to accept the federal
character of Canada and the special concerns of Quebec more fully
than the Conservatives. The latter, after all, in their pursuit of an
imperialist ideology, were prepared to ride roughshod over
Quebec's objections, for example, during the conscription crisis of
1917. Nor did many in their ranks entirely shed assimilationist aspirations with respect to French Canada, going back to the Durham
Report.

Faced with such opponents, Laurier found it relatively easy to
paint himself as a more valiant defender of French Canada's specificity. King, temporizer par excellence, inherited from Laurier the same
tradition and proved more adept than the Conservatives at manag-
ing English-French differences over conscription during the Second
World War. He also moved more cautiously, but surely, down the
road to the welfare state than had Bennett, with the constitutional
amendment on unemployment insurance of 1940 and a number of
other measures introduced in conjunction with the war (Family
Allowances, P C 1003, facilitating trade union certification).

The Liberals, for so long the "governing party," were not averse to
reinforcing the central state. Many of the crown corporations in this
country were either created or consolidated under their rule. The
same constraints – economic crisis, war, a shift to more collectivist
values – were at work during their long period in power. During the
Second World War, the Liberal government was to prove even more
vigorous in the exercise of emergency powers than the Conservatives during the First World War. Over 85 per cent of the vastly
expanded share of gross national product (G N P) in the hands of the
state (some 50 per cent of total G N P in 1944)[48] was accounted for by
the federal government. In the post-1945 period, the Liberals
embarked on Keynesian-type economic policies, laid the foundations for a significant welfare state, and moved to increase signifi-

cantly Canada's participation in international affairs, albeit as a junior partner to the United States.

Still, to speak of King or St Laurent (leader 1948–58) or Pearson (1958–68) in terms of Jacobinism seems grossly out of place. The first was too pusillanimous, the second too much the chairman of the board, the third too much the besieged leader of successive minority governments to project the kind of authority that the term *Jacobin* evokes. Nor, in their regard, can one really speak of a cult regarding the powers of the central state in the way that Macdonald and certain twentieth-century Tories were prone to project.

It is only with the era of Trudeau (leader 1968–84) that the term *Jacobinism* again comes into its own. Trudeau's motivation for entering federal politics was, first and foremost, to restore central authority faced with the challenge of Quebec nationalism: "One way of offsetting the appeal of separatism is by investing tremendous amounts of time, energy, and money in nationalism *at the federal level* ... Resources must be diverted into such things as national flags, anthems, education, art councils, broadcasting corporations, film boards; the territory must be bound together by a network of railways, highways, airlines; the national culture and the national economy must be protected by taxes and tariffs; ownership of resources and industry by nationals must be made a matter of policy."[49] The symbolism of the central state would be invoked against that of "tribal nationalism" and federal institutions remade so that French Canadians could feel themselves "masters in their own house" in the whole of Canada, not just in Quebec.

In Trudeau, Canadian encountered a figure who would not hesitate to make use of the military/repressive powers inherent in the notion of sovereignty. The "Peace, Order and Good Government" clause of the BNA Act, dear to Tory hearts, became the basis for the suspension of civil liberties and invocation of emergency powers in October 1970: "I think the society must take every means at its disposal to defend itself against the emergence of a parallel power which defies the elected power in this country and I think that goes to any distance."[50] The kidnapping of a British trade attaché and of a Quebec cabinet minister (later murdered) had been turned into a full-scale legitimacy crisis from which the authority of the central government would emerge greatly enhanced.

In October 1975, faced with the aftermath of the OPEC-related crisis and a serious economic downturn, Trudeau reversed his campaign position of 1974, introducing a system of mandatory wage and price controls. In a year-end interview, he told Canadians:

You can't live in a different world with the same institutions and the same values that you had before ... It's a massive intervention into the decision-making power of the economic groups and it's telling Canadians that we haven't been able to make it work, the free market system ... The government is going to take a larger role in running institutions, as we're doing now with our anti-inflation controls ... Things don't go necessarily better because we spend less on health and on welfare and leave the private sector free to spend more on producing baubles or multicoloured gadgets ... The state is important, the government is important. It means there's going to be not less authority in our lives but perhaps more.[51]

A Jacobin-type philosophy in many ways, but not one that either the corporate élite or the trade union movement, for that matter, was prepared to accept.

Trudeau's initiatives between 1980 and 1984 were the culmination of this philosophy. During the Quebec referendum campaign, he played an important role in support of the "No" side, defending the central state against the sirens of sovereignty-association: "It is this loyalty to the whole country upon which we must build if we want to vanquish the enemy within ... The feeling of being a Canadian, that individual feeling which we must cultivate, the feeling of being loyal to something which is bigger than the province or the city in which we happen to live, must be based on a protection of the basic rights of the citizens ... *The national interest must prevail over the regional interest*" (my emphasis).[52]

Pursuing a renewed federalism after the referendum, Trudeau proceeded to introduce a constitutional package which consolidated the powers of the central government, introducing a new, overriding, and unifying element into the operation of all political power in this country – the Charter of Rights. His preparedness to go over the heads of the provincial governments to Westminster, to use the threat of unilateral patriation to force recalcitrant provinces (except Quebec) to climb aboard, was in a tradition that goes back to 1793–94.

At the same time, the National Energy Program was a bold attempt to assert the primacy of federal economic priorities over provincial and ensure that oil revenues, despite formal provincial control over resources, would not accrue solely to the oil-producing provinces. The expanded activities of Petro-Canada were also part of a more conscious use of state enterprise as a means of nation-building, as opposed to province-building or multinational expansion. The legacy of Trudeau, in other words, was of a reinforced central state, prepared to assert its authority against recalcitrant provinces and to make extensive use of its military, economic, and reserve powers. Well could he denounce his successor at the time of the Meech Lake Accord as a man who would "render the Canadian state totally impotent."[53] So spoke the most Jacobin of our twentieth-century prime ministers.

Socialists, too, though but a minority force in Canada, have had their strongly Jacobin leanings. The Regina Manifesto (1935) had only the most grudging concessions to make to provincial power: "The present division of powers between Dominion and Provinces reflects the conditions of a pioneer, mainly agricultural, community in 1867. Our constitution must be brought in line with the increasing industrialization of the country and the consequent centralization of economic and financial power which has taken place in the last two generations."[54]

The League for Social Reconstruction, in its mid-1930s *Social Planning for Canada*, called for economic planning and socialization of finance and large-scale industry. The logic of its economic proposals, borrowed from the British Labour party, pointed to a strong, central government as the instrument of political and economic change. It was certainly not provincial governments, presided over by the likes of Maurice Duplessis and Mitchell Hepburn, that were likely to move Canada to the left.

This centralizing tendency was reinforced during the war years which saw concentration of economic decision-making power in Ottawa's hands and the first moves toward a Canadian welfare state. Despite its strong base in the prairies, the Co-operative Commonwealth Federation (c c f) was anything but a defender of regional power, given its broader world view. The machinery to begin moving Canada leftward lay in Ottawa, not the provinces.

By the 1960s, however, the c c f's successor, the New Democratic Party (n d p) had become more comfortable with the institutions of federalism or, as it came to be called in the party's founding program, "co-operative federalism"[55] The road to political power did not seem to lie so exclusively through Ottawa; the reality of strong provincial power and, more especially, the emergence of a potent Quebec nationalism after 1960 were further factors, as was *abandonment* of single-minded commitment to economic planning. As the n d p found itself in power for varying periods in three of the western provinces after 1969, a good deal of its centralizing thrust was muted.

Yet the pursuit of social democratic objectives, should the n d p transcend third-party status, would ensure a more vigorous, active

role for the central state. The policies for which the N D P has historically stood – social programs like unemployment insurance, old age
pensions, medicare, public ownership through such institutions as
the Canadian Development Corporation and Petro-Canada – had
centralizing implications. So did the nationalist measures the party
supported, such as the Foreign Investment Review Agency and cultural and economic sovereignty vis-à-vis the United States, though
the Canada- U s Free Trade Agreement will make any future action
along these lines immensely more difficult. The same centralizing
implications would be true for industrial policy and for programs
that might be developed regarding work sharing or a reformulated
social contract on a national scale.

It follows, therefore, from this survey, that the term *Jacobin* has appli-
cations to the study of Canadian politics and the role of the central
government, at least at key moments in our history. I am not seeking
to transpose the term from French to Canadian soil without recognizing the rather different conditions, economic no less than political, that characterized the two societies. Our sense of the state was
not born of revolution, nor was it grounded in the economic necessi-
ties of a war economy that culminated in the Jacobin republic. Ours
was not a core society, transmitting a code of values to Europe and
beyond. The business of state-building would be slower and less
dramatic in a society situated on the northern tier of North America,
made up of regions, many of them peripheral in their own right,
with linguistic and cultural dualism as a permanent feature.

Still, as the Jacobins had discovered, the logic of the modern world
pushed in the direction of centralization and a powerful state structure. Military considerations were one important factor; so too were
economic forces – transportation, trade routes, the capitalist division
of labour, and technology. Nationalism, that new and powerful credo
forged in the latter part of the eighteenth century, might unite populations and geographical regions that had been divided or loosely
administered until then. What took a radical form during the French
Revolution could take a quite conservative one in Germany or Italy
or in the overseas dominions of European states moving to statehood.

The Tories were our first Jacobins, the creators of the Canadian
central state. We might have done things differently, had 1837 not
turned out the way it did.[56] But in the end, commercial interests and
imperial sentiment, fear of the United States and the lure of a conti-
nent-wide economy, the spirit of the British constitution and a pinch
of American values combined to give us the institutions of 1867. The

state in question – centralized in practice, but not to excess; open to outside capital, though simultaneously promoting indigenous capitalism; and top-down in form, though subject to popular input through the electoral process – would preside over the filling in of a half-continent, the emergence of a substantial industrial capacity,[57] and a gradual increase in Canadian sovereignty, at least at the formal level.

Nationalism would come more slowly, with great resistance – from English Canadians wedded to a British form of identity and from French Canadians holding on to their own sense of nationality as the one defence against the alien economic, linguistic, and cultural forces that surrounded them. But the central state would grow, and its functions – from the railway-building and National Policy of the nineteenth century, to its role during two wars and the Depression, to its increased involvement in social as well as economic activities in the post–Second World War years – would more and more come to resemble the interventionist model that the Jacobins had first unveiled.

Liberalism and socialism would do much to further these centralizing tendencies. In the former case, the attempt to mediate capital-labour relations and to alleviate some of the dysfunctioning of capitalism through social spending led to an expanded role for the state, especially in the post-war era. The need to maintain Quebec within Canada would also lead, with time, to the strong assertion of state authority, as in October 1970 and again with the constitutional patriation of 1980–81. In the socialist case, one can speak of pressure for enhanced central state activities that led to legislation brought in by Liberal governments from the period of the Second World War on.

Province-building tendencies were not to vanish, and at various moments, from the Mowat and Mercier governments of the late nineteenth century, to the agrarian protest movements of the 1920s and 1930s, to the Quiet Revolution and the Parti Québécois government in Quebec, to the resource-based regionalism of western Canada in the late 1970s, to the Meech Lake Accord (whatever its ultimate fate), we were to see them powerfully at work. They were to act as countervailing forces to the spirit of centralization and ensure that what Jacobinism we got would be tempered and less fulsome than in unitary states. But we would do well to ponder the motivation that led the Fathers of Confederation to opt for a strong central government and the ideological, no less than economic, constraints that furthered the process at points in the twentieth century. Parts of the Jacobin legacy have been alive, even in this most unrevolutionary of modern states.

CHAPTER THREE

"Dominion" and "Province," "Government" and "State"

Concepts and terms are not the property solely of theorists and philosophers. As the currency of political debate, they enter into the direct practice of a society and shape the way in which both rulers and citizens see themselves. Thus, in Greece and Rome terms like *polis, res publica*, and *civitas* had a resonance that went well beyond the closed circles of political philosophy. They were, if writers as varied as Fustel de Coulanges, Victor Ehrenberg, and Claude Nicolet are to be believed, an intimate part of the daily lives of citizens: "Ce que les Latins appellent *res publica*, les Grecs *to koivov*, voilà ce qui remplace la vielle religion. C'est là ce qui décide désormais des institutions et des lois, et c'est à cela que se rapportent tous les actes importants des cités."[1] Similarly, imperium and Stände, estates and sovereign were key terms of political discourse in the Roman Empire, in the Middle Ages, and in the period of the emergence of the modern European nation-state from the sixteenth century on.

Hobbes shrewdly reminds us of the importance of definitions and words to the political enterprise: "In the right Definition of Names lyes the first use of Speech; which is the Acquisition of Science ... The light of humane minds is Perspicuous Words, but by exact definitions first snuffed and purged from ambiguity."[2] And since his day, much energy has been invested into the elaboration of terms and into the attempt to infuse these with particular meanings. One thinks of words like "people," "rights," and "liberty," and how much the vocabulary of both the American and French Revolutions would be denuded without them. One thinks of the play that "republican," "democratic," "proletarian," "revolutionary," "nation," and "national" have received over the past couple of centuries and can ill conceive of a political history of the modern world with them removed.

What I would like to do in this chapter is to examine the use of certain terms in Canadian political discourse. In one sense, this can be seen as a fairly practical exercise, charting the rise and fall of terms like "dominion" or "province" over time and addressing the relative weight of "government" and "state" in political speeches, debates, or diverse publications. This itself can be useful in bringing home the shift in symbolism between the time of Confederation, say, or the First World War and the post–1945 period. Yet there is more than a historical dimension to such a discussion. For in a deeper sense, the replacement of terms like "Dominion of Canada," "Province of Alberta," and "Province de Québec" with terms like "Government of Canada," "Government of Alberta," "Etat québécois," and "state sector" bespeak the larger role that government and state have come to play in all twentieth-century societies, including our own. It thus ties directly into the theme of the larger volume.

What does the historical record suggest? We know that the Preamble to the British North America Act refers to the desire of the provinces of Canada, Nova Scotia, and New Brunswick "to be federally united into one Dominion under the Crown." We also know that John A. Macdonald and others of the Fathers of Confederation had originally preferred the term *kingdom* to describe Canada but had been persuaded by the British, fearful of arousing republican sentiment in the United States in the aftermath of the Civil War, into accepting "dominion" in its stead.[3] The reference, we are led to believe, had come to Leonard Tilley from his reading of Psalm 72: "He shall have dominion from sea to sea, and from the river to the ends of the earth." And as the Earl of Carnarvon wrote to the British colonial secretary, it was "intended as a tribute to the monarchical principle which they earnestly wish to uphold."[4]

Well and good. But the first question that comes to mind must be to whom this "dominion from sea to sea" was being given, and by whom it was to be exercised. It would be one thing if sovereignty were being derived directly from the people and if it were unambiguously to Canada and Canadians that all governmental power – executive, legislative, and judicial – were being allocated. We would then have had much the same constitutional foundation for the Canadian state as the Americans were to have for their republic or the French for theirs. But this was not to be the case.

By insisting on the monarchical principle, with the British monarch exercising a similar function with respect to Canada as to the United Kingdom, and by further insisting on the preservation of intimate links to the British Empire, the imperial government and the imperial Parliament, the Fathers of Confederation, in good counter-revolutionary fashion, were ensuring that something less than sovereignty would be vested in this country, its people, and their governments under the BNA Act. According to the German *Geschichtliche Grundbegriffe*, the term *dominion* can be traced back to the term *dominium regis*, describing kingly rule between the eighth and eleventh centuries, and to the *dominus mundi*, describing the "world rule" of the Holy Roman Emperor.[5]

According to Blackstone's mid-eighteenth-century definition, a dominion was "a country conquered by British arms ... subject to the legislation of the Parliament of Great Britain."[6] This evocation of a subordinate status, the harping on the *British* character of the newly created Dominion, may well explain why the term would find less favour with French Canadians than English Canadians through much of the succeeding century and why even English-Canadian nationalists would ultimately turn against it: "I claim independence from the Parliament of Great Britain; and I object, therefore, to Canada being called a 'dominion,' for the word implies subjection."[7]

Nonetheless, "dominion," as in Dominion of Canada, Dominion Government, Dominion Parliament, or Dominion Courts, prevailed in Canadian political discourse from the passage of the BNA Act to the immediate post Second World War period. It was a favoured term in statute law, used, for example, in the Inland Revenue, Post Office, Bank, and Intercolonial Acts of 1867, or in the banking, life insurance, criminal law and railway acts of 1890. It figures in the title of the Dominions Land Act of 1909 and the Dominion Election Act of 1920. It is no less common a term in statutes of the late 1920s, for example, the Fisheries Act, Juvenile Delinquents Act, Opium and Narcotics Act, and Penny Bank Act, of 1929. A 1935 piece of legislation is entitled the Dominion Housing Act, while 1937 sees the establishment of a Royal Commission on Dominion-Provincial Relations. As late as 1949, annual reports of federal departments give the term *Dominion* prominence on their title page, as does the Canada Year Book.[8] In 1953-4, Hansard Debates were still published under the heading Dominion of Canada, House of Commons Debates, and a federal agency like the Dominion Bureau of Statistics retained the word in its title down to 1971, when it became Statistics Canada. Nor did Canada Day displace Dominion Day as the name of Canada's national holiday until relatively recently.

"Dominion" was also a favoured term in Canadian historiography, political discourse, and social science. The collection *Canada and its Provinces*, edited by Adam Shortt and Arthur Doughty, makes numerous references to Dominion or Dominion government, and none to state.[9] Sir Robert Borden uses the term throughout his Rhodes Memorial Lectures, published in 1929, in reference both to Canada and to the other British dominions.[10] The entry under the rubric "government" in the 1932 *Encyclopedia of the Social Sciences* has a two-page article by Robert McKay entitled "Dominion of Canada"[11] The 1940s was to see publication of Donald Creighton's *Dominion of the North* and Alexander Brady's *Democracy in the Dominions*.[12] This is but a tiny sampling of a much larger body of material.

The term *dominion* had, in fact, acquired further importance with the evolution in Canada's constitutional status. At imperial conferences, held with increasing frequency in the first decades of the twentieth century, "His Majesty's Overseas Dominions" came to be used with reference to all the self-governing members of the British Empire.[13] In 1919, it was the "Dominion of Canada" that achieved representation in its own name in the newly formed League of Nations. That same year, imperial acts of Parliament and imperial orders in council were no longer included in the bound volumes of the Statues of Canada where they had, until then, preceded Canadian orders in council and acts of the Parliament of the Dominion of Canada; only the latter would now be printed. The Statute of Westminster of 1931 recognized the full autonomy of the various British dominions from the government and Parliament of the United Kingdom for purposes of international law. And it was to the "Dominion of Canada" that Franklin Delano Roosevelt gave an assurance in 1938 that the United States would not sit idly by were it to come under threat from some other empire than the British.[14]

Yet the term was to die out in the decade following the outbreak of the Second World War. It was Canada, rather than the Dominion of Canada, that became a founding member of the newly formed United Nations in 1945. Increasingly in the following years, the term *Dominion* was to be dropped from official publications, statements and speeches, and all international references to this country, with the term *Canada* or *Government of Canada* taking its place. Its disappearance can be seen as a manifestation of a newly stirring national feeling, of which the Canadian Citizenship Act of 1947, abolition of appeals to the Privy Council in 1949, and the appointment of the first Canadian-born governor general in 1952 were examples.

In 1947, the British government itself had changed the title of the Office of Secretary of State for Dominion Affairs to Secretary of State for Commonwealth Relations, and Clement Attlee had given as the reason that the term *Dominion* was "liable to convey a misleading impression of the relations between the United Kingdom and the other members of the Commonwealth."[15]

In 1946, 1948, 1950, and 1951, private member's bills, initiated by francophone Liberals from Quebec, called for abolition of the term *dominion* and the renaming of the national holiday Canada Day: "One of the main reasons for this bill is that since Canada has become a sovereign state, the word 'dominion' as applied to Canada has entirely lost its original meaning."[16] "Be it moved that the government recognizing our status as an international power ... introduce legislation repatriating our constitution as a Canadian document deleting from the statutes of Canada, wherever it may be found, ... the word 'dominion.' "[17]

While none of these private member's bills carried on division, in practice the transition away from "dominion" was in full swing. This provoked much breast-beating and denunciation from anglophone Conservatives in the early 1950s:[18] "The Dominion of Canada is what I was taught to revere, but here for some reason or other, the word 'dominion' is now being left out."[19] "The work 'dominion' has begun to disappear. I regretted that. I regretted it very much."[20]

There were similar interventions by E. Davie Fulton and Howard Green in debate on the Dominion Election Act in 1951, by George Drew in the Throne Speech debate of March 1952, and by John Diefenbaker regarding the omission of the word "dominion" from the new building of the Dominion Bureau of Statistics in the summer of 1956.[21] Nothing, however, was done when the Conservatives came to power in 1957 to restore it. Instead, over the subsequent three decades the term has become anachronistic, effectively vanishing from all government publications, academic writing, and popular usage.[22] Government documents now invariably read Canada or Government of Canada on the cover and title pages, with a logo of the Canadian flag often alongside.

There is an interesting parallel between the rise and fall of the term *dominion* and the usage of the term *province* in official documents and publications. The historical practice between 1867 and the 1960s and 1970s is clear enough. Title pages read: Public Accounts of the Province of Ontario or Statutes of the Province of Ontario; Public Accounts of the Province of Alberta or Estimates of Revenues for the Province of Alberta; Province de Québec: Rapport du Surintendant de l'Instruction Publique, or Ministère de l'Agriculture et de la Colonisation de la Province de Québec. Then comes the break.

By the mid-1960s, "Province" is dropped from official Quebec publications. Instead, there is increasing use of "Gouvernement du Québec" or "Québec," with a fleur-de-lis logo or flag. For example, we now find Gouvernement du Québec, Ministère des Richesses

Naturelles, or Québec, Service des Assurances: Ministère des Institutions Financières, Rapport Annuel. The Quiet Revolution, a new sense of importance associated with the Quebec government, increasing restiveness about any subordinate position vis-à-vis the federal government would all have played their role. As Jean-Charles Bonenfant observed: "Il y a moyen qui consiste à dire ni 'la province de Québec' ni 'l'état du Québec,' mais simplement 'le Québec' tout comme à Ottawa pour faire disparaître 'Dominion' dans 'Dominion du Canada' on a pris l'habitude de dire 'le Canada.' "[23]

Ontario, as well, by the early 1970s, had curtly dropped the word "province" from the Revised Statutes of Ontario or its Public Accounts, suggesting that the symbolism of subordination was no more acceptable to the major English-speaking province than to Quebec. And Alberta, under Peter Lougheed's Conservatives, committed to province-building and regional affirmation, also dropped "province" from its publications. From 1973–4 one reads "Public Accounts Alberta," where these had read "Public Accounts of the Province of Alberta" until that date. As of 1976, the Estimates of Expenditure speak only of "Alberta" on the title page, and by the mid-1980s they read "Government Estimates Alberta." There exist an Alberta Hansard, an *Alberta Official Gazette*, and annual reports for various government departments, but nary any reference to the "Province of Alberta."

In place of "dominion" and "province" two other terms have come into use, *government* and *state*. Neither of these is new to Canadian political discourse, but their increased salience since 1945 is itself worthy of attention. Before I discuss their current status, however, let me say a little about earlier terminological practice.

The B N A Act, for all its reference to "Dominion" in its Preamble, has far greater recourse to "Government of Canada" (sections 16, 118, 132, and 145) and to "Government of the Provinces" (sections 68, 126, and 142). And numerous are the references from that point on in statutes and political speeches to the "Government of the Dominion of Canada" (Intercolonial Railway Act, 1867, Preamble), the "Government of Canada" (Official Secrets Act, 1890), or the "Dominion Government" (Canada Grains Act, 1929 40[7]). John A. Macdonald, during the Confederation Debates, speaks about "the future government of British North America,"[24] Tilley, as minister of finance in his 1879 budget speech refers to "the present Government,"[25] Laurier talks about "my Government be[ing] sustained,"[26] Meighen, with reference to railway subsidies speaks about "Government subsidies and guarantees" and "Government ownership."[27] References to

"Conservative Government," "Liberal Government," or "Union Government" are legion.

There is common usage of the term with respect to the governments of the Canadian provinces and with regard to the imperial government and the governments of other countries. What strikes me, however, in surveying this earlier period is the sense in which "dominion" and "province" seem to refer to ongoing geographical and political entities, over which governments, more provisional in character, preside. Or to carry this thought one step further, they have some of the attributes of permanence and, perhaps, sovereignty, that elsewhere is vested in the term *state*.

This may become more apparent when we canvass uses of the term *state* down to 1945. One early, very positive usage occurs in William Lyon Mackenzie's 1837 Draft Constitution on behalf of "the people of the state of Upper Canada."[28] The term *state* is used in the sense of sovereignty and plenipotentiary political power throughout this eighty-one-clause document, which provides for a republican system of government for Upper Canada. The aim is an independent "state," unbeholden to Great Britain and to monarchical institutions, which have brought the colony to an evil pass. "Dominion" will simply not do.

In the Confederation Debates, there are numerous references to 'the parent State," i.e. the United Kingdom,[29] to the role of an upper house in the "State,"[30] and to the question of state interference in religion.[31] There are, by comparison, few references to Canada itself constituting a state. George Brown comes closest to such a formulation when he claims: "In 1871 we shall stand equal in population to the 9th sovereign state of Europe ... it will make us the 3rd maritime state of the world."[32] But John A. Macdonald captures the underlying character of Confederation with the phrase "the junction of all the provinces in one great government under our common Sovereign."[33] There is little place in the Confederation scheme – essentially home rule within the British Empire – for something as grandiose as a sovereign Canadian state.

The term *state* is invoked, from time to time, in Canada down to the First World War. There is, for example, a Department of the Secretary of State dating from Confederation, though its functions were essentially related to ceremony, records, and correspondence.[34] When Canada acquired an interest in foreign affairs, the relevant department came to be known as that of the Secretary of State for External Affairs.[35] The Official Secrets Act of 1890 refers to communication of information to persons "to whom the same ought not, in the interest of the State, to be communicated at that time,"[36] though one strongly suspects it was imperial, as much as Canadian, state secrets that were involved. An occasional M P uses the term *state* like the Alberta Liberal, Michael Clark, in deploring the move to "state control" that he detected in William Lyon Mackenzie King's Combines Investigation Act of 1909.[37] Such uses, however, are relatively few and far between.

French Canadians displayed a greater propensity to use "state," even in this earlier period, than English Canadians. Laurier's addresses are replete with references to "a free state," to "the best-regulated State," to "the rights of the members of the State", to Quebec as "an independent state forming part of another independent state (Canada)," to "our constitution invit[ing] all citizens to take part in the direction of the affairs of the State," to "the security of the State" depending upon freedom of opinion.[38] His nationalist opponents of the 1900s, Henri Bourassa and the Nationalist League, made use of terms like "political state" and "state grants,"[39] anticipating the much greater recourse to the term in Quebec's subsequent political discourse.

The First World War, with its intensive patriotism, gave "state" a new importance in English-Canadian political life. A 1915 Ontario Government Commission on Unemployment argued: "If the state wishes to secure the fullest loyalty and efficiency of its citizens must it not assume a larger measure of leadership than in the past?"[40] During the conscription debate of 1917, Sam Hughes, Canada's militia minister, could declare: "Every citizen owes duty to the state; he must pay taxes, must be personally responsible for a share in the administration of justice. So also in every land, each is liable for service for the defence of homes and loved ones and against the common enemy of mankind."[41] Conservative M P George McCraney could ask:

What are the responsibilities which we owe to 300,000 men who are now in England, France and Flanders, in the King's uniform, under authority of this Parliament? We shall answer the question pretty much in the views we hold as to the relations which the citizen bears to the state. Some of us hold the view that the relations are reciprocal, that the citizen who is damaged in his person, in his right, or in his property, has a right to the protection of the state, and also that when the state is in danger, the state has a right to call upon the citizen for his property and for his person in its defence.[42]

For John Watson in his 1918 book, *The State in Peace and War*: "It is the function of the state to defend the conditions under which the best life is possible."[43] War suddenly brought home dimensions of political obligation and sovereign command that only the word "state" captured.

A little of this percolates over into the immediate post-war period. In reference to the Treaty of Versailles, one Conservative M P exclaimed: "We enter this League as a sovereign State."[44] In the context of the Winnipeg General Strike, some at least of the labour press was conscious of the coercive power that the "state" deploys: "And it was not until the state, through ... Meighen and Senator Robertson ... stepped in and laid it down as the policy of the government that collective bargaining could only be recognized when it was confined to local unionism."[45] "This fact of there being two lives – the 'life of the state' and the life of the working class, contradicts the popular view of the State being the people, the nation, the community ... Private property and the State go hand in hand. By means of the State, the ruling minority, through their monopoly of the social product, dominate the whole social group."[46] The indictment against the Winnipeg strikers, however, spoke of conspiracy "to bring into hatred and contempt the government, laws and constitution of the Dominion of Canada and of the province of Manitoba."[47] Until the Depression, "dominion" and "government" are far more prevalent than "state."

During the 1930s, "state" had something of a renewed appeal. For liberal and socialist-minded intellectuals in the midst of the apparent breakdown of the capitalist system, "extension of the state's functions was necessary;"[48] "the state could no longer remain an arbitrator between man and man."[49] Graham Spry, in his testimony to the parliamentary committee on broadcasting counterposed "the State or the United States" as the alternative facing the country,[50] while Harold Innis's economic essays are peppered with references, not all positive, to the state.[51] For the Liberals, Vincent Massey argued in 1933, "individualism, however 'rugged' it may be, can no longer be left to itself. It can, in fact, be safeguarded only by means of the control which the State provides."[52] The League for Social Reconstruction's *Social Planning for Canada* makes reference to "administration in the socialized State," to "State medicine," to the "planned state," to "state holding companies," and to "state trusts."[53] Even R.B. Bennett, in his radio broadcasts of January 1935, summoned "the power of the state" in support of his "New Deal" measures.[54] Here it is the state – as antidote to economic crisis, as articulator of social needs, as repository of a certain vision of nation – that has pride of place.

In Quebec, the late 1930s saw positive references to the notion of the state in nationalist circles. Best known is the Abbé Groulx's declaration of 1937, "Nous l'aurons notre état du Québec!"[55] Equally interesting is the 1938 article by a professor at les Hautes études commerciales, Maximilien Caron, entitled "La province du Québec est-elle un Etat?":

La conclusion nous paraît s'imposer. Le Québec est une entité politique, une personne morale. Celle-ci réunit sur un territoire qui est le sien, sous une autorité commune bien organisée et suprême, trois millions d'hommes dont elle peut régir les droits. Notre province, dans son champ d'activité, qui est trés étendu, possède la même souveraineté intérieure que l'autorité fédérale or l'autorité impériale. Elle est indépendante de tous pouvoirs; elle est auto-nome. Elle ne jouit pas de la souveraineté extérieure; cela n'importe pas, nous l'avons vu ... Elle constitue un Etat.[56]

There is an ambiguity to the term *état* that permeates French juridi-cal writings of the early twentieth century and here finds expression in Quebec. For Delbez, whom Caron seemed to be unconsciously echoing, "Les Etats membres d'une Union réelle et les membres d'un Etat fédéral sont seulement des Etats au sens du droit constitu-tionnel, pas au sens du droit international."[57] But this distinction between constitutional and international law is less evident in Hauri-ou's treatise, *Droit publique*, which Groulx seemed to be emulating: "L'Etat est la personnification juridique d'une nation, consécutive à la centralisation politique, économique, juridique des éléments de la nation, réalisée en vue de la création du régime civil."[58]

In English usage as well, there has been increasing identification of the term *state* with sovereignty. Thus Frederick Watkins, in the *International Encyclopedia of the Social Sciences* writes: "The state is a geographically delimited segment of human society united by com-mon obedience to a single sovereign ... As the above definition shows, the concept of the state is closely related to the concept of sovereignty."[59] And it is this sense that seemed to come home to Canada as a result of the Second World War and Canada's interna-tional position thereafter. As a founding member of the United Nations, whose Charter and publications make frequent reference to "original member states" or "peace-loving states,"[60] Canada itself came to be referred to by its political leaders as a "state." Mackenzie King, in a 1945 debate about the forthcoming San Francisco Confer-ence, at which the U N was to be constituted, used expressions like "Canada and other secondary states" or "all states, other than the five great powers, would have the same constitutional position in the organization."[61] In the 1946 debate on the Canadian Citizenship Act, M P F.E. Jaenicke noted: "There is no question but that Canada, especially during the past ten years, has been recognized as a sovereign state."[62] In the flag debate of 1964, Lester Pearson argued: "The flags we have used for Canada have already changed as Canada has evolved from a colony to a self-governing Dominion to an independent nation, to a sovereign state respected among the states of the world."[63]

Still, the period since 1945 has not seen "state" simply displace "government" in Canadian political discourse. Until recently, especially where domestic, as opposed to international, functions of the political sphere are concerned, "government" has been far more common. At most, what I shall be arguing is that there is increasing recourse to the term *state* on the part of English-Canadian and Québécois social scientists, jurists, philosophers, and historians and, from time to time, in official documents as well.

I have already made mention of the tendency for "Government of Canada" to displace "Dominion Government" or "Government of the Dominion of Canada" in federal publications after 1950. Similarly, at the provincial level, "Government of Ontario," "Gouvernement de Québec" and so on displaced the older formulae, "Province of Ontario," "Province de Québec," and so on from the 1960s. We speak of intergovernmental relations in Canada, of a federal form of government, of diverse governmental institutions, while we variously praise or blame the Trudeau government or the Mulroney government for the measures each undertakes. To this degree, we seem in Canada, especially in English-speaking Canada, to have preserved something of a distaste for the "heavier," more metaphysically tinged, continental European notion of the state. Even neo-conservative critics of an ostensibly too large public sector are prone to speak more of "government" as the villain of the piece than of the "state."[64]

Moreover, in Quebec, despite strong nationalist sentiment sparked by the Quiet Revolution, there was reluctance to use the term *Etat du Québec* in official government publications or in the media, despite a suggestion by the Office de la Langue française to do just this in 1963: "Au début de 1963, l'Office provinciale de la langue française du Québec demandait aux journalistes de remplacer la désignation de 'province de Québec' par celle 'état du Québec.' Cette suggestion, qui n'a pas été acceptée officiellement par le gouvernement, en a scandalisé quelques-uns qui sont allés même jusqu'à prétendre qu'un tel changement violerait la constitution de Canada."[65] Yet there is a considerable difference between official publications and actual usage and much evidence that the term *état* and its English equivalent, "state," have gained in currency in Canada over the past couple of decades.

On the francophone side, the mid-1950s saw attacks by the Quebec government and its Tremblay Commission on the "centralizing" intentions of Ottawa. One of the studies done for the Tremblay Commission was by Charles de Koninck, dean of the Faculty of Philosophy at Laval, and entitled *La Confédération: Rempart contre le grand état*. De Koninck, citing Aristotle, de Jouvenel, and others, argues against the so-called Grand Etat, which arrogates to itself "a certain divinity" and seeks to homogenize its subjects. "The centralized state is an evil in itself," and a smaller state, less blind to individual realities, is to be preferred.[66]

By the late 1950s and early 1960s, the focus in Quebec had shifted to viewing the Quebec state as a good in itself. Jean Lesage, in a political work published in 1959, attacks the Union nationale for what he calls "sabotage de l'Etat québécois," arguing: "Si l'Etat québécois est le principal moyen d'action politique des Canadiens français et si à ce titre on en exige le respect, la plus élémentaire décence requiert qu'on le respecte soi-même."[67]

The Institut Canadien des Affaires Publiques organized its 1962 annual conference around the theme *Le Rôle de l'Etat*, with participants focusing on the historical evolution of the state's role, on the traditional fear of the state – "L'Etat fédéral, donc étranger"[68] – on the part of French Canadians, and on the new consciousness about the state that the removal of political and clerical obstacles seemed to be promoting: "Il est à souhaiter, avec la démocratisation croissante de notre population, que l'Etat puisse noliser les compétences voulues et créer à chaque point stratégique le consortium capable à la fois de saisir la réalité social et économique et d'y engager à fond les forces qui peuvent la mouvoir."[69]

For Gérard Fortin, writing in 1966 about the proponents of a new Quebec nationalism, "leur idéologie du progrés et du développement s'appuie sur une conception égalitaire de la société et sur l'idée qu'il faut donner à l'Etat un rôle prédominant."[70] Arthur Tremblay, in 1970, talks about a new generation of Quebec civil servants, "équipée pour assurer intégralement le rôle dynamique de l'Etat dans le développement."[71] And social science and historical writing in Quebec is replete, from that point on, with references to "la légitimité de l'état," "les appareils d'état," "état et nation," "Etat québécois," and so on.[72]

What should we read into the word? At one level, perhaps, it is a synonym for the "government" of Quebec, albeit emphasizing the autonomy of the Quebec government vis-à-vis Ottawa and the quasi-sovereign powers it therefore deploys within its own particular sphere, whatever its shortcomings as an actor in terms of international law: "Il est sûr que l'Acte de l'Amérique du Nord britannique ne parle pas de l'Etat du Québec, mais l'absence du mot n'entraîne pas nécessairement l'absence de la chose ... On doit admettre que le Québec est souverain dans la sphère assignée aux provinces par la constitution. Ce qui lui manque, c'est la souveraineté extérieure, c'est-à-dire une existence véritable en regard du droit international. Les états membres d'un état fédéral sont dépourvus de toute capacité internationale, mais ils n'en sont pas moins des états, au sens du droit constitutionnel."[73]

At another level, however, following Hauriou's definition cited above, the state becomes "the juridical personification of the nation," and as such is invested with the defensive mission that might earlier have been associated with the church and with new tasks of social and economic development – l'épanouissement – and even international affirmation. Much like the word "nation," "état" takes on overtones that potentially look beyond the existing Canadian federation.

There are hints of such use in Daniel Johnson's positing of French and English Canada as "Etats associés" as one means of restructuring confederation.[74] There are much more explicit assertions of a sovereignty attached to the state in various Parti québécois documents of the 1970s. Its 1975 program, for example, talks about a P Q government pledging itself "To set in motion immediately the process of accession to sovereignty by proposing to the National Assembly a law ... If it becomes necessary to proceed unilaterally to assume methodically the exercise of all the powers of a sovereign state, having ensured beforehand that it has the support of the Quebec people by means of a referendum."[75]

The White Paper of 1979, *Quebec-Canada: A New Deal*, makes it clear that the P Q is talking in terms of "two States," associated with each other, but with each enjoying a large measure of sovereignty, if its referendum proposal carries: "Sovereignty for Quebec will have a legal impact on the power to make laws and levy taxes, on territorial integrity, on citizenship and minorities, on the courts and various other institutions, on the relations of Quebec with other countries."[76] And jurists like Jacques Brossard devoted hundreds of pages to analysing the legal position a sovereign Quebec state would find itself in with respect to international, no less than domestic, legal arrangements."[77]

It was this potential identification of state with sovereignty that, in turn, led an opponent of Quebec independence like Pierre Elliott

Trudeau to seek to invest legitimacy in the federal state: "Since a state needs to develop to preserve consensus in its very life ... much more nationalism would appear to be required in the case of a federal nation-state."[78] And one finds in Trudeau's political vocabulary terms like "the democratic state," "the Canadian federal state," "a parliamentary federal state," or "the Canadian state" *tout court*.[79] "State" is a term too charged with meaning, too important, to be left uncontested to one's political foes.

One notes also a tendency to use "état" in French where English would not use "state." One example is the NATO Charter of 1949. The English text, in its Preamble, refers to "the Parties to the Treaty," whereas the French text reads "Les Etats parties au présent Traité"; Article 14, speaks in English of the "governments of the other signatories," but in French about "Etats signataires."[80] Within Canada, where the term *crown corporation* is the most frequently used designation in English for government-controlled enterprises, French-speakers invariably refer to "société d'état."[81] While the explanation here can be linked to the antipathy in contemporary Quebec to the symbols of monarchy and crown, there is also a deeper reservoir of feeling that can be mobilized around "état" than is true for "state" in English Canada. Part of this is a function of the greater resonance "état" may have in French, going back to centuries of experience of centralization under the ancien régime and since the French Revolution, part of it of the nationalist investment in state-building at the provincial level in Quebec during the period 1960–1980.

As for English-language uses of "state," I think it is fair to note a distinct increase in its popularity, especially in the social sciences, in recent years. In the 1950s and 1960s, there were occasional articles with titles like "The State and Economic Growth in Canada."[82] But "government" was far more prevalent in Canadian political science, sociology and economics.[83] The one exception may have been the term *welfare state*, which entered the broad literature of the social sciences by the 1960s and would therefore have found echoes in Canada.[84]

It is with the revival of political economy in English Canada that one began to see more sustained use of the term *state*. The new political economy school, strongly influenced by Marxist and neo-Marxist currents, was more prone than its pluralist rivals, to recognize the class dimensions of political power and the pivotal role that the state plays within capitalist society. (Neo-Marxist writers also display a greater predilection for the term *state* than do those of a more classically social democratic hue.[85]) Moreover, relations between centre and periphery, especially between Canada and core powers such as Great Britain and the United States, were key to adherents of this school, for example, Mel Watkins, Kari Levitt, Tom Naylor, and Wallace Clement, leading them to focus on issues of state sovereignty or its absence. The year 1977 saw the publication of a Marxist-inspired anthology, *The Canadian State*,[86] the first contemporary work in political science/economy to put the concept "state" at the front and centre of its analysis. It was soon complemented by a variety of books and articles with a left-of-centre perspective, referring to "the provincial state," "state building," "state corporations," "state elite," "state enterprise," or "state capitalism."[87] A series was inaugurated at the University of Toronto Press, entitled The State and Economic Life, with monographs such as *The State and Enterprise: Canadian Manufacturers and the Federal Government, 1917–1931; An Impartial Umpire: Industrial Relations and the Canadian State 1900–1911;* and *A Staple State: Canadian Industrial Resources in Cold War* succeeding each other.[88] For journals such as *Studies in Political Economy* and *Labour/Le Travail*, the "state," with greater or lesser autonomy from the institutions of capitalist domination, has become a privileged term of analysis.

But not only the left would write about the "state." Increasingly the term found its way into the writings of other social scientists and historians. For some, like H.V. Nelles, writing about "the image of the state" or "the role of the state in the development of natural resources and the regulation of the economy" in Ontario,[89] it may have stirred echoes of Canadian political economic writings of the 1920s and 1930s, for example, Innis or Creighton. For those writing about foreign policy or international relations, references to "state system" and "state behaviours" reflected a so-called realism about international politics in which state sovereignty was privileged and civil society seen as relatively insignificant.[90] Students of public policy, caught up with the new importance of governmental and bureaucratic intervention in the post war era, began to refer to "the administrative state," "state enterprise" and "state behaviour."[91] Students of federalism preferred to contrast "interstate federalism" and "intrastate federalism," where the terminology of dominion and provinces had once sufficed.[92] Canadian philosophers argued about the relation between nation and state and whether one necessarily led to the other,[93] while a political scientist like Douglas Verney might call for a "broad secular state" with a good deal of linguistic as well as cultural tolerance to replace the nation-state of yore.[94] And two research volumes for the Macdonald Commission addressed the theme State and Society in the Modern Era[95] (cf. chapter 7), confirming that the term was now in wide use in Canadian political science.[96]

Something of this penchant for the term *state* carried over into official political discourse, though "government" is still far more prevalent. The *Canada Year Book* of 1985, for example, devotes several chapters to the institutions of government. But in the introductory overview to these, it tells us that Canada's "is a federal state with ten provinces and two territories" and that "the Canadian federal state ... had its foundation in ... the B N A Act, 1867."[97] The term here refers to type of regime and institutional distribution of power. The Canadian Security Intelligence Act of 1984 talks about "Ministry of State" and "Foreign state mean[ing] any other state than Canada."[98] The Canada- U S Tax Convention of that same year refers to "contracting states" in its first article, and later to citizens with homes "in both States or neither State."[99] The Macdonald Report makes frequent reference to "state" in its opening chapter, in its discussion of the welfare state in Volume II, and with reference to citizenship and the federal state in Volume III.[100] And Mme Justice Bertha Wilson, in her written decision in the historic Supreme Court case on abortion that struck down article 251 of the Criminal Code, invokes the term *state* repeatedly.[101]

I am tempted to conclude with the observation that social science in English Canada and Quebec and, to a lesser degree, official discourse may well reflect deeper transformations that have been occurring in twentieth-century practice. As the political, economic, social, and international roles of states have tended to grow (compare chapter 6) in periods of crisis, but also over the long haul, it is only natural that our terminology increasingly reflect this. "State" has connotations of permanence that "government" lacks, of sovereignty in the international arena, of an ongoing distributional role that can be counterposed to that of markets, of an institution to which legitimacy is owed, but whose power, with respect to citizens, must somehow be kept in check.

As issues of sovereignty or legitimacy, economic allocation or social security have loomed larger in Canada, so too has "state" become a more salient feature of the political vocabulary of francophones and anglophones,[102] of those who support increased state activity and of its opponents. If some, including this author, hanker after a face-to-face vision of political community with resonances of the ancient polis,[103] and if others, on the political right, look to the market-place as the be-all and end-all of political, no less than economic, good, our world remains one in which the state occupies, and will continue to occupy, the centre of the political stage. The political evolution of Canada since 1867 has been not from colony to nation but from dominion to state.

CHAPTER FOUR

Montesquieu Revisited

Bientôt la liberté civile du peuple, les prérogatives de la noblesse et du clergé, la puissance des rois, se trouvèrent dans un tel concert, que je ne crois pas qu'il y ait eu sur la terre de gouvernement si tempéré.
Montesquieu, *De l'esprit des lois*[1]

Canadians are not in the habit of looking to Montesquieu for an understanding of their political institutions. They tend not to be theoretical in their approach to politics, which sets them off from the populations of Europe and even from the intellectual practice of various New World societies, including the United States and much of Latin America. Lacking a revolutionary tradition, and wedded for the larger part of their history to a neo-colonial outlook, which, on the English-Canadian side, made them tributaries, intellectually speaking, first of Great Britain, then of the United States, Canadians have given a much more modest place to ideas than is true for countries with a stronger sense of nationhood.

Pragmatic, matter-of-fact propositions have generally sufficed for politicians, coupled with whatever wisdom could be distilled from the British constitution and from the working premises of parliamentarism and federalism, as adapted to the political-economic realities of a white settler dominion. As Frank Underhill pointed out many years ago, contrasting the Canadian experience with that of Britain and the United States, "Those two countries since the end of the eighteenth century, have abounded in prophets and philosophers ... Where are the classics in our political literature which embody our Canadian version of liberalism and democracy? Our party struggles have never been raised to the higher intellectual plane at which they become of universal interest by the presence of a Canadian Jefferson and a Canadian Hamilton in opposing parties. We have had no Canadian Burke or Mill to perform the social function of the political philosopher in action."[2]

From time to time, Canadian academics have attempted to introduce political theory into their analysis. On the English-Canadian side in recent times, Locke has been invoked, especially by adepts of Louis Hartz like Gad Horowitz, though usually to argue that Canada, unlike the United States, did not have an exclusively Lockean liberal tradition.[3] (The implication, however, remains that alongside the Tory and socialist elements, a powerfully Lockean strand did indeed exist in this country.) Reg Whitaker has talked about the Hobbesian underpinnings of the Canadian state, as in a way has Dennis Smith,[4] and there is much going back to the "Peace, Order and Good Government" passage in the British North America Act, or the invocation of authority over liberty by Canadian governments at crises in our history (the Winnipeg General Strike, the October Crisis) that would seem to bear this out. Rod Preece has talked about the Burkean streak in John A. Macdonald's political thought,[5] and certainly the prevailing Canadian view of Parliament and parliamentary sovereignty stems far more from Burke than from the revolutionary eighteenth-century idea of popular sovereignty.

On the French-Canadian side, despite the signal contribution of social scientists such as Bergeron, Dion, Rocher, and Rioux to a global-type analysis of Quebec society, there seems to have been even less of an attempt to look to political theory for inspiration. However, Thomism was a very powerful body of ideas in French Canada until recently, and through it something of classical discourse, for example, Aristotle, found reflection in Quebec intellectual life.[6] Marxism has had enormous influence in Québécois academic circles since the early 1960s, bringing with it a potent reading of the nature of political domination in capitalist societies of a nationally divided type.[7]

These contributions do not offer a convincing description of the theoretical underpinnings of the Canadian state and of the central institutions developed over time. This chapter suggests that such a perspective can in good part be generated from the writings of one of the major intellectual figures of the eighteenth century, Montesquieu. Although Montesquieu is usually held up as someone whose influence was far greater on the American or the French republics than on Britain and British-derived constitutions, I shall be arguing that his *Spirit of the Laws*, especially the famous discussion in book x I, section 6, entitled "Of the English Constitution," is a seminal text for understanding the Canadian political order, more so than anything in Hobbes or Locke or any other major theorist.

The reader might object that Montesquieu's reading of the English constitution of the mid-eighteenth century, with its ostensible separation of powers among executive, legislative, and judicial spheres, was perhaps itself profoundly mistaken, ignoring the real fusion between executive and legislative power that was to characterize the British system of cabinet government from that time on. It was the authors of the *Federalist Papers* who quoted "the celebrated Montesquieu" for his doctrine of the separation of powers[8] and who wrote it, with modification, into the American constitution of 1789, with its clear distinction among Congress, the presidency, and the courts. Similarly, article x v i of the *Declaration of the Rights of Man and the Citizen* of 1789 boldly stated: "Toute société dans laquelle la garantie des droits n'est pas assurée, ni la séparation des pouvoirs déterminée, n'a pas de constitution."[9] One looks in vain for similar formulations anywhere in the constitutional texts of Great Britain and, by extension, the dominions.

Yet if Montesquieu was so mistaken how is it that his *Spirit of the Laws*, in particular book x i, section 6, received so enthusiastic a reception in late-eighteenth-century England? As F.T.H. Fletcher argued in a study first published almost half a century ago,

The four principal interpreters of Montesquieu in England – Blackstone, De Lolme, Paley and Burke – were content to reproduce his account of the balanced three-power system almost without change ... In points ... too numerous to record ... we see Blackstone following faithfully in the wake of Montesquieu. The origin of the Constitution in the woods of Germany, separation of powers, nature and function of King, lords and commons, perishability of the legislature, money bills, representation and suffrage, assembly and dissolution of Parliament, the army and navy – everywhere the trace of Montesquieu is heavily impressed ... [As for] Montesquieu's most perspicacious and distinguished interpreter in England, Edmund Burke ... the surest testimony to Montesquieu's wisdom was the fact that it had reached its journey's end in the British Constitution.[10]

For M.J.C. Vile, author of the more recent *Constitutionalism and the Separation of Powers*, "Blackstone was not a very original thinker ... It was Blackstone's task to assimilate as much of Montesquieu as possible and to domesticate him."[11] Edmund Burke, for his part, spoke of Montesquieu's "aquiline eye," praising him as "a genius not born in every country or every time."[12] Something in Montesquieu's work had obviously impressed itself on important intellectual figures, who in turn influenced such nineteenth-century colonial politicians as John A. Macdonald and George-Etienne Cartier. What could it have been?

To answer this question, one must recognize that Montesquieu was the originator of more than a mechanical formula regarding the separation of powers: an encyclopaedic student of history and comparative institutions, he was also heir to a doctrine that comes down to us from antiquity, that of the mixed constitution. This doctrine, developed in its fullest form in the works of Polybius and Cicero, suggested that the ideal constitution (for example, that of the Roman Republic of the second century B C) was one that combined features of the three constitutions known to the ancients – rule of the one, rule of the few, and rule of the many – which in their good forms might be called monarchy, aristocracy, and democracy. Polybius, for example, argued that in Rome the consuls incarnated a form of monarchical authority, the Senate aristocratic, and the Tribunes as well as tribal assemblies a form of popular power.[13] Each might appear for certain purposes to possess plenipotentiary power, yet the powers of each were so blended with those of the other two that the Roman constitution could be said to represent a mixture of all three. Hence the term *mixed constitution*.

Now Montesquieu was himself an aristocrat of liberal inclination, writing under the monarchy of the ancien régime, at a period when the rising third estate was increasingly demanding admission into the political portals of the realm. A self-professed believer in the virtue of moderate government,[14] he saw in the England of his day (England almost a century before the first Reform Bill) the model of a state blending the three crucial political forces – monarch, aristocracy, and people (or gentry). For this triad, at the sociological level, underpinned the checks and balances that at the institutional level came to be called the separation of powers. "Tout serait perdu si le même homme, ou le même corps des principaux, ou des nobles, ou du peuple, exerçoient ces trois pouvoirs: celui de faire des lois, celui d'exécuter des résolutions publiques, et celui de juger les crimes ou les différends des particuliers."[15]

The solution he hit upon, ostensibly derived from the English experience, is ingenious. To the people as a body is given the legislative power. But since direct democracy of the ancient mould is for him impossible in the modern state, the people can act only through representatives. "Le grand avantage des représentants, c'est qu'ils sont capables de discuter des affaires. Le peuple n'y est point de tout

propre; ce qui forme un des grands inconvénients de la démocratie."[16] Moreover, only those who are not in such a lowly state – "un
tel état de bassesse" – that they cannot be said to have a will of their
own shall enjoy the franchise.

There are, however, in any state, men distinguished by birth,
wealth or honour. Were their voices simply drowned out by those of
the people, they would have no means of defending their own liberty and interests against the latter. Hence the need for a separate
legislative body grouping the nobility, with the power "d'arrêter les
entreprises du peuple, comme le peuple a droit d'arrêter les leurs."[17]

To the monarch is given executive power. Yet this power is not
hermetically sealed off from the legislative one. The monarch can
convene the legislature and veto such legislative measures as he/she
may oppose. While the legislature's control over the executive's day-
to-day actions is less complete, it does retain control over the voting
of all public funds, including those voted for the military, and this on
an annual basis. It can impeach ministers, though not the king himself. "Voici donc la constitution fondamentale du gouvernement
dont nour parlons. Le corps législatif y étant composé de deux parties, l'une enchaînera l'autre par sa faculté mutuelle d'empêcher.
Toutes les deux seront liées par la puissance exécutrice, qui le sera
elle-même par la législative."[18]

The checks and balances thus rest on the concert among monarch,
Lords, and Commons, or on the appropriate balancing of monarchy,
aristocracy, and democracy. It is the mixed constitution that lives
again under the guise of the England that Montesquieu describes.

This doctrine of the mixed constitution had enjoyed an important
revival in the England of the late seventeenth and early eighteenth
centuries and would have impressed itself upon Montesquieu both
from his travels in England and from his reading of such authors as
Bolingbroke and Halifax.[19] Yet it is given a new resonance in his
famous work. Such a mixed system is associated with the values of
honour, moderation, and virtue that Montesquieu, in book III, attributes to each of monarchy, aristocracy, and democracy, and which
come to be blended under a single constitution. This form of government, that of "a free people,"[20] is, by implication, contrasted with
the extremes of both despotism and democracy. One is tempted to
assert, along with Isaac Kramnick,[21] that the intellectual source of
subsequent arguments against democracy from Burke to de Tocqueville to latter-day critics of mass society is none other than Montesquieu. Montesquieu's formulation of the mixed constitution,
therefore, is a good deal more original and powerful than the version
advanced by his contemporaries.

The other major feature of his analysis – the one that American and French constitution-writers focus on – is the delineation of powers among legislative, executive, and judicial. While Montesquieu was not original in distinguishing the first two powers from each other, he placed the king outside the legislative, unlike authors such as Bolingbroke.[22] He was also the first to distinguish the judicial from the executive. Although this was the weakest of the three powers – "en quelque façon nulle"[23] – it bespoke the crucial importance of legal rights in the eighteenth-century delineation of citizenship and politics.

The imperative behind Montesquieu's three-tiered separation was rooted in his dislike for any form of despotic government, whether in its origins monarchical or republican. The separation of powers prevents the concentration of authority in a single set of hands, though it does not rule out close and continual interplay among and between the executive, legislative, and judicial powers. The original version of his doctrine, including royal executive power, reads like a blueprint for constitutional monarchy of a fairly traditional sort. Fate was to decree, in the late eighteenth century, that it would be adapted to the purposes of the American and French revolutions, gradually fading from British political debate.

The two aspects of Montesquieu's doctrine that have been singled out – the sociological theory of the mixed constitution and the separation-of-powers doctrine – are particularly apposite in explaining the constitutional development of this country. After Confederation, we acquired an institutional arrangement at the central level that mimed the British structure of monarchs, Lords, and Commons, together with a good deal of the political culture that went with it. The spirit of Montesquieu, with its blend of "honour," "moderation," and, more dubiously, "virtue," with its disdain for democratic excesses and for "extreme equality,"[24] seemed very much alive. Today, as Canada has moved closer to the United States, it is the Montesquieu of the separation of powers that seems to stalk the land.

In what sense was the British North America (B N A) Act a Montesquieuan document? We have been told by many historians and social scientists that Canada is a land of counter-revolution,[25] with a "greater acceptance of limitation, of hierarchical patterns" than the United States,[26] with a strongly monarchical flavour to its institutions.[27] Neither Cartier nor D'Arcy McGee hid his disdain for democratic forms during the Confederation Debates: "The weak point in democratic institutions is the leaving of all power in the hands of the popular element. The history of the past proves this is an evil. In order that institutions may be stable and work harmoniously there must be a power of resistance to oppose the democratic element."[28] "We run the risk of being swallowed up by the spirit of universal democracy that prevails in the United States ... The proposed Confederation will enable us to bear up shoulder to shoulder to resist the spread of this universal democracy doctrine."[29]

And John A. Macdonald, throughout his life, identified himself with the monarchical and class spirit that for him was the essence of the British Constitution: "Not a single one of the representatives of the government or of the opposition of any one of the lower provinces was in favour of universal suffrage. Everyone felt that in this respect the principle of the British Constitution should be carried out and that classes and property should be represented as well as members."[30] "The monarchical idea should be fostered in the colonies, accompanied by some gradation of classes."[31] "I have heard him express the opinion with much energy that no man who advocated universal suffrage had any right to call himself a Conservative."[32]

Class relations and social conditions in British North America during the second half of the nineteenth century were not, of course, identical with those of the England that Montesquieu had visited. For one, there was no native aristocracy, and hence no possibility of reproducing on Canadian soil a second chamber like the House of Lords. The spirit of democracy, for all the Loyalist ideology in the English-speaking colonies and ultramontane colouring of Quebec, was far more present than in the earlier period and could not be entirely contained. Monarchy could be distilled only in a derivative way, through governors general as representatives of the British crown. The existence of French Canada, and of strong regional sentiment in Atlantic Canada, and subsequently in the west, further ruled out a unitary form of government, introducing, despite Tory sentiment, a federal feature that was foreign to the British constitution.

And yet, within the limits of the possible, the BNA Act was a Montesquieuan-type mixed constitution. In its Preamble, it openly modelled itself on the prevailing constitution of Great Britain: "Whereas the Provinces of Canada, Nova Scotia, and New Brunswick have expressed their desire to be federally united into One Dominion under the Crown of the United Kingdom of Great Britain and Ireland, *with a Constitution similar in principle to that of the United Kingdom.*" The monarchical element dominates the opening sections, with the office of governor general, paralleling that of the crown, given pride of place over every other political institution. If the aristocratic element as such must be modified, we do end up with an appointed second chamber with a strong property restriction inserted to defend the interests of the wealthy. "The rights of the minority must be protected, and the rich are always fewer in number than the poor."[33] Had not Montesquieu, in describing the British nobility, talked about "la naissance, la richesse ou les honneurs" as setting the peers off from others in the realm? Under Canadian conditions, the Fathers of Confederation had to make do with "la richesse" and, to a much lesser degree, "les honneurs," in framing the Senate.

As for the Commons, it assured the element of popular representation which Montesquieu had singled out as being inherent to the British constitution. Yet the franchise, left initially to the provinces to determine, provided for significant property qualifications: "The qualifications in effect constituted a householder's franchise which allowed most heads of family to vote. These citizens did not compose a large portion of the total population ... for figures ... show average electorates to approximate 15 per cent of the population of the constituencies."[34] Nor did the franchise bill that Macdonald introduced in 1885 alter this. "The most striking point about the Conservative franchise bill of 1885 was that it was not a general extension of the franchise bill, but rather the opposite."[35] In spirit and in letter, those who were in "un état de bassesse,"[36] as Montesquieu had described them (in words that Blackstone reproduced[36]), were effectively disenfranchised at least to 1921.

It follows that the type of regime that we acquired in 1867 was a moderate government in which monarchical, oligarchical, and democratic features were combined. Nor would it be right, following on Bagehot, to see the first two elements as purely dignified or ornamental, and the third as the effective feature. This would be making light not only of the intention of the Fathers of Confederation but of the actual practice of Canadian politics through the first half-century of our existence.

James Bryce, in 1921, commenting on Canadian "deference to legal authority," noted that this had been "planted deep in days when authority was regarded with awe as having an almost sacred sanction ... under governments that were in those days monarchical in fact as well as in name."[37] For John A. Macdonald, "The Office of Governor General – the outward and visible sign of British connection – was an institution of the highest importance, and one that could not be safeguarded with too great care."[38] He remarked further that "the people of Canada like to see the dignity of the office fully maintained."[39]

The succession of governors general who incarnated the monarchical principle in Canada reads like a *Who's Who* of major and minor branches of the British aristocracy – Viscount Monck, Baron Lisgar, the Earl of Dufferin, the Marquis of Lorne (Queen Victoria's son-in-law), the Marquis of Lansdowne, Baron Stanley, the Earl of Aberdeen, the Earl of Minto, Earl Grey, the Duke of Connaught (Queen Victoria's third son), the Duke of Devonshire, Viscount Byng of Vimy, Viscount Willingdon, the Earl of Bessborough, Baron Tweedsmuir, the Earl of Athlone (Queen Mary's brother), and Viscount Alexander of Tunis.[40] Their presence lent an unmistakably Old World flavour to Canadian government, instilling a civic religion for the British Empire and constitution that can be contrasted with the republican civic religion south of the border. What else was the purpose served by speeches from the throne and by vice-regal levées and visits to far-flung parts of the Dominion? For the first decades after Confederation, moreover, these viceroys served as the direct liaison between British and Canadian governments, having special responsibility to ensure that Canada was fitted into the larger framework of British foreign policy.

Governors general, then, had both an efficient and an ornamental function, tying Canada to what, until 1931, remained in law as well as in fact the imperial power. In the words of Alpheus Todd, "The governor of a British province is a connecting link between the distant portions of a wide-spread empire and the august person of its monarch. [He] is in duty bound to foster, within his own sphere, loyalty and devotion to the sovereign and attachment to the institutions of monarchy."[41]

Montesquieu had emphasized the role of honour as the underlying principle of monarchy. The Canadian political élite would seem to have paid great attention to this value – witness a letter of August 1873 from Macdonald to the governor general: "I see that all the Chief Justices in India are knighted; and I think it will be found that the same rule prevails in most of the colonies of the Empire. Surely the chief judges of the Supreme Court of the Dominion, with its present population of four millions, should be placed on the same footing!"[42] He writes in another letter of 1889: "I can quite understand her Majesty's desire to raise the degree of Knight Bachelor from the discredit into which it has in some degree fallen. One would like to see a Victorian Knighthood as much esteemed as in the days of Queen Elizabeth ... Colonists should be taught to look to the Empress-Queen, as the *fons honoris*."[43]

Nor was Macdonald alone. Most Canadian prime ministers and leading political figures, industrialists, and financiers down to the

1920s looked to imperial titles as the dignified capping of their careers. This craving for status plays a role familiar to us from the history of the late-nineteenth-century European bourgeoisie, in an era that Arno Mayer has described, in a remarkable work, as that of the "persistence of the old regime."[44] Save that in the Canadian case the values in question had to be consciously, somewhat artificially, inculcated from Europe.

Earlier it was suggested that aristocracy proper could not be transposed directly to Canada. In one respect, however, even this feature of the British constitution as described by Montesquieu was to live on in Canada down to 1949. The Judicial Committee of the Privy Council acted as the final court of constitutional appeal for this country until that date. Most discussion of its role has focused, correctly, on its giving a more provincially oriented reading to the BNA Act than the letter and the spirit of both the Confederation Debates and the document itself might have suggested.[45] One further feature, peculiarly Montesquieuan, has not received quite the attention it deserves. By making British law lords the ultimate arbiters over Canada's constitutional destiny, our politicians allowed the aristocratic element (British in this case) a checking role on the activities of the popular branch. In good part, it is true, this was exercised in favour of the popular branch of government at the provincial level at the expense of that at the central. But, in a more general way, it was exercised in a manner to limit untoward expansion by the state in the industrial and social arenas, as in interference with property rights, to limit what early-twentieth-century writers such as Lord Hewart, echoing Montesquieu, liked to call "the new despotism."

The specifically Canadian institution that served in place of the Lords, namely the Senate, fulfilled a somewhat similar function at certain strategic moments. In failing to ratify some 100 government bills that had passed the Commons between 1867 and 1960,[46] the Senate, despite its appointed nature, showed itself to be a checking institution. Between 1900 and 1930, the Senate resisted a number of changes in the law designed to further the interests of organized labour, for example, union labels, the eight-hour day in federal public works, and fortnightly pay to railway workers.[47] More important, on four successive occasions between 1926 and 1930 it refused to sanction the repeal of section 98 of the Criminal Code on "unlawful association" passed at the height of the "red scare" of 1919.[48] It also vetoed the Old Age Pension Bill when it was first presented in 1926.[49]

These actions of the Senate can be interpreted, in good part, as an expression of the class interests of its largely oligarchical member-ship. On Montesquieuan grounds, such a checking function for an appointed, as opposed to an elected, upper house was both right and proper. "Des trois puissances dont nous avons parlé, celle de juger est en quelque façon nulle. Il n'en reste que deux, et comme elles ont besoin d'une puissance réglante pour les tempérer, la partie du corps législatif qui est composée de nobles est très propre à produire cet effet."[50] Admittedly, a second house based on "men of property" rather than on a nobility fell short of Montesquieu's pre-scription in book x I, section 6. Yet in a new society like Canada, privilege was not that far removed from property, even if it were not give a formally hereditary stamp. As Robert Mackay has argued, "In 1867 an upper house whose members were appointed for life was not contrary to the prevailing climate of opinion. Democracy had not yet arrived and was, indeed, distrusted in many quarters; prop-erty was still thought to be entitled to a special place in the govern-ment of the country; and privilege was still not an unacceptable social phenomenon."[51]

With respect to the Canadian House of Commons, Montesquieu's less than democratic convictions also seem to prevail. Montesquieu had argued for members of parliament as representatives, rather than delegates, from their constituencies. "Il n'est pas nécessaire que les représentants, qui ont reçu de ceux qui les ont choisis une instruction générale, en reçoivent une particulière sur chaque affaire, comme cela se pratique dans les diètes d'Allemagne ... Cela jetteroit dans des longueurs infinies, rendroit chaque député le maître de tous les autres."[52] This is precisely the way in which Black-stone and Burke, the models for our constitution-makers, interpreted an M P's functions.

Moreover, in counterposing representative institutions to any more direct expressions of the popular will, Montesquieu was noting a central aspect of the British system – the vesting of sovereignty in Parliament or, more correctly, the King/Queen-in-Parliament, rather than in the people. In Montesquieu's version of the mixed constitu-tion, the people (with the exclusion, as we have seen, of the poor) choose representatives who, in conjunction with the House of Lords and the monarch, each with a hereditary basis of designation, consti-tuted the legitimate government. The people's role is at best indi-rect, constituting but one element in three within the constitutional order. How different from the spirit of the French *Declaration of the Rights of Man and the Citizen* or the opening phrase of the American constitution, in which all political authority is derived from the people. Montesquieu's moderate government is, in fact, a repudiation of purely democratic principles, which he makes clear a little earlier in book x I: "La démocratie et l'aristocratie ne sont point des États libres par leur nature. La liberté politique ne so trouve que dans les gouvernements modérés."[53]

This is essentially what Cartier, Macdonald, and McGee, with considerably less theoretical sophistication than Montesquieu, were expressing with their repudiation of the spirit of democracy: "We, who had the benefit of being able to contemplate republicanism in action during a period of eighty years, saw its defects, and felt convinced that purely democratic institutions could not be conducive to the peace and prosperity of nations ... In our federation the monarchical principle would be the leading feature, while on the other side of the line ... the ruling power was the will of the mob, the rule of the populace."[54] The King/Queen-in-Parliament, on which the B N A Act is based, is thus Montesquieu's "moderate government," as opposed to more radical formulations that draw on popular sovereignty.

The reader may have noticed that considerably less weight has been placed on Montesquieu's institutional doctrine of the separation of powers in this analysis of the B N A Act, even though the terms *executive power*, *legislative power*, and *judicature* occur in the text. The reason is that checks and balances as among executive, legislative, and judicial compartments seem a less useful approach to illuminating the text than the underlying concept of the mixed constitution. There is no discussion of the powers of the judiciary in the B N A Act (whatever the role subsequently played by the Judicial Committee) – a signal omission if we are to take Montesquieu's doctrine literally. Nor by the latter part of the nineteenth century did the doctrine of checks and balances adequately describe the nature of cabinet government in Britain or the colonies. In so far as checks and balances were subsequently to arise, they would take the form of federal-provincial conflict, reflecting centrifugal versus centripetal interpretations of Confederation. But here we find ourselves looking not so much to Montesquieu's doctrine of book x I, section 6 (though Montesquieu has interesting things to say about federalism in book I x, sections 1–3), as to Madison's rationale for federalism in the *Federalist Papers*.[55]

Does it follow that Montesquieu's separation of powers has little application to this country? Had this chapter been written a couple of decades ago, we might have been tempted to answer in the affirmative. But in the light of a number of recent events, in particular the constitutional package of 1981, with its Charter of Rights, as well as more recent proposals for parliamentary, especially Senate, reform, we are drawn to a rather different conclusion.

In the period between the end of the First World War and the Second, the institutional bulwark underpinning the B N A Act began to dissolve. The monarchical principle, so potent in the decades after Confederation, began to give way almost at the same speed as Canada's attachment to Great Britain. A few nostalgic die-hards might invoke the fading past: "In contrast to the static perfectionism of the Whig-Republican system of individual liberty, the monarchical idea is that of a free and essentially historical order of life ... Kingship is innate in human life precisely because all life is essentially organic in form and function."[56] The finger of history, however, was moving both English Canada and Quebec in quite new directions. Canadians of neither British nor French backgrounds, moreover, could not "instinctively" find in the cobwebs of the old English constitution much to inspire them.

With Canada's shift to the United States from the British sphere, we began to adopt a more frankly American approach to government. Certainly, the Tory disdain for democracy that had coloured the first half-century of our existence was no longer in favour. The Supreme Court came to replace the Judicial Committee as the final court of constitutional appeal. Governors general were now Canadian nationals, and the institution increasingly a quasi-republican type of presidency along Indian or West German lines. The Senate, too, appeared more and more to be an anachronism in a more democratic age, tainted by its reputation as an expensive retirement home for party hacks or corporate directors.

Under these circumstances Montesquieu's separation-of-powers doctrine has suddenly acquired a new lease on life. It came to us refracted through American lenses, following the long encounter, both in popular culture and in political circles, with the institutions of American government. The American tradition of a written constitution with a codified bill of rights, in particular, exerted a magnetic influence on Canadian public opinion. Pierre Trudeau in the early 1960s might disdainfully dismiss the American (and continental European) penchant for written documents with a "thrilling bill of rights," contrasting the Canadian document of 1867, with "its absence of principles, ideals or other frills."[57] Within two decades, he had singlehandedly ensured that we would be living with precisely such a written document henceforth.

Ironically, it was John Diefenbaker, the most "British"-minded of our post-war prime ministers, who started us down that road, enacting a Bill of Rights as a non-binding statute in 1960. The Quiet Revolution in Quebec, the nationalist fervour that followed, the coming to power of the Parti québécois, and the subsequent referendum battle then set the stage for the second round in Canada's top-down constitution-making. Trudeau interpreted the victory of the "No" side in the Quebec referendum as a mandate to proceed with the renewal of Canadian federalism. He had in mind more specifically a written Charter of Rights that would institutionalize minority-language rights and a variety of classically liberal individual rights and freedoms. By and large the Charter that emerged, while somewhat altered from its initial draft form and subjected to opting-out provisions by various governments, was the document that Trudeau himself desired.

Such a written charter gives vastly increased power to the courts in interpreting fundamental rights. In this respect, as the Royal Commission on the Economic Union and Development Prospects for Canada (the Macdonald Commission) has recently argued, it has introduced a new element into the Canadian scheme of things, alongside parliamentarism and federalism.[58] To use Montesquieu's term, "la puissance de juger" has now acquired a solemnity and importance it did not enjoy before. While it is far too early to assess the full implications of the Charter for the Canadian political system, some things are clear. Federal and provincial law-makers must keep the Charter in mind; if not, the risk of constitutional challenge is high. Already there has been a spate of litigation invoking the Charter, with preliminary indications that the judiciary is indeed prepared to use the new weapon provided it: "Our Charter of Rights and Freedoms recently has imposed new and large responsibilities on the courts ... If the courts are to adjudicate credibly on those rights and fashion remedies for their infringement, the independent role of the courts must be maintained."[59] The Supreme Court, and the lower courts, are likely to become increasingly political institutions in the American sense, playing their part in checking and balancing executive and legislative powers. Two centuries after the Americans, we seem about to acquire an American-type system of constitutional adjudication and interpretation. "The celebrated Montesquieu," so dear to the hearts of Madison and Hamilton, is becoming our own.

But we still have the fusion between executive and legislative powers characteristic of the British system. There is no disposition to replace the parliamentary system with a congressional one (although in the early 1970s, the Parti québécois proposed an American-type system for an independent Quebec[60]). Looming on the horizon, however, is the very real possibility of Senate reform. The Macdonald Commission has added its voice to earlier studies, such as that of the Task Force on Canadian Unity of 1979, in calling for the remaking of this second chamber.[61]

If we look to Australia for an example of what might happen with a popularly elected upper house, it becomes clear that a new element of check and balance within the legislative branch and between the latter and the executive is thereby introduced. The mere fact that the basis for electing the upper house will be different from that of the lower ensures that, more often than not, it would have a different party composition. If one were to use a system of proportional representation, as the Macdonald Commission suggests, it is only the rare federal government, like the Mulroney one of 1984, which received 50 per cent of the popular vote, which could hope to have a clear majority in the Senate. (This is assuming, of course, that we do not go the route of coalition governments.) An elected Senate, moreover, could only with the greatest of difficulties be kept to a purely advisory or suspensive role. The members of such a chamber, elected directly from an entire province (or major portion thereof), by direct universal suffrage, would have at least as good a claim to incarnate legitimately the popular will as members from geographically circumscribed constituencies in the Commons. In the long run, their case for powers commensurate with their popular support might well lead to an American or Australian-type arrangement, in which the Senate is a major legislative power in its own right.

There is nothing inevitable about this, to be sure. But just as the Constitution Act, 1982, suggests that the pace of constitutional aggiornamento has speeded up, so the numerous calls for Senate reform suggest that before too long this institution will be replaced by a more effective, more responsible, and therefore more powerful upper house. In the process, something of Montesquieu's checks and balances will likely come to characterize the relationship between executive and legislative, between upper and lower house, in this country.

So we may yet come full circle. Having begun with Montesquieu, the theorist of the mixed constitution, of the gothic origins of moderate government, of a less-than-democratic British constitution based on monarch, aristocracy, and gentry, we may end up with the Montesquieu of more formalized checks and balances among executive, legislative, and judicial powers adhered to by republican schemes of government. It is the first Montesquieu, the monarchical-aristocratic author, who can be read as informing the Canadian constitution of our first fifty or seventy-five years, the period of British tutelage. It is the second Montesquieu, by way of the American experience and our own cautious moves toward constitutional reformulation, that may inform our institutional development in the contemporary period (the period of American tutelage?).

This chapter has not suggested that at the conscious level our constitution-makers looked to Montesquieu for theoretical inspiration. There is scant evidence that Macdonald, Cartier, or McGee had read Montesquieu or ever cited him with veneration. Rather, in a more mediated way, Montesquieu's synthetic reading of the British constitution, with its particular balance among monarch, Lords, and Commons, comes to occupy pride of place in such crucial statements of late-eighteenth-century constitutional theory as Blackstone's and Burke's and through them, in our own.

Are we wrong to call "Montesquieuan" what others might be tempted to interpret as Blackstonean or Burkean? A strong case can be made that Montesquieu, for all the influence that British political practice had had on the political formulations of Locke, Shaftesbury, or Bolingbroke, was indeed an innovator in bringing the understanding of the empirical nature of eighteenth-century British institutions to the highest of theoretical planes. It was he, not his English contemporaries, who gave the concept of the mixed constitution a new lease on life. It was he who formulated a version of the separation of powers that was to enjoy especial success in liberal constitutional theory from the late eighteenth century on.

One is, therefore, on solid ground in arguing the Montesquieuan foundations of a particular political system without needing to trace this literally back to Montesquieu. To be Montesquieuan in this sense is to believe in the virtue of moderate government and, therefore, in some blend among monarchical, aristocratic, and democratic principles and in a separation of powers that, at the institutional level, distinguishes among the executive, legislative, and judicial branches of government and incorporates an element of balance into the political system. These two elements may be directly linked to one another, as they were in Montesquieu's own thought. But they may also come to be separated, as they were by the late eighteenth century, with the British and the British-influenced constitutions accepting an element of the first and the Americans and French (and others influenced by them) republicanizing Montesquieu along the lines of the second.

In trying to come to terms with the nature of the Canadian state, at least at the central level, I have suggested that we have been a good deal more Montesquieuan, in both senses of the term, than our politicians or constitutional theorists have led us to believe. The direct connection that Montesquieu might have postulated between the mixed constitution and the separation of powers may not have been present in Canada; instead, we have been sequential in our assimilation of these two strains, accepting the first until the mid-twentieth century, and the second with a good deal less of the first since then.

There are good reasons why Montesquieu's amalgam between the mixed constitution and the separation of powers would have come unstuck in the twentieth century, an era in which the influence of both monarchy and aristocracy has waned. But there is less reason to discard Montesquieu's larger political theory or to underestimate the considerable contribution that the latter can make to an understanding of politics and constitutions in states of which its author had never dreamed. We speak of Machiavellians in politics, of Hobbesians and Hegelians, of Rousseaueans and Marxists. In a parallel vein, might one not argue that Canada, with its particular stress on "moderate" government and its appropriation of the two key features of Montesquieu's political doctrine over time, can be best interpreted as constituting a quintessentially Montesquieuan polity?

CHAPTER FIVE

Burke or Rousseau?
Parliament or People?

Sir, we in this house are representatives of the people, and not mere delegates ... If we do represent them, we have a right to see for them, to think
for them, to act for them.
John A. Macdonald, 1865[1]

The people spoken of by the political stump speakers and election campaign
literature as the "sovereign people" have, I might say, no direct efficient
control. They are sovereign de jure but not de facto, except at election times.
The actual power experienced by the people consists chiefly in the periodic
choice of another set of masters who make laws to suit themselves and
enforce them until their term of office expires, regardless of the will of the
people. We are governed by an elective aristocracy which in its turn is
largely controlled by an aristocracy of wealth.
R. C. Henders, 1911[2]

In this chapter I set out to explore two widely diverging notions of
sovereignty, one rooted in the power of King/Queen-in-Parliament,
the other more directly in the people. The first, which derives from
British constitutional practice, has tended to predominate in Canada
and has looked to elected politicians and appointed ministries as the
ultimate repositories of power and legitimacy. To be sure, the power,
at least of elected politicians, is ultimately traced back to some version of popular sanction through periodic election. But once elected,
members have a mandate that is beyond reproach and a power of
decision-making, be it on routine matters or monumental ones, that
is unlimited.

The origins of such a doctrine can be traced back to Edmund
Burke (among other sources) with his strong defence of the independence of members of Parliament˙ from their constituents and his

utter rejection of any notion of mandatory instructions or delegated responsibility. *"Authoritative* instructions, *mandates* issued, which a member is bound blindly and implicitly to obey, to vote and to argue for, though contrary to the clearest conviction of his judgement and conscience – these are things utterly unknown to the laws of this land. Parliament is not a *congress* of ambassadors from different and hostile interests ... Parliament is a *deliberative* assembly of *one* nation, with *one* interest that of the whole ... You choose a member, indeed, but when you have chosen him he is not a member of Bristol, but he is a member of *Parliament."*[3]

As Isaac Kramnick has argued: "Burke's is the classic repudiation of the radical theory which sets up the representative as no more than an agent, a mere delegate for his constituents ... His letters to his Bristol commercial constituents enjoined them to follow his views and in turn gave short shrift to any suggestion that he should follow theirs ... His position on representation was elitist ... and smacked of an aristocratic notion of natural leaders and natural followers."[4]

A quite different notion of sovereignty can be derived from the doctrines of the two great eighteenth-century revolutions, the American and the French, each of which traces sovereign power directly to the people. But even before the American constitution or the French Declaration of the Rights of Man and the Citizen had come to be drafted, the great iconoclast of the Enlightenment, Jean-Jacques Rousseau, had provided arguments for the inalienability of popular sovereignty and against the usurpation of the popular will by elected representatives: "Sovereignty cannot be represented for the same reason that it cannot be alienated; its essence is the general will, and will cannot be represented – either it is the general will or it is something else; there is no intermediate possibility. Thus, the people's deputies are not, and could not be, its representatives; they are merely its agents; and they cannot divide anything finally. Any law which the people has not ratified in person is void; it is not law at all."[5]

For Rousseau, the concept of representation could be traced back to feudalism and stood in sharp contrast with the type of participatory practice associated with face-to-face communities like Geneva, the Swiss cantons, or the Corsica of his dreams. There is a radically anti-élitist quality to his notion of citizenship and an aspiration to political equality that cannot find realization in the luxury-driven European nation-states of his day.

I do not want to get into a wide-ranging discussion of Burke's or Rousseau's larger political philosophies. There are volumes enough that do precisely this, and little is to be gained for our purposes in once more going over their deeply diverging readings of human nature, of political community, or of the foundations of property and wealth. The one tends toward a conservative defence of the existing order of things, what one writer has called a "bourgeois conception of civil society and aristocratic conception of state";[6] the other toward a more radically egalitarian vision of community, with agrarian underpinnings and democratic practice potentially joining civic freedom with civic virtue.[7] Neither is without his inconsistencies and contradictions, and neither is wholly relevant to a conception of the state in the late twentieth-century.

Yet there is in the deep divergence between Burke and Rousseau over the nature of representation something directly relevant to that function of the modern state called legitimacy (cf. chapter 6). Burke tells us: "The people, indeed, are presumed to consent to whatever the legislator ordains for their benefit ... This they owe as an act of homage and just deference to a reason, which the necessity of government has made superior to their own."[8] He is identifying here a partly elected, partly hereditary or appointed institution, with a higher reason that commands obedience. The institution in question – Parliament, or more correctly King/Queen-in-Parliament – far from being a mere reflection of the popular will, is itself the effective source of constitutional legitimacy. Its members are "the expert artists," "the skilled workers," who transform the people's "gross wants" into "perfect form ... to fit the utensil to use."[9] Not for Burke, who denounces "the tyranny of the multitude" as "multiplied tyranny,"[10] any notion of unmediated popular rule.

Rousseau conversely argues: "The instant the People is legitimately assembled as a Sovereign body, all jurisdiction of Government ceases, the executive power is suspended, and the person of the least Citizen is as sacred and inviolable as that of the first Magistrate."[11] He is underlining the legitimacy of direct popular sovereignty as the source of all authority – legislative and executive – in the state. Whether we take this literally or metaphorically, we have here a conception of the relationship between citizens and their representatives vastly different from Burke's. Governmental authority is, at best, contingent, subordinate to the overriding will of the people, which, at frequent intervals, makes itself known. For Rousseau, this entailed annual citizen assemblies, in which the form of the constitution and those charged with its administration came up for reconsideration.[12] For others, over the past two centuries, this may have involved a belief in citizen initiatives, recall procedures, referenda on key legislative or constitutional proposals, or other devices of direct citizen participation.[13]

I would like to suggest that both Burkean and Rousseauean notions of sovereignty have been present in Canada, albeit in very unequal measure. And I want to argue further that a Burkean notion of legitimacy can be as damaging to public liberties and the democratic well-being of a society as, pushed to its extreme, the most effusive or intolerant version of Rousseau's general will. In other words, a society can suffer from an excess of institutional legitimacy, as surely as another can suffer from the reverse. Canada is an almost textbook example of the former.

In turning to the place that parliamentary sovereignty occupies in Canada, let me begin with two observations, one by Frank Underhill, the other by Alexander Brady. "In Canada we have no revolutionary tradition; and our historians, political scientists and philosophers have assiduously tried to educate us to be proud of this fact. How can such a people expect their democracy to be as dynamic as the democracies of Britain and France and the United States have been?"[14] "Notable is the extent to which Canada has preserved the basic elements of the British parliamentary regime, especially the symbolism of the monarchy, the intimate tie between executive and legislature, the presence of parties disciplined by parliamentary leadership, the very meagre reliance upon direct appeals to the people in referenda."[15]

There was in the Canadian decision to "perpetuate British institutions on this continent" and "adhere to the protection of the British crown"[16] an implicit rejection of more popular notions of sovereignty. The very way in which the British North America Act of 1867 came to be adopted, through a series of closed-door meetings among the leading colonial politicians and without any direct recourse to the people, showed on just what foundations Canada was to be constructed.

For John Ross, there was no need to bring the Confederation scheme directly to the people for their approval: "This mode of appealing to the people is not British but American, as under the British system the representatives of the people in Parliament are presumed to be competent to decide all the public questions submitted to them."[17] For Col. Arthur Rankin: "We were made to taste the consequences of self-government [during the 1837 Rebellions]. We were taught that questions like these must be decided by the will of the majority of the people, as made known through their representatives in Parliament."[18] And for John A. Macdonald, writing to Leonard Tilley: "The measure must be carried per saltum – with a rush and no echo of it must reverberate through the British provinces until it becomes law ... There will be few important clauses in the measure that will not offend one interest or individual ... The people will soon learn to be reconciled to it."[19]

A few might argue differently, suggesting that "in voting to change the constitution of the Government without consulting the people on the subject" the members of the Canadian House were exceeding their powers,[20] or that "the taking of a direct vote – yea and nay" would allow the people "a more decisive way" of pronouncing on the constitutional changes proposed than was possible "through their representatives in this House."[21] Their voices were drowned out in a cacophony of anti-democratic sentiments that would have done Burke proud.

The truth of the matter is that the constitution-making from above that we got in the 1860s reflected a counter-revolutionary set of values. Not only would there be no direct popular ratification of the handiwork of the Fathers of Confederation, but "the people" itself would nowhere merit a mention in the text of the B N A Act. In the absence of the political mobilization, however fleeting, of the revolutionary experience – what England of the late 1640s experienced with the Levellers and the debates within the Parliamentary Army; the United States, in the current that gave rise to the American Bill of Rights and Jeffersonian democracy; or France with the sectional democracy among the sans-culottes of 1792–4 – the advocates of a deferential, passive notion of the citizen's role carried the day in Canada.

Could a John A. Macdonald have proudly proclaimed the absence of support for universal suffrage among members of the colonial assemblies[22] in the aftermath of a successful struggle for independence from Britain? Could George-Etienne Cartier have deplored "mob rule ... supplant[ing] legitimate authority" as the inevitable consequence of a democratic system[23] or D'Arcy McGee extolled "a large infusion of authority" as essential to a conservative constitutional order,[24] in a Canada where the rebellions of 1837 had ended differently? The upshot has been the exclusion of popular sovereignty as an operating construct or ideal for the larger part of Canadian history. "The Canadian fathers copied the English doctrine of the sovereignty of Parliament when framing the British North America Act ... There is no sovereignty reserved to the people."[25] "In Canada there is no sovereignty in the people. So far as we are concerned, it is in the Parliament at Westminster, and our powers to legislate are such, and only such, as that Parliament has given us."[26]

Few are the politicians, Conservative, Liberal, or for that matter CCF/NDP, who have questioned the hegemony of parliamentary sovereignty, or who have been prepared to accord the people more than an auxiliary role in the operation of government and state. Macdonald's repudiation of the notion of the MP as delegate "voting according to the instruction of the commission which he holds in his pocket from his constituents"[27] bespeaks the deeper antipathy that the Canadian political class would have to any abdication of its powers.

Laurier's definition of political liberty hinges almost entirely on the electoral dimension of citizenship, to the exclusion of a more active, ongoing role: "The moment the people exercise the right to vote, the moment they have a responsible government, they have the full measure of liberty."[28] William Lyon Mackenzie King, in his comments on the constitutional crisis of 1926, seems to anticipate Joseph Schumpeter's redefinition of democracy as a choice between competing élites,[29] when he writes: "I was simply asking that the people who are, or who, at least, ought to be the sovereign power in the nation, might in the necessity of the circumstances, be given an opportunity of themselves deciding by whom they desired their Government to be carried on."[30] And in his very next breath, it is the sovereignty of Parliament, not of the people, that he extols: "The supremacy of Parliament, the rights, the dignities, the existence of Parliament has been challenged by the present Prime Minister [Meighen] in a manner that surpasses all belief."[31]

Of M.J. Coldwell, long-time leader of the CCF, Walter Young writes, "The CCF's reputation as a parliamentary group was decidedly high ... Coldwell, more than his predecessors, accepted the parliamentary rules of the game. He was, more than Woodsworth, part of the institution, a confidant of Mackenzie King, a conscientious legislator ... Coldwell saw Parliament as something important in itself."[32] There was a strongly parliamentary streak to the national CCF/NDP that overrode whatever populist impulses might have accompanied its birth on the prairies.

Pierre Elliott Trudeau, one of the few Canadian politicians to have quoted Rousseau on occasion,[33] was anything but Rousseauean when it came to defining the powers and privileges of government vis-à-vis the people in a parliamentary system: "If any doubt exists about the good faith or the ability of any government, there are opposition parties ready and willing to be given an opportunity to govern. In short there is available everywhere in Canada an effective mechanism to change governments by peaceful means."[34] In the

Charter of Rights that he did so much to introduce, there is a notably narrow definition of democratic rights under sections 3–5, limited to the rights of citizens to vote in elections and run for office and to the need for the re-election of parliaments and legislatures at least once every five years. No echoes of participatory democracy or face-to-face community here, but a soberly instrumental substitution of parliamentary for popular sovereignty.

Indeed, the way in which the Charter and the patriation of the constitution came to be engineered – through a series of closed-door meetings, with only grudging popular input through a joint parliamentary committee and without submission of the package for the direct approval of the electorate – was in the tradition of undemocratic constitution-making of the 1860s. (The Meech Lake Accord is but a more recent sequel.) Parliamentary (and legislative) sovereignty has come to mean the right of prime ministers and premiers, with no explicit mandate from their constituents, to undertake fundamental constitutional change. The legitimacy of their actions derives from a Burkean-type notion of the privileged knowledge, judgment, and power that legislators, unlike the mere mortals who elect them, enjoy.

In general, Canadian politicians have shown minimal willingness to consider making use of referenda for purposes of constitutional amendment. The only important instance in which it has been advocated (and in one case employed) at the federal level has been in relationship to war-time conscription. Here the Liberals, with their Quebec supporters strongly opposed to compulsory overseas service and their anglophone supporters no less in favour, found themselves prepared to consider a referendum as the way out of their dilemma. Hence Laurier's stance during the 1917 election campaign[35] and Mackenzie King's resort to a plebiscite in 1942 to win release from an earlier election pledge.

Too much, however, should not be made of this experience, and the arguments deployed against it, for example, by the Conservatives in 1917, have in fact tended to prevail on most occasions: "We are told that this [conscription] is a fit subject for a referendum. Governments in this country have not frequently shifted their responsibility and placed upon the people the lead that they themselves should take."[36] "Parliament has a duty to perform. Who else could perform that duty except Parliament ... The Government of a country must govern the country – a country cannot govern itself, it must be led, it must be governed."[37] "I trust the people. I trust implicitly to their judgment when they have had opportunity for information and consideration. But I do not conceive the functions of a representative of the people to go around to meetings throughout the country, addressing people who have not the necessary information, stirring them up to express an opinion in a certain sense, and then walk into this House and say: There is nothing more to be said, I am here to express the opinions of the people."[38]

The Canadian political élite strongly resists anything that might diminish its monopoly over political decision-making. This is, of course, nothing unique to Canada, though in our case it is magnified by the type of political tradition handed down through generations of English-Canadian loyalism and Québécois ultramontanism.

Our intellectuals have usually been as hostile to directly democratic impulses as the princes whom they have not infrequently served. Take the views of O.D. Skelton, professor at Queen's University and later Under-secretary of State for External Affairs under Mackenzie King, bemoaning "the cultural and political dominance of 'farmers and shopkeepers' ... deny[ing] the usefulness and practicality of the popular idea of the referendum on the grounds that issues were too complex for the average man to become informed upon."[39] Or those of Robert McIver, University of Toronto political scientist, denouncing in 1926 the attitude "that democracy en masse can legislate or make executive decisions" as naive, "confined to Rousseau's mind and the people of the United States of America."[40]

Instead, what has tended to prevail is a concept of legitimacy closely associated with parliamentary institutions and the constitutional order handed down in derivative fashion from Great Britain. Textbooks of Canadian political science are replete with eulogies to the institution of Parliament,[41] though none has gone further than André Bernard in underlining the legitimizing function of parliamentary institutions: "La fonction de légitimation que remplissent les institutions parlementaries est très importante et elle établit, de ce fait, l'importance du Parlement lui-même ... Le Parlement est en effet le garant du consensus général et l'instrument priviligié du système en ce qui concerne la conversion des questions politiques en décisions impératives. Il puise son autorité souveraine dans les représentations collectives (idéologies, croyances, valeurs) qui le légitiment et le valorisent et qui inspirent et encadrent son action."[42]

There is much truth at the empirical level to what Bernard says. But before we get carried away with the normative implications of such a statement, let us remember that the "sovereign authority" that he associates with Parliament may well have come at the price of other, more radical manifestation of collective beliefs and values. As A.O. Hirschman has noted: "When the vote was granted to the people of France, and in particular to that obstreperous, unruly, and impulsive people of Paris which had just made the third revolution in two generations, it became enthroned in effect as the *only* legitimate form of expressing political opinions. In other words, the vote represented a new right of the people, but it also restricted its participation in politics to this particular *and comparatively harmless* form ... The vote *delegitimizes* more direct, intense, and 'expressive' forms of political action that are both more effective and more satisfying."[43] And as the German constitutional theorist Hans Kelsen once observed:

If political writers insist on characterizing the parliament of modern democracies, in spite of its legal independence from the electorate, as a 'representative' organ, if some writers even declare that the *mandat impératif* is contrary to the principle of representative government, they do not represent a scientific theory but advocate a political ideology. The function of this ideology is to conceal the real situation, to maintain the illusion that the legislator is the people, in spite of the fact that, in reality, the function of the people – or more correctly formulated of the electorate – is limited to the creation of the legislative organ.[44]

Does the legitimacy of Parliament simply serve to render a more participatory version of politics illegitimate? Instead of enhancing our liberties, have parliamentary institutions, much as Rousseau argued, merely provided more effective chains with which to bind a people?[45]

Let me now explore Rousseauean impulses that may have been at work in Canada and the extent to which they point to a countervailing principle of legitimacy to that of Parliament. As I implied earlier, these have been a good deal weaker than Burkean impulses and certainly less prominent in Canada than in the United States, France, or Switzerland, with their traditions of referenda; certain American states, with their citizen initiatives; and some New England towns or Swiss cantons, with their annual citizen assemblies.[46] Yet even Canada has not been immune to more popular notions of sovereignty. I want to explore this under three headings: (1) western populism in the 1920s and 1930s; (2) Quebec nationalism, especially since 1960; and (3) arguments for or examples of participatory democracy – political, economic, social – today.

(1) The eruption of agrarian revolt in western Canada in the decades following the First World War was rooted in the exigencies of the grain economy and a sense of both regional and class estrangement from the country's dominant political and economic powers.

The forms this discontent took, ranging from the Progressives to the United Farmers of Alberta, from Social Credit to the c c f, have been the subject of numerous monographs and studies.

The underlying democratic nature of this thinking merits our attention. The sources of Canadian interest in "direct legislation, the single tax, the recall of public officials, direct primaries, women suffrage ... and proportional representation" were indisputably American,[47] reflecting critiques of the party system and of the power of monopolies and trusts that ran through American populism. The marriage between a strongly "Jeffersonian faith in the virtue of the people"[48] and the British parliamentary mould would not prove easy. But as David Laycock has argued in his excellent study, *Populism and Democratic Thought in the Canadian Prairies*: "[Radical democratic populism] is the only theory of government and the state to have rejected the British parliamentary model and still commanded more than a marginal degree of support in a mass democratic movement in Canada."[49]

Of the parameters to this thinking I would stress three directly relevant to participatory democratic theory. The first was a belief in direct legislation, which would "establish self-government in place of government by council and legislature, democracy in place of elective aristocracy, government by and for the people in place of government by and for the politicians and the corporate interests."[50] Such a measure, which was actually passed by the Manitoba legislature in 1915, provided a means for citizens to initiate legislation that they wanted or veto laws that they opposed through recourse to binding referenda. The bill in question, denounced by the Conservative leader, Rodmond Roblin, as "a form of degenerate republicanism," was held ultra vires by the Appeal Court of Manitoba in 1916, a decision subsequently upheld by the Judicial Committee of the Privy Council in 1919.[51]

A second was the doctrine of group government advanced by political activists like H.W. Wood and William Irvine in the 1920s, which won the support of the United Farmers of Alberta: "Democratic organization among the people means that the people must organize themselves and organize in such a way that they can initiate, direct and control all the activities of the Group thus organized. This is distinguished from autocratic organization by being self-governing or governed from the 'bottom up' instead of from the 'top down.' If the farmers succeed in establishing organizations on this basis, it will be the first successful attempt to develop democratic organizations to any considerable extent."[52] "The people must learn to think of themselves, not as individuals, but as groups ...

There must be a common interest to bring them together. As a group advances in its thinking powers, it will become conscious of itself in relation to other groups and will find its fuller life in a group of groups; and from that group of groups will come the consciousness and expression of a whole people. The people have only been voting together as individuals; they have not been thinking and acting as individuals, and, consequently, there is no democracy."[53]

In both these passages one finds echoes of a Rousseauean concern with the communitarian dimension of identity and a corresponding emphasis on the shared experience and "hands-on" democratic practice possible only within grass roots–based political units. The group theory of democracy was developed for the relatively homogenous farming communities of the prairies, with their rough equality of condition among citizens.[54] Whether such a construct can be transferred to a more heterogeneous society, with a complex division of labour and more inequality, is another matter. But it certainly points to a more active notion of citizenship than purely electoral theories allow and toward a delegated theory of representation.

A third feature of populism relates to its co-operative ethos. The same grain growers who were taking on the elevator companies and pushing for public ownership of utilities were strongest in their support for direct legislation or recall. Opposition to economic monopoly seemed to go hand in hand with disdain for the political monopoly exercised by elected politicians under the parliamentary system. Co-operatives provided the economic counterpart to the type of political practice to which radical democratic theory aspired. It is, therefore, not preoccupation with quaint terminology that led the more anti-capitalist of western populists to talk about a "co-operative commonwealth," to make it the name of Canada's first important social democratic party, or to foster a co-operative strain side by side with the more technocratic element in socialist theory.[55]

Prairie socialists like Norman Priestly argued that "the Cooperative Commonwealth will provide against the too great dominance of the state by the use of cooperative associations of citizens grouped as producers or as consumers."[56] Carlyle King, in his pamphlet *Socialism and Cooperatives*, argued the parallel objectives of the co-operative movement and socialism, "each advocating a pluralistic democratic political life, equality through the abolition of class distinctions and equal opportunities for participation and development, and an ethic of 'comradeship.'" Co-operatives, moreover, provided "one of the most practical training grounds for democracy," where "democracy means running our own affairs," and helped guard against over-centralization.[57] The anti-statist component of the co-operative movement went very well indeed with a political theory that stressed decentralized decision-making and ongoing popular control.

Populist aspirations in and of themselves did not, of course, add up to a coherent theory of the state, and we cannot simply go back to the Manitoba Grain Growers Association or William Irvine for relevant democratic models. But I think that the western experience shows the pertinence of Rousseauean principles, even in a society characterized by an "almost religious admiration of English parliamentary usages" and institutions.[58] David Laycock reminds us: "Canadians have not always deferentially accepted the determination by contending federal and provincial governments and elites of the legitimate scope and character of democratic politics ... One of prairie populism's most valuable legacies to the jaded and alienated common folk of Canada should have been a recognition of the value of participatory democracy and decentralized control over power in both popular movements and entrenched structures of economic and political power."[59]

(2) There is a second, somewhat different source for Rousseauean notions of popular sovereignty, linked this time to Quebec nationalism. In chapter 10, I suggest that nationalism in Quebec (unlike the English-Canadian variant) has been strongly grounded in civil society, since well before Confederation. To the degree that political legitimacy comes to be invested in nation and nationalism, the people itself may come to be seen as the subject of political discourse. This was certainly the direction in which the Patriotes were headed in the 1830s, and Papineau, in a speech to the legislative assembly of Lower Canada of 1833, singled out Burke, "the persuasive champion of the nobility's privileges,"[60] for attack, even as other Patriotes might identify with Rousseau.[61]

By later in the nineteenth century, however, French-Canadian nationalism had taken on an increasingly conservative hue, in which obedience to established institutions displaced any notion of popular sovereignty.[62] G.-E. Cartier was speaking for the ultramontane hierarchy and all that was counter-revolutionary in Quebec when he proclaimed, "We are French in origin, but French of the old régime."[63] A political world dominated by the likes of Lomer Gouin, Alexandre Taschereau, and Maurice Duplessis would not prove very receptive to democratic ideals.

The Quiet Revolution was another matter, inaugurating as it did two decades of political ferment and modernizing reforms. Liberal ideas took hold, social democratic ones gained a foothold, and the whole sweep of twentieth-century values, especially those of national self-affirmation or determination, came to the fore. While governments like those headed by Jean Lesage and René Lévesque provided much of the leadership, diverse social and political movements, from students to trade unions to counter-cultural organizations, provided a quite different impetus for change.

To the legitimacy of legislatures or national assemblies was now added the call for more direct popular participation in resolving Quebec's constitutional status within Canada. In the spring of 1965, members of the Students' Council at Université Laval set the stage by organizing an informal referendum among the student body: 3,000 students voted yes or no (mostly no) to the Fulton-Favreau formula then being discussed. In a speech at the university shortly thereafter, Daniel Johnson, then leader of the opposition in Quebec's National Assembly, observed:

C'est bien la première fois que des citoyens canadiens ont l'occasion d'exprimer leur avis sur une affaire constitutionnelle. Dans la plupart des grandes démocraties du monde, notamment en France, en Suisse, et en Australie, toute modification constitutionnelle doit être soumise par référendum à l'approbation du peuple souverain. Mais au Canada, jamais le peuple n'a été appelé à se prononcer en pareille matière. C'est pourtant lui qui est reconnu comme la source de l'autorité constituante dans les pays vraiment libres.

Est-ce que l'avenir de la nation canadienne-française serait moins important qu'un amendment au code municipal? La constitution appartient-elle au peuple ou à un parti politique?[64]

The logic of asking the sovereign people – not some legislature – to determine Quebec's constitutional future gained increasing support in the late 1960s and the 1970s. In particular, the newly formed Parti québécois (P Q) made this part of its party platform after 1973, pledging to hold a referendum on its sovereignty-association option during its first term in power. The language of P Q party programs in this period had resolutely Rousseauean overtones, talking about "the adoption of a national constitution elaborated by the citizens at the constituency level and adopted by the delegates of the people meeting in a constituent assembly," to be followed by a referendum.[65] Once in power, the P Q within two years enacted a special version of the Electoral Law for the holding of referenda. In the words of the minister, Robert Burns, introducing the measure: "Le projet de loi-cadre sur la consultation populaire offre à l'électeur un nouvel instrument permanent de participation qui permettra à celui-ci d'apprendre à vivre progressivement avec cette institution nouvelle du référendum au niveau québécois."[66]

The period 1979–80 was taken up with laying the groundwork for the referendum, designing the actual question, and then allowing the debate between "yes" and "no" to unfold until the dénouement of 20 May 1980. The battle was clearly more dramatic than that in any ordinary election. Not only was the issue at stake of the highest importance, but the direct involvement of Quebec's people in the decision was a notable breach with the tradition of parliamentary sovereignty. René Lévesque, in kicking off the referendum debate in the National Assembly, was not wrong to note: "Nous n'avons pas l'habitude de rendez-vous comme celui du référendum, c'est la première fois de toute notre histoire que se présente une telle occasion de décider par nous-mêmes, collectivement, de ce que nous voulons être et de la direction que nous voulons prendre dans l'avenir."[67]

Such an experience is not necessarily to be repeated every day. But the precedent of the referendum has ensured that there is now a clearer sense of sovereignty lying with the population, at least in Quebec, than in English Canada. Submitting the repatriated constitution and the Charter for direct popular approval was, thus, an idea that Lévesque and, for a brief moment, Trudeau were prepared to countenance, but the English-Canadian premiers, true to their Burkean heritage, refused.[68]

Even on the issue of Canadian- U S free trade, a number of voices in Quebec suggested that this would have been a fitting issue for resolution through a Canada-wide referendum. Réjean Pelletier, citing the precedents of Norway, Denmark, and the United Kingdom, which held referenda regarding membership in the European Community, suggested that free trade fell into the same category: "Pour retenir une telle solution et engager le pays dans un débat référendaire en demandant à la population elle-même de se prononcer sur une question qui la concerne au plus haut point, il faut du courage politique, beaucoup de courage politique et la conviction profonde qu'une consultation référendaire est une processus éminemment démocratique. C'est peut-être ce qui manque le plus à nos dirigeants actuels, tous partis confondus."[69] And Stéphane Dion offered an explicitly Rousseauean argument: "Un référendum sur pareil enjeu constitue bel et bien un droit démocratique tant il est vrai que la souveraineté réside plus fondamentalement dans les citoyens que dans leurs représentants."[70]

The experience of nationalism – both its ups and downs – over the past twenty-five years and the significant democratization of

Quebec's political life have given popular sovereignty a basis of support in Quebec civil society.

(3) Since the 1960s, there has been renewed interest in participatory democracy in Western societies. The student movements of the 1960s adopted it as one of their key demands – the American Students for a Democratic Society, in the Port Huron statement of 1962; the West German student movement, with its argument that "In a democracy the people, not Parliament, is supreme"; the French, with such May 1968 slogans as "Elections = trahison."

The Canadian and Quebec student movements, as well, made extra-parliamentary opposition something of a leitmotif: "People in Extra-Parliamentary Opposition ... have a principled position against electoralism and parliamentarism ... The new left student and youth movement demands that producers should control what they produce using the operating principles of 'self-government,' 'autogestion,' 'workers councils,' 'participatory or direct democracy' ... They seek to organize new centres of power among ethnic and racial minorities, urban and rural workers, youth, the poor, and other groups on a neighbourhood and group level."[71] "La prétendue souveraineté populaire finalement, est donc réduite à la participation au rituel électoral. Les élections sont le moment où les mécanismes de la pseudo-démocratie sont peut-être le plus sérieusement investis par le pouvoir de la classe dominante ... Les citoyens sont appelés à voter ... La 'démocratie' ne les fait pas participer au pouvoir, mais simplement décider qui l'exercera 'en leur nom.' "[72]

To the degree that the new left gave legitimacy to grass roots organizations and consensual decision-making, it helped introduce a salutary new dimension to politics in the West. Women's groups, environmental organizations, the peace movement, minority and native groups, and residents' associations have at various moments engaged in forms of direct action and civil disobedience in support of their objectives or in opposition to the actions of what they see as unresponsive governments. No wonder the Trilateral Commission, speaking here for the ruling élites in all Western societies, could decry the dangers stemming from these new forms of political mobilization.[73] From a Burkean point of view, Rousseauean demons were on the loose.

In practice, the electoral and parliamentary mould of Western polities has held good, despite the successful breakthrough, here and there, of anti-system parties like the West German Greens, or the wholesale initiation of popular referenda – over the opposition of most of the political establishment – by parties like the Italian Radicals in the late 1970s and early 1980s. It is a good deal easier to criticize the limitations of elections and parliamentary institutions than to advance viable, participatory democratic alternatives. In this area, by and large, the new left, both in Canada and elsewhere, floundered.

Still, there have been some limited experiments with Rousseauean notions of democracy in Canada in the 1970s and 1980s. Probably the most important structural examples have been attempts to decentralize the administration of medical and social services in a number of provinces. Quebec introduced the Centres Locaux de Services Communautaires (C L S C) in 1971, and today these constitute a province-wide network of 108 bodies with some 5000 employees and with elected community representatives constituting the majority of their boards of directors.[74] British Columbia, during the N D P government of 1972-5 established a network of Human Resource Boards in Vancouver and Victoria, with boards of directors elected at the local level.[75] (The Boards were promptly disbanded once Social Credit returned to power.) And there has also been a fairly well-developed system of community-run clinics in Saskatchewan through much of the past three decades.

One must be careful not to romanticize the degree of actual community control within these bodies. The turn-out in elections for the Human Resource Boards in Vancouver in 1975 did not exceed 10 per cent, and there is evidence of a similar lack of large-scale involvement in the C L S Cs in Quebec. In fact, as Jacques Godbout has argued in two interesting essays, participation can become a legitimizing device through which the permanent staff of a body like the C L S C in fact runs the organization, with relatively little input from those who use its services: "Nous avons vu apparaître une façon de prendre les décisions qui échappe au mécanisme démocratique à l'intérieur même des organisations les plus démocratiques; nous avons vu des intentions participatives se pervertir et se transformer en légitimation d'une pratique non démocratique, devenir le support du pouvoir des professionels et des permanents. Le contrôle des permanents se produit au détriment de celui des clients, des utilisateurs, des 'bénéficiaires.' "[76]

Yet the limited nature of the functions that community service organizations like C L S Cs provide may, in and of themselves, prevent more effective participation. To the degree that larger issues become open to community-level decision-making and a broader cross-section of society can become involved, we may have a fairer test of participatory democracy in practice.

In an essay written a few years ago, I sketched one possible model for moving in such a direction.[77] I call it base-level democracy, and it would entail a dual system of power, with representative structures as we now know them being complemented by a network of some 17,000 base-level organizations across the country, each grouping 1,000 citizens on average, in short, covering the entire adult population of Canada. Each base unit would meet once a month and would be free to consider matters of local, provincial, and national importance. Each would have an executive chosen by lot from among its members, serving for a period of one year, and acting as a liaison with the executives of other base units. If there were sufficient support for some initiative (or opposition to some measure proposed or enacted by a government) – say 20 per cent of the base-level units within a province, or the same number nationally, voting for some proposal – this would automatically trigger a referendum. The results of such a referendum, with due respect for constitutional provisions like those in the Charter, would be binding. We would thus have more ongoing citizen participation than is possible within a purely parliamentary system and periodic decision-making on important matters by the whole citizen body. In short, such a scheme would introduce a degree of popular sovereignty into a system from which it has been studiously excluded.

For such a proposal to work, one would need evidence of wide-scale popular support and, equally important, willingness on the part of elected members of parliaments or legislatures from the existing political parties to move in such a direction. This idea is not for tomorrow, given the deep hold of Burkean notions of representation on Canadian political culture. Yet it is also not out of the question that one of the political parties, especially at the provincial level, might move in such a direction. For example, several of the provincial wings of the N D P have recently expressed an interest in decentralized, community-based development, while more generally, many on the left have taken their distance from the statist version of socialism that predominated fifty or seventy-five years ago.[78] It does not strike me as too far-fetched to see the N D P, if it returns to power in British Columbia or Saskatchewan, enacting some significant democratic reforms. There may also be a stronger basis in Quebec, if my arguments above are valid, for engendering more extensive forms of citizen participation in the future.

In the economic arena, there have been some experiments with worker-controlled firms and with worker-elected directors in existing companies.[79] Economic democracy remains a putative ideal in a political economy dominated by large banks and multinational corporations. But there are economic reasons – plant shut-downs, problems of productivity, competition – that may make worker participation in decision-making or worker control more important in the years to come, both to workers and to owners of capital. And there is a large financial network of credit unions, caisses populaires, and co-operatives to be tapped in trying to diversify economic decision-making out of the small number of hands in which it is currently concentrated.

The point I am trying to make is that there is the *potential* for more Rousseauean-type initiatives in Canadian society. This is, perhaps, more common already at the municipal and local level, where citizen groups of diverse sorts abound and where the practice of submitting various proposals to the electors, in conjunction with the renewal of municipal councils, is not uncommon. There is, at the same time, a deeper feeling of rootlessness or alienation from power structures – both state and corporate – that many experience and that shows little sign of abating at the end of the twentieth century. To the degree that we have moved toward a more organized capitalism (cf. chapter 8), neither market nor nation-state can provide a satisfactory vision of community. To the degree that power becomes more concentrated and centralized, governing institutions like Parliament, cabinet, and courts become more removed from those they ostensibly serve.

That some of this powerlessness is a consequence of an ever-greater division of labour, of international, no less than national, factors that cannot simply be wished away, is undeniable. There can be no re-creating of Rousseau's agrarian, face-to-face society, nor is it evident that many would wish to live in such a society, even if they could. (One thinks of the ill-fated experiments with rural communes in the late 1960s and the 1970s.) We must adapt any democratic proposals we may develop to the exigencies of the large-scale nation-states within which we live and to the realities of an increasingly post-industrial order.

A society like Canada's, nonetheless, suffers from a surfeit of institutional legitimacy which gets in the way of authentically democratic initiatives from below. If the picture I have been painting is correct, Canada has had an overdose of Burkean-type legitimacy, stemming from our political leaders' unwillingness to risk turning over some power to the people in whose name they rule. Such initiatives, we were told by the Fathers of Confederation, were perniciously American or associated with the worst excesses of the French Revolution. We were to be protected against the "multiplied tyranny" that democracy, for writers like Burke, entailed.

I happen to believe that Canadians as a people suffer from a degree of political immobilization and disempowerment that accounts, in good part, for the diffidence of our political culture and our less than developed sense of national identity. The legitimacy of institutions like Parliament and cabinet has come at the price of the corresponding illegitimacy of actions originating directly with the people. The supersession of doctrines like the divine right of kings opened the door in Great Britain (and subsequently in dominions like Canada) to a doctrine of sovereignty no less anti-democratic in its implications: "In every state, there is and must be supreme, irresistible, absolute, uncontrolled authority in which the rights of sovereignty reside ... [Such is Parliament] ... the tripartite indenture of King, Lords, and Commons."[80] What Pocock refers to as "the revolutionary sovereignty of that body [i.e. Parliament]"[81] could become the justification for a quite counter-revolutionary theory of sovereignty, as we saw in this country.

We could do with a good deal more of American and French influence in our thinking about democracy and about the sources of legitimacy in the Canadian state. I conclude with a passage from the American Rousseau, Thomas Jefferson, that speaks clearly to the theme I have been addressing:

The article nearest my heart is the division of counties into wards. These will be pure and elementary republics, the sum of all which, taken together, composes the State, and will make of the whole a true democracy as to the business of the wards, which is that of nearest and daily concern. The affairs of the larger sections, of counties, of States, and of the Union, not admitting personal transaction by the people, will be delegated to agents elected by themselves; and representation will thus be substituted, where personal action becomes impracticable. Yet, even over these representative organs, should they become corrupt and perverted, the division into wards constituting the people, in their wards, a regularly organized power, enables them by that organization to crush, regularly and peacably, the usurpation of their unfaithful agents, and rescues them from the dreadful necessity of doing it insurrectionally. In this way we shall be as republican as a large society can be; and secure the continuance of purity in our government, by the salutary, peaceable, and regular control of the people.[82]

We need more radical imagination and experimentation, if we are to develop our practice of public liberties further than it has gone. We need more of Rousseau (and Jefferson), to counter the deadly weight of Burke on the Canadian body politic.

PART TWO

Political Economy and Sociology

CHAPTER SIX

Functions of the Modern State

In world history, one talks only about peoples who have built a State.
Hegel

In the late 1960s, a British political scientist observed: "The concept of state is not much in vogue in the social sciences right now."[1] This was less true for continental Europe, where concepts such as état and Staat have roots going back over centuries than for the English-speaking world, where the term *state* has seldom enjoyed a good press, but Nettl's point was none the less well taken. The year 1968 – the high point of student protests and challenges to established state systems East and West – was not a propitious time for theorists of the state. Two decades later, with state power more firmly in the saddle than ever before, with the economic and non-economic functions of the state experiencing continuous enlargement or refinement, writings on state power pour from the presses in English, French, German, Italian, and a score of other languages.

My purpose in this chapter is to try to make sense of the ever-growing literature on the state. My focus will be primarily thematic and descriptive, leaving in abeyance the much thornier issue of developing a theory of the state – on the assumption that such a quest is more than a twentieth-century version of the search for the Holy Grail. Much can be gained from critically scrutinizing recent efforts. In a sense, the problem of the state is at the very heart of the twentieth century, of ideologies ranging from Marxism through Fascism,[2] of political systems in every corner of the globe.

To be sure, the problem of the state is the current expression of a much older problem – the nature of political power. And there have been forms of power in earlier societies, so anthropologists tell us, in which the state as such does not seem to have existed.[3] This helps explain why classical writers were preoccupied with uncovering the origins of the state, whether through contract theories (Hobbes, Locke, and Rousseau), conquest theories (Herbert Spencer), or class theories (Marx and Engels).

Another aspect of the definitional problem has been the difficulty of disentangling the concept of state from society. In so far as power is dispersed through various levels of complex societies, boundary problems of the first order arise for any would-be theorist of the state. Hence juridical writers going back to Bodin sought to ground discussion of the state in terms of sovereignty, sociological theorists like Weber hoped to define the state in terms of "a legitimate monopoly of force," and twentieth-century Marxist theorists, from Gramsci to Althusser, tried to extend the concept of state to elements of civil society.[4]

These persistent questions of genesis and definition are not my chief concern. The most interesting question posed by the twentieth-century literature on the state has less to do with its abstractly conceived nature than with its actual *functions* – economic, sovereignty, and legitimation – in different societies. It is here that debate is joined among Marxists and non-Marxists, economic historians, sociologists, and political theorists. It is through this debate that we can perhaps come better to underline the protean character of state power.

What then are the principal functions of the modern state, and to what extent have they taken on a special importance in the twentieth century? Let us begin with the economic, which probably is the most important, and certainly the one that has attracted the greatest attention. Contrary to what neo-Marxist writers like Nicos Poulantzas contended,[5] there is an important non-Marxist literature on this subject going back to the late nineteenth century, when Adolph Wagner, the German conservative political economist, coined his famous law of increasing state expenditure relative to community output.[6] For Wagner, the development of capitalism brought with it certain new needs that could be met only by the state. For example, the national and international division of labour and more complicated commercial and legal regulations entailed a more important role for the police, army, navy, foreign service, and judiciary (Rechts- und Machtfunktion). As civilization developed, there was also a tendency for the state to become responsible for the 'higher and finer needs' of society, even while accepting greater responsibility for its economically weaker members (Kultur and

Wohlfahrtsstaat). Wagner's organicist sympathies, not unrelated, one suspects, to the strain of romantic anti-capitalism that pervaded German universities in the decades prior to the First World War,[7] also made him sceptical of the ability of joint-stock companies to handle large amounts of capital effectively or to develop new technical processes, further reinforcing the trend toward increased state expenditure.

While Wagner's law has been subjected to criticism in the literature of public finance, it has helped spark some of the most important empirical research into twentieth-century state expenditure. More important still, its broad predictive role has overall been sustained – i.e., state expenditure as a percentage of gross national product (GNP) has shown a secular tendency to increase in both relative and absolute terms in this century, though the curve has been neither as continuous nor the causes nearly as simple as Wagner might have believed.

The most important empirical studies that make reference to Wagner's law include those of Fabricant, Peacock and Wiseman, Andic and Veverka, Bird, and André, Delorme, and Terry.[8] Fabricant's study, for example, documents the increase in total American capital assets held by government from 7 per cent in 1900 to 20 per cent by 1949 and the parallel increase in the government labour force from 1 million to 7 million, stressing the growing importance of public welfare, health and public works, alongside defence, as the chief factors in state growth.

Peacock and Wiseman document the growth in government expenditure in the United Kingdom as a proportion of GNP from 9 per cent in 1890 to 37 per cent by 1955 and try to develop a more sophisticated explanation for leaps in patterns of state spending, linked to what they see as the inspection, displacement, and concentration effects of war. In a nutshell, situations like war provide a setting for leaps forward in state expenditure, making people more aware of injustices in social conditions, displacing public expenditures to new levels, and concentrating power at the centre, where it can later be brought to bear more effectively on these problems.

Peacock and Wiseman's conceptualization was in turn influenced by Titmuss's study of the levelling effects of war: "The aims and content of social policy, both in peace and war, are thus determined – at least to a substantial extent – by how far the cooperation of the masses is essential to the successful prosecution of war. If this cooperation is thought to be essential, then inequalities must be reduced and the pyramid of social stratification must be flattened."[9] It was also indirectly influenced, though its authors do not sufficiently acknowledge it, by Pitrim Sorokin's apocalyptic view of the role of calamities in history.[10]

For Sorokin, a major calamity such as war, famine, plague, or revolution concentrates both the individual's and society's attention on that calamity to the exclusion of everything else. Old loyalties and social ties are loosened while "a favourable ground [is laid] for the swift transformation of social institutions ... The main uniform effects of calamities upon the political and social structure of society are an expansion of governmental regulation, regimentation and control of social relationships and a decrease in the regulation and management of social relationships by individuals and private groups."[11]

The Zwangsökonomie of the First World War, the development of collectivistic economic policies in post-revolutionary Russia, and the turn to a totalitarian economy among all belligerents in the Second World War are modern versions of a much more ancient phenomenon. From the war and famine economy of ancient Egypt to the increase in governmental functions in republican and imperial Rome, from the role of medieval communes and states in periods of plague or famine down to today, government intervention has been the direct result of calamity.

War and depression have certainly been major contributors to increased state expenditure in this century. Andic and Veverka's study on Germany, for example, underlines the importance of the First World War and the economic crisis of the late 1920s to the growth of the public sector. "It was the virtual breakdown of the economic system based on private initiative and national circulation which explains the continuation of the displacement after the end of hostilities."[12] A study on France also shows a major leap upward in state expenditures as a result of the First World War and again in the 1930s.[13] And the same would probably hold good for Canada and the United States.

But do we yet have an adequate explanation for the economic function of the state? How does one account for the continuing growth in state expenditures in Western countries through much of the post-1945 period, not a period of calamity, so that by the mid-1970s OECD data could show most Western societies with state expenditures ranging from 30-50 per cent of GNP?[14] Are there not perhaps other structural explanations that must be brought to the fore?

It is here that Marxist theory has attempted to fill the void. While Marx never completed his projected volume on the state, while Luxemburg and Lenin in their economic writings focused more on the international process of accumulation than on the domestic economic activities of the state, others paid greater attention to the latter.

On the Marxist-Leninist side, the Third International, influenced by Bukharin, developed the germs of a theory dubbed "state monopoly capitalism," which essentially saw the capitalist state as acting at the behest of the giant monopolies, organizing and integrating the process of capital accumulation on their behalf, and repressing the working class and traditional democratic liberties, as under fascism. Since the Second World War, this theory, with some modifications, has become the official doctrine of Soviet, East German, French, and other communist parties in analysing contemporary capitalism. While some, such as the French, have shown greater sophistication than others,[15] the theory of state monopoly capitalism tends to an instrumentalist theory of state action. The state is seen as acting pretty well in the interest of the large monopolies, with only minor concessions here and there to other classes, and having little autonomy; hence French communist analysis in the early 1960s of de Gaulle and the Fifth Republic as "the agents of monopoly capital."[16]

A much more interesting formulation, I would argue, can be traced back to the writings of Rudolf Hilferding, the Austrian theoretician of finance capital and "organized capitalism." Already, in his oft-cited but seldom read *Finance Capital* of 1909, he had underlined the interests of large-scale finance in a less competitive form of capitalism: "What finance capital wants is not liberty but domination. It has no sympathy for the independence of the individual capitalist ... It abhors the anarchy of competition and demands organization in order to be able to engage in the struggle for competition at an ever-higher level. To achieve this, it requires the state."[17]

In a 1915 article in the Austrian socialist newspaper *Der Kampf*, he perceived the movement sparked by the war, from an economy of individual entrepreneurs opposed to state control to a highly concentrated, bureaucratically organized economy, entailing much state intervention.[18] And, to be sure, such ideas were being voiced by von Moellendorf and Rathenau, the economic tsars of wartime Germany.[19]

Some ten years after the war, Hilferding, in an address to the 1927 Kiel Congress of the German S P D, analysed what he considered a more permanent trend in twentieth-century capitalism: "Finance capital has a tendency to temper the anarchy of production and bears the seeds of a transformation of an anarchist-capitalist into an organized capitalist economic order ... The formidable strengthening of the state's power works in the same direction. Instead of the victory of socialism, we see the possibility of a society taking shape organized, to be sure, but along authoritarian (herrschaftlich) and non-democratic economic lines."[20]

To Hilferding, capitalism had by the mid-1920s become stabilized, the proletariat tamed, while the capitalist economy had gone from the road of competition to monopoly, with ever greater emphasis placed on organization and planning. While Hilferding was clearly wrong in emphasizing the stability of the system, his analysis of organized capitalism did draw attention to the decisive role the state had come to play in the operation of the European capitalist economies. A number of contemporary historians have drawn on his work, and one can find in his term *organized capitalism* the germs of an explanation of the growth of the twentieth-century state.

The term *organized capitalism*, once shorn of its subordination to finance capitalism, has certain advantages over "state monopoly capitalism." It is less ideologically charged and, more important, does not ignore the relative autonomy of the state apparatus from monopoly capital. What is common to both terms, as a German historian suggests, are the following factors: the tendency to centralization and concentration of production and capital, fusion of financial and industrial capital, changes in productive forces sparked by the growth of new industries, the increased role of knowledge and science, the organization of class conflict, the role of imperialism, and the increased linking of politics with economics.[21]

It also has certain advantages over the term *corporatism*, which experienced a certain vogue in western Europe and North America from the mid-1970s on. Not only does the latter term involve a rather dubious throw-back to the fascist economies of the interwar years, but it lacks precision. It has been used by some writers to describe "Japan Inc.," by others to describe European social democracy at its zenith, by still others with reference to more peripheral capitalist economies from southern Europe to Latin America, where military regimes have often prevailed.[22] We can save ourselves unnecessary anguish by recognizing the more organized and statist quality of capitalism in our time, without having to dub the phenomenon corporatist.

At the heart of current Marxist and neo-Marxist discussion of the state, then, lies the attempt to relate its increased economic role to transformations in the nature of contemporary capitalism. Of course, non-Marxist writers have recognized some of this as well (Shonfield, Galbraith, not to mention Keynes). But in explaining the state's new role, the Marxist school focuses on structural changes in the capitalist mode of production, on the ever-greater need for organization and centralization of the process of capitalist accumulation.

Within the contemporary Marxist camp, there are major differences of emphasis. Some, a bit foolishly, try to read an economic theory of the state back into *Capital*.[23] Others explain increased state expenditures as a form of devalorization of capital,[24] still others as a mean of arresting the falling rate of profit.[25] Some would emphasize the role of military expenditures,[26] while others, more accurately in my view, stress the increased importance of social spending in most Western economies, which O'Connor rather narrowly terms the "legitimation function."[27] What contemporary Marxist theorists share is a view of the state as a sort of 'overall capitalist,' not without contradictions, but entailing greater planning, state expenditure, and organization of the economy than in earlier periods of capitalism.

Overall, I would hold the Marxist emphasis on changes in the capitalist mode of production to be most useful in accounting for the state's increased economic function. Yet, as I shall shortly argue, when we examine the non-economic functions of the state, Marxism proves much less adequate. One of the ironies of the increased role of the state under "organized capitalism" is that the much-vaunted distinction between base and superstructure formulated by Marx has broken down (on the assumption that it was ever entirely accurate). The state becomes a good deal more than "the executive committee of the whole of the ruling class," coming to influence and shape human behaviour in ways more reminiscent of Sophocles than of Marx: "Crafty inventions, subtle beyond believing, now onto evil bring them, now onto good" (*Antigone*).

From the economic, let us turn to a more traditional function associated with the state, namely sovereignty. Not surprisingly, jurists tend to pay it the greatest attention. For example, the influential early-twentieth-century French jurist, Carré de Malberg, defined the state in the following terms: "A human community, established on a territory of their own and possessing a higher power of command and coercion."[28] And a Hungarian jurist, reflecting the ideology of "real socialism," if not the reality of certain practices, wrote in turn: "Sovereignty is nothing else but independence of state power from all other powers both within and without the borders of the state ... The socialist state is not subordinate to another state, to the power of either a capitalist or socialist state."[29]

Sociological and political writers have not been far behind. Werner Sombart, in his classical study of capitalism, looked to the external arena in explaining the state's increased power. Economic competition, military threats, and imperialistic rivalries had all strengthened the state system of Europe, and with it the importance of sovereignty.[30] For Charles Eisenmann, "the international function" is one of the three main functions of a modern state,[31] while Bertrand de Jouvenel points to the development of a popular conception of sovereignty, from the eighteenth century on, authorizing the extension of state power: "As long as we represent sovereignty concretely in a single man, since we know that all men are fallible, we cannot admit an unlimited sovereignty. But, on the other hand, we cannot conceive of limits to the sovereignty which is that of all. It would be unfair to say that the idea of popular sovereignty dictates a very great governmental power, but it would be fair to say that it authorizes it."[32]

For many Marxist writers, sovereignty has been a less certain value. While the twentieth-century world is clearly one of nations and states, which Marxism has pragmatically come to terms with, its original impulse was strongly internationalist. Moreover, its emphasis on the underlying class nature of institutions such as the state, its tendency to regard foreign and military policy, along with domestic policy, as the emanation of a ruling class in capitalist society, and the absolutist origins of the very term *sovereignty* have considerably reduced its attractions to Marxist writers, especially in the West. Not surprisingly, then, contemporary metropolitan Marxist treatments of the state, for example those of Miliband, O'Connor, and Poulantzas, give little or no place to sovereignty in their discussion of state functions.

Elements of sovereignty have, however, been reintroduced into Marxism through Third World literature. The Marxist theory of imperialism emphasizes the domination of certain powerful states over others within the international system and the impediment this constitutes to the sovereignty of smaller powers. Concepts of national liberation and self-determination are twentieth-century forms of sovereignty much influenced by Marxist thought. In a related way, distinctions between national and "comprador" bourgeoisies or metropolitan and peripheral capitalism, so fashionable today, are attempts to come to grips with the implications of the international system for ostensibly sovereign states. The work of Samir Amin, André Gunder Frank, and Immanuel Wallerstein comes to mind here, helping to elucidate the connection between sovereignty, at least in its economic aspects, and accumulation at the world level. Some of this had penetrated into Western Marxism, though, arguably, not enough.

There is another aspect to the discussion of sovereignty – the claim of the state to represent some absolute or ultimate power against its own citizenry. Recent challenges to the modern state have stemmed from this, whether on the part of student radicals, militant workers, ecologists, "autonomists," urban guerrillas, and other practitioners of extra-parliamentary activity in the West or on the part of workers and dissidents from party rule in the East. Pierre Elliott Trudeau in October 1970, Helmut Schmidt in the autumn of 1977, de Gaulle on 30 May 1968, and the party leaders of the Soviet Union, Poland, Czechoslovakia, and China – all faced with dissidents – shared a belief in the higher interests of the state they ruled against some ostensibly small and disloyal group of citizens. The wholesale scuttling of civil liberties in various countries around the globe, the limits to dissent even in so-called liberal societies in times of trouble, and the role of police, intelligence services, and military establishments attest to the continuing importance of sovereignty as the doctrine of governors against governed and as the justification for the state's repression of threats internal, no less than external, to its authority. Marxism has usually recognized this where capitalist societies are concerned, but it is no less true of socialist regimes.

This comparative neglect of sovereignty by Western Marxists points to a more fundamental deficiency in Marxist thought. It is a failure to recognize that there may be a uniquely political dimension to social life (a perception, after all, that goes back at least to Aristotle) and that the origin of the political division of labour in society as between rulers and ruled is not in some mechanical or determinist sense coterminous with the economic division of labour. When Poulantzas tells us that "the state is the strategic centre of organization of the dominant class in its relations with dominated classes. It is the place and centre for the exercise of power, but lacks any power in its own right,"[33] he is echoing the reductionism that creeps into some of Marx's own writings on the state[34] and that certainly dogs most twentieth-century Marxist writers. It underlines an inability to recognize the autonomy of the political – not merely some relative autonomy in which the economic instance always wins through in the end – but one that itself often determines the final outcome.

Is the state used as an instrument of domination over the citizenry, regardless of institutional safeguards? Is the state, as the examples of Hitler, Stalin, Idi Amin, Pinochet, and countless others suggest, a demonic power in no ways explicable in purely economic or material terms? Should we not in Hobbesian-Freudian fashion speak of a libido dominandi, at least where rulers are concerned?[35]

For certain theorists, the answer is crystal clear. Carl Schmitt, for example, student of Max Weber and Nazi supporter in the 1930s, made the distinction between enemy and friend the very essence of politics.[36] A theory of the state could only be grounded in a view of human nature as corrupt, imperfect, trying to arrogate power onto itself, and designating its rivals as the foe. Whatever classical liberalism, with its religion of progress, harmony, and minimal state interference, may have posited, the logic of history pointed to a powerful state grounded in domination. It was the state that came to define the economic system, rather than the other way round, reserving to itself the power to designate its enemies and crush them. Hence for Schmitt, the Bolsheviks, with the rediscovery of the enemy in the form of the bourgeoisie, were better students of politics than their liberal rivals.

Schmitt's French pupil, the sociologist Julien Freund, follows his master in speaking of an essence of politics: "There is an essence of politics ... There are no politics without a real or potential enemy."[37] For Freund, politics is based on divisions, external no less than internal, and on the affirmation of "relations of command and submission" in society. Class struggle is but one aspect of struggles between city-states, as in ancient Greece, between collectivities and groups aspiring to domination one against the other. Politics, accordingly, is to be seen as a fully autonomous activity, and the state as the expression of the friend-foe distinction and of an inherent desire for domination in human nature.

The Social Darwinian, not to say worse, undertones of such a political theory scarcely need underlining. Yet we would be foolish to discard it entirely in our analysis of the modern state. The attempt to locate a uniquely political form of activity merits consideration. We may not wish to limit this to the friend-enemy distinction – fortunately there is Rousseau to counterbalance Hobbes's view of human nature. But we will, however reluctantly, have to recognize that the exercise of domination seems to be an all-too-human activity in this century and has in numerous instances led to the extermination of "enemies of the state."

A less chilling theory of domination is outlined by Michel Maffesoli. Not unlike Marcuse, he sees all aspects of daily life, from language to sexuality, integrated into a system of value: "The legitimation of domination ... constitutes itself through work and its organization. Planning, efficacy, productivity become the modern gods."[38] Marxism comes to resemble liberalism, ceasing to be a critique of political economy as opposed to a critique within political economy. The symbolic aspect of state domination recalls that of religion: "A profane form of religion, politics reproduces the same scheme of delegation and substitution."[39] This analogy between state power and religion is, of course, not new. The Greeks had made it a central aspect of the polis.[40] Cicero, some centuries later, had exclaimed: "Nowhere do men so approach the power of the Gods as in the founding of new states,"[41] Rousseau had argued the case for a civil religion in his *Social Contract*, with Hegel in his deification of the state not far behind. In the twentieth century, the analogy between politics and religion has come to be applied to political parties (e.g. between Leninist parties and the organization of the Catholic church), to significant state occasions (e.g., coronations, assassinations),[42] and more generally as well: "The concept of the state with the distinction it implies between power and those who govern is as socially indispensable as were, in their time, the *mana* of the chief, the superstition of warriors, and divine anointment."[43]

Yet Marxist and neo-Marxist writers have great difficulty tackling the symbolic dimensions of power. The psychological dimensions of rule are ignored, along with the symbolism attached to state offices such as president or prime minister, or the quasi-religious authority exercised by successful political leaders. This does not mean that economic relations should be neglected or that we should take the symbolic level as constituting the essence of politics, any more than the friend-enemy distinction of Schmitt and Freund. But we should at least recognize that forms of political domination cannot be explained solely by economic domination.

After all, twentieth-century capitalism has known a variety of political regimes, from fascism through to liberal democracy, all presumably within the same mode of production. The same was true for pre-capitalist modes of production, for example, ancient Greece. How then is one to account for the different forms of political power the same mode of production gives rise to? To be sure, the position a state occupies within the international system, the level of class struggle, and the degree of development of the forces of production provide partial explanations. But are they sufficient to explain why fascism came to power in Germany rather than England, why socialism in the Soviet Union engendered Stalinism rather than some twentieth-century variant of the Paris Commune? It is not the political theory of Marxism that is sorely deficient?

A few contemporary Marxists have seen as much. For example, the Yugoslav philosopher Rudi Supek acknowledges the overwhelming power of party and state bureaucracy, not only in the sphere of production but also in daily life. If under classical capitalism political power derived primarily from economics, under eastern European regimes the contrary is true.[44] In the latter, ideological and political sanctions may play a more important role than economic, in the operation of the system.[45]

Henri Lefebvre, the French sociologist-philosopher, advances a more ambitious theoretical formulation in his four-volume treatise *De l'état*. He subjects classical Marxist conceptions of the state to critical scrutiny, discerning the emergence of a new mode of production dominated by the state: "When each member of a civil society, each individual, group or class has the state as its partner, when the latter enters directly into each relationship, then begins the statist mode of production."[46] Lefebvre underlines structural similarities between state growth East and West and the predominant role the state per se has come to assume in the world political economy. To be sure, he recognizes other structural forces as having potentially equal power, for example, the multinational corporation, but his interpretation challenges much of the current neo-Marxist literature that continues to read the state in terms of an ongoing capitalist mode of production.[47]

There are hints of a similar approach in Claus Offe, Jürgen Habermas, and a number of other German writers, though few seem to have gone as far as Lefebvre. Offe, for example, argues that "any attempt to explain the political organization of power through the categories of political economy becomes implausible."[48] And Habermas credits the state with a legitimation function in late capitalism that transcends the purely economic: "It is not possible to derive all the socio-economic-political problems of our community exclusively from the process of capital formation ... The assumption that capitalism, through state policies, has merely been stabilized, but otherwise unaltered, is fundamentally untenable."[49]

Fruitful as these openings may be, they leave unresolved a crucial question. If political domination is indeed as important as various writers, past and present, suggest, is it still meaningful to search for a theory within the confines of Marxism alone? Or is it not more honest to recognize that there are important areas of state activity in which Marxism proves just as inadequate as does non-Marxist theory in other areas?

This question becomes all the more important when we turn to one final function, which more than any other defines the limits of the modern state – legitimacy, or legitimation. Ever since Max Weber's delineation of three types of legitimacy – traditional, bureaucratic-rational, and charismatic – this term has enjoyed great popularity in the social sciences.[50] The term, however, is much older, having roots in Roman and medieval times and coming into widespread use in the modern period.[51] Racine speaks of "légitimes princes" in *La Thé-baïde*,[52] while the early-nineteenth-century liberal Benjamin Constant rhapsodizes: "There is something miraculous in the consciousness of legitimacy."[53]

That legitimacy is more than mere legality has been recognized by a number of writers, pointing to such cases as the Weimar Republic, as an example of legality without legitimacy, or de Gaulle's leadership of the wartime French Resistance from London, as an example of legitimacy without legality.[54] Be this as it may, one element in definitions of legitimacy bears particular attention: "Whatever is founded on values and recognized as such by public opinion is legitimate."[55]

Now there are enough cases in the contemporary world as in the past of regimes lacking popular support by any measurable index, yet able to endure. Force, just like tradition, can create its own legitimacy and for long periods dispense with any measure of popular support. Yet one of the permanent effects of the democratization of European and world politics over the last century has been to make popular support, even if manipulated, an important aspect of political rule. All states, in the long run, like to consider their authority as grounded in popular support. It is when such support is put into question by elements of the military, the working class, the peasantry, student movements, or the bourgeoisie – in short, by important social forces – that one can speak of a crisis of legitimacy, of institutions, or in relations of production.[56]

Some Marxist theorists pay considerable attention to legitimacy/ legitimation as a function of the modern state. O'Connor focuses on the large expansion in social expenditure by Western governments since the Second World War as evidence of attempts to win working-class support for the system.[57] Miliband also stresses ideological factors – the role of education, religion, or the mass media – in explaining legitimation, while Habermas, traumatized, like other German writers, by the historical crisis of legitimacy of the 1930s, makes it central to his analysis.[58] Earlier, Gramsci and members of the Frankfurt School had placed much emphasis on ideological factors in shaping the organic interests of a hegemonic class or manipulating mass public opinion, as in the fascist state.[59]

Much of their analysis carries us a good deal further than any mechanical interpretation of the relationship between base and superstructure, economy and state, would allow. In particular, it counteracts the tendency in Marxist economic discussions of state action to reduce the latter to a mere agent of capital accumulation, with little regard to cultural, ideological, or institutional factors in state behaviour. But do these writers provide an altogether adequate theory of legitimacy in the modern state?

De Gaulle, addressing the British Parliament in 1960, observed: "In your success, for how much did the value of your institutions also count? At the worst moments, who among you questioned the legitimacy and the authority of state?"[60] He put his finger on the role of political institutions and national traditions in assuring the legitimacy of the state. Was he altogether wrong? When the German Admiral Von Tirpitz argued that "the German cannot afford to abandon that uprightness which was the palladium of his old civil service ... It is only by proud, unselfish devotion to the State that [Germany] can counterbalance the deficiencies of its geographical position ... its religious differences, its too young and too uncertain national sentiment,"[61] was he not invoking a concept of legitimacy that marked Germany far more than Britain or the United States? Is not the legitimacy of the centralized French state rooted in a national tradition from Louis x i v's "L'Etat c'est moi" to Georges Pompidou's "C'est l'Etat qui doit commander,"[62] from the Jacobins to the French Communist party, that historically transcended right-left divisions?

Forms of legitimacy, then, would seem to be bound up with questions of national history, geographical situation, and cultural values, no less than with class relations or mode of production. Can Marxism do full justice to these phenomena without a Copernican revolution that turns much of the base-superstructure division upside down? Would the ensuing theory, by any traditional standards, still be Marxist? At the very least, some doubts are in order.

What is required, then, is a reformulation of the problem of the state. Classical Marxist theory has paid little attention to non-material factors in developing a theory. But if political economy, as Marx and Marxism would have it, is the matrix within which the modern state develops, the modern state is itself the matrix for economic and non-economic forms of power.

Whether this quite adds up to Lefebvre's statist mode of production is another matter. I fear that such a formulation mutes the very real differences that exist between the still predominantly market-based politics of the West and the more centralized, planned polities of the East. Such a formulation, moreover, pays insufficient attention to the specificities of different Western states and uses the concept of "mode of production" as a deus ex machina to maintain some ongoing continuity with an earlier Marxist orthodoxy.

This is not my concern here. There is a serious crisis in Marxist theory, no less serious than the crisis of liberal theory, and there is nothing to be gained in minimizing its extent. It is not a matter of looking for the appropriate quotation in *The Communist Manifesto, The 18th Brumaire,* or *The Civil War in France,* of bringing Rosa Luxemburg to the rescue or of making Gramsci the patron saint of a democratized Western Marxism. The crisis is thorough-going, rooted in a chasm between theory and practice and in the inability of Marxist theory adequately to address crucial aspects of power.

Marx nowhere developed the political theory of a transitional society, let alone of a fully fledged socialist one. Marx and Engels's formula of the withering away of the state, while fine as a Utopian fantasy, bears no relation to the reinforcement of power in this century in societies both capitalist and socialist and seems an uncertain star by which to guide our fortunes into the indefinite future.

Perhaps Marxism is simply not radical enough in its analysis of political power, too prone to believe that, with the ending of bourgeois domination and market capitalism, the problem of political power is itself solved? Classical Marxism, by and large, failed to address the problem of limits to state power and in the process opened the door to the abuses that have characterized twentieth-century state socialist societies. It is well and good to underline the bourgeois premises of classical liberal theory in its search for checks and balances on state power. Can Marxism, after all that has been committed in its name, seek for less?

What is the Marxist explanation of the disputes and wars between socialist states? Is the nationalism of one socialist state objectively more progressive and proletarian than that of the other? Does sovereignty really take a back seat to material relations of production in the modern world?

Are we better off when we turn to questions of personality and leadership? At least Plato could talk of "philosopher kings," Hegel of "world historical personalities," Weber of charisma. What is the Marxist explanation of the role of personality in history, of the revolutionary founders like Lenin or Mao? A Marxist theory of the state that is to go beyond ritual denunciations of capitalism must address this.

The same is true when one thinks of the question of bureaucracy. Weber's theory of bureaucracy has had a greater influence on twentieth-century social science than any Marxist alternative. This is not because Marxist analyses of bureaucratic tendencies or deformations in capitalism or in socialism are valueless. But they fail to recognize sufficiently the link between bureaucracy and the political domination that characterizes the modern state.

To be radical in thinking about the state is to restore politics to a central position in our analysis. It is to recognize that different forms of sovereignty and styles of leadership, centralized versus decentralized types of politics, unified versus separated governmental structures, historical concepts of legitimacy and national traditions can decisively affect a society's development. These interact with material relations and modes of production, but the interaction is by no means unidirectional and the consequences are not easy to predict. To echo the position advanced by Theda Skocpol: "In contrast to most [especially recent] Marxist theories, [ours] refuses to treat states as if they were mere analytic aspects of abstractly conceived modes of production, or even political aspects of concrete class relations and struggles. Rather it insists that states are actual organizations controlling (or attempting to control) territories and people."[63]

Political power through time and across national boundaries shows a Protean character, ever-changing and difficult to pin down. Brief reference to a number of major twentieth-century states may help us to bear this out.

In France, state expenditure had grown from some 12 per cent of GNP in 1815-19 to some 29 per cent a century later (1920-4) and to an even higher 37 per cent by 1965-9,[64] a pattern not without parallel in other capitalist states. The French state employed some 25 per cent of all salaried workers in 1974 – some 3 million directly, and more than another million in nationalized industries – a far cry from the less than half a million who worked for the state on the eve of the First World War.[65] Most significant, however, is a tradition of centralization and state power antedating the revolution: "The furbishing of the greatest Kingdom, the construction of a great state for long absorbed the energies of a whole people. Who needed an America? In France, the state was an America."[66] Nor is the modern French state, with the tremendous power which, as study after study shows, the administration exercises,[67] to be reduced to a mere appendage of the bourgeoisie: "The determinism of the [administrative] milieu is greater than ever. The administration cannot be simply confused with the dominant bourgeoisie. It constitutes a force of domination in its own right."[68]

The issue here is not the exact degree of power the énarques and other senior civil servants have, and how much greater this may be than that of their counterparts in somewhat more decentralized societies, such as the Federal Republic of Germany, the United States, and Canada. Rather, the French state, to no small extent, constitutes a force for domination in its own right, and its "autonomy" vis-à-vis the economy has, if anything, increased with the reinforcement of executive power under the Fifth Republic.

That the French state is not immune from attack was shown by the events of May 1968. But its legitimacy is not so easily destroyed. Nor is its sovereignty function likely to disappear, despite the thirty-year experience of the European Community. It is no accident that Marx and Engels's concept of the withering away of the state should have been penned with the example of the Paris Commune in mind. Nowhere in the capitalist world is the weight of the state so heavy. Indeed: "France is the country of the state ... We have offered the world this superb thing ... an unfeeling Leviathan amongst unfeeling Leviathans."[69] Nowhere has the dream of its imminent demise been more persistently, and probably hopelessly, kept alive.

Germany in this century provides, even more than France, a model of the autonomy of state power. We shall leave the discussion of the whys and wherefores of Germany's lateness in developing a unified state to the historians and theorists of world systems. Suffice it to say that the absence of such a state preys heavily on German national and philosophical consciousness from the French Revolution on – for example, in Fichte and Hegel – and that the Bismarcks and Wilhelms found relatively little opposition from a politically supine bourgeoisie and an as yet untempered working class to a fairly authoritarian Reich. The economic role of the state was a great deal more directive, even in the pre-1914 period, than in other European countries.[70] This was further intensified during the First World War, with the state coming to appropriate nearly 60 per cent of G N P and to mobilize "all the nation's resources, human and material."[71]

The defeat of Germany in the First World War ushered in a liberal democratic regime whose legitimacy was continually in question. The revolutionary left had been crushed in 1918–19, and any socialist transformation headed off. Instead, a system of organized capitalism, embracing the major industrialists and trade unions, carried on in the early post-war years,[72] while a weak parliamentary regime presided over an unreformed and unpurged state apparatus. The punitive clauses of the Treaty of Versailles weakened the German economy and undermined its sovereignty.

We shall not enter the debate concerning the relative importance of big business as opposed to other forces in the coming to power of Hitler. Only the ideological blinkers of the Third International, however, would allow anyone to characterize the Nazi state as a mere servant of monopoly capital or underestimate its autonomy and freedom of action.[73] From the Nuremberg Decrees to the invasion of the Soviet Union, there is every reason to believe that politics, not economics, was in command – which is not to say that, where economic policy was concerned, there was not the closest possible interaction between big business and the state. But that is quite a different proposition from one that would see Hitler as a mere puppet of the big capitalists.

The post–Second World War state in the Federal Republic ostensibly tried to reverse the statist current. The federal structure was one important element in decentralizing and delegitimating a too powerful state, as were the neo-liberal policies pursued from 1948 onward. Yet the state has hardly proved an economic dwarf. Fully 44.1 per cent of GNP passed through the state in 1958, a slight increase from the 42.2 per cent in 1938, after years of Nazi regime.[74]

Nor in the political field has it been all that weak. Willy Brandt, the least authoritarian of chancellors, once stated his political credo: "The democratic state cannot be organized without a strong structure. It must have a right to sovereignty and, in certain precise cases, use force to assure peace inside the country, defend justice and combat criminality."[75] The state in the Federal Republic has not hesitated in using an iron fist against internal dissenters, such as the Berufsverbot of 1972 or anti-terrorist legislation passed in early 1979, in the process renewing a tradition of legitimacy with venerable roots in pre-1945 times.

Let us turn to the United Kingdom, which Tom Nairn has characterized as "the first state form of an industrialized nation."[76] What is most striking about Britain – and by extension the United States and the white dominions – is a political tradition that rejects the strong state in its continental form, placing major emphasis on limited government well into the twentieth century. True, the British state played no small part in fostering colonial expansion from the time of Elizabeth I, through Clive's plundering of India, to the partition of Africa in the nineteenth century. Nor was its role in policing the lower classes – the Peterloo Massacre, anti-combination legislation – or in alleviating some of the worst features of capitalist exploitation – such as the Factory Acts –negligible, even in the nineteenth century. Yet ideologically it was a state that for long refused to know its name.

We may make light of this ideological tradition, but it continues to characterize the English-speaking world down to the present day. It is not only the word 'state' that rings much less true in English than in French or German, but the very concept of unified governmental, bureaucratic, and legislative power.[77] De Jouvenel has pointed to the distinction between the English "the people are" and the French "le peuple est" as underlining the pluralist and individualist assumptions characterizing the English-speaking conception of government.[78] One might also point to the role of voluntary organizations independent of state action,[79] to a tradition of juridical independence from the executive, and to the autonomy of municipal government and even state enterprises (the nationalized industries, the BBC) from Whitehall in contrasting British with, say, French or pre-1945 German practice.

To be sure, the move to increased economic and social intervention by the state had been part and parcel of British history in this century and as such accepted by leaders of all political parties, at least until Thatcher. The experience of two world wars and a depression, the need to mediate deep-rooted class inequalities, and the long decline in Britain's competitive position within international capitalism all contributed to increasing the economic role of the state. Monetarist policies pursued after 1979, and privatization more recently, suggest that the earlier suspicion of the state in British political culture has considerable popular appeal to this day.

The question of the degree of state autonomy from the economy or of the importance of non-economic factors to state domination is not resolved by simply analysing the rate of state expenditure in twentieth-century Britain. A writer such as Miliband seeks to underline the common interests between state and capitalism and, within certain limits, does this effectively. Those limits, however, are the ones pointed to earlier: the functions of sovereignty, of legitimacy, of political domination – which can be only partly explained through Marxist analysis. To what extent do questions of sovereignty, as in two world wars, the debate over the European Community, or the 1982 war over the Falklands/Malvinas, defy a purely materialistic explanation? To what extent is legitimacy in Britain grounded in ideological values – monarchy, religion, parliamentarism – that have over time become independent institutional factors in determining political behaviour? Are those who hold political power coterminous with the economically dominant bourgeoisie, and if not,[80] may we not find a degree of autonomy to state action that cannot be explained by the larger interests of the capitalist class? And what of the role of political leadership? Would Churchill have been as quick to disengage Britain from India as the Labour party was? Would Macmillan have acted in the same way as Eden over Suez? Would Heath have pursued the same economic policies as Thatcher? Whatever the logic of the capitalist system, political leaders somehow develop wings of their own.

The United States, even more than Britain, denies the concept of the modern state. The roots of this attitude go far back in time, to the agrarian underpinnings of the American republic. The American governmental structure, carefully divided between federal and state governments, further subdivided into separate executive, legislative, and judicial compartments, was meant to stay small and serviceable, compared to the more powerful, absolutist states of much of Europe.

The imperatives and contradictions of capitalist development from the very beginning, coupled with the emergence of the United States as a global power of the first order in this century, were none the less to make the state, especially the federal part thereof, a much more important economic force. Still, certain major differences from twentieth-century European experience can be singled out.

The most important is the relatively smaller proportion of state spending that goes to social security, coupled with generally lower overall state expenditure as a percentage of G N P, compared to western Europe. O E C D figures, for example, show this percentage for the United States in the 1970s to be in the range of 30–35 per cent, as compared to 40–50 per cent in western Europe.[81] At the same time, defence spending for much of the post-1945 period accounted for over 40 per cent of overall federal expenditure and close to 10 per cent of G N P,[82] a figure far larger than in any other major capitalist country. This vast military expenditure was of course linked to the nation's dominant political and economic position within the so-called free world after 1945. War spending proved attractive to important sections of American big business otherwise hostile to state expenditure and enjoyed a legitimacy in American public opinion, unchallenged until the period of the Vietnam War, and revived in the Reagan years.

The second distinguishing feature of the American situation has been the continuing importance of an anti-state ideology. Even as public employment soared to some 14 million by 1974,[83] as the international role of American corporations and the American state loomed ever larger, the myths of laissez-faire and limited government continued to enjoy widespread support.[84] The United States is the capitalist country with the least public enterprise, with one of the least developed social security systems, with no socialist or social democratic party of any importance. Despite movement toward enhanced executive power during the Cold War years and the so-called imperial presidency, its state structure lacks the unity and coherence of older nation-states such as Britain and France. Institutional factors such as federalism and the separation of powers provide part of the explanation. Even more important, one suspects, are the country's geographical position, its extensive resources, its lack of a feudal tradition, and its place within a larger world system, all of which allowed a process of capital accumulation with relatively little support from the state.

What remains unresolved, however, are larger questions concerning political domination and the nature of legitimacy in the American system. A crisis of legitimacy such as the United States experienced during the late 1960s or the Watergate period went far beyond the issues of social expenditure that O'Connor stresses in his discussion of legitimation. The roots of legitimacy are moral and political, no less than economic: the challenge to the Moloch character of the modern state in the United States, for example, in the late 1960s, was rooted in questions of political domination and the external uses of sovereign power. To be sure, such questions were not unrelated to the nature of American capitalism or imperialism. But it is far from clear whether they are subsumed under the latter or whether in a socialist United States questions of state power, political domination, citizen participation, and sovereignty would be any less acute.

It we need to be convinced, let us turn to one final example of a twentieth-century state, the Soviet Union. Without getting into a long digression on the nature of the Soviet state, one thing is clear: it is not a Western-style capitalist state with the institutional structures or clusters of private economic power characteristic of France, West Germany, the United Kingdom, the United States, or Japan. What exactly it is has of course been subject to much dispute.

For Soviet and eastern European orthodoxy, the Soviet system is based on socialist relations of production; class exploitation has been abolished, and the state reflects the economic, cultural, and social interests of the people. While some theorists continue to talk of the council system as 'the classical political form of dictatorship of the proletariat'[85] and others of forms of direct democracy that contrast with the fake pluralism of the capitalist system,[86] all acknowledge the leading role of the party: "Under our historical conditions, it is impossible to conceive a political system which would provide for the development of new political centres, or political centres whose centre of gravity lies outside the party."[87] The withering away of the state is retained as an ultimate objective under socialism, but this is impossible until "the respective internal conditions – the building of the communist society – and the consolidation of socialism in the international arena" prevail.[88]

In practice, the history of the Soviet Union since 1917 and, more particularly, what the French historian Jean Elleinstein modestly calls "le phénomène stalinien"[89] pose problems for state power that go far beyond the confines of Marxist-Leninist theses. Not only has the state not withered in the Soviet Union, but its power over civil society has known few restraints. The question is not to assess how much of Russia's earlier history – absolutism, centralization – contributed to the type of regime that emerged by the 1930s, or how much economic conditions or Bolshevik ideology played a part. What matters is simply to recognize that the state apparatus can be the source of an extraordinary degree of control in its own right. It is the economic base and civil society which, until the accession of Gorbachev, have lacked autonomy. In Gramsci's telling phrase about the pre-revolutionary period: "In Russia the State was everything, civil society was primordial and gelatinous."[90]

Where then does our discussion of the modern state lead us? I stated at the beginning that I would not be so daring as to attempt to formulate an actual theory of the modern state. A number of strands can, however, be brought together.

(1) The state, as the modern form of political power, is here to stay into the indefinite future, regardless of what certain anthropologists[91] or Marx and Engels may have thought. The worthwhile questions then become what limits can be placed on its repressive qualities and how much power can in fact be devolved back to its citizens. That debate has scarcely begun.

(2) The economic functions of the state have grown by leaps and bounds, confirming the predictions of Old World conservatives like Adolph Wagner and imparting a new character to Western economic systems, even where large-scale private ownership over the means of production has been maintained. An updated Marxist economic theory of capital accumulation and concentration can account for a good part of this trend, coupled with an analysis of international capitalist relations and uneven development. As Hilferding suggested, the twentieth century has seen the emergence of "organized capitalism" at an increasingly global level.

(3) Concerning non-economic functions of the state, such as sovereignty, legitimacy, and domination, Marxism proves much less adequate. Indeed, some features of the modern state are better discussed by non-Marxist theorists, from Weber on legitimacy to Schmitt on the friend-enemy distinction, from Maffesoli on the logic of domination to various liberal writers on the autonomy of the state.

(4) There is no single type of capitalist state, as the different experiences of France, West Germany, Great Britain, and the United States show, and the argument could as well be extended to other countries. National history, international position, and various cul-

tural factors play roles that make difficult all-embracing theorization about the modern state. By the same token, socialist states also come in different guises – the Soviet Union, China, and Yugoslavia, to name but three – and the political form socialism might take in the West would conceivably differ even more. The relationship between political domination and forms of economic relations is thus highly complicated; we need new typologies of possible political regimes, in the manner of Aristotle's classical delineation in the *Politics*, relating them to both capitalist and socialist modes of production.

(5) The state must not be elevated into a fetish towering over society, nor should it be reduced to a mere expression of the relationship of social forces at any point in time.[92] A product of human history, it must be studied historically, and, in that endeavour, philosophy, political theory, and historical imagination have no less a contribution to make than political economy.

CHAPTER SEVEN

The Limits of a Royal Commission

The relations between citizens and states, between the market and the polity, and between rights and obligations involve the classic themes of Western political philosophy and the ideological controversies of the present era.
Alan Cairns and Cynthia Williams[1]

Over the past decade there has been a remarkable increase in social science literature in the West dealing with the state. In part, this reflects one of those epochal shifts in conceptual priorities that seem to mark now a generation concerned with system equilibrium or behavioural constraints (the late 1940s and the 1950s), now another concerned with social justice or ethnic/national liberation (the 1960s), and now one concerned with economic retrenchment and crisis management (the 1970s and early 1980s). In part, the literature reflects a search for organizing tools in the social sciences, especially on the part of political scientists eager to come up with a more convincing definition of their own discipline than the rather open-ended term *power* long in vogue or the simple mapping of different political structures that is the mark of the empiricist. More fundamentally still, it corresponds to a growing recognition by those on the political left, the centre, and the right of a new salience that the state has acquired as a result of economic crisis, war, and societal development.

For neo-Marxists, a state that has become responsible for a good deal of economic policy-making and gross national product can no longer be reduced to a mere superstructure, with an economic base controlled by a dominant bourgeoisie. For social democrats and Keynesian liberals, the legacy of the past forty years is a welfare state and a set of interventionist mechanisms at both the international and domestic levels that they have largely crafted. For neoliberals or neo-conservatives, the state has acquired the same demonological qualities once associated with "radicalism," "socialism," and "democracy." The result, according to them, is an "overloading" of political institutions, the weakening of both civil society and its privileged instrumentality, the market-place, and a road down which serfdom and totalitarianism inevitably lurk.

It should come as no surprise, therefore, that the Royal Commission on the Economic Union and Development Prospects for Canada (the Macdonald Commission) and many of its background studies should take the state as the major point of departure. The report, in its opening chapter, contrasts "the positive big state of the contemporary era" with "the limited distant state" of an earlier day.[2] It underlines the ongoing "social and symbolic roles of the state" and more particularly "the stabilizing integrating contribution of the welfare state," without which "support for the relative autonomy of capitalist markets would crumble."[3] It further postulates the "embedded" character of the state "in society and economy as a result of innumerable past policies which tie it down" and the limitations this places on any "significant change in direction."[4]

Variations on these themes reverberate through many of the commission's studies. Two whole volumes, 31 and 32, entitled *State and Society in a Modern Era*, examine such issues as the image of the modern state, the growth of government spending in comparative perspective, state-society relations in Canada, the nature of political authority and state legitimacy, experiences with tripartism, and the politics of employment and welfare. There are references to state intervention in general and to the role of the administrative or welfare state in particular in several of the papers in volume 26, *Approaches to Economic Well-Being*, and volume 40, *The Politics of Economic Policy*. And, in a slightly different vein, several papers in volume 33, *Constitutionalism, Citizenship and Society in Canada*, address the relationship between citizen and state in the modern period and develop arguments regarding the nature of Canadian democracy. Many of the commission's economics volumes (1–25) are also clearly concerned with the role of the state, though a strongly marketeering approach pervades them. The constitutional/institutional dimensions of state activity loom large in volumes 36–39 and again in many of the Law, Society and Economy volumes (46–51). The question of sovereignty with respect to the international political economy is a focus of volumes 28–30. And no less than thirteen volumes (59–71) explore the ramifications of divided sovereignty in a federal state like Canada's.

There is a division of labour characterizing these studies, and a far from perfect unity of definition or purpose among the economic, political, and legal components. Nor is there anything resembling unity of view among the contributors to many of the individual volumes. Still, if the Canadian state in its wisdom, through two successive governments, saw fit to lavish $20 million on a royal commission with a mandate as free-wheeling as this one, if so many of our academic colleagues were prepared to put pen to paper in a version of state-fostered research without parallel in the annals of this country, we must at least take notice. Not everyone will consider this money well spent or agree that the University of Toronto Press should have committed itself to publishing the whole of the commission's research effort, when scholarly manuscripts in various fields go begging for publishers. Nor will the irony of Canadian social scientists undertaking research into the nature and functions of the Canadian state, while funded by that very state, entirely escape certain members of our community.

I propose to focus on one specific theme: the image of the state that emerges from some of the articles in the five research volumes cited above and from the opening chapter of the commission report itself. These studies illuminate the way in which Canadian political scientists are likely to approach the study of the state in years to come and some of the limitations that may attend this.

How should we define the state? What ought to be its proper sphere of activity? Is there some boundary between civil society and state? What is the relationship between state authority and that other crucial mechanism of modern society, the market? What scope does the modern state leave to the individual citizen, and what mechanisms might we envisage to enhance citizen input and control over those – in public and private spheres – who act in their name? These are some of the questions any discussion of the state should seek to address.

The concept "state" points to a set of ongoing institutions that the more elusive "government" does not always capture. The functions one associates with the modern state include sovereignty, authority (or domination), economic accumulation and development, social policy, and the maintenance of legitimacy vis-à-vis the citizenry. The range of state activity has expanded by leaps and bounds over the last century. Some of this has been the result of war or crisis, some a product of more deeply rooted demands for state intervention to right the inequities and depredation of the market-place.

Yet in Western societies, at least, there continues to be an ongoing division between activities taking place within civil society (most economic undertakings, speech, writing and belief, social activities) and those associated with the state sphere. The boundary may be imprecise, as shifting institutional norms lead to new delineations between the two. But the distinction is crucial, especially when comparing such societies with non-Western ones or those of the ancient world. Further, the market – the power of capital – is a crucial feature of Western-type societies, mitigating and in some cases overshadowing the power of the state entirely. This is all the more true given the institutional power of capital and the ability of large corporations and financial institutions to shift investments from one country to the next within the international division of labour. Multinationals assume a role, alongside states, as gladiators on the world stage, their power of domination none the smaller for being masked behind market laws and relationships. This leaves the problems of democratic participation intact. Just as alienation so often characterizes the position of the individual citizen with respect to the nation-state, so a fortiori are powerlessness and inequality inherent features of concentrated economic power. To address the one without addressing the other is to evade the hard issues of political restructuring and democratic reform in our time.

The commission's report and research studies give much play to the term *state*. Yet there is a good deal of ambiguity surrounding the use of this term. There is a tendency, for example, throughout the opening sections of the report itself to oscillate between the "state" and "government," without careful delineation of the two.[5] To the degree that any specific definition of the former is advanced, it seems to be caught up with the sovereignty function of that state, its role as part of an international system that privileges nation states above all others, leaving to governments those domestic functions that Charles de Gaulle once scornfully referred to as l'intendance. Still, this does not quite capture the difference, since the commission goes on to discuss the domestic role of the state in relationship to the economy at some length later in chapter 1, while also focusing on its international role. Nor do the words "government," "governors," or "governed" vanish from these latter sections, tout au contraire. One must, therefore, begin by asking whether the commission, for all its new-fangled commitment to the term *state*, has not muddied the waters considerably by hanging on with equal determination to the rival (?) term *government*.

This is more than a terminological quibble. Writers like Badie and Birnbaum have posited a distinction between more state-centred polities like France or West Germany and society-centred polities like the United Kingdom or the United States.[6] In the latter, which Canada resembles more closely than the former, there has been

much more talk about "government" than about "state," for the
very good reason that political institutions there seem more firmly
subordinated to various societal institutions than on the Continent.
One imagines with some difficulty a Canadian (or British or American) author echoing the metaphysically tinged sentiments of Thomas Mann in his *Reflections of a Non-political Man*: "As a boy I liked to
personify the state to myself in my imagination: I thought of it as a
stern, stiff figure in a dress coat, with a full black beard, with a star
on its breast, and decked out with a mixture of military-academic
titles that appropriately symbolized its power and legality: as
General Doktor von Staat."[7] Or that same Canadian, for that matter,
elevating the cult of the republic into a veritable myth, as in mod-
ern-day France.[8]

To suggest, accordingly, that Canada has crossed the boundary
that separates "government" from "state" is potentially to suggest a
degree of concentrated power and autonomous political authority
that one might associate with the political philosophies of Bodin,
Hobbes, or Hegel. It is to evoke the majesty of sovereignty, the
symbolism of Leviathan, the world-historical determination that
resides with the construction of strong states. Is all this to prepare
the terrain for an ideological counter-offensive against an all-perva-
sive state, to highlight the dangers of this cancerous Behemoth prey-
ing upon us, to point to a world where civil society, and more especially the market-place, play the ascendant role? This seems to me
an important part of the commission's intentions in deploying the
term *state* so effusively.

Thus the commission argues: "States are concentrations of coercive authority backed by force which govern particular citizenries
with fixed boundaries ... There were occasions in Commissioners'
hearings when powerful private economic actors, whose fortunes
closely depended on government discretion, were afraid to voice in
public their opinion of government policies for fear of the consequences ... The momentum behind the existing links between the
state and society in Canada, as elsewhere, is akin to the momentum
behind a huge loaded oil tanker steaming full-speed ahead."[9] The
clear implication is that state authority is coercive and expansive,
that even the largest of corporate entities falls within its grasp, that
all are so caught up within its gargantuan tentacles that only an
extraordinary effort of the will can hope to reverse it.

The term the commissioners use, *the embedded state*,[10] is the title of a
paper by Alan Cairns in volume 31. For Cairns, we are living in
"politicized societies caught in webs of interdependence with the
state."[11] With the resulting fusion between state and society, the

state comes to be tied down by the very programs it inherits and administers. "The contemporary state manoeuvres in an ever more extensive policy thicket of its own creation, interacting with a society that is tied to the state by a complex network of benefits, dependent relationships and coercion."[12]

It follows that the state is simultaneously fragmented and powerful, a prisoner of clientele expectation yet capable of autonomous actions at the margin, embedded in society yet pressing that very society to ever greater politicization. If *interdependence* is the term Cairns prefers to describe this, there are more than passing hints that the state plays a nefarious role in the entire process. "Our conceptions of community and identity are often inadvertent by-products of the massive role of the state in our day-to-day existence ... We now operate in terms of many state calendars indifferent to the movements of the solar system ... Political man and political woman ... constitute a new species qualitatively different from their predecessors, who could be defined by the adjective 'economic' or 'religious.' "[13]

To suggest, as Cairns does here, that everything has become permeated with politics is to neglect the pervasive role of private goods and individual interests in advanced capitalist societies. Ours is hardly the world of the classical city, where public liberties, to use Benjamin Constant's powerful metaphor, outweigh private ones.[14] To evoke a state calendar is to make light of the time-clock that regulates the movements of business executives and office stenos, assembly-line workers and aerobics instructors every working moment of their lives. Capitalism and industrial civilization seem more important forces here than the state. Yet they have no place in the Cairnsean version of the political universe. To argue the fusion of civil society and the state, moreover, is to revive the classical liberal attack on democracy (de Tocqueville, Mill) with a contemporary twist – Buchenwald-Belsen and the Gulag Archipelago as symbols of twentieth-century state tyranny.[15]

Even though Cairns is prepared to recognize the somewhat more "benign" role played by the state in Western societies,[16] negative imagery colours his own account. It leads him to the "overloaded" government thesis of the Trilateral Commission in the mid-1970s,[17] of a citizenry interested only in maximizing its rights. As he (and Williams) put it in their paper that opens volume 33: "The imbalance between rights and duties is fed by the politics of democracy which stresses the benefits of policies and minimizes their costs ... Not only is this bias productive of a magnified state sector, but it contributes to a distorted and thin conception of citizenship."[18] "La faute à l'état" here becomes the refrain for a neo-liberal or neo-conservative type of argument.

But is the state the source of all our problems? What are some of its strengths? And what light do some of the other research studies shed on the nature of this nebulous, but powerful, institution?

To the commission's credit (and here it is *very* Canadian), a fair degree of pluralism pervades the research studies in the politics section. (The economists were a good deal less pluralistic!) Meticulous care was taken in volumes 28-45 to ensure that theses echoing the Trilateral Commission's concerns about overloaded governments and the bureaucratic state were matched by others of an unimpeachably Keynesian complexion, and that here and there neo-Marxist arguments were also allowed expression.[19] The result is a considerable blurring of the negative image of the state that we have just encountered and a countervailing tendency to accept the legitimacy of a good deal of state activity in the economic and social arenas.

Before turning to some of the arguments, it might be well to explore a little further the use of the world "state" in the research studies. Probably the most ambitious definition occurs in Bruce Doern's introduction to volume 40: "The state is much more than government in executive form. The state is an amalgam of institutions, some formally constitutionalized, others less formally entrenched but nonetheless omnipresent. Thus, the state is simultaneously cabinet, parliament, government, federalism, and now the Charter of Rights, but it is also political parties, a complex structure of interest groups and interests, the courts and even the mass media."[20] This is quite a mouthful, recalling Louis Althusser's all-encompassing concept of state ideological apparatuses, embracing spheres of activity well beyond the traditional three powers – executive legislative, and judicial – of eighteenth-century constitutional theory.[21] For someone who wishes to focus "on the evolution of the administrative state,"[22] as Doern intends to, there is something to be gained from an extended rather than narrow "stocktaking of institutions." Doern also shows considerable realism (a good deal more than the commissioners) in defining capitalism itself, "based on belief in the political and economic value of free markets,"[23] as one of the overarching institutions of the Canadian political order.

Doern's definition of the state, however, is not without its pitfalls. Pushed to the extreme, it abolishes the frontier between civil society and state even more than Cairns does, by incorporating pressure groups and the mass media into the state realm. While for certain purposes this may make sense – a corporate-controlled press or broadcasters do provide an organic defence for the underlying political and economic values of the system, as does a crown corporation such as the Canadian Broadcasting Corporation – for more analytical purposes it blurs the edges. If every institution engaged in political activity or socialization is located within the state sphere, then the economic, ecclesiastical, and educational hierarchies characteristic of Western societies have lost their specificity. We have no means of distinguishing between Western societies and those in which civil society enjoys little or no autonomy from the political sphere.

Much narrower, through probably more functional, definitions of the state are suggested by David Laidler and Keith Banting. Concerned with contrasting the voluntary exchange characteristic of the market with "forms of economic organization that vest more responsibility for economic matters in various collective agencies," Laidler loosely calls the latter "the state."[24] While the well-being of the individuals who constitute society is the state's raison d'être, the socially beneficial role of collective action goes well beyond establishment of a legal or taxation system. No Friedmanite, Laidler is prepared to accept an element of distribution in his version of welfare economics, one grounded in propositions about society "providing a decent minimum living standard for its poorest members."[25] Since market mechanisms do not always generate maximum economic efficiency, cope adequately with risk, take account of the interests of future generations, or address the problem of equality, powerful incentives are created for the growth of the "welfare state."[26]

Banting, for his part, equates the term *state* with the public sector.[27] Public expenditure in Canada had grown from 15.7 per cent of G N P in 1927 to 47.9 per cent by 1983; the public sector employed almost one-quarter of the labour force; crown corporations played a major role in the economy. As government regulation has become more pervasive, the image of the state has increasingly become that of Leviathan. Yet Canada has had a rather conservative variant thereof, Banting hastens to add, citing evidence of relatively modest Canadian spending patterns when compared to other O E C D countries. The upshot, in his opinion, is a more fragmented and vulnerable state than neo-conservatives or neo-Marxists might suggest.[28]

We here have three definitions of the state gleaned from the research studies – "more than government in the executive form," "collective agencies responsible for economic matters," and "the public sector." Each tends to highlight the economic dimensions of state power, while having relatively little to say about such key functions as sovereignty, authority, and legitimacy. This may not appear surprising, given the commission's mandate and the strongly economic orientation of so much contemporary discussion of state activity. But it clearly should leave political scientists wondering whether these other functions of the modern state have not received short shrift.

For the moment, let us examine the principal areas of state economic activity covered in the studies under review: social expenditure, state-corporate-labour relations, deficit management, and taxation. The first receives a good deal of attention from Ake Blomqvist, David Cameron, Andrew Martin, Lars Orsberg, and James Rice, as well as Banting, Doern, and Laidler. Overall, these studies defend the logic of the welfare state against a purely marketeering philosophy. Rice speaks for the majority of contributors to the politics sections of the research studies when he writes: "As concerned as Canadians may become about the size of the welfare system and the effect it may have on welfare recipients, they are continually conscious of the threats of illness, injury and unemployment to their own incomes. Canadians will not treat kindly any government which destroys the security provided by the income security system. Family allowance, old age security and medicare are seen as important programs for the middle class."[29] Yet there is considerable difference of opinion regarding the genesis of the Canadian welfare state, the constraints on its past or present development, and the nature of any future reforms.

David Cameron, in "The Growth of Government Spending,"[30] attempts to relate the Canadian record on welfare expenditure to that of other O E C D countries. One of his major arguments, echoed in other papers, is that there is a positive correlation between large increases in government spending and two variables: control of government by parties of the left and the organizational strength of the trade union movement. This finding, consistent with that of Walter Korpi,[31] helps account for the higher levels of social spending in Scandinavia, Holland, West Germany, and Austria. (It works less well, however, for a country like Australia.) Cameron's other major argument, borrowed from Peacock and Wiseman,[32] emphasizes the role of the Depression and war, the so-called "displacement effect" of levels of state expenditure to a higher percentage of G N P compared to that of fifty or seventy-five years ago. To this is joined an element of economic vulnerability, flowing from our close economic relationship with the United States, leading to large Canadian expenditures in areas like unemployment insurance.

I am not entirely happy with Cameron's reasoning. While the

Depression and war did indeed pave the way to higher aggregate levels of state expenditure in Canada (as elsewhere) and set the stage for the introduction of the Keynesian-type economic policies, they do not explain the introduction of major new programs like Medicare, the Canada Pension Plan, or the Canada Assistance Plan in the 1960s, two full decades after the end of the war. Nor was Canada the only Western country expanding social services in the 1960s, at the crest of the long wave of post-war economic prosperity. Paradoxically, the social programs of governments ballooned at the very moment (low unemployment, high rates of growth) when Keynesian fiscal policy would have prescribed budgetary surpluses and state retrenchment. Political agendas and economic agendas do not neatly coincide, a truth that came home in a sharper fashion with the economic crisis of the 1970s and the sundering of the post-war consensus. Neo-conservatives like Buchanan and Wagner and neo-Marxists like Offe and O'Connor may have things to teach us on this score.[33]

As for American influence over Canadian social spending, Andrew Martin provides a much more systematic account than does Cameron. Martin's article, one of the two or three first-rate pieces in the commission's studies, also takes as its point of departure "the political strength of organized labour" in explaining government pursuit of employment and welfare goals.[34] But it argues that "the relative weakness of labour in the United States, compared with some of the other countries, has given employment and welfare goals a lower priority in the u.s. than in those other countries. *U.S. policies can therefore be expected to inhibit the attainment of these goals in the other countries.*"[35] What follows is a magisterial account of us policy toward the international political economy in the post-war world, which would favour trade liberalization over state intervention as the way of stimulating Western domestic economies. This can be contrasted with the more strongly interventionist policies of various European governments, such as the post-war Labour government in Britain and the dirigiste ones of France under both the Fourth and Fifth republics. Martin is particularly acute on the dilemma of combining full employment and the welfare state with participation in an open capitalist international economy. The inflationary impulse generated by the Vietnam War was to be transmitted abroad by the United States in early 1970s. In a similar fashion, the pursuit of deflationary politics by the Americans in the early 1980s was to have devastating implications for countries like France trying to reflate their economies.

What would this spell for a country as closely integrated with the

United States as Canada? If Martin is correct, the argument that the
Macdonald Commission makes about combining free trade with the
preservation of distinctive Canadian social policies collapses like a
house of cards. Far from being able to have our cake and eat it too,
Canadians could not afford to pursue employment and welfare goals
if support for these were low in the most influential of countries.[36]
Now Martin may overstate the case, since despite American hegemony in the post-war period many countries did set out to build
welfare states a good deal more developed than anything that was to
appear in the United States. And even Canada, with a labour movement only modestly more influential and politically organized than
the American, did substantially better in areas like health and hospital insurance. But the outer limits to welfare spending, in an integrated international economy, may well be set by the dominant
capitalist powers, and this can only be compounded under a bilateral arrangement like North American free trade.

Finally, as regards the welfare state, let me make brief reference to
the articles by Blomqvist and Laidler. These two form part of the
economics studies and fall far more firmly within the "public choice"
tradition than do the articles in the politics studies. Accordingly,
they are haunted by the spirit of Mancur Olson, the "free rider"
problem, and the instrumental goal of making the welfare state more
cost-efficient. Blomqvist is prepared to recognize the role of altruism
(what Titmuss would have called "the gift relationship") in providing an underlying rationale for the welfare state, but he is driven
(like most of his fellow economists and the majority of the commissioners) to ultimately individualistic, profit-maximizing views of
human behaviour.[37] Laidler notes "a failure on the part of economists to appreciate the pervasiveness of self-interest as a motivating
force in economic life" – one wonders who these altruistically/collec-
tively inclined economists might be! – and argues "the usefulness of
analysis which posits self-interest" as "a way of looking at the public
sector."[38]

The upshot is less a commitment to the welfare state as a means to
economic solidarity or egalitarianism à la Beveridge or Marsh and
more a questioning of "the possibility of using the state to enhance
society's well-being,"[39] a belief now fashionable on the political
right. Blomqvist, following in the footsteps of Bismarck, is prepared
to acknowledge the usefulness of social spending in heading off
more serious challenges to the capitalist system; yet the costs of
such spending must be balanced against any possible reductions
these may cause "in the productivity of our economic system."[40] The
emphasis in his recommendations, therefore, lies on making social

insurance programs actuarially sound and on more careful targeting of the recipients of government largesse in health or education. Social spending will be retained, with market tests of cost effectiveness and self-interest applied more rigorously. The logic of markets will come to pervade the logic of state behaviour, setting the stage for a possible retreat from universal social programs.

The relationship between markets and state figures prominently in the discussion of tripartism or corporatism. Banting refers to the close integration between government and business through much of Canadian history, including the immediate post-war years. With the adoption of Keynesian economic policies and expensive social programs, however, this relationship began to weaken. The result has been a now conflictive, now consultative pattern of relationships, with the state, no less than business, enjoying considerable autonomy.[41]

William Coleman, more tellingly, prefers to emphasize the "privileged yet conflictual relationship" between business and the state in market-based economics like Canada's. The state depends on business for both information and support. "The generation of resources by the state is directly affected by the level of profits and the accumulation of capital in the private sector." Moreover, where party funding or interest group lobbying are concerned, "business has more political resources at the ready than any other social category."[42] While business may be increasingly critical of the rise of large public bureaucracies and of various governmental priorities in the management and regulation of the economy, there is a "reciprocal dependency of the state and business" and "a privileged relationship" between the two.[43]

Labour is something of a ghost at this banquet, at least in Canada, despite calls for greater common understanding among what, in Europe, would be designated as the "three social partners." Leo Panitch provides a sweeping view of the operation of tripartite arrangements in four different European states – Britain, Sweden, West Germany, and Austria.[44] His historical summaries are incisive and the data suggestive of the very real limits against which corporatism comes, with regard to economic redistribution or high rates of growth. The presence of a strong social democratic and labour movement seems essential in the evolution of tripartite systems, although the experience, particularly in times of economic downturn, is a lot less glowing than Canadian enthusiasts (certain members of the Canadian Labour Congress research staff, Keynesian economists like Barber and McCallum) would believe.

Panitch points out the limits of corporatist-type arrangements and that these constitute no substitute for "a form of democratic social-ism" or for "ridding our society of class power, privilege and inequality."[45] Yet he chooses to put less weight on the relative suc-cess of countries like Sweden, West Germany, and Austria (and he might have added Australia, since 1983) in keeping unemployment relatively low and in preserving trade union rights, when compared with neo-conservative governments in Britain or the United States. Nor has the economic crisis of the past decade been anything as fatal to "the old social democratic tripartite option" as he suggests.[46] Note, for example, the relative popularity of the Australian Accord; the increasingly rightward, rather than leftward, turn in the eco-nomic thinking of the British Labour party, the French Socialist party, and our own N D P; and the attraction of consultation on larger issues of public policy for our trade union leaders and their suppor-ter, who have not enjoyed the privileged access to state power that business, as Coleman correctly underlines, has. With revolution of a classically proletarian sort hardly on the agenda of late capitalist societies, with the nature of work itself undergoing qualitative change, tripartism and income policies are likely to remain an inte-gral component of social democratic thought for a long time to come.

Still, the prospects for introducing a full-fledged tripartite system in Canada are slim, as Banting, McRae, Coleman, and Panitch him-self seem to recognize. Both the labour movement and our social democratic party are relatively weak; business is fragmented and unlikely to develop a single, authoritative, national voice; federalism and linguistic dualism limit what the central government can under-take. "The Canadian political system has long and deeply-rooted traditions of divided jurisdiction and majoritarian styles of decision-making. It should not surprise us if more consensual approaches to large-scale problems are likely to win acceptance only slowly."[47]

The one dissenter is Pierre Fournier. Yet his paper[48] is content to sketch the limited moves to greater consultation in Manitoba, Onta-rio, and Quebec (the economic summits) and to extrapolate from this into the future. There is little of the careful analysis of organiza-tions and ideology that characterizes Coleman's study of the politi-cal organization of business, the rich detail of Panitch's survey, or the informative overview of McRae's foray into linguistic diversity and its impact on economic decision-making in Belgium, Finland, and Switzerland. Nor does his view of the converging reasons that business, government, and labour would have for increased joint action – the pursuit of a stable investment environment, the legiti-mation of government programs and policies, the decreasing impor-tance of collective bargaining[49] – take into account the significant increase in corporate power over the last decade and the correspondingly rightward shift in the political agenda. Why should corporations, faced with a weakened trade union movement, offer their adversaries a consultative olive branch? Why should they take kindly to governmental involvement in economic consultation, given their memories of a "statism" associated with the hated wage and price controls or National Energy Program of the Trudeau years? Fournier seems to have misread the decade and the continent in which we live.

This is not a charge one could level against David Wolfe, who convincingly explains the politics of the federal deficit: "Most arguments about the appropriate size and role of deficits are in reality concerned with the appropriate relationship between the state and economy in advanced capitalism."[50] He pinpoints the very diverging positions on the deficit taken by representatives of financial institutions and of social agencies or labour unions. For the former, whose testimony loomed large before the commission, budgetary deficits spelled reduced personal spending, lower business investment, high levels of borrowing, and the transfer of the real cost of current public consumption to future generations. For the latter, budgetary deficits were a "positive" instrument to aid the government in sustaining its post-war commitment to full employment and to the provision of necessary social services.[51] Wolfe does not merely echo the latter's Keynesian refrain. Instead, he examines the experience of some other O E C D countries and the evidence from Cameron, Korpi, and Schmidt to the effect that high levels of state expenditure do not necessarily coincide with fiscal crisis and budgetary deficit. The relevant variable seems to be level of taxation and the greater political difficulty that governments of the right have in implementing tax increases on the income and wealth of their upper-income supporters, adequate to sustain government expenditures.

Unlike the economists in the Laidler volume, who advocate a consumption tax coupled with a flattening of personal tax rates as the summum bonum of tax reform,[52] Wolfe points to elimination of major tax expenditure items – from investment-income deductions to the non-taxation of capital gains – as opening the door to significant deficit reduction. It is the tremendous increase in tax expenditures over the last decade and a half that accounts for much of the fiscal shortfall that critics on the right (the McCracken Report submitted to the O E C D in 1977) and on the left (James O'Connor) have highlighted. The solution lies in more equitable sharing of the tax burden, in other words, on the revenue side of the federal-budget equation rather than on the expenditure one.[53] Wolfe is not playing

down the significance of ongoing deficits for state activity in the way
that some liberals or social democrats are prone to. But he situates
the problem within the terrain of political economy and class forces,
recognizing what the Macdonald Commission economists blithely
ignore – that taxation is where the ideological conflicts between
right and left on economic policy often play themselves out. Is it any
paradox, then, "that countries that have run the largest deficits and
the ones in which deficits have emerged as the most significant
political issue, are the ones where centrist or right-wing governments have predominated in much of the postwar period"?[54]
Reversing the argument of many of the right, Wolfe points to a
symbiotic relationship between right-wing ideology and the fiscal
difficulties experienced by certain Western states on the revenue
side.

All of this is not to reduce the fiscal policy of states to being the
mere plaything of dominant economic interests. Doern points out
that "high deficits have been tolerated despite continual business
pressure against them."[55] And Canadians have the evidence of the
1986 federal budget, suggesting the reluctance on the part of a Conservative government to buy the whole of the business agenda on
expenditure cuts and deficit control. But if "business power may not
be as great as advertised,"[56] it also seems considerably greater in the
present context than the research co-ordinator of volumes 40-43
seems prepared to acknowledge. Wolfe's article is a useful corrective
to conventional arguments about the cause of deficits – overly generous social expenditures – and a reminder of the power of market
ideology in shaping the political agenda, at least in the English-
speaking world.

The economic functions of the state, then, come under considerable
scrutiny in these different studies. The political studies, at least,
defend current levels of social expenditure and argue against any
wholesale compression in funding or services. The boundary
between state and market-place is identified as an open one, while
there is considerable diversity of views on just how tightly business
and government interact. Few authors expect movement to the kind
of tripartite arrangements that exist in a number of western European states. The state, moreover, while clearly important, is not
about to devour the autonomous economic actors in society.

Well and good. The shadow of the state appears less omnipresent
than Cairns and chapter one of the report assert. What about those
who have talked about a potential crisis of legitimacy flowing from
the contradictory political and economic functions that the state

pursues or from the overloading of government? Is the Western state a fragile bloom, destined, in foul weather as opposed to fair, to relive the haunted fate of Weimar? Anthony Birch addresses such a question.[57] And in the process, he helps move discussion of state activity from specifically economic terrain to a larger one, in which authority, legitimacy, and sovereignty play their part.

For Birch, the roots of contemporary legitimacy are three-fold: congruence between government, society, and territory; the character of a regime, in particular its representative or unrepresentative nature; and the success of government policies in safeguarding peace and security, maintaining law and order, providing full employment, avoiding rapid inflation, providing adequate social services, and pursuing fair fiscal policies. On all three accounts, he is prepared to give Western states in general, and the Canadian one especially, a clean bill of health. This is not to deny the presence of protest movements, civil disobedience, and even violence at various moments over the past two decades. But, according to Birch, revolutionary challenges to the regime have not sparked widespread support and are unlikely to do so in the future. He refutes the claims of Rose and Peters[58] that the increase in public expenditures in OECD countries during the 1970s was dramatically out of control. He next examines survey data suggesting fairly low citizen alienation from the governments of Western democracies. Finally, he touches on sub-state nationalism, for example in Quebec and Scotland, concluding "that proposals for secession are probably less of a threat to the national community than is commonly supposed."[59] Canada, in particular, seems to be in a relatively fortunate position as compared to the United Kingdom where legitimacy of governments is concerned.

Birch's analysis is generally satisfactory for the two decades he surveys. But I find much less acceptable his underlying identification of democratic practice with the representative principle and his tendency to see dissent and protest as faintly illicit forms of citizen behaviour. Seen from the point of view of the state, legitimacy becomes a matter of ensuring that orders are not defied and laws not broken by the members of civil society. This encompasses the problem that Cairns points to of "the startling discrepancy between the size and the weakness of the modern state"[60] and the need to provide sufficient authority for the state within its own sphere of activity. It is the problem Carl Schmitt alluded to in his striking discussions of sovereignty, of legality and legitimacy, at the end of the 1920s.[61] Yet seen from the viewpoint of the citizen, the world looks somewhat different. It is not evident that political parties and parliamentary bodies incarnate the whole range of citizen concerns. It may well be a symptom of the weakness of democracy, not of its strength, when robust citizens' groups opposed to various state policies do not make themselves heard on the political stage. A state that routinizes citizens' concerns along suitably antiseptic lines, that has immunized itself against sudden outbursts of passion within the body politic, threatens to deaden the practice of public liberties.

There is in Birch's evocation of the protest movements of the 1960s and disdainful reference to movements like Solidarity in British Columbia in 1983[62] a Burkean tendency to identify with the governors against the governed. With this comes a celebration of the existing Western order of politics as the best of all possible worlds. We are back to the vision of Schumpeter and the post-war revisionist theorists of democracy, to a "thin" as opposed to "thick" conception of citizenship in its relationship to the state and to the exercise of political power. Do we really wish to return to this again?

This brings us to the themes of volume 33, *Constitutionalism, Citizenship and Society in Canada*, which in turn, spill over into the report: the evolution of citizenship and community in Canada, the significance of the Charter of Rights, and the question of political participation. Cairns and Williams refer to "a complex dialectic between state and society"[63] and to the emergence of demands linked to welfare and social rights, to language and community, to gender, and to aboriginal questions, over the last several decades. As Williams shows, a fair number of these have become caught up in the evolving Canadian discussion of rights going back to the 1947 Citizenship Act, the 1948 UN Declaration of Human Rights, the 1960 Canadian Bill of Rights, and the political battles surrounding the Charter of Rights and Freedoms of 1982.[64] Canadians have not only become "rights conscious."[65] The substantive content of those rights now goes well beyond the individual legal ones highlighted in the largely unenforceable 1960 Bill of Rights to encompass social, linguistic, and community ones today. The Charter has emerged "as a third pillar of Canadian constitutionalism,"[66] while "the citizen has a new status as a bearer of rights."[67]

In the article by Knopff and Morton, the Charter is elevated into an instrument of nation-building.[68] We are given an account of the symbolic role of the Charter for politicians like Trudeau in helping to overcome a purely regional definition of citizenship, of the mobilization of interest groups in its support, and of the potential limits to too centralized a version of judicial statesmanship on the part of future supreme courts. For these two authors, no less than for Cairns and Williams, the Charter becomes the harbinger of a newer and richer version of democracy: "It ensures that the Constitution is at long last concerned 'at least as much with relationships between citizen and the state' as it is with relationships between governments. Sovereignty of the people is thus emphasized."[69]

The language of the commission is scarcely different. The report tells us: "The extension of democracy which is required by big government is not one of more fragmented participation, but one which addresses Canadians as citizens ... The charter has recently strengthened the citizenry in its possession of rights and reminded governments that their power is not without check. Citizens, no less than the state, have obligations."[70] This deeper sense of citizenship, with the Charter a key component, is seen as the way to counteract the tendency to big government with more democracy. In a passage that has surprising echoes of Rousseau, rather than Burke, the commission asserts: "We do not view democracy as a cycle of infrequent elections between which citizens revert to apathy. Governing is an every-day activity, while elections occur only every three or four years."[71]

For this reviewer, the Charter is here being used as an ideological weapon in legitimizing not the extension of democracy but its diversion into narrowly juridical/legal channels. To celebrate the top-down version of constitution-making that this country went through in the early 1980s as some kind of vindication of popular sovereignty, to equate the individual rights that citizens, according to the Charter, can now invoke against the actions of the state as the resolution of the broader question of political participation, are little more than a hoax. Citizenship in the political sense, in the collective sense, in day-to-day practice, has not been enhanced simply because of this Charter. There has been little rebirth of Constant's public, as opposed to private, liberties as a result of the political events of 1980–2. We may even have moved further into the realm of private liberty than before, one in which the market, rather than civil society and community, becomes the powerful determinant of citizens' identity.

There is one article, however – the single most impressive piece by far in all the research studies here examined – that addresses some of these issues. Charles Taylor's "Alternative Futures"[72] probes the philosophical and theoretical roots of our condition in the late twentieth century. For Taylor, there is a malaise about modernity that is closely connected to the atrophying of citizens' power. We view ourselves as autonomous individuals, our values are caught up with a 'subjectivist' civilization, and our relations to one another are reduced to purely contractual ones. It is the atomism at the heart of the modern conception of freedom and, one might add, the sphere of capitalist production that is at odds with community. While Taylor is not content to indulge in nostalgic evocation of the polis or the ancient republic, his argument is powerfully grounded in a classical notion of citizenship: "Participatory politics ... presupposes that these institutions and practices are valued and cherished as the locus of the citizen life ... The condition for a successful participatory model is a strong identification with the fate of the community."[73]

This has enormous implications for how we conduct our economic relationships (the Marxian theme of alienation), for the emphasis we choose to place on consumer goods "as a central purpose of life"[74] as opposed to other values, and for whether we wish to maximize individual rights or citizens' participation in our model for the good society. It is not that Taylor has succumbed to a purely Rousseauean version of the "general will." He acknowledges the importance of individual liberty and of rights pleas more generally. But unlike our Charter of Rights enthusiasts, he knows that litigation and courts are no substitute for "the sense of citizen dignity" that is caught up with "having a voice in deciding the common laws by which members live."[75] This leads Taylor toward a strong defence of decentralization and of regionalism in the development of any participatory model of citizenship for Canada. And with this conclusion comes an evocation of collective decision-making by the community as a surer road to the development of a democratic order than a continual emphasis on individual rights.

Taylor's position underlines the shallowness of so much of the commission's rhetoric about the state. Viewed from the perspective of citizens' participation, the problem we face today is neither the embedded state nor that of redrawing the boundary between state and market-place. We can turn market forces completely loose, as the neo-conservatives in our midst would have us do, and find ourselves even further away from a meaningful sense of community. We could prune certain branches of the "embedded state," such as the bureaucracy, or promote individual rights as a panacea against big government, without restoring the sense of authenticity so clearly lacking from the exercise of modern citizenship. Put another way, the state alone is an unsatisfactory institution to guide our every step, as unsatisfactory as the unregulated market-place. What is needed is a revitalized version of community, which in turn is caught up with a more participatory form of politics, economics, and social life.

Little of this filters into the report. There is no call for the democratization of existing state structures, save for that old bugbear, the Senate, or of economic institutions in the private sphere. There is little sense that civil society can provide a vital countervailing power to both the state and the large corporation. There is an obsession with the state that gets in the way of thinking creatively about less statist forms of public life, for example, ones combining features of community ownership, citizen and worker control, and market relationships.[76]

What seems to be embedded is less the state than the thinking of the majority of the royal commissioners and some of their key advisers. Those who come looking to the studies and report in search of some fresh vision of democracy, political and economic, will be sorely disappointed. Those expecting the same careful attention to problems of sovereignty or legitimacy that is given to the economic or social activities of the state will have equal reason to throw up their hands. There is both a narrowing of political horizons and an almost technical preoccupation with details of specific state behaviours that offers little conceptually new to the revived debate about the nature of the state. A jagged quality pervades the research studies overall, despite the excellence of certain individual contributions.

Such may be the fate awaiting any large-scale royal commission. Innovative scholarship, as opposed to the compilation of information, is seldom their hallmark. No one can expect so grand a theme as the state to survive the conflicting interpretations of economists, political scientists, or legal scholars. The economists, in this regard, with their single-minded commitment to free trade and market principles, have been a good deal more successful in stamping their own preferences onto the report and the research studies than political scientists, with their invocation of the state. At best, the latter have been engaged in a defensive operation, heading off a frontal attack on social spending and on the state's institutional autonomy, while leaving the issue of sovereignty – the political issue par excellence – for others to negotiate. Nor have they been successful in incorporating more than a 'thin' sense of citizenship into our working definitions of democratic politics.

There is a great deal more that remains to be said about the nature of the Canadian state, about its relationship to civil society, and about its interaction with that other crucial force of the modern era, capitalism and the large corporation. There is the larger task of reviving public liberties as a meaningful concept in societies where private liberties become all-encompassing.[77] There are notions of community and democracy to be developed, and functions of the state, such as sovereignty and legitimacy, to be explored and refined.

The neo-liberal critique of the state that permeates the report and many of the background studies does little to address such problems. Moreover, it leaves the power of the modern corporation unchallenged. The neo-Keynesian or neo-Marxist defence of the welfare state, while providing useful arguments against the marketeers in both government and the corporate world, does little to develop alternative and ultimately more appealing visions of the public sphere than ones inherited from socialist (social democratic or Marxist) or Keynesian/dirigiste discourse of forty or fifty years ago. It will take a good deal more theoretical imagination and philosophically and historically grounded argument of the kind that Taylor deploys to begin to come to grips with the long shadows cast by both state and capitalist market-place in the late twentieth century. And here, despite the laudable efforts made by individual contributors, our overall assessment of these research studies must remain negative. Far from being the last word on the subject, the research studies and the commission's report suggests that in this country writing about the state (and indeed civil society) has barely proceeded beyond square one.

CHAPTER EIGHT

"Organized Capitalism" and the Canadian State

In Canada, as in other Western societies, there has been enormous expansion in the role of the state over the past century. How can we best interpret this, bearing in mind the pattern of state expansion observed elsewhere?

Various approaches and interpretations of the growth of the Canadian state have been put forward. These range from largely statistical accounts of the growth of state expenditure in relationship to gross national product (influenced by Adolf Wagner and his "law of increasing state expenditure")[1] to more neo-conservative versions of the same, bemoaning the Leviathan-like character state activity has assumed.[2] They would include J.A. Corry's study for the Rowell-Sirois Commission ("In a new country the state is saddled with positive duties of helping people to help themselves."[3]) or Alan Cairns's invocation of 'the embedded state' in his writing for the Macdonald Commission.[4] Mention would have to be made of the "defensive expansionism" thesis advanced by Hugh Aitken in underlining state activity undertaken as a defence against the United States[5] or of some of Harold Innis's aperçus on the role of "hard frontiers" in shaping Canadian state behaviour.[6] One might note Herschel Hardin's book, *A Nation Unaware*, with its argument about the unsung public enterprise tradition marking Canada most clearly off from the more private enterprise–dominated republic to the south.[7] And account would also have to be made of neo-Marxist analyses, such as that by Leo Panitch and his co-authors, for whom the Canadian state has been largely engaged in furthering the process of capital accumulation while providing legitimizing programs, such as social services, to fend off potentially antagonistic class forces.[8] Clearly, there is enough in the above-mentioned material to make any would-be theorist of the Canadian state hesitate before embarking on yet another formulation.

Yet that is precisely what I intend to do in this chapter. Rather than engage in a long and potentially exhausting review of the existing literature on the Canadian state, or take the approaches outlined above as the focus for argument and debate, I propose to make use of a theoretical construct I referred to in chapter 6 – Rudolf Hilferding's concept "organized capitalism" – in clarifying the economic and social functions of the the twentieth-century Canadian state.

In adapting the theory that Hilferding, the Austro-Marxist economist and author of *Finance Capital*,[9] first developed in the 1920s with Germany in mind and bringing it to bear on Canada, I am taking certain risks. As I have discovered with chapters 2 and 4, there are some in the Canadian social science community who do not welcome the cross-fertilization that comes from harnessing European theory to our own circumstances. Such a theory, however – modified to take into account Canada's semi-peripheral position in the capitalist world economy (at least till mid-twentieth century) and the different relationship between state and civil society existing here as compared to central Europe – may clarify the economic role of the state in this country. I intend to use Hilferding's construct as a sort of ideal-type toward which Canadian development, at least at certain key junctures, has tended. Yet there are "disorganized" as well as "organized" features to capitalism and to the role of the twentieth-century state, and one must avoid overstating the case.

Hilferding's original thesis posited the increased importance that finance capital had assumed within Germany and beyond by the turn of the century. Through their extension of credit to the largest German industrial enterprises, the banks had become involved in the long-term planning and development of these industries and thus the ultimate masters over them. Uniting industry, commerce, and finance under a common hegemony, the banks were less interested in competition and laissez-faire than in a more organized type of economy which they would dominate. This led to a reinforced role for the state:

Finance capital does not want freedom, but domination; it has no regard for the independence of the individual capitalist, but demands his allegiance. It detests the anarchy of competition and wants organization, though of course only to resume competition on a still higher level. But in order to achieve these ends, and to maintain and enhance its predominant position, it needs the state which can guarantee its domestic market through a protective tariff policy and facilitate the conquest of foreign markets. It needs a politically powerful state ... which will ensure respect for the interests of finance capital abroad, and use its political power to extort advantageous supply contracts and trade agreements from smaller states; a state which can intervene in every corner of the globe and transform the whole world into a sphere of investment for its own finance capital.[10]

Such a state, with its tendency to colonial expansion and unlimited power politics, seemed faithfully reflected in the reality that was to bring the major European powers to war in 1914. That war saw a far greater reinforcement of links between the state and large-scale capital in all the belligerent countries, especially Germany, than anything Hilferding had described in his book of 1910. But it was not during the war as much as in the 1920s, in a Weimar Republic in which the German working class and the Social Democratic Party (s p d) had acquired a moderate degree of influence alongside the trusts and banks and bureaucratic and military apparatuses of the state, that Hilferding elaborated his thesis of "organized capitalism" to the fullest degree.

In a speech to the 1927 Kiel Congress of the s p d, he characterized the contemporary era as one in which "we are moving ... from an economy regulated by the free play of forces to an organized economy."[11] This move was furthered by four tendencies: a more complex technological base, symbolized by the new prominence of industries such as synthetic chemicals; further organization of cartels and trusts to take advantage of this new scientific knowledge and extend it as far as possible on a world-wide scale; the internationalization of capitalist industry and the attempt to unite various national monopolies, trusts, and cartels at an international level; and elimination of competition where individual business is concerned and increasing emphasis on scientific methods of planning and business organization within the capitalist firm. Questions of productivity, efficiency, and the running of economic firms had ceased to be a strictly private affair, becoming a matter for society as a whole. "This planned and consciously directed economy supports to a much greater extent the possibility of the conscious action of society; that is to say, action by means of the only conscious organization in society, equipped with coercive power, namely the state."[12]

The upshot of this was growing interpenetration of economy and state. Even in the earlier period of free competition, the state had already assumed control over money markets. Now, state regulation was directly affecting the lot of the working class through the labour market. Unemployment insurance, wage agreements, and courts of arbitration underlined the political regulation of wages and working hours. For Hilferding, this enhanced state role was partly the result of the increased importance that working-class organizations, both inside and outside parliament, had acquired in Weimar Germany and held forth the promise of breakthrough to a more democratically organized economy. But the structurally salient feature of this new phase of capitalism was its organized character, "subject to ever-increasing conscious organization by society and by the state."[13]

Hilferding's insights into the development of capitalism in the core countries are remarkably prescient, pinpointing tendencies to consolidation and merger within the corporate sector, the importance of science and technology, the emergence of a more internationally oriented political economy in which global corporations loom large, and the co-ordinating and planning roles that characterize both state and corporate sector in the Western world. If his theory overplayed the stabilization of the capitalist system (cf. the Depression) or the elimination of competition, it correctly pointed to the symbiotic relationship between large-scale capital and the state in the pursuit of a more patterned, i.e., organized, economic system. Nor does Hilferding's concept of "organized capitalism" suffer from the defects of other Marxist writings on the subject – for example, the state monopoly capitalism theory dear to orthodox Marxism-Leninism, with the state reduced to being the mere agent or instrument of large trusts. Rather, there seems to be a congruence between economic concentration or technological change and the increasing importance of economic planning and state economic intervention generally. There is room in Hilferding's delineation for the influence of other social actors – say, trade unions or parties of the left – on state behaviour, which enhances our understanding of the rise of the welfare state. At the same time, war comes to be understood as both cause and consequence of transformations taking place in the economic sphere, heightening tendencies to centralization and co-ordination within the major capitalist economies. In short, Hilferding's theory encapsulates key factors to which a variety of post-1945 accounts point in explaining the growth of the twentieth-century state.

How might we apply this theory to Canada? To begin with, we would need to recognize that a new settler society with a thin ratio of population to territory and a strong pattern of dependence – political, economic, and cultural – on Great Britain would have somewhat different characteristics from the core powers of the day. Before you can have "organized capitalism" you must first lay the infrastructural basis for capitalist development. "In a new country, the state ... must help to build the playing field before the game can begin."[14] In the Canadian case, this entailed wholesale reliance on outside capital, both portfolio and investment, to finance railway-building and manufacturing activities. The state's role was important here, providing the grants and lands for railway development, tariff protection through the National Policy, and incentives for immigration and capital inflow.

One way of looking at this process is to see governments in Canada, both federal and provincial, responding to indigenous strategies of development, in which the opening of the west to agriculture and resource extraction would come to coexist with a more industrial-type vocation in the east. Another would relate Confederation to the interests of outside investors, originally British, in a stable investment climate guaranteed by strong central government. According to this latter interpretation, outside capital, at a higher stage of development than what existed inside the British North American colonies in mid-nineteenth century, was the prime mover in "organizing" the integrated economic and political ensemble called the Dominion of Canada.[15]

Adherents of the first approach might see Canada as a late developer in which the state, much as in Germany or Russia, is a key element in fostering industrial take-off.[16] Adherents of the second might interpret the very creation of the Canadian state and its activity in terms of Canada's peripheral or semi-peripheral status within a larger capitalist sphere, in which finance capital was beginning to play the commanding role that Hilferding had described. "Capitalism is now imported into a new country in its most advanced form ... All capitalists with interests in foreign countries call for a strong state whose authority will protect their interests even in the most remote corners of the globe."[17]

I am not convinced that it is necessary to choose between these two interpretations, since each captures one part of the reality. The priorities during the first half-century after Confederation were dictated simultaneously by Canada's emerging position as a semi-periphery with regard to both Europe and the United States – something that outside capital would promote – and by the desire of our political, financial, and industrial élites to see a staple-derived capitalism, indigenous and branch plant, take root in this country. If the primary emphasis would be on private entrepreneurship and ownership (except for the Mackenzie government's ill-fated railway building of the 1870s, there is no major example of state enterprise in Canada before 1900), the state contributed signally to the process. It helped organize the infrastructure for capitalist expansion and fostered the entrepreneurial climate within which a more concentrated Canadian-based capitalism could develop. "A persistent pattern developed whereby entrepreneurs looked to the central government for leadership in the definition of economic and industrial opportunities."[18] "The role of the state in the economic life of Canada is really the modern history of Canada."[19]

The state, therefore, played an organizing role, in conjunction with indigenous capitalist interests and outside investors, in implanting capitalism in this country. The organizing of a capitalist economy, however, entails more than state-fostered accumulation. To this degree, the emergence of strong financial consortia like the Canadian Bankers' Association, railway oligopolies, and a variety of industrial combines also enters into my usage of the term *organized capitalism*.

There is a qualitative change in the level of concentration within Canadian capitalism by the first decades of the twentieth century. For Tom Naylor, "from 1896 to 1907 many new mergers were created, mainly by the participating firms ... Supported by British industrial bond privileges, the merger wave created an industrial structure totally dependent on the tariff ... Simultaneously, Montreal and Toronto capitalists undertook substantial exports of long-term capital to the u.s., to the Caribbean, and to South America."[20] For Abram Epp, in an exhaustive study of 106 major mergers in nine leading industrial sectors between 1909 and 1913, Canada seemed to be following the trend to consolidation evident in Great Britain and the United States.[21] As Gustavus Myers noted in the preface to his 1914 study, *History of Canadian Wealth*: "It is estimated less than fifty men control $4,000,000,000 or more than one-third of Canada's material wealth ... Perhaps nowhere in the world can be found so intensive a degree of close organization as among the bank interests in Canada ... The amount of British capital put in Canada is stupendous ... u.s. capital ... is represented in factories which, to a great extent, are branches of the American trusts ... This process of centralization is continuing."[22]

It is not necessary to suggest that the merger movement in Canada was identical to the cartelization process Hilferding described for Germany to see certain parallels. The most important of these was financial consolidation within the country – with a handful of major banks intricately interconnected with all the major industrial sectors[23] and concentration in both branch-plant and indigenously controlled Canadian industries.

As for the Canadian state, it clearly lacked the imperial ambition with regard to foreign markets that Hilferding attributed to the major European powers in the era of finance capitalism.[24] At best, it aspired to the role of junior partner to Great Britain in the defence of its own empire – the Boer War, naval subsidies in the lead-up to the First World War, and participation in the conduct of that war. At home, however, federal and provincial governments were bolstering railway development (the second and third transcontinental lines), encouraging domestic processing in sectors like pulp and paper, and, in the case of Ontario, providing with Ontario Hydro the first major example of Canadian state enterprise, brought about by a Conservative government with the enthusiastic backing of most of large- and small-scale business in that province.[25]

There was the beginning of a more activist approach with regard to labour, if creation of a department bearing that name or passage of the Industrial Disputes Investigation Act in 1907 can be taken as symbolic. And there were halting commitments to social expenditure (though these remained predominantly philanthropic) and hints of new legislation to come with the Ontario Workmen's Compensation Act of 1914, emulated subsequently by the other provinces. True, the Industrial Disputes Investigation Act did little to secure the legitimacy of trade unions in a property system stacked in favour of large corporations,[26] while Canada's was but a "reluctant welfarism," as Moscovitch and Drover have argued, when compared to Europe or the South Pacific dominions.[27]

Still, one measure of state activity, aggregate expenditures for all three levels of government, stood at approximately 11.4 per cent of GNP in 1910, up substantially from an estimated 6.8 per cent in 1870, and not all that far behind the figure of 14.5 per cent estimated for Germany in 1914.[28] Capitalism itself – with the increasing division of labour that it engenders, its developmental needs, its obsession with profitability and competitiveness in an internationally oriented system, and its determination to shuck off ensuing social costs onto the public sphere – had much to do with this transformation.

This is not a matter of reducing the Canadian, or any other, state to being the mere handmaiden of a few large corporations or banks (though there are moments, as in the financing of the Canadian Pacific Railway or the bail-out of the Bank of Commerce at the time of the bankruptcy of the Canadian Northern, Grand Trunk Pacific, and Grand Trunk railways in 1917–18, when that seems the case). Despite a significant overlap between the personnel of government in Canada and membership in the dominant economic élites, there has been autonomy to state actions stemming from the need to respond to the interests of other social forces, for example, farmers and labour, to regional pressures, and to the all-important national division (English Canada/Quebec). But the underlying pattern of property-holding in a capitalist society is such that the interests of large-scale capital loom large where state behaviour, particularly in the economic field, is concerned.

The First World War saw an intensification of state-corporate inter-penetration throughout the Western world. The process went furthest in Germany, cut off from trading routes, starved for resources, and with a tradition of an administrative state in Prussia going back to the seventeenth century.[29] The so-called Zwangsökonomie brought a degree of state planning, centralization of resources, and cartelization without precedent, with close to 60 per cent of G N P by 1916 passing through the state.[30] In Great Britain as well, as Leslie Hannah has observed, "The First World War marked a watershed in economic and business development as well as in political and social life ... The Ministry of Munitions began to play an increasing role in planning, financing and directing the activities of manufacturing firms ... The internal practices of firms were also profoundly changed by the war ... Many of these wartime industrial developments – mergers, large-scale enterprise, new industries, standardization and mass production – were, of course, associated with the stirrings of what became the modern corporate economy."[31]

In Canada the organizing role of the state also loomed larger during this period. Some of the impulse for this came from the outside. Britain's inability to produce enough shells and rifles for trench warfare placed Canada in a strong position to plug the gap. The Imperial Munitions Board, which promoted consolidation and co-ordination within the British war economy, played a similar role in Canada. Through 1915, 1916, and 1917 orders flowed into this country, with figures like Joseph Flavelle, the board's Canadian representative, helping to spark a degree of hot-house industrialization without parallel in Canadian history. As Flavelle's all-too sympathetic biographer has recorded, "In a sense, Flavelle was running the biggest business that had ever existed in Canada ... He had more men working on his contracts than any Canadian business had ever supervised ... The production network for the Imperial Munitions Board covered far more territory than the old empires of the fur trade; the factories employed far more than the C P R; the Board spent far more money than the Government of Canada had ever spent before the war."[32]

If businessmen like Flavelle helped to shape the state sector, the state similarly affected the way in which the economic life of the country would be carried on, through rationing and war-related production; assumption of new taxing powers, e.g., the Income Tax

Act of 1916; creation of a domestic bond market;[33] and creation of an independent Civil Service Commission and the National Research Council. War raised the overall level of G N P going to the state, reinforced the market position of those large enterprises best able to profit from war-related orders – for example, Flavelle's own meat-processing firm, Davies Co. – and imparted a more organized and, in the short term, coercive character to the lives of farmers and labourers, westerners and Québécois, men and women.

Peacock and Wiseman's term *displacement effect* nicely describes the long-term change in state behaviour resulting from war.[34] The level of G N P allocated to state expenditures was to remain higher in the 1920s, at approximately 16 per cent, than in the lead-up to the war[35] (even if a good part of this was accounted for by government debt contracted in relation both to the war and the buy-out of the bankrupt railways that became the C N R). More important, however, was the change in mentality that the experience of more collectivist forms of organizing during the war seemed to have brought about: "The obligation to die must carry with it the right to live. If every citizen owes it to society that he must fight for it in the case of need, then society owes to every citizen the opportunity of a livelihood."[36] "The War ... contributed to the decline of laissez-faire as a social philosophy ... Recalling the War-time activity of governments, many were led to hope that governments could organize for social welfare as they had organized for War. The War hastened considerably the acceptance of the philosophy of the social service state in Canada."[37] This shift in thinking was not to bear fruit immediately, if the parsimonious approach to social expenditures of the 1920s is anything to go by. But it was to set the stage for the acceptance of a more interventionist-type state in the 1930s.

Even before that, there had already occurred further concentration of power in the corporate sector. In the United States, business centralization, as measured by the enlargement in the average size firms, had increased markedly between 1900 and 1929.[38] In Britain, the so-called "rationalization" movement was gathering steam, leading to emphasis on scientific research and industrial consolidation, the better to meet challenges from abroad. As British industrial publications argued: "What has been drilled into us in Great Britain is that there is far too little of 'Big Business' amongst us. While Germany and the United States have been developing huge industrial consolidations, with ample resources ... and with a full equipment for scientific research, we in Great Britain have been trying to get along with a multitude of small, rather old-fashioned, manufacturing units ... If we are to hold our own in the future we must revolutionize our scale of doing things."[39] In Canada in 1923, the 100 largest companies controlled 25.5 per cent of the capital of all companies reporting; by 1932, the figure had risen to 35 per cent.[40] It was corporate and financial enterprises themselves, not politicians and civil servants, that were orchestrating the move to an ever more oligopolistically organized economy.

This greater corporate concentration, therefore, made it increasingly difficult after 1929 for the proponents of unhindered laissez-faire to argue for an unregulated market system. Some of the pressure for more interventionist policies came from farmers; faced with a collapse in grain prices and the dust bowl conditions of the early 1930s. (The Canadian Wheat Board was the result). Some of it came from labour and the unemployed, whose ranks had swollen to over 20 per cent of the work force – relief and unemployment insurance were to follow.

Intellectuals, too, whether associated with the newly created Co-operative Commonwealth Federation (c c f), the Liberals, or the Conservatives, were to press for a substantial degree of state planning, ownership, and fiscal and monetary intervention: "The state could no longer simply remain an arbitrator between man and man ... allowing the individual members of that society to work out their economic destiny unhindered within these limits."[41] "Government will have to take steps at once to enact measures which will put into practical form the controls that even a cooperating society must have ... Private enterprise must keep its freedom to attend to the localized practical details of community life. But in its general and social aspects ... private enterprise must also be subjected – against its will if need be – to the social control of government."[42] So at least some of the impetus for new crown corporations and increased levels of social spending came from them.[43]

But equally significant, many in the corporate sector by the mid-1930s had come to accept the need for a more interventionist state. Alvin Finkel has documented support for the Bank of Canada, for unemployment insurance and manpower agencies, and for stronger federal power from key business organizations and individuals, referring to a "new business ideology of conservative state planning to maintain stability in the capitalist system."[44] The same imperatives that led R.B. Bennett, with links to the Canadian Cement Co., Imperial Oil, E.G. Eddy, and the c p r, to argue in his radio addresses of January 1935, "I am for reform. I nail the flag of progress to the mast. I summon the power of the state to its support,"[45] were leading other stalwarts of capitalism to call for an enhanced economic and social role for the state.[46] The groundwork for what was to become a more interventionist set of policies in Canada was being laid in the 1930s.

Donald Creighton once observed that Canada has two different constitutions – one for periods of European war, one for peacetime.[47] There can be no doubt that federalism proved an obstacle to the emergence of a more organized capitalism in the 1930s, as was shown by the history of Bennett's New Deal legislation, ruled ultra vires by the Judicial Committee of the Privy Council, or the debates surrounding the Rowell-Sirois Commission. So the Second World War, with federal emergency powers in effect, marked a major development for the Canadian state.

It was the war, far more than the Depression, that saw the tentative coming of the welfare state to Canada. Agreement was reached in 1940 on a constitutional amendment giving the federal government jurisdiction over unemployment insurance. In early 1943 came the Marsh and Heagerty reports, Canadian versions of the Beveridge Plan, calling for recasting of old age assistance and income assistance programs and for universal health insurance, family allowances, and public housing. Family Allowances were introduced in 1944, the same year that saw the federal order in council, P C 1003, that brought state-supervised certification procedures for trade unions and, like the American Wagner Act of 1935, helped consolidate their position.

Even more than in the First World War, a good deal of economic concentration characterized government activity during the Second World War. Rationing and wage-and-price controls were the order of the day, with the state, through such agencies as the War Supply Board and the Wartime Price and Trade Board, becoming the great organizer, in conjunction with the so-called dollar-a-year men, of Canada's war production: "The Department of Munitions and Supply became, when war production reached its peak in 1943, one of the world's biggest business operations. It is by far the largest industrial organization ever established in Canada and it attracted some of the best business and industrial brains in the Dominion."[48] About 120 committees, commissions, administrative bodies, and crown corporations helped co-ordinate Canada's war efforts, with 765,000 people in uniform by 1944 and one million directly engaged in war production. By 1944, the share of G N P passing through the state (essentially federal) reached an all-time high of about 50 per cent, with the federal civil service growing from 46,000 in 1939 to 115,000 by 1945.[49]

Not only did the war greatly bolster the role of the state; it helped turn Canada into an industrial power: "It is under the pressure of events that Canada developed the means, almost overnight, to become a major industrial power."[50] "Canada in the summer of 1939 was an agricultural country with a thin veneer of mass production industries in her central provinces ... Two years after war began Canada had creased to be an agricultural country and had become one in which agriculture and industry were almost equal partners. Two years later, industry had become more important than farming ... The birth of industrial Canada is one of the significant events of the Second World War."[51]

From the production of aluminum and steel to that of airplanes, ships, or tanks, Canadian capitalism was winning for itself a more salient place within the world economy. For Canada, the organized capitalism of the Second World War signalled the beginning of the passage from semi-peripheral status to something a good deal closer to the core (cf. chapter 9).

The collectivist impulse of war, with a much-enhanced role for the state and a redistributionist ethos favouring social expenditures, would not necessarily persist into peacetime, at least not in a Canada governed by the likes of C.D. Howe: "The government rejected consciously the early 1940s version of post-war planning and political control of the market expressed by the Marsh Report and the Advisory Committee on Reconstruction."[52] Instead, there was wholesale dismantling of crown corporations, a rapid move away from controls and regulation, and a decline in aggregate state expenditures, to 22 per cent by 1950. (The comparable figure for the last pre-war year, 1939, is 20.7 per cent.)[53] It might seem that "organized capitalism" had simply given way to the more familiar market variety.

This, however, would be a superficial reading of events. There is room for disagreement about just how far Canada was to travel down the Keynesian road after 1945, and indeed, over how one interprets the term *Keynesian* in the first place. Robert Campbell has contrasted the likely policy orientations of socialist and liberal interpretations of Keynes: the former would probably emphasize "a somewhat comprehensive socialization of investment [as] the only means of securing an approximation to full employment," and the latter, more optimistic, might focus on private economic activity and its ability to generate employment and stability.[54] Clearly the latter version, what J.L. Granatstein has dubbed "free enterprise Keynesianism,"[55] won out in Canada.

This liberal philosophy was spelled out in the 1945 White Paper on Employment and Income, drafted by W.A. Mackintosh, which served as the Liberal party's economic manifesto in the June 1945 election: "The Government will be prepared, in periods when unemployment threatens, to incur deficits and increases in the national debt resulting from its employment and income policy ... through increased expenditures or reduced taxation ... The Government's policy will be to keep the national debt within manageable proportions and maintain a proper balance in its budget over a period longer than a single year."[56]

Between these grand principles – a more activist role for the state in monetary and fiscal policy, job creation, investment, and trade expansion – and Hilferding's "organized capitalism" there is, to be sure, some considerable distance. The imperatives behind the White Paper flowed from the economic conjuncture of the post-war period mediated by lessons from the Depression. Hilferding's scenario had been sketched out in the 1920s, taking as the benchmark for state economic activity trends to concentration and planning within the most technologically advanced sectors of capitalist industry. The adepts of the former were, in good part, economists, civil servants, and politicians, for whom Keynesianism seemed to reconcile state activity with a still predominantly market system. The supporters of the latter, according to Hilferding, should have come from the large trusts and cartels, for whom the market system itself had lost its meaning.

Yet if we use Hilferding's term flexibly, denoting, as he meant it, the move toward more integrated state–private sector relationships and greater conscious direction of the economy, then much is to be gained from applying it to post-1945 Canada. The organizing of capitalism was what a good deal of state economic activity, at both federal and provincial levels, would be about: state investment in infrastructure, taxation policies, regional development, and industrial and employment policies. Social expenditures, on education, health, social assistance, and unemployment insurance, would follow a steadily rising curve, especially in the 1960s and early 1970s, leading Canada closer to the more socialized western European norm. Corporate concentration continued apace, with a combination of foreign-controlled and indigenously controlled corporations our real economic potentates. Organized interest groups – big and small business, farmers, trade unions, professionals, and consumers – loomed ever larger in public policy debates, leading some, a little glibly, to speak of corporatist tendencies. And other factors – technological innovations and multinational investment flows, shifting commodity prices, and a new international division of labour – forced the state, corporations, and even trade unions to think in a more concerted fashion about Canada's place in the world economy and on the North American continent.

The state since 1945 has grown substantially in terms of share of GNP for which it is responsible, percentage of the work-force it employs, number of crown corporations, regulatory activity, and redistributive role – this is generally agreed to by writers across the political spectrum. For example, the state's share of GNP (including income transferred), which was 22.4 per cent in 1950, has risen to 34.1 per cent by 1967 and, by one estimate, to a height of 47.9 per cent in 1983, declining slightly since.[57] The total number of state employees – those working for federal, provincial, or municipal governments and crown corporations and in the para-state sector (education and health) – increased dramatically, from about 8.9 per cent of the total labour force in 1946 to 21.2 per cent by 1974.[58] There were well over 400 federal crown corporations and some 230 provincial ones by the early 1980s,[59] and some of these, like Ontario Hydro, Hydro Québec, Petro-Canada, and the CNR, were among the country's largest corporations in terms of assets.

Does it follow from all this that Canada has become a government-centred society, with government threatening to overawe us, as some on the right are prone to argue?[60] Are we to interpret Canada's as a mixed economy, with "a greater genuine liaison and rapport between government and business than in any other country?"[61] Or is the state, as a version of neo-Marxist analysis would have it, hopelessly engaged in a political-economic attempt at squaring the circle: trying to reconcile its accumulation function (securing high profitability for capital), with its legitimation function (making the economic system acceptable to the working class and others through rising income levels and social expenditures)?[62]

I would suggest that Canada between 1945 and the mid-1980s embarked down the road to a more organized type of capitalism. I would not single out the state as the independent variable in this regard, since corporate concentration, both domestic and international, has played a large role. Edward Herman observes about the US situation: "[T]he enlargement in size and role of government has been parallel to and has partly been induced by the growth in size and power of the large corporation. Big business has wanted big government – in selected spheres – and the spread of large firms across international boundaries and their increased mobility has led to demands for governmental aid by injured business people, abandoned workers, and ailing communities."[63]

As writers from Andrew Shonfield to John Kenneth Galbraith noted, "The taming of the market ... is the condition for a style of private enterprise which tends to grow like the behaviour of certain public institutions."[64] "Industrial planning is in unabashed alliance with size ... Vertical integration, the control of prices and consumer demands, and reciprocal absorption of market uncertainty by contracts between firms all favour the large enterprise."[65] Mergers, takeovers, investment syndicates, transnational capital, and technology flows hardly bespeak the small-firm, competitive capitalism beloved of earlier economic theory.

In Canada, too, concentration has been the rule: "As the economy has grown so have the dominant corporations ... For the corporate world the decade of the 1950s was one of continuing consolidation, merger and takeover. Big firms got bigger, not only from internal expansion, but also by joining together."[66] Through merger and acquisition, John Porter's 183 dominant corporations of the late 1950s and early 1960s had become Wallace Clement's 113 of a decade later, controlling well over 50 per cent of all assets in finance, transportation, mining, and most branches of manufacturing.[67] Corporate capitalism itself – with or without the state – is a great force for centralization and organization in our age.

It so happens that the state has played an important role in Canada, as elsewhere, in furthering this process. And the state, in certain regards, has been an important economic organizer in its own right. In the remainder of this chapter, then, let me try to isolate some of the particular contributions that the Canadian state has made to the emergence of a more 'organized capitalism' and then, by way of conclusion, briefly consider whether the turn to more neo-conservative policies in the 1980s is likely to alter this situation drastically.

There are at least three rubrics under which one could examine state economic activity: the *stabilization of capitalism*, including Keynesian-type counter-cyclical policies, welfare expenditures, and more episodic interventions ranging from price and wage controls to corporate bail-outs; the *forward development of capitalism*, e.g., support for scientific research, education and manpower training, industrial policies, export drives, and integration into larger, world markets; and *nation-building* (and province-building), e.g., government attempts to impart a more national complexion to the structure of capitalist ownership within its own borders, using measures ranging from tax incentives and legislative restrictions to crown corporations and the active channeling of investment. Let us look at each of these in turn.

A crucial difference between pre-war and post-war capitalism has been the greater acceptance of responsibility by governments for the overall management of their economies. In the English-speaking world one was prone to speak of Keynesianism, in France and certain continental countries, of statism or dirigisme.[68] Through the thirty years of prosperity that the French economist Fourastié has dubbed "les trente glorieuses,"[69] governments were prepared to use monetary and fiscal policy, social programs, "concertation" with key economic actors, and forms of indicative planning to introduce a stability into the capitalist system that had been sorely absent in the 1930s.

In the Canadian case, as already suggested, there was an ideological commitment to Keynesianism beginning with the White Paper of 1945. This Keynesianism would not put into question the prevalence of a corporate-dominated economy, nor would it attempt to tilt the balance, as did some northern European states with strong social democratic parties (and sometimes Christian Democratic), in the direction of labour. Some have suggested other peculiarities of Canadian Keynesianism, for example, a strong commitment to the freeing up of international trade, reflecting our resource staple base.[70] To this one might add federalism as an impediment to European-type notions of planning and our increasing integration with the United States, making it difficult to pursue economic policies radically different from our neighbour's.

How effective was Keynesianism in ensuring the prosperity that Canada, along with the Western world, came to experience? Alan Noël suggests that removal of wartime controls and release of pent-up consumer demand were probably sufficient, at least in North America, to prime the economy, with Keynesianism at best a political device serving the interest of C C F or Liberal politicians.[71] Robert Campbell suggests that Keynesianism was applied unevenly over a thirty-year period (1945–75) and that, more often than not, it had to be supplemented by more interventionist programs, such as regional development, social expenditures, and the Anti-Inflation Board.[72]

Yet most economists and politicians in Canada embraced a more active role for government – "fiscal and commercial policies ... to maintain the right kind of economic climate,"[73] "increased responsibility in respect to short-term economic instability"[74] – something at the heart of post-war Keynesianism, as many have interpreted it: "Keynes directed systematic attention – especially in his essay on The End of Laissez-Faire and then in the General Theory – to one of the fundamental problems of our time, the growing role of the state in economic life ... In the final analysis, his General Theory can be regarded as a great intellectual effort to see how the State can intervene to save capitalism, making it function in a socially acceptable way."[75]

A further feature of the stabilization of capitalism involved the integration of labour. This was achieved, in part, through an industrial relations framework that entrenched the certification procedures introduced at the federal level in 1944. More tellingly, it entailed labour's sharing, through wage increases – usually worked out at the bargaining table, sometimes through strike action – in the fruits of post-war prosperity. It also involved governments' willingness to meet periodically and consult with representatives of labour, as at annual meetings of the federal cabinet with the Canadian Labour Congress, to appoint some labour representatives to various boards and commissions, to extend (in the 1960s), the right of collective bargaining to its own workers, and to introduce social legislation which labour strongly backed. I see nothing corporatist about state-labour relations in Canada over the post-war period, though I do discern a move to a more organized, state-regulated system of industrial relations. (Some of this regulation could be turned against labour, through injunctions, repressive legislation, arrests, and jail sentences, and has been much more noticeable in recent years.)[76]

It is in the same light that I think one can best approach the emergence of the welfare state. It did not come about in one piece: unemployment insurance and family allowances date from the war; universal old-age pensions and hospital insurance from the 1950s; medicare, the Canada/Quebec Pension Plans, and a comprehensive system of social assistance from the 1960s; and enriched unemployment insurance and a revamped family allowance scheme from the 1970s. These measures, it is fair to say, met with strong support from organized labour and the broadest cross-sections of Canadian society; support from big business was either lacking or a good deal more muted.

That social expenditures in 1981 accounted for 57.8 per cent of total government expenditures and some 22.1 per cent of Canadian G N P and that they showed a tendency to increase more rapidly than other government expenditures for a number of decades,[77] underline just how much of the enhanced role of the post-war state they help explain. Canada, in this regard, has followed the trend observable in other O E C D countries, even if many western European countries have had aggregate levels of social expenditure greater than our own.[78] Programs like unemployment insurance, income assistance, pension plans, and health insurance provide a safety net for large sections of the work-force against the vagaries of the economic cycle, of illness, or of old age. They introduce some stability, predictability, and security, where none was present before. They thereby provide a more organized dimension to social life.

I think we gain from emphasizing the parallel imperative that leads the state to play a more interventionist role in both the economic arena and the social. If depression and abrupt down-turns in the business cycle are the great evils action in the first sets out to forestall, then the breakdown in social solidarity stemming from the capitalist division of labour may be the great evil action in the second sets out to correct.[79] Social cohesion is as much of a prerequisite for the stabilization of capitalism as is the intelligent management of monetary or fiscal policy. It is for good reason that the two came to be linked in the policies of post-war societies such as Canada's.

This is not to suggest that there were no differences in the welfare policies pursued by different political parties in the Western world or that there was a homogeneity to the organized social behaviour of states. Major examples of social policy in Canada such as Medicare or the Canada/Quebec Pension Plans were not introduced until the 1960s, fully two decades after the White Paper and after similar measures had already been institutionalized in western Europe. Clearly, political culture and leadership, class and social relations, and economic conditions would have to be examined in explaining why this was the case. Nor would I want to interpret the welfare state as solely an attempt to stabilize capitalism, since a more generous social philosophy than capitalism inspired many of its strongest adherents.[80] But its emergence has had a lot to do with making post-war capitalism a more organized system, better able to withstand economic and political crisis than its pre-war predecessor.

Other state policies have sought to stabilize capitalism in new ways: (1) import controls during 1947–8, following the breakdown of the North Atlantic triangle and an increasing Canadian trade deficit with the United States; (2) regional development policies, from the Atlantic Development Board to a full-fledged Department of Regional Economic Expansion; (3) the Anti-Inflation Board and subsequent wage and price controls 1975–8, to cool down an "overheated" economy; (4) the 6 and 5 program at the federal level in the early 1980s, with encouragement to the provinces and the private sector to follow suit (cf. the Quebec government wage roll-backs in the public sector in 1982–3, or the B C government's 'restraint' program of July 1983); (5) bail-outs of corporations or banks threatening to go under, from Chrysler and Maislin Trucks to the Canadian Commercial Bank and the Canadian Northern; and (6) regulation of whole sectors of activity, ranging from communications to energy, environment to finance, food production to transportation.

In all these programs, government tried to supply a visible helping hand to the market. Such action could involve rectifying breakdowns in the system, whether caused by international factors, corporate (mis)behaviour, or previous governmental policies. It could involve trying to organize a more "rational" framework for agricultural producers or public carriers, broadcasters or financial institutions. Or it could impinge on the actions of key economic actors, like capital or labour (though more frequently the latter), when government determined "higher" public interests were at stake: "The Government is going to take a larger role in running institutions, as we're now doing with our anti-inflation controls ... The state is important; the government is important. It means there's going to be not less authority in our lives but perhaps more."[81] The upshot of such interventions was to move us collectively toward a more organized type of capitalism – at least until the mid-1980s.

There is a second set of policies, somewhat different in purpose, that has led us in a similar direction. These are ones which, for analytical purposes, can be called the "forward development of capitalism," though there is some inevitable overlap with the stabilizing function referred to above.

Education, for example, which accounted for 6 per cent of G N P in Canada in 1981, compared to 3 per cent in 1960,[82] is normally classified under social expenditures and, as such, has been central to the development of what we call the welfare state. Yet an important part of education, broadly conceived, is manpower training, particularly at the secondary and post-secondary levels, and this is the way in which politicians have frequently come to see it.[83] In an era in which technological innovation and scientific discovery have become crucial to the renewal and development of capitalism in the advanced countries, in which traditional types of employment in the primary and secondary sectors are fast decreasing, educational policy has attained greater salience.

The role of government is not only to provide job training, from which the private sector stands to benefit, but to devise an educational policy with such ends in mind. The close interlocking between university boards and the corporate sector that Harold Innis decried back in 1946, when he wrote about "the descent of the university into the marketplace,"[84] had gone a good deal further by the late 1980s, with university presidents and representatives of the corporate sector alike subordinating the very purpose of higher education to the logic of the capitalist market. "Universities are a major source of free enquiry, providing the ideas that can later be exploited by free enterprise. We need both the push of free enquiry and the pull of free enterprise for success in our society."[85] "Each university faculty should be able to catalogue the expertise of its members and then market these talents to corporations or other clientele."[86]

What holds for education holds also for the funding of research and development generally. While Canadian spending in this regard was for much of the post-war period well below the level of the major OECD countries, government provided the lion's share of funding: "Technology ... put the problems of planning beyond the reach of the industrial firm. Technological compulsion ... will require the firm to seek the help and protection of the state."[87] Research could be done directly in government labs (the NRC, Agriculture Canada, Fisheries Canada, and so on), in universities largely paid for by government, or in the private sector, with government tax credits and deductions the order of the day. The more complex technological base that Hilferding saw leading to cartelization and international concentration in his time has in our own spawned a government-university-industry complex, ever more tightly organized in the attempt to conquer new technological frontiers: "Technology is like oil. You cannot do without it ... However, contrary to oil, you can create technology. It is one of the rare resources which is inexhaustible."[88] The hubris of this statement is mind-boggling, underlining just how much of a dystopia the technological imperative can become. Yet the organization of research and development is a cause that politicians as diverse as Harold Wilson and Brian Mulroney have embraced.[89]

Industrial policy is another theme in contemporary discussion of the state. On the one hand, it can refer to support programs for ailing industries or regions or to direct bail-outs that fit under the "stabilizing of capitalism" rubric. On the other, it can refer to a more developmental range of policies, the attempt to separate out "winners" from "losers," to foster mega-projects, for example, in the resource sector, or to encourage certain types of exploration or investment. In a highly integrated economy, with indicative planning as in France for much of the post-war period or in Japan with MITI and the larger firms mapping out global strategies, industrial policy of the "forward development" sort becomes very important.[90] In Canada, we have tended to pursue more ad hoc measures,[91] with only occasional attempts, as in the National Energy Program (NEP), to develop a more comprehensive approach.

Yet before we take the Business Council on National Issues at its word, when it argues "that a comprehensive national industrial strategy is (n)either feasible (n)or necessary,"[92] we might do well to note a variety of ways in which the state pursues such an end. Blais, for example, notes that all levels of government in Canada in 1983 paid over $8.6 billion in operating grants to business, representing 2.2 per cent of G D P and 5.5 per cent of all government expenditures.[93] Trade fairs, export development corporations, procurement policies, and loans at reduced rates are but some of the techniques used by federal and provincial governments to prod the private sector to invest or act in certain ways.[94] Business leaders who may be quick to criticize dirigiste policies like the N E P, are much less hostile to industrial policies "supportive of the principles of an open economy and freer trade ... developed with the full cooperation of capital and labour,"[95] or stemming from "a shared perception of Canada's vulnerable position in the global economy."[96] In this area, Conservatives like Mulroney begin to sound positively corporatist, talking about the challenge "to secure effective linkages among governments, financial institutions, well-established business, and the community of entrepreneurs,"[97] while Liberals like Trudeau have been prepared to be unabashedly statist, as in the 1980–4 period.

Perhaps the most telling contribution of the state to the forward development of capitalism has been in the international field, furthering our insertion into a world capitalist economy, dominated through most of the post-war period by the United States. Support for arrangements like Bretton Woods and G A T T served notice of a desire for an open currency and trading framework. Similarly, post-war Canadian governments fostered close economic relations with the United States, accepting the position of resource supplier during the Cold War and a major American capital inflow into this country. Canadian governments contributed to the emergence of a continentally integrated economy through direct intercession in Washington and appropriate policies back home – infrastructural development, the Trans-Canada Pipeline loan, tax and royalty structures.[98] It was only in the late 1960s and the 1970s that, for a limited period, one was to see a greater degree of Canadian economic nationalism.[99]

By the mid-1980s, the same Canadian state, through such agencies as the Economic Council of Canada and the Macdonald Commission, was proposing further integration between Canada and its neighbour with a Free Trade Agreement. That Agreement, reached in October 1987 and implemented in January 1989 in the aftermath of a bitterly divisive election, would, according to External Affairs, "ensure our industries can grow from their Canadian base; encourage new investment in world-class enterprise."[100] As François Houle has correctly noted, the Canadian state by the late 1980s had adopted "a strategy of economic development which [would] allow the most productive, profitable and competitive sectors within the new world economic conjuncture to expand."[101] This may not be the strategy of designating "winners" and "losers" associated with the interventionism of the N E P era. But it did bespeak a state orientation to the interests of the most organized section of Canadian capitalism, namely, our own multinational corporations.

A third major component to state economic activity can be referred to as nation- (or province-)building. It has been important in the creation of many crown corporations – the Canadian Broadcasting Corporation, Air Canada, Petro-Canada, and Hydro Québec – and has lain behind some of the bolder post-war attempts at state intervention, such as the N E P and Bill 101 in Quebec. Not only has it legitimized an extensive public sector in a society where private enterprise is otherwise the rule, but it has also provided – alongside Keynesianism, social spending, research and development, and international trade – an additional impulse to the development of a more organized capitalism.

As we saw, the two wars justified a co-ordinated harnessing of resources by the state and the creation of a more planned, even collectivized economy. We also have a number of instances between 1867 and 1945 when defensive nationalism against the United States resulted in the creation of crown corporations. I would not want to explain all forms of public enterprise in these terms – Ontario Hydro, the C N R, the Canadian Wheat Board, and the Bank of Canada were not set up primarily for this reason. But the use of the state for nation-building, especially in English Canada, where the sense of nation was weak (see chapter 10), is of cardinal importance.

In the post-1945 period, both federal and provincial governments would create major public enterprises to serve national (or regional) ends. Thus, the nationalization of most of the remaining private power companies in Quebec after 1962 was part of a strategy of making Québécois masters in their own house, using the provincial state as a lever to promote greater French-Canadian presence in the economy: "We need powerful means ... to put the French-Canadian people at the level of the present-day world. The only means we possess is the State of Quebec, our own State. We cannot afford the luxury of not using it."[102] Hydro Québec was soon joined by the Société Générale de Financement and a host of other crown corporations in the 1960s. The Caisse de Dépôts grew into a major financial institution in its own right, with an equity portfolio of over $3 billion in the early 1980s, said to be the largest in Canada,[103] and total assets in the $25-billion range.

At least some post-1960 exponents of Quebec nationalism set themselves the explicit goal of creating a French-Canadian–controlled capitalism. As Jacques Parizeau argued in 1970: "In Quebec we must have state intervention. It is inevitable. This is what gives us the appearance of being more to the left; if we had 25 enterprises like Bombardier, our situation might be different. But we don't have large institutions. We therefore have to create them."[104] Over the next decade and a half, Quebec and Ottawa put much energy into promoting a more vibrant French-Canadian capitalism. Direct grants and procurement policy were games both levels of government could play. Languages policy was another, with the P Q government, through Bill 101, enforcing the francization of large and small-scale firms in Quebec, and with the federal official language policy offering a larger, pan-Canadian and international perspective to successful Quebec firms like Lavalin, Bombardier, and Power Corp.

As the nouveaux guerriers of Quebec capitalism began to make their presence felt in the 1980s, as stock purchase schemes generously subsidized through the Quebec tax system took the place of direct government funding, one thing became clear. The state had been the "indispensable animator" and "supreme coordinator"[105] in the transition from an English- and foreign-dominated Quebec economy to one in which Québécois capitalism now played a more central part.[106] Can there be a more eloquent example in the Western world of a state using nationalism to foster and organize capitalism?

The federal government, for its part, was committed to supporting greater Canadian control over the economy in the late 1960s and the 1970s, after two decades of continentalism. There was a strong nationalist motif behind creation of the Canadian Development Corporation (C D C) and the Foreign Investment Review Agency (F I R A). The 1973 oil crisis provided reason to go the route of a state-controlled oil company, as was the case in many European and Third World countries: "I must say that when I first came here I was not at all that sold on the idea of Petro-Canada or a Canadian oil corporation. But when I found out that we had been misled by the oil companies back in 1971 and 1972, when they told us we had all the oil we would require for the next hundred years, and then almost overnight there was a shortage, it was then I knew, and became convinced, that we needed a national oil company – and so did the majority of Canadians."[107] Again in the early 1980s, the government reiterated its intention "to promote Canadian ownership and control over the economy" and, through the N E P, to pursue "an active acquisition program" to promote these ends.[108]

Provinces besides Quebec were also seeking vigorous economic growth, using public enterprise. The takeover of B . C . Electric in 1961 by a "private enterprise" premier committed to a two-river development strategy for his province is one example. The establishment of the Alberta Heritage Foundation by an equally "private enterprise" – oriented government is another. The takeover of the potash industry by Saskatchewan's N D P government in the 1970s is a third. There were an estimated 233 provincial crown corporations in existence by the early 1980s; 75 per cent of these had been created after 1960, in sectors ranging from agricultural development to mining, from power to transportation.[109] Yet these crown corporations, much like the 464 federal crown corporations then in existence,[110] were not so much in competition with the private sector as larger or smaller players in a more integrated capitalist ensemble.

This period of more advanced state presence coincided with further mergers and consolidations within Canadian capitalism and with corresponding Canadianization of the commanding heights of the economy. Figures for foreign ownership by the late 1970s, according to Statistics Canada data, were a good deal lower than a decade before;[111] as a recipient of direct investment inflows, Canada had dropped from first to seventh place among the top ten Western countries between 1960 and 1980;[112] and direct outflow of foreign investment from Canada had risen from $ U S 90 million in 1960 to $ U S 3,668 million by 1981.[113]

Two observations follow. First, Canadian crown corporations such as Petro-Canada, the C D C, and the Potash Corporation of Saskatchewan had themselves contributed in no small way to the Canadianization of the economy. Second, Canadian-based and -controlled capital was now better able to compete with other multinational corporations, especially with American capital relatively weakened.[114] Nation-building and province-building had coincided with greater concentration in the corporate sector, making for a more strategically positioned Canadian capitalism in the 1980s.

I have been attempting to illustrate how the concept of organized capitalism can explain the economic role of the state in Canada since 1945. I have not been exhaustive, and there have been counter-tendencies at work, especially in recent years. Price and wage controls, despite the 1975–8 episode, have not become a permanent feature. Nor can we profitably speak about corporatism in Canada, at either federal or provincial levels, unlike the case in a number of western European countries.[115]

More important, still, neo-conservatism, which gained ascendancy in the United Kingdom and the United States over the past decade, has not left Canada unscarred. This process has gone furthest in provinces like British Columbia, where governments since 1983 have been engaged in a binge of public-sector bashing that sought to turn the clock back to an earlier period where labour rights and social services were concerned.[116] At the federal level, there has also been the beginning of privatization of crown corporations, most notably Air Canada, and strident questioning of the role of the state by business, large and small. A full-scale neo-conservative onslaught on social services has thus far been warded off, though no one can say for sure what the Conservative government, into its second Parliament, may do – despite all manners of reassurance about social spending during the 1988 election. (The changes to U I C announced in April 1989 along with Michael Wilson's budget suggest that the gloves are now off where roll-backs in social expenditure are concerned).

What is clear is that the switch to free trade coincides with a shift to greater emphasis on market forces and, to that degree, away from the more interventionist type of state that the economic nationalism of the 1960s to early 1980s tended to foster.[117] There is a new emphasis on deregulation and a retreat from the hands-on approach of governments to the economy that held sway over the previous four decades. It may just be that the type of organized state activity that served Canadian capitalism well during its formative stages, or in the transition to a more industrialized economy around the time of the two world wars, has run its course, and that Canadian capitalism in its new position on the perimeter of the core that I depict in the next chapter has less need for state economic intervention. Such, at least, is the argument we hear from big business in this country, and it is one that the Conservatives seem to share. So perhaps, as Claus Offe suggests, we should begin talking about "disorganized capitalism"[118] and about ways in which state and private sector may come to disengage.

These factors, however, are not reason enough to abandon the concept of "organized capitalism" outright. "Organized capitalism" as an ideal-type construct allows us to synthesize a number of approaches that have been taken to the state – "defensive expansionism," response to war, the emergence of social security, the integration of labour, the adoption of Keynesianism – and see these in a more unified fashion. Twentieth-century capitalism, in Canada, as elsewhere, has taken on an ever more technologically oriented, economically concentrated form. The growth in state activity and functions has been part and parcel of that process – neither a wholly independent variable, as some who would hypostatize the state might believe, nor a purely dependent one, as others who might reduce it to a mere expression of class domination would argue.

I happen to believe that the factors that have led to a stronger state role, economically speaking, than a century ago will not simply vanish in an age of capitalist restructuring and global economic interdependence. If Keynesianism at the international level may not be for tomorrow, even less probable is the return to some kind of night-watchman state. Technology, international competition and concentration, warfare, Third World famine, environmental catastrophes, the inherent instability of markets (of which the stock market crash of October 1987 was a reminder), and the ongoing need in liberal democracies (and other societies) to allay a variety of social and class forces suggest that, despite neo-conservatism, organized capitalism will remain a powerful construct into the future. Hilferding may, after all, have been this century's most sobering prophet, and his "organized capitalism" one of the more persistent masks that Proteus has come to wear.

From Semi-periphery to Perimeter of the Core: Canada in the Capitalist World Economy

The question of Canada's position within the capitalist world economy has been the subject of much discussion among political economists over the past two decades. There are some who have argued Canadian dependency vis-à-vis metropolitan powers like Great Britain and the United States, in the process suggesting significant parallels between Canada's position, with a truncated industrial sector and significant foreign ownership, and that of the Latin American countries.[1] Others have stressed the First-World character of Canada's financial, manufacturing, and income structures, thereby playing down the role of outside capital and powers in Canadian development.[2] And there are many intermediate positions, placing emphasis now on the absence of a military determinant to Canadian industrialization when compared with other major powers,[3] or on the unique resource component to our economy,[4] or on a relative maturation in Canadian capitalism in the contemporary period as compared to an earlier day.[5] The subject promises to continue to elicit vigorous controversy, as Canada takes a giant step toward greater continental integration through the Canada- u s Free Trade Agreement and as the simultaneous decline in American hegemony makes the capitalist world economy a more complex one than at any time since the Second World War.[6]

My purpose in addressing such a topic in a volume on the state is fairly straight forward. Sovereignty has been seen as the prime dimension of state power in writings of both political theory and international relations going back to the sixteenth and seventeenth centuries. Yet the realization of a state's sovereign power, particularly in the international arena, has had a lot to do with that state's position within the larger nexus of economic, political, and military relations that make up the state system. In trying to come to terms with the Canadian state, therefore, and the question of just how sovereign it has been, we must consider how Canada has fitted into the larger capitalist world economy and how that position may have altered since 1867.

As the title of this chapter would suggest, I think there is virtue to the classifications that Immanuel Wallerstein has developed in a succession of studies since his *The Modern World System* appeared in 1974. In particular, I find Wallerstein's three-fold distinction among core, semi-peripheral, and peripheral states to be a potentially fecund way of looking at a world capitalist system in which the influence of states varies enormously. There are, however, limitations to Wallerstein's delineation, particularly where the category of semi-periphery is concerned, and a need to introduce further gradations into the typology. And we should also make use of political, and not solely economic, criteria in any assessment of the relative influence and power of states like Canada in the larger scheme of things.[8]

Let me state my primary thesis. The Canadian economy and state developed in the late nineteenth century within a capitalist world in which Britain was a hegemonic power, but in which a number of rival powers, including Germany and the United States, were challenging its ascendancy. Canada's position with respect to Britain, following Confederation, and vis-à-vis the United States for the First two-thirds of the twentieth century, can be seen as that of a semi-peripheral country. It provided many of the raw materials for the core but also engaged in industrialization and infrastructural development that would give it a gross national product per capita and mix of economic activities typical of a core country. At the diplomatic and military level, however, Canada throughout its first century remained a junior partner, first to Britain and later, through much of the post-1945 period, to the United States.

The sequel to my argument is that there has been a qualitative change in Canada's position over the past two decades and that, economically at least, Canada has now reached a stage where it must be seen as one of seven leading capitalist powers in the world. From a net importer of capital, it has become a net exporter; its mix of primary, manufacturing, and service-sector activities and its growth in G N P or productivity are those of a highly advanced, even post-industrial society; and its influence in world affairs, in a period of declining American hegemony, is relatively greater than when the United States (or earlier Great Britain) dominated the world capitalist economy. The new position Canada occupies lies on the perimeter of the core.

Before I develop my argument any further, let me say something about what these terms (and the two related ones of core and periphery) signify. Core countries, according to Wallerstein's definition, dominate the world economy, tend toward variety and specialization in their economic activities and the use of free labour, and develop a strong state machinery along with a national culture.[9] Core countries are not necessarily hegemonic, though a hegemonic power like Britain in the nineteenth century or the United States in the mid-twentieth "will produce goods that are largely competitive even in the other core states ... and will be the primary beneficiary of a maximally free labour market."[10]

Peripheral countries, in contrast, produce "primarily lower-ranking goods, i.e. goods whose labour is less well rewarded" but that are an integral part of the overall system of the division of labour.[11] They tend toward monocultures and in earlier periods toward the use of forced labour (for example, slaves, coerced cash-crop labour).[12] Their state structures are weak, ranging from non-existence to ones with a low degree of autonomy (for example, neo-colonial situations).[13]

Semi-peripheries fall somewhere between core and periphery. There is a "fairly even mix" between core-like and periphery-like activities, they enjoy fairly high land-to-labour ratios, and they may develop strong indigenous bourgeoisies and a state machinery that seeks to enhance the country's relative position in the world economy.[14] Sweden, Prussia, and the United States are seventeenth- and eighteenth-century examples of semi-peripheries that Wallerstein cites; in the nineteenth he adds Russia and Japan.[15]

"Perimeter of the core" is a neologism that Peter Lange coins in a recent discussion of Italy, signifying that "the country in question is *newly arrived* in the core" measured along a range of dimensions that might include G N P per capita, structure of national production, structure of national trade, class structure, wage structure, patterns of development, and political response.[16] I had originally intended to advance the term *semi-core* to describe Canada's current position, but I find Lange's term more elegant, and it will allow us to focus on the core-like features that a country like Canada has achieved, even while remaining at the perimeter of the grouping of core states in today's world.

What then is the evidence for treating Canada as a semi-peripheral state within the world capitalist system for the century or so after Confederation? There are three main reasons: a mixture of primary production and staple exports with an import substitution–driven industrialization that situated Canada somewhere between the core industrial countries and the primary-producing peripheral ones; a level of G N P per capita and a wage structure that resembled those of the core countries rather than the low-income societies of the colonial world, coupled, however, with a degree of foreign ownership over key sectors of the economy resembling the latter; and a state structure which, while not fully autonomous in foreign relations (for example, British control over treaty-making down to the 1920s, Canada's automatic entry into the First World War at the same time as Britain's), did control such vital features of development as tariff structure, railway construction, forest and mining policy, and electricity generation.

First, the central role of staples – furs, wheat, lumber, minerals, or energy – in Canadian exports has been a leitmotif of Canadian economic analysis since at least the time of Harold Innis. At one level, this yields a "hewers of wood and drawers of water" – type argument, with Canada seen as trapped within its primary commodity-producing role for the international economy.[17] And even today such commodities loom larger in Canada's export trade than is true for the major industrialized O E C D countries.[18] At another level, it underlines the notion of Canadian dependence, suggesting an analogy between our penchant for primary exports and Third World economies beholden to international circuits of capital and metropolitan centres.[19] Among dependency-influenced theorists, some suggest an ultimately truncated type of development, setting Canada off from the normal road of metropolitan capitalism; others talk about an "advanced resource capitalism," and still others recognize Canada as an example of late-developing capitalism, with industrial and resource activities coexisting, albeit unequally.[20]

The existence of an industrial sector – iron and steel, farm machinery, electric trams, pulp and paper, textile – in the Canada of the late nineteenth and twentieth century is indisputable.[21] What is more in dispute is how exactly to characterize this industrial sector – as essentially staple-related industries with forward and backward linkages, as import-substitution industrialization, with British, and especially American, firms leaping over tariff walls to take advantage of a relatively high income market, or as a technologically derivative capitalism? And there is the related and vexing question of ownership and control that leads a number of writers to play down the specifically "Canadian" character of any industrial capitalism that developed.

But Canada, unlike the countries, colonial or independent, of the periphery, very early set out toward some kind of industrialization.

As Tom Kemp has written: "There was a difference between the countries of white settlement with self-government and the rest of the 'colonies' inhabited by non-Europeans. Investment in the former, although mainly attracted by staple products, was not only much greater in per capita terms, but also permitted a start to be made along the road to industrialization. A comparison between India and Canada is instructive in this respect."[22] J.-C. Asselin observes along similar lines: "Contrairement à l'Inde, soumise à "l'impérialisme du libre-échange" dans toute sa rigeur, comme le sont aussi du reste bien des économies semi-coloniales, les dominions ont la maîtrise de leur politique tarifaire, même à l'égard de la métropole."[23]

Canada by 1913 was covering 77 per cent of its industrial needs domestically, compared to 97 per cent for the United States, 90 per cent for Germany, 87 per cent for France, 83 per cent for the United Kingdom and 66 per cent for Japan.[24] Canada was the seventh largest industrial economy, though very reliant on the importation of industrial technology and capital.[25] Moreover, the distribution of national product among the three major sectors of the economy, agriculture, industry, and services, was quite similar for Canada, the major European countries, and the United States.[26] At the very least, therefore, we must assign Canada a higher position on the scale of economic activity than the primary resource economies of the periphery.

Second, by the standards of G N P growth and per capita income as well, Canada resembled the core countries from the very beginning. Kuznets shows growth rates in total product between 1870 and 1967 of approximately 40 per cent per decade, double the rate for countries like Britain and France. Per capita income in Canada also grew at a rate higher than for most developed countries.[27] An 1896 study showed Canadian earnings at £36 per capita, compared to £38.8 for the United Kingdom, £44 for the United States, and figures ranging between £14 and £31 per capita for nine European countries.[28] Yet another study calculates Canadian output per capita in the late nineteenth century as only slightly under the British figure (but greater than in most European countries), coming to exceed that for the United Kingdom itself from 1910 on.[29] Canada, in other words, enjoyed high levels of output and a high wage structure.

Canada also enjoyed privileged access to outside capital. The country was literally awash with sterling, with the state guaranteeing the yields of both government and railway securities. As Michael Edelstein notes: "When Canada gained Dominion status in 1867 ... perhaps half of Canadian gross domestic capital formation was funded by foreign savings. By the 1890s ... foreign borrowing was down to about 1/3 of Canada's gross domestic capital formation ... Almost 1/2 of the nation's gross capital formation was funded by British and to a lesser extent American savings during 1911–15."[30]

As for American capital, according to Mira Wilkins, the spillover into Canada was promoted as much by the potential market for U S goods as by greater access to staple production.[31] By 1914, "the greatest U S direct investments were in Canada," a pattern that would hold for the next half century. And the element of direct control in this case, as Kari Levitt, among others, has noted, was a good deal more significant than in the British case.

This is the fly in the ointment that makes it necessary to downgrade Canada's status within the world capitalist economy. Had the Canadian economy in 1914 or 1926 or, jumping ahead, 1950 been unambiguously under Canadian control, there might have been good arguments to see Canada as one of the smaller members of the core group. But despite an important element of indigenously controlled capital in the banking sector, as well as in trade and industry, the Canadian economy remained highly reliant on outside investment and to that degree subordinate to the two leading economies – British and American. The relative autonomy of Canadian capital was no doubt greater than that of indigenous capital in Chile, Brazil, or even Argentina.[32] Here and there, moreover, as in electric tramways and banking, one even saw the first hints of Canadian capitalism expanding abroad. But Canadian capitalism was small potatoes indeed in global terms; nor did Canadian capitalists control the commanding heights of their economy in the way that British or German or French or American capitalists controlled theirs.

Third, what best of all defines Canada's semi-peripheral position is the nature of the Canadian state. One does not have to agree with Otto Hintze, for whom "all state organization was originally military organization, organization for war."[33] But certainly warfare enters into the development of the European nation-state,[34] and military power had much to do with the relative ranking of states in the nineteenth, no less than the sixteenth, century. To be sure, military power without economic underpinnings can be self-defeating, as the comparative histories of France and England would suggest. But Britain did not acquire or maintain its empire through trade or goodwill alone, nor did the United States or Germany or Japan or Russia, in their respective rise to core-power status, disdain the use of arms.

By this standard, Confederation marked a banding together of the British North American colonies for defensive purposes, under the protective umbrella of one of the core powers against another. Such naval or military aid that Britain might have accorded Canada would not have gone very far in the event of real hostilities with the United States. But the British connection did serve as symbolic protection for Canada and, in turn, entailed Canadian involvement in the destiny of the empire of which it was a part. Dominion status, by definition, symbolized something less than complete sovereignty (cf. chapter 3). Yet it did set the stage for increasing consultation between the imperial government and those of the white-settler dominions and for the eventual emergence of the latter as full-fledged sovereign states by the second quarter of the twentieth century.

Another feature of military organization (and its relative absence in Canada, save for periods of war) is its symbiotic relationship with industrialization. Gautam Sen, in a recent study, has pointed to the military origin of industrialization in a number of major states: "The state in the late-comer countries of Europe, Japan, the United States and eventually elsewhere, felt compelled to industrialize their own country in response to the threat posed by the presence of industrially, and therefore militarily, powerful nations elsewhere."[35] Sectors as diverse as iron and steel, coal, textiles, and chemicals were affected by military developments, and significant technological breakthroughs were the result of war. To this degree the Canadian path to industrialization, as Gordon Laxer has acutely observed, was different from that of the core countries, something that may also help to account for a singularly high degree of foreign ownership: "The creation of an independent armaments and engineering sector was not a strategic requirement because Canada did not develop its own armed forces to an appreciable level before World War 1. Canada's voluntary position as a dependency of Empire (until near the end of World War 1) coincided with the period when the industrial structure was established in its branch plant mould. The result was clear: no strategic logic, no compelling motive to block foreign ownership."[36]

The issue of state sovereignty is not related only to military capacity. In the larger world of diplomacy and foreign policy, Canada was for all intents and purposes a non-power down to the end of the First World War and at best a very timid participant in international forums like the League of Nations between the wars. If the Department of External Affairs traces its origins back to 1909, it is only in the mid-1920s that Canada began to negotiate treaties in its own name, in 1931 that Canadian sovereignty was formalized by the Statute of Westminster, in 1946 that Canada acquired a full-time Secretary of State for External Affairs.

It is, I think, perfectly fair to describe Canadian foreign policy down to 1945 in terms of our relations with two major powers, Britain and the United States, and our participation in two world wars as a function of our ties with the former.[37] It is the mark of a peripheral or semi-peripheral power to play an auxiliary role in international affairs and to count for relatively little in the grand strategic struggles of the day. In a world dominated by a small number of core powers, very much the case down to 1945, Canada's was a limited role.

This does not mean that the Canadian state was unimportant where domestic policy was concerned. In chapter 8, I sketched the important activities that the state performed in organizing capitalism in the late nineteenth and through the twentieth centuries. We saw the crucial importance of tariffs and infrastructural activities, for example, canal and railway building, state enterprise (Ontario Hydro, the c n r, the Canadian Wheat Board, the Bank of Canada) and wartime state procurement, in laying the basis for capitalist take-off and development. Nor should one neglect issues of industrial relations or social policy in which Canadian governments at all levels began to play an increased role in the twentieth century. Does one, therefore, to employ the current language of political science, describe the Canadian state as having been strong or weak?[38]

In the aggregate, I would think it was strong. To be engaged in fostering economic accumulation within one's own borders through cheaper electricity or railway developments, to be able to administer one's own population effectively and with a modicum of bureaucratic rationality, and to be furthering a country's integration into international circuits of trade and capital on terms that lead to long-term growth and development do not bespeak the weak state structures of the periphery. I do not want to overstate the case – Canada has had its share of venality and corruption in government, of authoritarian-type leaders, especially at the provincial level, of dysfunctional economic policies (the second and third transcontinental railway lines), of excessive dependence on capitalism's booms and busts. But when one thinks of societies where "public institutions are used as private assets" routinely and systematically,[39] where there is no administrative expertise, precious little diversity to the economy, and next to no bargaining power with respect to core states or their economic institutions, the Canadian situation appears in a very different light.

The Canadian state may not have enjoyed the full panoply of sovereign power of the core countries, especially in foreign policy and military affairs. But in close association with the capitalist class that it helped to foster, it was an effective agent of industrialization (branch-plant and indigenous), of the agricultural settlement of the country, of the opening up of the resource sector, and of increasing integration into the capitalist world economy via its two leading powers, United Kingdom and the United States. If "semi-peripheral" refers to a situation lying between the core and the periphery, then there is every reason to consider the functions and activities of the Canadian state semi-peripheral.

The Canadian state was neither as supine nor as weak as most states in the colonial (or neo-colonial) world, nor in a position to project its power and influence like the core states. Its legitimacy was better grounded than that of many European states, yet it remained in the shadows of Britain and the United States. Its economy was more diversified than that of a strictly commodity producer but more dependent on resource production than the highly industrialized countries of the core and more beholden to foreign ownership. If some have preferred the term *semi-industrial* to describe Canada,[40] and others "dependency" or "rich dependency"[41] with its implications of subordination, my own preference goes to "semi-peripheral." For this term properly recognizes the intermediate status that a country like Canada enjoyed with respect to the world capitalist economy along a range of criteria and leaves open the possibility of upward or downward change in status over time.

It is to this possible change in status that I want to turn. It seems to me that there are a number of indices by which Canada would now have to be classified as one of the core countries in the world, in economic terms especially. Yet in terms of military or diplomatic influence, Canada can hardly be considered one of the leading powers in the world, but, at best, as lying on the perimeter of the core group. Let me outline my arguments regarding Canada's status in point form and develop them further.

(1) Economically, there has been a maturing of Canadian capitalism over the post-war period, with Canadian banks and corporations increasingly in control of leading sectors of the Canadian economy and better able to project their influence abroad. The Canadian state has played a crucial role in furthering this process.

(2) Closely related to the above, there has been a shift in the international capitalist economy away from undisputed American hegemony in the two or three decades after the Second World War. Within a "polycentric" world economic order, Canada's position has marginally improved.

(3) Canada has maintained a strongly competitive position in

terms of overall trade, productivity, and growth in G N P. Moreover, its mix of primary, secondary, and tertiary activities may even be an advantage in a period of deindustrialization in the industrial heartlands of western Europe and the United States.

(4) In the post-war period, Canada became a visible actor in alliance politics – the North American Treaty Organization – and international organizations – the United Nations, the Commonwealth – even while, for long, functioning as a junior partner to the United States. Canada has tended to act more independently over the past two decades, though its influence lies only on the margins of the core.

(5) As the concept of sovereignty itself comes under challenge in a more regionally integrated and open world economy, we may need to reassess its usefulness in evaluating a particular state's position. Since few, if any, of today's core states have the untrammelled sovereignty that would have been associated with core status a century or two ago, Canada may be in good company.

(1) For the first two decades after 1945, there would have been little reason to see the Canadian political economy as more than an appendage of the American. With the sundering of the old North Atlantic triangle linking Canadian trade with Britain and the United States and with the United States in a hegemonic position in the Western world, the stage was set for continentalism in the economic arena no less than in military and in foreign policy. U S capital flowed into Canada at an unprecedented rate, into the resource sector which had acquired strategic significance in a period of Cold War,[42] but into manufacturing as well. Fully 40 per cent of new capital formation in 1956 was American in origin, with the level of foreign (principally American) ownership in mining, oil and gas, and manufacturing ranging from 57 to 74 per cent in the 1950s and early 1960s.[43] True, Canadians controlled banking and finance, utilities, and most of wholesale and retail trade. But a significant component of the Canadian corporate élite was made up of individuals in the branch-plant sector of the economy.[44] Canadian governments, federal and provincial, had encouraged the process of continental integration, with nary a protest to be heard. Nor was there any reason to anticipate any early reversal in a process of American capital inflow whose roots went back to the late nineteenth century.[45]

Such a reversal did begin to get under way, however, in the 1960s, gathering steam rapidly from that point on. Economic nationalism in Canada became a more potent force during this period, for a combination of internal and external reasons.[46] From the establishment of the Canadian Development Corporation and the Foreign Investment

Review Agency to that of Petro-Canada or the National Energy Program, a strong nation-building current was manifest at the federal level; certain provincial actions like the nationalization of the remaining private electricity companies in Quebec in the early 1960s or of the potash industry in Saskatchewan in the early 1970s pointed in the same direction. As a result, state enterprises accounted for close to 20 per cent of the total assets of the largest enterprises in Canada by the late 1970s.[47] As Jeanne Laux and Maureen Molot argue in a recent study: "The state in Canada has moved beyond the circumscribed role that liberal ideology assigns to it. No longer is it limited to ensuring conditions favourable to private investment and involved in production only exceptionally, in instances of market failure. We now find the state itself owning the means of production, employing wage labour, selling on commercial terms, and reinvesting earnings. Contrary to orthodox Marxist assumptions, the state is clearly not excluded from the accumulation of capital."[48]

No less important was what was happening in the private sector. Canadian banks and major corporations were taking on a larger international role. On *Fortune* lists of the leading 500 non-American industrial corporations in 1981, Canada ranked fifth, with thirty-three[49] (including ten subsidiaries of foreign companies; but even with these removed, Canada edged out Sweden for fifth place). Three Canadian banks were among the fifty leading world banks in 1986, with five among the top 100.[50] The U N Centre on Transnational Corporations, in a 1983 study, showed that Canada, "which had traditionally been an important recipient of direct investment (largely originating in the United States)," had itself become an important source of direct investment by the 1970s. (See Tables 1 and 2.) As the chairman of the Royal Bank of Canada put it in 1985: "We used to be a large Canadian bank with international operations. But now we are a large international bank with a strong national base. There's a difference."[52]

For some reason, certain Canadian political economists have great difficulty acknowledging these changes. Leo Panitch, writing in 1985, argued: "Optimists in the late 1970s and early 1980s, observing the rising new 'arriviste bourgeoisie' in Quebec and Alberta, a marginal decrease in foreign ownership and the National Energy Program, began to foretell the emergence, finally, of a national bourgeoisie in Canada. Unfortunately, such observers made too much of too little."[53] And Michael Clow could observe: "Canada would seem to represent the highest state which a dependent economy can attain and the great difficulty such economies have in becoming a member of the Northern 'club' of advanced industrial economies."[54]

TABLE 1
Investment Flows

	1960	1965	1970	1975	1979
Flow of Direct Investment from Canada (Millions of $US)	52	116	302	782	1,849
As a Percentage of Flow from Developed Market Economies	1.3	1.6	2.5	3.1	3.9
Flow of Direct Investment into Canada as a Percentage of Direct Investment in All Developed Market Economies	32.1	11.7	11.5	5.9	6.7
As a Percentage of Canada's Gross Capital Formation	7.9	4.1	5.0	1.7	2.9

SOURCE: UN Centre on Transnational Corporations, *Salient Features and Trends in Foreign Direct Investment*, New York, 1983, Tables 1, 2, 8, 11.

TABLE 2
Investment Stock

	1967	1973	1978
Stock of Canadian Investment Abroad			
Billions of US dollars	3.7	7.8	13.6
As a percentage of total in developed market economies	3.3	3.8	3.7
Stock of Inward Direct Investment to Canada			
Billions of US dollars	19.2	32.9	43.2
As a percentage of total in developed market economies	26.6	23.4	17.7

SOURCE: As Table 1.

Yet the evidence suggests the opposite. The *Globe and Mail's Report on Business Magazine*, beginning its report on the top 100 for 1986, noted: "This year's list is dominated by the big Canadian banks and industrial conglomerates. Not long ago, the top companies were mostly U S-owned branch plants."[55] Andrew Malcolm, former *New York Times* correspondent in Canada, observed: "Canada has become one of the largest foreign investors in the United States. Its total of more than U S $11 billion in *recorded* investment falls short of only the Netherlands, Great Britain, and Japan."[56] Statistics Canada data show that Canadian direct investment in the United States as a percentage of U S direct investment in Canada has grown significantly, from 15.2 per cent in 1964 to 48 per cent in 1984, with the trend line clearly upward.[57] And other Statistics Canada data showed annual rates of growth for Canadian direct investment in the United States of 19.8 per cent for 1974-7, 52.7 per cent for 1978-81, and 11.9 per cent for 1982-4, while the rate of U S direct investment in Canada averaged 11.0 per cent in 1974-7, 9.7 per cent for 1978-81, and 7.6 per cent for 1982-4, a clear reversal of the 1950-65 patterns.[58]

It seems to me, therefore, that political economists like William Carroll, Jorge Niosi, and Paul Kellogg are right when they state: "In an era of rising and then declining American hegemony, the dominant faction of Canadian capital has consolidated control over circuits of finance capital at home and abroad."[59] "L'économie se "canadianise" aux dépens du contrôle américain. Le déclin relatif des firmes multinationales américaines dans le monde est évident aussi au Canada."[60] "Canada's economy must be seen as relatively strong and advanced when compared to the other western economies."[61] There is a different structure to the Canadian political economy than a half-century ago, something I have elsewhere referred to as "the maturing of Canadian capitalism."[62]

Let me add the heretical thought that the strong support that organizations like the Business Council on National Issues and the corporate capitalism that it represents gave free trade[63] may reflect the new position of Canadian capitalism. In an earlier period, for example, 1911, when Canada was still a "late developer," to use Alexander Gerschenkron's term,[64] the Canadian Manufacturers' Association stood front and centre in opposition to reciprocity with the United States, seeing in it a threat to a Canadian industrial base. In the Cold War period, despite the continental integration referred to above, Canadian capitalists had few illusions about their ability to compete on equal terms with the Americans either on their home turf or in Canada.

But by the mid-1980s, there was a new confidence, even hubris, to Canadian capitalists, whose mergers and consolidations at home and successful incursions abroad, especially into the United States, led them to see world capitalism and the North American part of it from the perspective of the core. Canadian banks participated in major financial consortia on the London and New York markets, placed an increased percentage of their total investments abroad, and through their interlocking directors were becoming part of an international circuit of finance capital.[65] Canada numbered 11 corporations among the top 430 multinational corporations in the world, while in terms of direct investment abroad Canada, at the end of the 1970s, was in eighth position.[66]

There is no question that North American interlocks predominated in the Canadian case, as Wallace Clement, for one, has shown.[67] But it is far less obvious that this signifies a lopsided dependence of Canadian capitalism on American. Rather, there is occurring an internationalization of capitalism which has affected the relative position of the United States itself and which makes North American free trade a viable strategy for both Canadian and American capitalism, faced with a new conjuncture in the world economy. In writing this, I am in no way expressing support for North American free trade or playing down the hidden agenda – in terms of attacks on the trade union movement or social spending and, of course, on Canada's political and cultural identity – that such an agreement entails. But free trade does reflect the logic of the relatively more favourable position of Canadian capitalism today – precisely why our largest corporations and banks are such fulsome supporters.

(2) The decline in American hegemony over the world economy since the 1940s and 1950s is a crucial new element for our understanding of the ranking of core powers in today's world. When American G N P accounted for 50 to 60 per cent of goods and services in the advanced capitalist countries, when American technology held the cutting edge and the American dollar was the undisputed reserve currency of international trade, the position of other countries could not but, by comparison, appear weak. A prostrate West Germany or Japan, a war-battered Britain or France, could not hope to give the Americans much of a run for their money. What one had in the immediate post-war world were much weakened core countries, with the United States crowding out the field. As Robert Keohane defines it: "Hegemonic powers must have control over raw materials, control over sources of capital, control over markets, and competitive advantages in the production of highly valued goods."[68] This seems an accurate description of American economic power at the height of the Cold War, which was, of course, refined and bolstered by American military power throughout the world.

For a variety of reasons, American power began to unravel from the 1960s on. It was natural that Japan and western Europe recover from their post-war situation and that the American share of total

O E C D gross national product decline – to 40 per cent and eventually about one-third.[69] It was also likely that in a liberal trading regime, such as the Americans had engineered, the high-cost/high-currency producer would begin to lose out to certain competitors. At the same time, the political dimensions of American power looked much less appealing in the era of the Vietnam War and significant internal strife over civil rights. The American share of the export of manufactured goods for the developed market economies decreased from 22.3 per cent in 1960 to 13.3 per cent by 1984.[70] American productivity, measured in terms of output per hour, increased at a much lower rate between 1967 and 1977 than in the other O E C D countries, save for Britain.[71] And American multinationals suddenly found themselves faced with growing rivalry from both the Europeans and the Japanese. Thus American companies had been the largest in the world in 11 of 13 major industries in 1959; by 1976 this had shrunk to 7 of 13. If 111 of the top 156 industrial firms in the world had been American in 1959, this was true for only 68 of the top 156 in 1976.[72] American banks accounted for only 8 of the top 50 in the world in 1986, compared to 19 for Japan, 5 each for West Germany and France, 4 for Britain, and 3 for Canada.[73] The American share of world production of steel, autos, textiles, and electronics plummetted, as did the ratio of American direct investment abroad to foreign investment in the United States and the overall American balance of trade.[74]

The significance of all this, as Robert Gilpin has noted, is that "the competitive position of important sectors of the American economy has been permanently damaged and the structure of the economy has been distorted."[75] There has been a meteoric rise in the economic power of Japan and a shift from the Atlantic to the Pacific in the world economy.[76] At the same time, the "embedded liberalism" of the post-war period, with its Keynesian policies at home and Smithian trading policies abroad, has become less plausible in an international division of labour in which the newly industrialized countries of the Far East no less than Latin America are beating at the trade doors of the developed capitalist countries.[77]

When one looks at the symbolic significance that the economic summits of the O E C D countries have acquired since 1975, at the periodic meetings of the finance ministers of the G-5 (now G-7, with the inclusion of Italy and Canada), and at the enhanced role of agencies like the International Monetary Fund and the World Bank where the global debt or North-South relations are concerned, one is strongly tempted to argue that the capitalist world has become much more polycentric. What the United States wishes – in trading relations, currency rates, fiscal and monetary policy, or a host of other matters – is not within its exclusive power to dictate.

If it would be too much to talk about a unified transatlantic and transpacific ruling class,[78] it is less far-fetched to see a three-continent basis to core power in the capitalist world economy (i.e. North America, western Europe, and the Far East). Regional arrangements, such as the EC, a North American free trade area, some similar arrangement among the ASEAN countries and Japan, may well be part of the reshuffling that is going on. But it is more and more a world economy to which individual countries and their capitalist classes find themselves obliged to adapt. Wallerstein's insight of 1974 – "The distinctive feature of a capitalist world economy is that economic decisions are oriented primarily to the arena of the world-economy"[79] – had by the late 1980s become the conventional wisdom of mainstream writers: "From now on any country – but also business – that wants to prosper will have to accept that it is the world economy that leads and that domestic economic policies will succeed only if they strengthen, or at least do not impair, the country's international competitive position. This may be the most important – it surely is the most striking – feature of the changed world economy."[80] "The greatest change [in economic policy] required appears to be that the unit for policy thinking must become the world economy rather than the national economy."[81]

What about Canada's place in all this? It is perhaps more affected by the relative decline in US power than any other country, precisely because of the privileged position American capital, until recently, enjoyed within its borders. Is there a cause-and-effect relationship between low American rates of growth and the worsening US trade and investment position and the new vigour of Canadian-controlled capitalism? "The periodic difficulties of world capitalist accumulation present *a few* semiperipheral states with their opportunity. For one thing, a world squeeze on profit intensifies competition among core powers and weakens their hold on given semi-peripheral states."[82]

If there are suddenly more core-like characteristics to Canada's economic structure, if the country has emerged as one (albeit the weakest) of the seven leading capitalist countries in the world today, as measured by UN and OECD data, should we not at least take modest notice? It is for this reason that I propose that we see Canada as on the perimeter of the core countries, not quite with the economic or geopolitical clout of the United States, Japan, or the major

European countries, but with a more elevated position than the semi-peripheral one it occupied until recently.

To make such an argument is not to deny that there are still characteristics that mark Canada off from the other leading powers. Arrighi and Drangel have suggested that a country like Canada may "have in all respects attained core status but present features of "structural dependency"."[83] Niosi has pointed to the fact that Canada's international expansion was based on foreign technology.[84] Williams has highlighted the weaker Canadian manufacturing base in exports.[85] The 1983 UN Report on Transnational Corporations does not include Canada among the principal countries receiving royalties and fees from abroad.[86]

But I tend to agree with Carroll, who in his *Corporate Power and Canadian Capitalism* suggests that predispositions to primary resource extraction and technological borrowing are not symptoms of a 'truncated' or 'arrested' or 'aborted' development, as the proponents of dependency theory have tended to argue. Rather, "The regime of accumulation in Canada in this regard is the product of Canadian business strategies to take advantage of Canada's cultural, commercial and spatial location within the international structure of capital. It is not the result of any congenital deficiency in entrepreneurship."[87] Far from condemning Canada to permanent backwardness, the much-berated strategy of staple extraction and industrialization by substitution seems to have placed Canada within the top echelon of capitalist powers. It has taken a long time for this to occur, and there is no guarantee that Canada will be able to hold on to its new-found position on the "perimeter of the core" into the indefinite future. Still, for all our single-minded focusing on the Canadian-American relationship, accentuated by the free trade debate, we would do well to recognize the improvement in Canada's relative position in a period that has seen a decline in American economic hegemony in the world at large.

(3) The core-like features of the Canadian economy merit some further enumeration. A 1987 IMF study of the 7 major OECD countries, for example, shows Canadian GNP growth at 5.1 per cent per annum between 1950 and 1973 and 3.3 per cent per annum 1974–85, substantially better than the British and American performance for both periods, and better than that for France, West Germany, and Italy 1974–85.[88] A projection for 1989–95 shows Canada with an overall growth rate exceeded only by Japan's.[89] In industrial productivity growth for the top OECD counties over a 23-year period, Canada ties with France for second place, behind Japan, but ahead of the United

States, the United Kingdom, and even West Germany.[90] Canada's job-creation record in recent years has been quite good, while the country's "natural unemployment rate" between 1985 and 1995 is projected to be lower than that for France, Britain, or Italy.[91] At the same time, the structure of civilian employment in Canada is somewhat more strongly weighted toward the service sector – 69.3 per cent of all employment in 1985 – and less toward the industrial one – 25.5 per cent – than in other O E C D countries. (By comparison, the service sector accounts for between 53.5 and 68.8 per cent of employment in the six other countries, and industry for a range between 28 and 41 per cent.)[92]

While some have interpreted such figures as proof of deindustrialization or the nefarious consequences of branch-plant capitalism, an alternative interpretation might hold that Canada is particularly well positioned for the increasingly post-industrial orientation that faces the advanced capitalist countries. As more and more industrial activities come to be sited in the periphery or semi-periphery, the leading O E C D countries will see the service sector gaining in importance. Nor does deindustrialization account for Canada's performance in total exports of manufactured goods among the developed capitalist countries. Canada's share of these exports increased from 3.3 per cent of the total in 1960 to 4.1 per cent in 1980; by comparison, the United Kingdom's share declined from 14.6 to 7.2 per cent, the American from 20.1 per cent to 15.9 per cent, and even that of Sweden, with which Canada is often compared, from 3.4 per cent to 2.6 per cent.[93] While the Canada- U S Auto Pact certainly accounts for part of this, Canada's overall performance does not suggest problems of restructuring any more intense than those faced by other core countries.

By a whole series of other criteria, Canada also comes out in a strong position. Its share of O E C D industrial production amounted to 3.1 per cent of the total in 1984, putting it in seventh place; aggregate G N P in 1984 was about the same as Italy's, while in terms of G N P per capita, Canada was third out of twenty-four, preceded only by the United States and Switzerland. And its overall rate of economic growth placed Canada fifth out of twenty-four.[94] As for social indicators, whether measured by levels of education or medical services or the provision of unemployment insurance or old-age security, Canada's profile resembles that of the other welfare-type states of the West.[95]

True, Canada's export position remains more heavily weighted toward primary production than the other core countries (see Table 3). And there is still a significant foreign, especially American, com-

TABLE 3
Exports of Primary Commodities as Percentage of All Merchandise Exports

	1970	1983
World	27.1	17.6
Canada	42.5	30.1
United States	25.5	23.9
France	21.7	21.6
West Germany	7.2	9.0
Italy	11.0	6.8
Sweden	24.1	16.0
Japan	5.0	2.4

SOURCE: UN *Yearbook on International Commodity Statistics*, 1985, 3.

ponent to Canada's manufacturing and mining sectors (44.5 per cent of total assets in manufacturing and 35.35 per cent in mining in 1983, compared to 69.4 per cent and 59.63 per cent respectively in 1970).[96] Nor is Canada's overwhelming orientation to bilateral trade and investment with the United States, which any free trade agreement will reinforce, an altogether healthy arrangement for a would-be core country concerned about its autonomy. But none of these constitutes sufficient reason to modify the assessment of Canada as lying on the perimeter of the core group today.

(4) In turning to Canada's position in the post-1945 world, we can begin with an observation by Lester Pearson: "The postwar world was one of changing power relationships in which Europe was relatively much weaker and Canada much stronger than in earlier years. The most important change, however, was in the position of the United States, now the Western superpower and inevitably the leader of the free world. Britain and France had become lesser Great Powers, not far above Canada in strength and resources."[97] This captures rather well the shake-up in status that would be occurring, with both Britain and France losing their empires and the United States experiencing a long period of hegemonic domination over the non-communist world.

The question of Canada's status is another matter. Canada's relatively strong position in 1945 was profoundly flawed, since it rapidly became contingent on massive American dollar inflows into the country and on exports to that one market.[98] The best Canada could aspire to was junior partnership with the United States and to an activist role as one of the second-tier states in the United Nations and in the emerging Western alliance. This is what the so-called golden age of Canadian diplomacy was all about,[99] though its boosters fail to emphasize sufficiently just how much Canada's role hinged on the closest of alignments with the United States.

The Cold War period saw a Canadian deference to American power that at points approached the craven: "The power of the United States in the world, a power now decisive, was established against the will of the Americans who were content without it ... It is in the hands of a people who are decent, democratic and pacific, unambitious for imperial pomp or rule."[100] There was little evidence of independence in foreign policy and defence matters, whether the issue was Canadian recognition of the People's Republic of China, the Canadian role on the International Control Commission in Indo-China,[101] or the use of Canadian air space (cf. the radar lines in northern Canada and the North American Air Defence [NORAD] Agreement of 1958).

This is not to suggest that a semi-peripheral Canada vis-à-vis the United States drew no profit from its close alignment. As Keohane has argued:

We should not assume that the leaders of secondary states are necessarily victims of false consciousness when they accept the hegemonic ideology, or that they constitute a small, parasitical elite that betrays the interests of the nation to its own selfish ends. It is useful to remind ourselves, as Robert Gilpin has, that during the *Pax Britannia* and the *Pax Americana*, countries other than the hegemon prospered, and that indeed many of them grew faster than the hegemon itself. Under some conditions – not necessarily all – it may be not only in the self interest of peripheral elites, but conducive to the economic growth of their countries, for them to defer to the hegemon."[102]

In this sense, Canadian junior partnership was not without its logic, since it did coincide with the rapid post-war economic development of Canada under American auspices. This was, however, the logic of a semi-peripheral state, prepared to eschew autonomous development and to turn "quiet diplomacy" into a testament of faith.

Have things changed dramatically since the mid-1960s? "Yes" and "no." With the decrease in American hegemony, Japan and western Europe, as well as some of the countries of Latin America, of the Middle East, and of the Third World generally, have become more assertive. At the same time, relations between the communist and non-communist world have slowly broken from their earlier Cold War mould (despite the relapse of the early 1980s). It is against this backdrop that Canada too has fitfully, though not consistently, pursued more independent policies from the United States and acquired enhanced status in a number of important arenas.

The economic nationalism of the late 1960s and early 1970s found its diplomatic counterpart in such gestures as Canadian recognition of China in 1971 and the pursuit of a so-called third option in Canadian foreign policy, aimed at broadening Canadian ties with Europe, Japan, and Latin America. Canada adopted a generally more progressive position on North-South issues than did the United States, showed greater concern for reaching East-West arms agreements and limiting nuclear weaponry, was less than enthusiastic about the Strategic Defense Initiative (Star Wars), and was reticent about hardline American policy in Central America.

In 1976, Canada became a participant in the OECD economic summits. If only symbolically, this did place the country among the top tier of capitalist states, something exemplified further with the expansion of the G-5 group of finance ministers to include Canada and Italy in 1987. Canada took the initiative in helping to organize the Cancun Conference of heads of government from North and South in 1981 and has, more recently, played a leading role in supporting economic sanctions against South Africa within the Commonwealth, with Thatcher's Britain the odd country out. Canada has also become a force, along with France, within the francophone group of nations.

By a number of standards, then, one might say that Canada has become a more important actor in international affairs. James Eayrs has gone so far as to call Canada a "foremost power,"[103] Lyon and Tomlin speak of a "major power,"[104] while Dewitt and Kirton have termed Canada "an ascending principal power in an increasingly diffuse, non-hegemonic international system. Placed in the context of the most prevalent global configuration, Canada is argued to be part of the classically defined "top-tier" group."[105]

I am hesitant to embrace this terminology, though I do think Canada, for certain purposes, has joined the top-tier group. If I prefer the term "perimeter of the core," it is because there are still a number of features that make Canada something less than one of the core powers in geopolitical terms. (This, incidentally, is also where I have my strongest disagreement with Wallerstein and his school, who tend to use economic criteria almost exclusively in their ranking of states within the world system.)[106] The most obvious of these weaknesses is military power, with Canada very much a second-rate state when compared to Britain and France, let alone the United States. True, Japan and West Germany are no longer the military powers they once were. But their aggregate economic strength, their technological inventiveness, their hard currencies, and their zones of economic influence place them in the uppermost ranks of today's core states.

One would be hard-pressed to see Canada as having a determining voice in the councils of the I M F or the World Bank or the O E C D, or the U N or N A T O, or as a country that much affects what Washington or Moscow, or even London or Paris, does. (One need but recall Trudeau's futile peace initiative of 1983-4.) In the same way, it is not Canadian media that the world watches or reads, Canadian art, music, or literature that influences others with its coded values, or Canadian science to which other pay attention. Nor does a relatively small population, a highly federalized system, or a diffident domestic political culture give the Canadian state the means to engage in international politics as it has been historically played. The best Canada can aspire to, and the stage currently reached, is that of a core-like power economically, but one on the perimeter of the core in terms of influence in the hard currency of international politics – power.

(5) Having delivered myself of so peremptory a judgment, let me turn finally to the question of whether sovereignty is still the meaningful criterion in assessing state power (and, therefore, rank in the world economy) that it once was.

Sovereignty is rooted in the philosophy of order (cf. chapter 1), with its notion of a summa potestas, or absolute and perpetual power, within the state. This power was originally attributed to a single individual (or monarch), though the seventeenth century saw the term applied to legislative bodies such as parliaments as well.[107] In the eighteenth century, both in philosophies such as Rousseau's and through events such as the American and French revolutions, it came to be associated more directly with the people, hence the term *popular sovereignty*.[108] Yet whatever the grounding of authority, it was linked with the state and those who ruled over it. A key attribute of sovereignty was the demarcation of one state's territory, its political, cultural, and economic space, from all others, with the notion of the inviolability of that space. War might be the ultimate form in which state sovereignty came to be asserted or defended. But sovereignty was caught up in a whole gamut of other developments, from mercantilism and colonial exploration to nationalism and industrial take-off.

From the point of view of the state system, sovereignty was rarely absolute. Smaller states were always subject to the influence of larger ones and in extreme cases, such as Poland after the three partitions, might find themselves wiped off the map of Europe altogether. Larger states, though they could impose their wills with greater impunity, could not always count on having their own ways either (as Britain discovered when the thirteen American colonies revolted, or Napoleonic France between 1812 and 1814, or Russia during the Crimean War, or Germany twice in this century). Still, there seemed to be something plausible about the notion of sovereignty, when nation-states set down political or economic or social paths of their own choosing. Britain, for example, might embrace free trade from 1846 on, while Germany and the United States pursued industrialization behind tariff walls; Britain, the United States, or France of the Third Republic were increasingly liberal democratic in character, whereas imperial Germany, tsarist Russia, and Japan combined capitalist development with more absolutist forms of governance; laissez-faire might predominate in Britain and the United States, whereas elsewhere, the state was used more actively as an instrument of economic development.

As a normative value, sovereignty has not lost its appeal in the twentieth century. It has been the bedrock for organizations like the League of Nations and the United Nations and underlies international relations both in peace and in war. Despite the increased importance of multinational corporations and non-governmental organizations of all sorts, states remain privileged actors in the modern world. And the difference in the power of states, for example, between the United States and the Soviet Union on the one hand and Gabon or Laos on the other, measured along a scale of military, diplomatic, economic and other criteria, is evidence of the differentiated sovereignty each enjoys.

It does seem to me, however, that there has been some lessening in the exercise of sovereignty since 1945, when compared to eighteenth-, nineteenth-, or early-twentieth-century practice. This was already apparent during the two or three decades of American hegemony, when all other capitalist countries came under the aegis of the American security umbrella, despite the protestations of a de Gaulle, and when American economic power was transcendent. (In the Soviet sphere as well, the invasions of Hungary and Czechoslovakia and the enunciation of the Brezhnev doctrine showed how attenuated a concept sovereignty had become.) Within western Europe, where the concept of sovereignty had originated, countries have found themselves drawn into forms of economic and political association – the Treaty of Rome and the European Commission and Parliament – corrosive of traditional notions of sovereignty.

At the same time, the political, ideological, and cultural underpinnings of Western states have grown more and more alike. Liberal democratic institutions are well-nigh universal, mixed economies, with a greater or lesser welfare component, the general rule, and ideological currents, be they of protest and dissent, as in the 1960s, or of neo-conservatism, as in the 1980s, not easily confined within national borders. Science and technology, forms of popular culture, and the artifacts of mass consumption are less and less nationally determined, undermining in the process the uniqueness of each nation-state.

This is equally perceptible in the economic arena. Bob Rowthorn has written about Britain: "As the British economy became more integrated with a global capitalism over which the British state had no control, it became increasingly vulnerable internationally, and the potential benefits to big capital of a straightforwardly aggressive nationalist development have dwindled accordingly."[109] Nor is Britain the only country subject to the constraints of global capitalism. France, which between 1981 and 1983 attempted to pursue expansionist policies at home in the face of monetarist restriction elsewhere, was faced with capital flight and balance-of-payments problems and forced to change course.[110] The United States was not able to withstand the competitive surge of Japan and the four "dragons" (Hong Kong, Taiwan, South Korea, and Singapore) or to avoid the effects of the 1973 oil crisis. All Western countries find themselves caught up with the ramifications of the international debt crisis, with the new international division of labour, with industrial production decreasing in the core countries, with growth in information-based activities, and with qualitative expansion in the importance of trade for their national economies.

This does not mean that, by the classical criteria of military, diplomatic, or even economic power, the United States is not a good deal stronger than other core states, or that Britain and France cannot still occasionally flex their muscles (the Falklands or Chad, nuclear deterrents) in ways that recall earlier theories of statecraft. It, nonetheless, puts a different complexion on how we measure the power of states to know that the relatively impervious walls that surrounded sovereign nation-states of a century of two ago have given way to something much more porous. There is increasing interpenetration among what once would have been purely national capitalisms, and there are pressures for co-operation among the leading capitalist states to assure a modicum of stability for the global capitalist system. While state sovereignty remains, and will continue, as the formal basis to any such co-operation – I see no trend to the supra-capitalist or supra-imperialist state that Kautsky talked about at the beginning of the century[111] – there is reason to see core power today as collective, rather than purely national, in character. The core today is a collective grouping of states, with a privileged position vis-à-vis global production and distribution. Canada, I think, can be seen as lying on the perimeter of this grouping. It is not certain that Canada would have qualified for similar status within a state system like that of 1914, which strongly emphasized sovereignty. But there is a better case for such a claim in the more collective type of core grouping that exists today in the capitalist world economy.

There is a paradox to the picture I have been painting. On the one hand, I have been suggesting an improvement in Canada's relative position within the capitalist world economy from the time of Confederation which, in traditional terms, would have spelled enhanced Canadian sovereignty. And I have suggested that the state has been an important instrument – though not the only one – in this transformation. On the other hand, I have been reluctant to argue Canada's core-like character in strictly political and military terms and have even suggested that sovereignty may be more elusive for all core powers today, including Canada, which I place on the core's perimeter. It may be the changing nature of the core itself, as much as any improvement in Canada's real position, that would justify the change in ranking I have been suggesting.

Still, the time has come to bid good-bye to the old images of Canadian dependence or semi-peripheral status. Just as the world capitalist economy today groups a much larger network of states and actors than a century ago, so too the Canadian political economy is much more developed and internationally integrated, with many core-like features. This is neither to over-emphasize Canada's importance nor to suggest that it is in any way immune to crises arising within the world system. The contradictions between the wealth of the North and the poverty of the South; the diverging, no less than converging, interests of the United States, western Europe, and Japan; the destructive, and not merely creative, impulses of capital at the global level – environmentally, socially, politically; ongoing divisions between East and West; and conflicts within the periphery may yet bring the whole structure crashing down. Nonetheless, we need to recognize that Canada today occupies a more privileged position with respect to the larger system than in an earlier day, and our actions must be increasingly geared to this arena.

To be on the perimeter of the core means that Canada cannot simply restrict its horizons to the North American continent or to the bilateral relationship with the United States. Canada now has a more direct share of involvement in and moral and political responsibility for the shape of the capitalist world economy and for the actions and depradations carried out therein in our collective name. Here lie a new and critical function for the Canadian state to play and a new focus of attention for the Canadian left.

PART THREE

Nationalism, Federalism, Socialism

CHAPTER TEN

English Canada and Quebec:
State v. Nation

The very conception of a civil state does not seem to have ever taken root in French Canada.
André Siegfried[1]

If nationalism founded on cultural, racial, or religious sentiment is the cult of the day, the French of Canada have a far better claim to political independence ... than the Irish of the British Isles.
H. McD. Clokie[2]

The purpose of this chapter is to explore the rather different roles played by state and nation in the development of English Canada and of Quebec. My argument, in a nutshell, is that on the English-Canadian side one began with a state structure, that of 1867, with which in turn the concept of nation would come to be intimately associated. On the French-Canadian side, however, the sense of nationhood preceded 1867, so that only with the greatest difficulty would it come to be associated with the institutions of a federal state within which French Canadians constituted a permanent minority.

My intention is to go beyond the familiar argument of many Quebec nationalists that French Canadians were to look to the one government, that of Quebec, over which they had palpable influence, in preference to the federal one, over which they had less. This position, in my opinion, does not give enough weight to the relative absence of a state tradition in Quebec. It is only after 1960 that Quebec governments became a good deal more interventionist, leading them into increasing friction over financing and powers with Ottawa. That particular battle was to culminate in the Quebec referendum on sovereignty-association of 1980, which, for the decade that followed, appeared to put paid to the belief that the Quebec state was destined to replace the Canadian as the sole repository of the loyalty of Quebec's population. But Quebec nationalism as such is far from dead.

English-Canadian historians and social scientists, for their part, have made something of a cult of the importance of the state in fostering a sense of nationalism in Canada. One thinks of the arguments of J.A. Corry in his study for the Rowell-Sirois Commission, of the "defensive expansionism" thesis of Hugh Aitken, of the "red Tory" position associated with George Grant.[3]

What has been lacking on the English-Canadian side has been recognition of the implications of a largely state-fostered version of nationalism for their polity. Insofar as the sense of nation springs less spontaneously from the population at large, must be inculcated, often artificially, from above, it cannot but be a rather weak bloom beside the kind of nationalism that flourishes in Quebec: "Recent English-Canadian nationalism has been notoriously devoid of distinctive myths and symbols capable of evoking strong emotional responses."[4]

I think, therefore, that we have something to gain from exploring the rather different relationship between state and nation among the two founding groups that make up Canada. Not only may it help our understanding of the roots of English-French conflict down to today, but it may also suggest why permanent resolution to this tension is highly unlikely. For in embryo, English Canada and Quebec incarnate the two quite distinct roads that peoples have taken to modern nationhood – the one beginning with the state, the other developing in its absence. The first recalls the experience of such state-centred polities as England, France, Spain, and Russia; the second, that of a host of nationalities, many seeking statehood, from Italy, Germany, and Poland in the last century, to most societies in what we now call the Third World.

Let me begin with English Canada. In chapter 2, I develop the argument that Canadian Tories resembled French Jacobins in their commitment to a strongly centralized state structure: "The fatal error which [the Americans] have committed ... was in making each state a distinct sovereignty ... The true principle of a Confederation lay in giving the General Government all the principles and powers of sovereignty ... The subordinate or individual states should have no powers but those expressly bestowed on them. We should thus have a powerful Central Government, a powerful Central Legislature, and a decentralized system of minor legislatures for local purposes."[5] The "national state" that emerged in 1867 did more than unite three colonies into a federal union. It established a new pole of loyalty for the citizens of the fledgling union, a sense of continental vocation symbolized further by the building of the railway and establishment of the National Policy. It helped constitute Canada as a semi-peripheral actor within the larger interstate system that Immanuel Wallerstein has referred to as underpinning the state.[6] While Canada was clearly not a fully sovereign state in 1867, given British suzerainty over foreign and defence policy and the residual powers of the British government and Parliament with respect to constitutional amendment and interpretation, many of the attributes of statehood, such as emergency powers, fiscal powers, control over economic development, and control over the militia, did come to be vested in the central government as of that year.

True, fifty to seventy-five years would elapse before Canada could achieve such marks of sovereignty as membership in the League of Nations and that equality of status with Britain sanctioned by the Statute of Westminster. This would be reason enough for critics to argue: "We are not sovereign. We are subordinate. We are not a nation, but a colony."[7] Moreover, the take-off of state activities, on the social side and on the economic, would be far more dramatic as a result of the two world wars and the Depression than during the long developmental decades stretching down the First World War. That a Canadian state had been formed in 1867, however, can scarcely be the subject of historical dispute.

It is much less evident that 1867 led to the formation of a new nation or nationality. Macdonald and the other Fathers of Confederation were perfectly aware of the special character of French Canada, using the very term *nationality* to describe it: "The people of lower Canada [are] a minority with a different language, nationality, and religion from the majority."[8] For all Tories and most Liberals the national feature that bound Canada together, however, was its "British"ness. During the parliamentary debate of 1865 on Confederation, Alexander Campbell argued a "duty to unite with us in bringing about that which is so dear to all of us – a closer connection with the Mother Country, and a better means of perpetuating British institutions on this continent."[9] For Alexander Morris, "A community of British freemen as we are, deliberately surveying our past ... and looking forward to our future, we in effect resolve that we will adhere to the protection of the British Crown ... We will cling to the old Mother Land ... We have no desire to withdraw ourselves from that protection we have so long enjoyed."[10]

There was precious little aspiration to a uniquely Canadian sense of identity in the long decades after Confederation. We were given a constitution that was frankly imitative of "the British constitution."[11] Macdonald's proud boast in his final election campaign was "A British subject I was born, a British subject I shall die."[12] Many were the English-Canadians adherents of imperialism who could echo the sentiments of the headmaster of Harrow, speaking to his charges in the early 1900s: "An English headmaster, as he looks to the future of his pupils, will not forget that they are destined to be citizens of the greatest empire under heaven; he will teach them patriotism ... He will inspire them with faith in the divinely ordained mission of their country and their race."[13] The symbolism of country in Canada – flags, uniforms, holidays, anthem – was British, not Canadian; it was as a component part of the British Empire that Canada went to war in 1914.

It follows that a Canadian state did not necessarily engender in its wake a consciousness in the population of forming a specifically Canadian nationality. The strongest defenders of unhyphenated Canadianism in the period before the First World War were the members of the francophone Nationalist League, with their call for "the largest measure of political, commercial, and military autonomy" from Britain and for "the adoption of a policy of exclusively Canadian economic and intellectual development."[14] They were seen as traitors by leading sections of political and intellectual opinion in English Canada.

We have, therefore, more than a terminological problem at hand. Used as we have become to analysing the modern state in terms of the nation-state, what are we to make of a polity where for the dominant linguistic grouping nationality was for long identified with an outside power? How are we to come to terms with the division between English and French as regards the nature of the federal union and, more particularly, Canada's role in the external arena, divisions that were to become acute during the run-up to the First World War and during the conscription crises of both wars? As André Siegfried observed back in 1906: "After a hundred and fifty years of life in common ... under the same laws and the same flag [the French and English] remain foreigners, and in most cases adversaries. The two races have no more love for each other now than they had at the beginning."[15] And for Alexander Potter, writing in 1923: "There is neither common racial origin, nor common language; neither common customs, nor common aspirations."[16]

If we pursue the matter a little further, we come to the realization that for English Canadians nationalism was itself the slowly developing by-product of a state structure whose origins can be traced to 1867: "There are nations that instead of creating states have themselves been created by long-established states. If there is a Canadian nationality it must be of this latter kind."[17] The identification with Canada, as distinct from Britain, would come out of the slaughter of the First World War and again the Second and out of the shift, economically, culturally, and politically, between the 1920s and the 1940s, from the British to the American spheres. It would take sustenance from the greater international recognition that Canada as a state achieved through membership in the League of Nations, the Commonwealth, and the United Nations; from those nation-building activities associated with crown corporations such as the Canadian National Railways, the Canadian Broadcasting Corporation, and Trans-Canada Airlines; with the sense of national solidarity associated with the social activities of the state – old age pensions, unemployment insurance, and family allowances; and from the symbolism of post-1945 Canadian nationalism – the Canadian Citizenship Act (1947), abolition of appeals to the Privy Council (1949), naming of Canadians to the position of governor general (1952 and on), creation of the Canada Council (1957), the Bill of Rights (1960), adoption of a new Canadian flag (1965), Expo '67, and patriation of the Canadian constitution (1982). The federal state was the prime architect of this transformation, engaged in what historians Eric Hobsbawm and Terence Ranger have labelled "the invention of tradition"[18] – forging a Canadian identity.

How successful would this prove to be in a state that occupied a semi-peripheral position in the international scheme of things, one caught somewhere between the old British symbols and the reality of American hegemony in the post-1945 capitalist system? In truth, the process would prove a lot more faltering and incremental than in a good many other nation-states. The world-view of the Canadian political and economic elites through much of the post-war period was that of junior partnership to the United States. Canadian foreign policy and defence policy were so suffused with this relationship that nothing else, for long decades, seemed to exist. Three-quarters of our trade was with that one country, and a good deal of our resources and manufacturing, of our trade union movement, and our culture was under American control. A country so beholden to an imperial power could only cautiously begin to develop the symbolism and values associated with independence.

The federal structure of Canada further weakened the nation-building abilities of the central state. For all the centralizing features associated with wartime expenditure and the coming of Keynesianism and of the welfare state, a good deal of power remained with the provincial governments. Their role in the post-war period, particularly from the mid-1950s on, increased at a faster rate than that of the central government, as whole sectors under their jurisdiction – health, education, social security – burgeoned. Province-building in the economic arena – infrastructural development, hydro, and resource extraction – was also of great importance, giving a regional basis to governmental activities from British Columbia and Alberta to Quebec.

There were ideological constraints as well on too-powerful a state role in the fostering of nationalism. Big business (and small), influenced by American practice, were not inclined to welcome an excessively interventionist state, nor to forgo short- or middle-term profits in the name of some erstwhile national interest. Market values were one thing, political another; in a capitalist society like Canada's the former would probably win out. If they did so less perfectly and completely than in the United States, it was, in good part, because other social forces – the new middle class, the working class – were somewhat more effective in making their voices heard and because the very nature of the Canadian political economy, on the margins of empire, had entailed a more powerful state role from the nineteenth century on. As a result, we may be less individualistic that the Americans,[19] though there are limits to our collectivism.

It follows that those who preside over the Canadian state must tread more carefully in the economic arena than their counterparts in European states with traditions of interventionism and that in the pursuit of nationalism, a number of conflicting interests must be reconciled. In the particular circumstances of the 1960s, 1970s, and early 1980s – a weakened United States, a modernizing and potentially independentist Quebec nationalism – the temptation to enhance the nationalist functions of the central government increased. At other moments – the late 1940s, the 1950s, the late 1980s – the state's keepers seemed to march to quite a different drum beat.

It also follows that in English Canada nationalism is, more often than not, something instilled from above. There have been few genuinely grass-roots movements to articulate English-Canadian nationalism. The Canada First movement of the 1870s was a small élite grouping of passing importance. The League for Public Broadcasting was a good deal more successful in mobilizing support for its particular objectives, establishment of the C B C, in the 1930s, but could hardly go beyond this. The Committee for an Independent Canada, while on paper a large organization, with 200,000 members at its height about 1970, proved ephemeral.

The one ongoing organization that has maintained a vested interest in Canadian nationalism, albeit of a moderate stripe, has been the

Canadian state itself. Whether we go back to the National Policy of 1879, to the invocation of patriotism during two world wars, or to recourse to the language and symbolism of nationhood – in parliamentary debates and statutes, on civic holidays, in connection with governmental programs and activities of the most diverse kind – we will find a consistent pattern. Elected politicians, civil servants, military people, and diplomats have an interest in positing at least some minimal version of nationalism compatible with their own positions. They are also inclined, faced with any challenge from provincial governments, to assert the unity of the country against any purely regional or sectional interpretation. In the words of Trudeau at the time of the Quebec referendum: "The national interest must prevail over the regional interest."[20]

All of this is not to argue that Canadian nationalism is without a basis of popular support. That would be a rather extraordinary phenomenon after 120 years of existence as a self-governing state in a world where nationalism, moreover, is a key ingredient in the exercise of state sovereignty. One could, indeed, argue that public opinion in English Canada has over the last couple of decades become more vigorous in its support of an unhyphenated Canadian nationalism, unbeholden to either Britain or the United States, than had been true in any earlier period. In Quebec, as well, the result of the 1980 referendum suggested more than a vestigial commitment to a Canadian (as well as a Quebec) nationalism by the majority of the population.

Yet nationalism is a weaker force in Canada than in a good number of other Western states. This may be partly a function of size; compared to the Americans or to the densely populated major European states, Canadians, with their small population, must have fewer illusions about their place in the world. Other small countries, however, for example, in eastern Europe or in Latin America, have much keener nationalist histories. Being on the periphery or the semi-periphery can be a powerful inducement to nationalism, not an obstacle to it.

More important, in my opinion, would be the dependent nature of our economic and, linked closely to it, our political development which, on the English-Canadian side, ensured a prolonged gestation period as a colony/dominion of Britain. Having turned our backs on revolution as the road to independence, we never developed within civil society the type of heightened nationalist consciousness that comes out of struggles against external rulers or internal class enemies. Nationalism was something for the élites to worry about. What nationalism there was would be associated with the state and with the little bits of Canadian identity our political and economic rulers, closely tied to imperial centres, would see fit to appropriate into a *British* North American society. This would be a generally unexciting affair, with a little drama provided by external events in which we played a tributary role (two world wars) and by internal English-French conflict. The fact that French Canada's sense of identity was less firmly linked to the Canadian state and, a fortiori, to the British Empire than English Canada's only highlights the point I have been trying to make. In English Canada, nationalism was more a by-product of Confederation and the British connection than the generating cause of a distinctive state structure.

If we turn to French Canada, however, we encounter a quite different dialectic at work. Here, the sense of nation is strong, the sense of state a good deal weaker, at least until recent times. The reasons for this situation are threefold.

(1) French Canadians had never controlled their own state, either during the French regime or from the period of the Conquest down to 1867. Theirs was the unenviable fate de Tocqueville had described, following a short visit to Lower Canada in the 1830s: "I have never been more convinced ... that the greatest and most irredeemable evil that can befall a people is to be conquered."[21] Nor were they in anything but a minority position vis-à-vis the new federal state in which the major economic and developmental powers were vested in 1867. At best, they controlled a provincial government whose powers, for a variety of reasons, would not be deployed in a dynamic way for at least three-quarters of a century.

French-Canadian nationalism was therefore of the intra-state variety Wallerstein describes, "defined by and constrained by (a) necessary relationship to a state-structure,"[22] confined within a larger sovereign entity that alone enjoyed international recognition. Far from aspiring to statehood, it had, more often than not, to fend off the encroachments of the stronger central state, which was generally beyond French-Canadian control. Such a nationalism would develop less in connection with the state than outside it and even against it. The Negro-king parallel that André Laurendeau first postulated in relationship to Duplessis[23] can be applied more generally to the role of the Quebec state to 1960. Such a state would provide only limited defence for traditional values, while permitting outside capital access to and control over Quebec's resources: "The period 1867–1897 is characterized by the financial weakness of the Quebec state ... Government intervention was limited to certain number of sectors ... Social policy was for all practical purposes, non-exist-ent."[24] "In comparison with every other provincial government, the government of Quebec was relatively inactive in the investment field ... Developmental policies had little place in the provincial budget. The public works undertaken were for the most part those that could not be avoided. At a time when the Dominion was engaged in the construction of the National Transcontinental, and the other provinces were frequently expanding their public programmes and supporting developments in the railway and other utilities fields, Quebec was expanding its public works programme slowly and leaving utilities to others."[25] Or, as Gerard Bergeron has written: "Sometimes venerated, more often hated, the term 'State' has had a varying fate in history, of which the most common has been indifference."[26] It is not until 1937 that it is solemnly invoked in a strongly nationalist sense by Lionel Groulx, at the Congress of the French Language: "Nous l'aurons notre Etat francais!"[27] And not until a quarter-century later was the formula "Etat du Quebec" to become a buzz-word of the Quiet Revolution.

(2) After 1759, English control over capital, land, and surplus value ensured that the subsequent development of a merchant and industrial class, as epitomized in institutions like the Northwest Co., the Bank of Montreal, the Grand Trunk Railway, the C P R, and Montreal Light and Power Co., would not be "a realization of the main ethnic group in the province."[28] The English-French division of labour was of a classically colonial sort, with the former dominating the upper reaches of the economic structure, and the latter the bottom levels.[29] English-Canadian and foreign capitalists would have little reason to encourage a dynamic French-Canadian – controlled state, certainly not one that interfered too fulsomely in the economic arena.

The inclination of "the ruling provincial group under Sir Lomer Gouin, Alexandre Taschereau, and others ... was to express the ideas of the business interests of the province."[30] The position taken by provincial governments down to the 1960s was that associated with a resource-dependent periphery. Alexandre Taschereau's defence of American investment in Quebec's staple industries in the 1920s is symptomatic: "We do not have enough American capital interested in our enterprises. For you know how difficult it would be to find the $75 million necessary for the development of the Caron Falls ... We need our neighbour's gold for our own development. We will be the first beneficiaries. And do you really think that if American capital were not involved in our pulp, that our paper industry would have an easy or natural market in the United States?"[31] French-Canadian nationalism, based on the notables and intellectuals of the traditional petty bourgeoisie, could dream its dreams of la survivance, agrarian vocation, and social order. Industrialization, carried out under the auspices not of a francophone bourgeoisie but of alien English-speaking groups, would be required to transform Quebec society sufficiently to bring about a sea-change in the attitude taken toward the state.

It was a revitalized Quebec nationalism, based on the new middle class, coming into its own during the Quiet Revolution, that brought a veritable take-off in state activities.[32] The state sector would be used throughout the 1960s and 1970s in ways analogous to the practice in such "developing" societies as late-nineteenth-century Russian or the contemporary Third World – namely, to promote development of an indigenously based capitalism.

Let me cite a short passage from Teodor Shanin's incisive study of turn-of-the-century Russia:

The Russian State was a massive economy in two distinct senses. It was a gigantic enterprise *sensu strictu* and at the same time a powerful system of political and administrative intervention ... The concept of "triple alliance" coined for Brazil of the 1970s to define the complex relations between local capitalists, foreign capital and the state economy was remarkably apt for Russia of the period described. Despite considerable dependency on foreign credits and investments, the Russian state administrators were able to face major Western financiers from a position of strength using as much the state's own riches as the monopoly of politico-territorial control.[33]

Of course the analogy is not perfect (Quebec, unlike Russia or Brazil, was not a sovereign state), but the use of the state and publicly controlled enterprises (Hydro Québec, the Caisses de Dépôts) was monumental. Moreover, it helped spark the emergence of a more significant French-Canadian private-sector bourgeoisie, a full century and a quarter after the coming of capitalism to Quebec.[34]

(3) There was a powerful competitor to the state within civil society, one which, after the defeat of the 1837 Rebellion, could in a hegemonic manner associate its own interests with the linguistic, cultural, and religious interests of French Canada – namely the Church: "In a certain measure the Church was more present than the state; through its network of parishes and dioceses which dot the inhabited space, through the essential social character of the institutions it controls."[35]

For an observer like André Siegfried: "Not only is the Church independent of civil society – she is superior to it by reason of her extent and of her goal ... It is not the Church that is comprised in the State; it is the State that is comprised in the Church."[36] Clerical control over education, over freedom of speech, and over the press, and clerical intrusions into the political arena, so frequent at the turn of the century, led Siegfried to argue: "The Church really achieves the perfect condition of complete independence of which its high functionaries love to talk. It lives outside the jurisdiction of the civil power; *above* it ... No one ventures to assert in Canada, as in France, the supremacy of the state."[37] For Jean Hamelin, "the central position which the Church occupie(s) in the structures of power (gives) teeth to its moral authority and allow(s) it to confine its old enemy, the State, to a subordinate role."[38] And as Fernand Dumont puts it succinctly: "The State was above all the Church – so what need was there for any other?"[39]

The situation in Quebec thus recalled the dualism that had permeated medieval societies, with church and state (empire or kingdom) struggling for supremacy. With the legitimacy of Quebec governments so deeply rooted in the maintenance of traditional, church-interpreted values, with the government in Ottawa that of les autres, the relationship was often one-sided. This is not to deny that Quebec governments under the control of strong premiers like Duplessis sometimes controlled the funding and dictated various measures to the church itself – note Duplessis's cynical remark, "The Bishops eat from my hand." But the church remained a privileged actor in Quebec society for almost a full century after Confederation.

These three dualities – federal v. provincial power, English-Canadian v. French-Canadian economic domination, and church v. state – highlight the impediments that existed to a strong, interventionist state in French Canada. What is more elusive, but significant, in light of the earlier discussion of English-Canadian nationalism, is the concomitant strength of nationalism within French-Canadian society.

Instances of nationalism in post-1867 Quebec history are frequent enough. Most often, this nationalism was linked not to political parties as such but to movements that swept the population at large – sympathy for Riel in 1885; alarm over the fate of French-Canadian minorities, in Manitoba in the 1890s or in Ontario in the 1910s; anticonscription sentiment, leading to riots in Quebec City in the spring of 1918 or to the formation of a mass organization like the Bloc populaire to spearhead the 72 per cent 'no' vote in Quebec during the conscription plebiscite of 1942 (the French-Canadian nation v. the English-Canadian–controlled state). Many were the nationalist-type organizations engaged in "the invention of tradition," from the Action nationale to the Ordre Jacques-Cartier and the Société St-

Jean Baptiste, linked to the church, the parish, the universities, or economic actors. Many were the French-Canadian associations, organizations, and publications for which the word "national" figured in the very name.

The strength of this nationalism may well have been a reflection of the state's weakness. This is especially true where the religious element is concerned. Siegfried, for example, emphasizes defence of "the passionate integrity of the Canadian race"[40] as a crucial feature of the church's influence in Quebec. As in a number of other strongly Catholic societies (Spain, Ireland, Poland), the church marked the expression of national identity with its own stamp, the "Religion and Fatherland" motif dear to ultramontane circles late in the nineteenth century.[41] No secular interpretations, as the demise of the Institut canadien had shown, could really compete. When, in turn, politicians before 1960 defended Quebec's autonomy against federal encroachment, it was in the name of traditional values which denigrated an all-powerful state:

The French-Canadian culture is communal. Three great traditions – family, autonomous work and the parish have been the lines of force in the social history of French Canada ... They correspond to the permanent requirements of human life ... With the progress of the idea of social insurance and public pensions, the Anglo-Protestant provinces ... met new situations by creating new institutions subsidized by the state ... The Province of Quebec remains at heart faithful to its Catholic-inspired social traditions ... It must take care to give itself a social security system consistent with its religious convictions, culture and the social traditions of the population.[42]

Pierre Trudeau might regret the excesses to which nationalism had been carried in Quebec, the social and economic backwardness it had fostered, and the failure to make proper use of provincial powers.[43] Far more common was the exaltation of nationalism as the one bulwark against assimilation that runs like a red thread through most Quebec political writing of this century: "If Dollard were alive, how ardently, how forcefully, how convincingly he would argue for the patriotic option! ... Should you command it, O Dollard, O powerful leader, we are ready to follow you to the supreme holocaust for the defence of our French tongue and our Catholic faith."[44] "A powerful reason conditions the existence and destiny of [our] people ... Much like the sentiment of family, the sentiment of nation has never ceased to give it life."[45]

This nationalism changed significantly after 1960, taking on a modernizing, state-coloured flavour. From denigrating the interventionist policies of federal governments, Quebec governments had now acquired an appetite for intervention all their own. For Jean Lesage in 1961: "The present situation forces us to re-think our traditional position. We need powerful means, not only to overcome the inevitable challenges of the coming years, but also to put the French-Canadian people at the level of the present-day world. The only means we possess is the State of Quebec, our own State. We cannot afford the luxury of not using it. I do not have the right as Prime Minister to tell you that we can rely solely on the efforts of individuals or organized groups."[46] For René Lévesque: "Without seeking to play the prophet, I am persuaded that in the coming years French Canada, thanks to the State of Quebec, will achieve that measure of emancipation indispensable to a normal nation."[47] For Daniel Johnson: "The French Canadian nation is striving with all its force ... to realize itself through the state and its aspirations are absolutely normal and legitimate."[48]

The size of Quebec government expenditures, expressed as a proportion of gross provincial product, almost tripled, going from 7.7 per cent in 1961–2, to 26 per cent by 1979–80,[49] even as the battle over Quebec's status within Confederation became sharper. The sociological nation was increasingly investing the state with a larger mission.

In attempting to travel the route from nation to state, recent Quebec nationalists were following in the footsteps of nationalist movements elsewhere. They sought, out of group consciousness and shared history, language, and culture, to develop an independent state structure that would more perfectly incarnate nationhood: "The modern state both shapes nationalist politics and provides that politics with its major objective, namely possession of the state."[50] In doing so, however, they came up against the logic of the federal system. Most English Canadians could not envisage anything but a pan-Canadian rubric for their own national consciousness. The state that would be undermined by a sovereign Quebec would be the Canadian state, the fountainhead, as I argued earlier, of any English-Canadian nationalism. For federalist French Canadians, as well, the force of history, of economic integration, and of habit militated against independence.

In the end, the Canadian state has prevailed – at least for the moment. Whether we are any further along the road to genuine cohabitation and to a common nationalism between English and

French Canada is another story. Religion may have waned as a divisive factor; the English-French division of labour within Quebec, or at least Montreal, is a good deal less one-sided than before.

Nationalism, however, remains a libidinal factor, rooted in civil society and popular consciousness, which can, moreover, well up from below at any moment, whatever the formal division of powers between Ottawa and Quebec, whatever the current state of English-French relations. One need but note the wave of protest unleashed in Quebec by the federal Supreme Court's ruling of 15 December 1988, striking down the sign provisions of Bill 101, and the haste with which the Bourassa government had recourse to the "notwithstanding" clause of the Charter in the language legislation that followed (Bill 178). Quebec nationalism may not be able to remake the federal state entirely to its own liking, but it is never likely to be completely circumscribed by it either. Its origins antedate 1867, and its fate is not nearly as tied to passing political events, even sovereignty-association referenda, as its staunchest adherents (and opponents) might believe.

Conversely, in English Canada, nationalism remains closely tied to the federal state. There may be a little more vibrancy to English-Canadian culture today (that part that has survived American bombardment); patriotism evokes a measure of spontaneous support within the population, as witnessed by the emotional tone of the 1988 federal election campaign in much of English Canada. English-Canadian nationalism, however, remains linked to governmental programs and policies, and the key debates – from free trade to foreign policy to public v. private ownership – typically revolve around the use (or misuse) of state power. There is little of that autonomous sentiment that John Breuilly points to when he writes: "Only if there is a distinct notion of a private civil society which is regarded as the source of sovereignty can one claim that power ultimately rests with the nation defined in 'private,' that is, in cultural, terms."[51] Insofar as there is an (English)-Canadian nation, it is the by-product of 120 years of a central state structure. In contrast, the concept of a French-Canadian (or Quebec) nation has been around for longer in Quebec society than the concept of the state.

Is it any wonder, then, that English Canada and Quebec have so often resembled two ships sailing off in opposite directions on a northern sea, one from an embarcation point called state, the other from one called nation? And that their itineraries have so often led and will continue to lead to collisions and crises that can rock the Canadian federation to its very foundations?

CHAPTER ELEVEN

Federalism and Socialism: A Reconsideration

The twentieth century will open the age of federations, or else humanity will undergo another purgatory of a thousand years.
Proudhon[1]

Centralism goes hand in hand with democracy and progress, while federalism and particularism are linked with reaction and backwardness.
Rosa Luxemburg[2]

Socialists, historically, have not been supporters of federalism. As a modern political idea, federalism is linked closely to the bourgeois political institutions that developed in Holland, Switzerland, and the United States from the sixteenth to the eighteenth century, spreading thereafter to the far-flung corners of the globe. True, nineteenth-century anarchists like Proudhon and Bakunin were strong advocates of federalism, while even Marx had favourable things to say about it in *The Civil War in France*. The tenor of socialist and Marxist thought in the late nineteenth and early twentieth centuries, however, was strongly centralizing and ensured at best reluctant toleration for what was seen as weakening the possibility of vigorous state action on behalf of the working class and its allies. Here social democrats and Marxist-Leninists after 1917 tended to see eye to eye, though each might, for tactical reasons, have to come to terms with federal structures in the particular circumstances of western Europe and the British dominions or the Soviet Union and post-1945 eastern Europe.

In the first part of this chapter, I want to explore the historical origins of federalism and why it is that socialists, for a long time, could not identify with it. I will then examine how the twentieth-century socialist experience with the national question led to modifications in the traditional stance and how developments in the capitalist political economy further influenced the attitudes of socialists on this question.

In the second part, I want to address the Canadian experience more directly. The Canadian left, historically, was no more comfortable with federalism than was the left internationally, and for very similar reasons. How do post-1960 developments in Quebec and more recent events within English Canada colour its attitudes? What place should federalism occupy in a socialist conception of the Canadian state?

Let me begin with the historical foundations. The ancient world saw various confederations and leagues, grouped around Sparta (the Peloponnesian League), Athens (the Athenian Confederacies), Thebes (the Boetian League), and, from the fourth century B C on, the Achaean and Aetolian leagues, formed to head off the danger from Macedonia.[3] It is through Polybius, the aristocratic defender of Rome's "mixed" constitution, that the last two came to be known to the early modern world, influencing both the founders of the Republic of the United Netherlands in 1579 and of the United States, some two centuries later.[4] There was nothing particularly democratic about the member states of these leagues.[5] What characterized them, rather, was their delegation of authority to representatives or even restricted councils for defensive purposes against an external threat.

This loose federal system appealed to the merchants and aristocratic regents of Holland who sought unity against the Spaniards; it still allowed the cities and provinces "ample opportunity for seriously promoting the essential interests of their own citizens and subjects."[6] The system worked well in the seventeenth century, with Dutch commercial power at its height, but fell on evil times in the eighteenth, with rising public debt, rivalry among the provinces, and the powerlessness of the estates' assembly. Just prior to the French Revolution, conservative forces had abolished federalism and replaced it with a unitary monarchy. After 1789, progressive and radical forces, influenced by the Jacobins, supported the "absolute unity and indivisibility" of a Dutch republic, denouncing the late Union of Utrecht as "a Gothic monstrosity, a hideous constitutional abortion."[7] Dutch federalism, for the left, was damned by its aristocratic origins.

The roots of federalism in Switzerland were not aristocratic, if one thinks back to the original confederation of the peasants of the Forest Cantons in 1291 against the Hapsburgs. But by the eighteenth century, the Swiss Confederation had developed, through expansion and economic transformation, into an increasingly anti-democratic affair, dominated in the more advanced cantons, such as Geneva, Zurich, and Berne, by the bourgeois oligarchs lording it over the disenfranchised inhabitants. (Cf. Rousseau's criticisms in his *Letters from the Mountain*.) This did not hider Rousseau, here following in the footsteps of Montesquieu, from doing much to popularize the argument for a potential link between federalism and democracy.

In the case of Montesquieu, the prevailing principle of a republic was virtue, something more clearly realized in a small state than in a large. But smallness left the republic open to attack from the outside. Hence the republican dilemma: "If a republic is small, it is destroyed by a foreign force, if it be large, it is ruined by an internal imperfection" (*The Spirit of the Laws*, IX, 1). The solution lay in confederation, uniting its members for certain ends, such as defence, while preserving their independence for others.

Montesquieu's federalism must be related to his larger theoretical outlook. His separation-of-powers doctrine, which bears some resemblance to Polybius's mixed constitution, was the attempt of an aristocratic liberal to limit absolutism, not to allow those in a "low state," i.e. the rabble, a voice in political affairs. His republicanism was of the Roman mould, anti-democratic and oligarchical, and it was for this type of state that federalism was conceived. Whether it could be transferred to a republic, founded on popular sovereignty and with expanding, rather than limited functions to fulfil, was another matter.

Though Rousseau did not share Montesquieu's aristocratic inclinations, his diagnosis of the problem of republics was strikingly similar. As he advised the Poles: "I would wish, if this were possible, that you could have as many states as the Palatinates, each with its local administration. Perfect the local Diets, enlarge their powers within their territory. But clearly demarcate their limits so that nothing can sever the tie of a common legislation to bind them or their subordination to the body of the Republic. In a word, extend and perfect the system of federated governments, the only one which unites the advantages of large and small states and thus the only one which can suit you."[8]

Rejecting representative institutions, championing direct democracy at the level of the small agrarian republic, Rousseau had strong additional reasons to support federation. It was the sole means of reconciling efficacy with democracy, executive flexibility with genuine citizen participation. True, the system was not conceived for large-scale industrial-type states. But just like Jefferson's ward republics, Rousseau's concept of inalienable citizen sovereignty has inspired recurring visions of participatory democracy down to this day. As such, it must be a component of any revitalized socialist theory of democracy, a theme to which I shall be returning in my conclusion.

There were, however, ambiguities in Rousseau's defence of small-scale democracy and of federalism. To begin with, in *The Social Contract* he limited the sphere of direct citizen sovereignty to two questions: "1. Do the people wish to preserve the existing form of government? 2. Do the people wish to leave the administration in the hands of those who are currently charged with it?" (book I.11, chapter 18). The first of these, to be fair, goes a good step beyond what most liberal-type regimes practise in the writing of their constitutions. Compare the indirect way in which the delegates to the American constitutional convention of 1787 or to the Indian Constituent Assembly of 1946 were chosen, or the Bonapartist means by which Pierre Trudeau rammed through his constitutional package of 1981–2, without any express mandate from the Canadian people. Rousseau's second stipulation, however, is little different from the periodic occasions that modern electorates have to vote political parties in or out of office – it provides no occasion for direct legislation, let alone execution, by the people.

More important still was Rousseau's emphasis on the general will, opening the door to a centralizing definition of the common good. Just as the general will of the collectivity never erred and, therefore, overrode the particular wills of individual citizens (*The Social Contract*, book I, chapter 6 and 7), did not, by extension, the general will of the larger community, such as the nation-state, overrule that of the smaller, particularistic communities, given to error? This would seem to follow from the passage in *On the Government of Poland* cited above and underlay the Jacobin interpretation of Rousseauean popular sovereignty as "the Republic one and Indivisible."[9] Proudhon was not altogether wrong in arguing "that in the social contract as imagined by Rousseau and the Jacobins the citizen divests himself of sovereignty, and the town and Department above it, absorbed by central authority, are no longer anything but agencies under direct ministerial control."[10] Rousseau's ambiguities on the nature of federalism anticipate those of later socialist theory.

A comparative examination of the American and French revolutions will help us pinpoint the problem. If both of these can be seen as quintessentially liberal revolutions, one resulted in a federal system of government and the other in a strongly unitary one. I will not attempt to probe the differing historical legacies behind each revolution, or the geographical and economic positions in which the United States and France found themselves at the end of the eighteenth century. Suffice it to note that revolutionary France was emerging out of centuries of despotism and monarchical centralization and found itself surrounded by enemies on all sides, while the United States had no feudal or absolutist past and had an ocean between itself and the Old Word.

The American founders, in trying to overcome the weaknesses of the Articles of Confederation, strove for a strong central government, independent of the states: "Was, then, the American Revolution effected ... was the precious blood of thousands spilled, and the hard-earned sustenance of millions lavished, not that the people of America should enjoy peace, liberty, and safety, but that the government of the individual states ... might enjoy a certain extent of power and be arrayed with certain dignities and attributes of sovereignty?" (*The Federalist Papers*, x l v). The economic and military powers vested in Congress, the strong powers of the presidency, and the latent power of the Supreme Court served to ensure that the patriotism coming out of the American Revolution would be channeled into the creation of a nation-state where capital could have continental, and not strictly regional, aspirations. The debt would be consolidated and placed on a sound foundation; the threat to property that might surface in one region could be more easily headed off at the national level (x).

Yet the American constitution was federal, not unitary, in character. In part this was a necessary concession to the sentiment for state rights, and more particularly to those agrarian interests who resented the potential domination of commercial interests in a national government. Insofar as these interests are identified with Jefferson and his very favourable reading of popular rights and freedoms as against government, this element of federalism had a decidedly democratic flavour. And there is an obvious continuity, through the Populist movement of the late nineteenth century, to twentieth-century arguments.

Something else was involved. Federalism could also go hand in hand with fear of popular democracy, and it was this concern that led the authors of *The Federalist Papers* to look to it, along with the separation of powers, as a bulwark against "the abuses of liberty" (l x i i i). Not only, in good Montesquieuan fashion, was the legislative power to be divided into different branches, elected in different ways, and in turn distinguished from the executive and judicial powers, but also "in the compound republic of America, the power surrendered by the people is first divided between two distinct governments and then the portion allotted to each subdivided among distinct and separate departments." In such a system "society itself will be broken into so many parts, interests and classes of citizens that the rights of individuals, or the minority, will be in little danger from interested combinations of the majority (L I)."

The minority rights that the *Federalist* authors were most concerned about protecting included property rights threatened by "a rage for paper money, for an abolition of debts, for an equal division of property, or for any other improper or wicked project" (x). Federalism here functioned as an institutional bulwark against untoward government initiatives that interfered with capitalist rights.

As de Tocqueville was to observe some fifty years later: "In the United States the majority, which so frequently displays the tastes and propensities of a despot, is still destitute of the most perfect instruments of tyranny ... When the central government which represents that majority has issued a decree, it must entrust the execution of its will to agents over whom it frequently has no control and whom it cannot perpetually direct: the townships, municipal bodies, and counties form so many concealed backwaters, which check or part the tide of popular determination."[11]

If the American system spawned a federal system, the opposite was true of France. There the third estate, from the very beginning, associated the cause of liberty with a strong central government, subordinated only to the higher rights of man and of the sovereign people. France might be divided into eighty-three administrative departments; the indivisibility of the republic was another matter: "France is a Republic; her constitution is representative; national representation in no way results from a division of the territory nor from the separate wishes of parts of the population; it emanates expressly from the general will."[12] Attacked by the Prussians, the Austrians, and the English, the revolution could brook no internal opposition. To call for decentralization, for federation, as the Girondins did in 1793, was from the Jacobin point of view to play into the hands of the enemy: "Federalism and superstition speak Breton; the emigration and hatred for the Republic speak German; the counter-revolution speaks Italian and fanaticism speaks Basque. Let us smash these instruments of fanaticism and error."[13] The nation constituted a single bloc, into which provinces, communities, orders, and classes were all dissolved. Regional particularisms had given way to the "natural rights of all the French."[14]

St-Just, Robespierre's faithful disciple, argued the case unequivocally: "If the authority of the centre has been broken, its debris will weigh down everything ... Federalism is even more hideous than civil war. There exist under it no more social relations between one city and another, between one village and another. Federalism does not only mean a divided government, but a divided people."[15] The Jacobins and after them Napoleon and the republican, no less than monarchical, regimes of France reaffirmed the fundamental unity of the nation. Federalism and regionalism had, until recently, only epi- sodically found their way onto the national agenda, as in the Paris Commune of 1871 and de Gaulle's ill-fated referendum of 1969. (I shall withhold judgment as to whether the regional reforms intro- duced by the Socialist government in the early 1980s will drastically change this situation.)

Insofar as the popular party in the French revolution, the sans- culottes, tended to go along with the Jacobins' anti-federalism (though not with its suppression of sectional democracy),[16] the die may also have been cast for nineteenth-century socialism. Gracchus Babeuf, tribune of the people, leader of the Conspiracy of the Equals of 1796, was no federalist. Nor was Buonarroti or Blanqui. The Giron- dins, such as Condorcet and Roland, were condemned to the role of liberal backsliders, potential traitors to the revolution, by progres- sive or socialist historians of the revolution as diverse as Michelet, Jaurès, and Mathiez.

It is important to dwell on these distant events. Until the Russian Revolution, the French was the one that marked socialist and revolu- tionary thought throughout Europe. Centralism seemed the inevita- ble accompaniment of the nationalism that 1789 had launched. The logic of capitalist development in the nineteenth century, moreover, was pushing in the direction of ever-larger units of capital, ever- larger nation-states, as in Germany and Italy, and imperialist spheres. Socialists might advocate the overthrow of capitalism – they could not help but be impressed by the processes of capitalist concentration and growth (cf. *The Communist Manifesto*).

In an article in the *Neue Rheinische Zeitung* of the 1840s, Marx could write: "Today, because of the huge process of industry, trade, and communications, political centralization has become an even more pressing need than it was in the fifteenth and sixteenth centuries. What is not yet centralized is being centralized."[17] Engels was even harsher in his assessment of the Swiss: "The struggle of the early Swiss against Austria, the famous oath of Rytli, the heroic shot of Tell, the immortal victory at Mortgarten – all of this represented the struggle of restless shepherds against the thrust of historical devel- opment, a struggle of hidebound, conservative, local interests against the interests of the entire nation ... They won their victory over the civilization of that period, but as punishment they were cut off from the whole later progress of civilization."[18] Nor were European socialists given to any particular sympathy for the South, the party of state's rights and slavery in the American Civil War, as against the more centralizing and industrial North.

To be a federalist in the nineteenth century seemed to be standing against the forces of history. It came, even for constitutional writers like Bryce or Dicey, to be associated with weak government, "in which intricate legal dispute replaces, frustrates or distorts much of the play of political argument and influence, leading to a pervasive 'conservatism.' "[19] Why would socialists have been more friendly to it?

True, anarchists like Proudhon argued the contrary view, looking toward an agro-industrial federation as an alternative to the capitalist state, to mutualism in the economic sphere and decentralization in the political. But Proudhon's writings on federalism were, at points, inseparable from classical liberalism: "The federal principle, *liberal par excellence*, has as its first corollary the administrative independence of the localities composing the federation, as the second, the separation of powers within each of the sovereign states, as its third, the agro-industrial federation."[20]

Bakunin was less suspect on this score, making democracy rather than liberalism the keystone of his federalist theory: "Every organization must proceed from the bottom up, from the commune to the central unit of the country, the state, through federation ... The base unit of a country's constitution must be the absolutely autonomous commune represented by the majority of adult suffrage of all its inhabitants."[21] Bakunin, however, was not the world's most lucid political thinker.

It was through anarchism, more especially through the experience of the Paris Commune of 1871, that federalism came into contract with mainstream socialist theory. Marx, in his eulogy for the commune, seemed to adopt something of its decentralizing philosophy: "The Paris Commune was, of course, to serve as a model to all the great industrial centres of France. The communal *regime* once established in Paris and the secondary centres, the old centralized government would in the provinces, too, have to give way to the self-government of the producers ... The unity of the nation was not to be broken, but, on the contrary, to be organized by the Communal Constitution and to become a reality by the destruction of the State power which claimed to be the embodiment of that unity independent of and superior to, the nation itself."[22]

To make of Marx or his successors fulsome believers in federalism would, however, be going to far. Marx may well have believed in the ultimate withering away of the state and with it in "the self-government of the producers." He may have felt the need, just after the crushing of the commune, to celebrate its spirit. But he never returned to the theme of federalism, nor had he dwelt on it before. When in 1875, in his *Critique of the Gotha Programme*, he turned briefly to sketch the transition that lay between capitalism and socialism, he referred not to federalism but to the "dictatorship of the proletariat." Whatever else this term *dictatorship* entailed, it evoked a centralizing form of power, closer to the Committee of Public Safety of 1793 than to a communal-type federation.

Socialists of the next generation, from Karl Kautsky to Rosa Luxemburg to Jean Jaurès, had no particular fondness for federalism as a theory. Stressing the class interests of the working class, as opposed to those of the bourgeoisie, and the democratic reforms to be carried through by a socialist-controlled state, they looked to a strong central authority. The only socialists prepared to deviate somewhat were those in the multinational empires of eastern and central Europe, faced with the problems of nationalism.

Writing in the Austro-Hungarian empire, with its nine significant national groupings, Otto Bauer argued for the cultural autonomy of distinct nationalities within a multinational state: "The socialist society of the future will unite all its members in an autonomous national union. Here, common origin will no longer cement the nation, but a community of education, of work, of the right to culture."[23] He sought to reconcile this position with the internationalist tradition in socialism which pointed toward a United States of Europe: "Little by little socialist society constitutes a confederal state above diverse collectivities ... The principle of nationality is transformed into one of national autonomy."[24]

In Russia, the national question was as acute as in Austro-Hungary. Some form of political autonomy was clearly in the cards for the "prison house of nationalities," and had already been accorded to some of the national groups represented within Russian social democracy. By 1913, the Bolsheviks had come to argue the right of nations to self-determination as a solution to the problems of national oppression. In practice, this opened the door to a form of federalism, though with a strong centralizing overtones: "The closer a democratic state system is to complete freedom to secede the less frequent and ardent will the desire for separation be in practice, because big states afford indisputable advantages, both from the standpoint of economic progress and from that of the interests of the masses ... Recognition of self-determination is not synonymous with recognition of federalism as a principle. One may be a determined opponent of that principle and a champion of democratic centralism but still prefer federation to national inequality as the only way to full democratic centralism."[25] In the years immediately after the Russian Revolution, Finland, Poland, and the Baltic states achieved their independence. But Ukraine, White Russia, the Caucasus, with its skein of nationalities, and the Asiatic Near East were not such obvious or successful candidates. Federalism was a solution, first recognized in the constitution of 1924 and reaffirmed in 1936 and 1977.

The federal element would, from the beginning, be subordinated to the "democratic centralism" of which Lenin had spoken. If the constituent territories had been marked by different historical pasts, languages, and standards of living, the long-term goal, as Stalin expressed it in 1918, was the building of a closer socialist union.[26] This did not rule out recognition of cultural and linguistic uniqueness of the constituent republics, "the principle of socialist federalism" as the 1977 Soviet constitution terms it (article 70).[27] The emphasis clearly lay and lies on "the state unity of the Soviet people [which] draws all its nations and nationalities together for the purpose of jointly building communism" and on the superiority of "the decisions of the highest bodies of state authority and administration of the U S S R" over those of the union republics (article 77). This is notwithstanding the formal sovereignty granted the republics under the Soviet constitution (article 76), their right to secession (article 72), and their representation in one of the two chambers of the Supreme Soviet, the Soviet of Nationalities (articles 109, 110). Federalism in the Soviet Union is an organizational form, reflecting the multinational character of the country. It in no way hindered an extreme centralization of economic and political decision-making power, a legacy from the Jacobins. (Recent events in Armenia, Azerbaijan, Georgia, Moldavia, and the Baltic republics, however, suggest that in the Gorbachev era the nationalist tensions underlying Soviet federalism will be increasingly coming to the surface and that real power will have to be devolved to the constituent republics.)

In post-1945 Yugoslavia, the multinational character of the country also led to a federal arrangement. The model for the constitution of 1946 was the Soviet constitution of 1936, although the Yugoslavs made the peoples, rather than the republics, the basic components of the federation.[28] By 1953, five years after the break with Stalin, the Yugoslavs had begun to move in a new direction. In the constitution of that year, they placed emphasis on the democratic nature of their socialism, on decentralization and "social self-management" in both economy and society.[29] In contradistinction to the Soviet model, Yugoslav socialism would be less statist and less centralizing. Workers' councils were one facet of this practice; a more co-operative form of federalism was another, combining a measure of republican autonomy with genuinely federal elements in such central institutions as the federal executive council and the state presidency. This did not prevent the central government from interfering when, from its point of view, nationalist forces threatened to get out of hand in Croatia (1972–3) and Kosovo province (1981) or Serbia from doing the same in 1988–9. Still, there seems to be a fair degree of polycentrism in the operation of Yugoslav federalism, something that has been much reinforced since Tito's death.

Federalism may thus entail a more democratic form of socialism. Czechoslovakia, however, which moved in a federalist direction in 1969, after the Soviet invasion of August 1968 and the suppression of the Prague Spring, may provide a counter-example. A binational Czech and Slovak state did not spell greater democracy – quite the opposite[30] – though a new chapter began in late 1989.

What about other twentieth-century federal states? One must first observe that federalism has proved more enduring than a mechanistic reading of the tendencies in capitalist development might have suggested. Capitalism may have entered on a stage of higher concentration, but federalism has not simply vanished as a vestige of feudalism, in the way that Kautsky had argued in 1908.[31] Indeed, by that year, two of the British ex-colonies, Canada and Australia, had for some time been federal states, just like a number of Latin American republics inspired by the American example. In the decades since, the model has spread to other countries, including Kautsky's own Germany, both under the Weimar Republic and the Bundesrepublik since 1949, Austria, India, Malaysia, Nigeria (off and on), and, for a short period, the former British West Indies. Regional groupings of nation-states with federal-type structures, such as the European Community, have also become part of our times.

The persistence of federalism does not mean that the balance between central and regional power is the same from one country to the next or from one period to another. As a general rule, the increase in state functions that has taken place in this century – in the social no less than in the economic spheres, in Third World countries like India no less than in First World ones like Canada, Australia, and the United States – has been accompanied by reinforcement of central power, particularly in periods of war or economic crisis, like the 1930s. Foreign policy and imperial management may have reinforced this tendency in the United States after the

Second World War, while nation-building may have been the key factor in India after 1947. Governments of the left, such as the S P D in West Germany, the Congress Party in India, and Labour in Australia, may have centralizing tendencies, though the pattern escapes any easy categorization. (Cf. the reinforcement of central power by both Republican and Democratic administrations in the United States, by Liberal governments in Canada and Australia, and by authoritarian governments of the right in Brazil and Argentina.) What is clear is that federalism need no longer imply the weak, non-interventionist state of an earlier, liberal theory.

It does not follow, moreover, that the only trend is toward greater central power. As K.C. Wheare pointed out in 1946: "It has not been the general governments alone which have grown in strength. The regional governments also have expanded. In all federations the regions now perform functions which, at the establishment of the federations, they performed either not at all or to a much lesser degree than now."[32] Many of the governmental functions that have grown most rapidly in the decades since – education, health, social security – have been regional, rather than national, responsibilities. There may be periods of alternation between strongly centralizing administrations and more decentralizing ones (cf. Australia and India in the early and late 1970s, Canada in the early and late 1980s) – between what I would call Jacobin and Girondin moments. Sub-state nationalism may run more deeply at times than that of the federation (cf. Tamil Nadu in the late 1950s and early 1960s and Punjab today, Biafra in the late 1960s, and Quebec in the 1960s and 1970s and again today). Regional economic blocs, in alliance with outside interests, may pull in ways that weaken central power (cf. Alberta vis-à-vis Ottawa, or Western Australia and Queensland vis-à-vis Canberra, during the resource boom of the 1970s). In short, federal states are not subject only to centralizing pressures.

Where, then, do socialists stand on the federal division of power? Would they agree with Mr. Justice Subba Rao, of the Supreme Court of India, who defended federalism in these terms: "It helps to decentralize power: it gives the people of different parts of the country a feeling of participation in the affairs of state ... It moves the machinery of state much quicker and more efficiently than in a unitary state ... It enables each state to work out its destiny to suit its genius afford[ing] emotional satisfaction to different linguistic, religious and ethnic groups. It safeguards more effectively individual rights."[33] Or would they lean to the views of the Australian constitutional writer Geoffrey Sawer, who argued: "Believers in non-government are the only people likely to be positively attracted by the qualities of federalism, and today they rarely achieve political prominence. To political activists, advocacy of federalism seems like an invitation to political frustration."[34]

Are the economic arrangements for state concentration, the nationalist arguments for sovereignty, and the class arguments for the common interests of the working class and its allies more important than any would-be case for decentralization? Under which arrangement, unitary or federal, are individual and collective rights and genuine political participation more likely to thrive? Let me try to answer some of these questions with reference to Canada.

In Canada, federalism was not at its origins a matter of heading off that popular sovereignty that might come to reside in an elected central legislature. So oligarchical were our traditions following the defeat of the 1837 rebellions that democracy posed much less of a threat for the Canadian founding fathers than for Madison and his co-authors of *The Federalist Papers*. Not that Macdonald and his confrères were any less convinced that "unless property were protected ... we should cease to a people altogether free."[35] But the federal Senate, an appointed body with a high property qualification, and the office of governor general, with its monarchical trappings, seemed adequate to protect against levelling instincts.

The main reason federalism was adopted at all, despite Macdonald's clear preference for a legislative union, was recognition that "the people of lower Canada, being a minority with a different language, nationality, and religion from the majority,"[36] would never assent to this. Canada, in other words, had to come to terms with its national question.

The form of federalism established corresponded to the national and territorial divisions of a political economy which Tom Naylor has characterized, at least in its origins, as an essentially mercantile form of capitalism. The financial and economic primacy of the central government, something the Baring Brothers in London avidly sought, was clearly established, as was the federal disallowance clause against provincial legislation. To the provinces were reserved property and civil law and what Macdonald characterized as legislation for "sectional prejudices and interests." To the centre fell the task of securing "a strong and lasting government under which we can work out constitutional liberty as opposed to democracy."[37]

There are interesting parallels between the centralizing thrust of the British North American Act and that which I attributed earlier to the Jacobins (cf. chapter 2). But there are no less striking differences. Jacobinism was born of revolution, out of a doctrine of popular sovereignty and the general will. The spirit of Canadian state-building was cautious, conservative, and openly hostile to doctrines of popular, as opposed to parliamentary, sovereignty and to the "excesses" of democracy. If the economics of semi-peripheral capitalism pointed to a strong centre with powers analogous to those of the imperial power, the political imperatives were anything but democratic. One need but compare the Confederation Debates, held behind closed doors, and the B N A Act, never submitted to the electorates of the founding provinces and proclaimed by London, with the Oath of the Tennis Court, the storming of the Bastille, the night of 4 August, and the other events that in France led to "the republic one and indivisible." There was never the same political, nay libidinal, investment in the Canadian state by the people of this country.

Despite the strong federal power in the B N A Act, provincial consciousness developed in the decades after Confederation. Mowat in Ontario, Mercier in Quebec, and several Maritime politicians articulated regional agrarian and commercial concerns against the centre. This clamour was amplified in the west, where the newly settled population saw itself in a colonial position; it came to spawn various agrarian and political movements that defended class and regional interests in the idiom of populist democracy: "The history of Canada since Confederation – the outcome of a politico-commercial conspiracy – has been a history of heartless robbery of both the people of the Maritimes and of the Prairie sections of Canada by the Big 'Vested' Interests of the political and financially stronger Central Provinces. High prices for manufactured goods ... overbuilding of subsidized railway lines ... excessive freight charges ... trusts, mergers, and other forms of monopoly ... are some of the consequences of the unholy alliance of politicians and plutocrats, aided by shyster lawyers."[38] Initiatives, recall, referenda and delegate democracy won support in western Canada, as did the struggle for provincial control over resources. Provincial power and grass-roots democracy seemed to go together.

At the same time, from another direction, the Privy Council in London, starting with the *Local Prohibition* case of 1896, defended the autonomy of the provinces against any literal reading of the centre's residual powers. Whether the judges were reflecting laissez-faire biases against too interventionist a state, or a native conservatism that took a paternalistic liking to provincial power, the result was a scaling down of the powers of the federal government, leading to major crisis in the 1930s. The result, following the near-bankruptcy of several provinces and the Privy Council's overturning of Bennett's

New Deal–inspired initiatives, was appointment of the Rowell-Sirois Commission.

For the Canadian left, both the social democratic Co-operative Commonwealth Federation (C C F) and the much weaker Communist party, the need in the 1930s and 1940s was for greatly increased central power to cope with the economic crisis and to move to socialization of the commanding heights of the economy. The only concession the Regina Manifesto made to federal structures was with respect to "existing rights of racial and religious minorities." Otherwise it called for vastly greater powers for the central government: "The present division of powers between Dominion and Provinces reflects the conditions of a pioneer, mainly agricultural, community in 1867. Our constitution must be brought in line with the increasing industrialization of the country and the consequent centralization of economic and financial power – which has taken place in the last two generations."[39] "The eradication of capitalism" which the C C F, unlike its N D P successor, proudly proclaimed, and its accompanying "full programme of socialized planning" brooked little interference from provincial governments. These should return to the sphere the Fathers of Confederation had intended them to occupy: "control of local matters in their respective sections."

Nor was that all. The amendment of the B N A Act to bring about this increased federal power was to be by action of the Dominion Parliament alone. Charting the course that Pierre Trudeau, with the support of the federal N D P, was to follow some forty-five years later, social democratic theorists of the 1930s argued: "Parliament alone represents all provinces, speaks for every Canadian, and should properly be held responsible for a matter of such national importance. It has been due partly to our luck as heirs of British practice, partly to the wisdom of succeeding generations of Canadian statesmen, that we have hitherto avoided in Canada the paralyzing rigidity which renders the American Constitution so unworkable."[40] Socialism and a decentralized federal system were perceived to be incompatible, while democracy, in good British Fabian fashion, was equated with the sovereignty of Parliament.

The Communist party was less theoretical in its arguments, but given to similar views. In its brief to the Rowell-Sirois Commission, it proposed that responsibility for all social legislation be assumed by the Dominion government, along with control over all legislation affecting capital and labour. Given the national emergency Canada was passing through, the only action that made sense was "on a *national* scale."[41] The crucial issues in Canadian society did not revolve around the federal-provincial division of power: "The constitutional history of Canada is really the history of the struggle between the democratic masses of workers and farmers and the vested interests and monopolists. The material basis of real political equality and democracy is lacking because the exploiting class dominates the economic life of the nation."[42] Given the forces then in provincial office, the Communist party, much like the CCF, would have had little reason to favour enhanced provincial power: "Hepburn and Duplessis are the political representatives of the extraordinary powerful group of financiers and industrialists in eastern Canada who see the necessity of curtailing the political and economic rights of the people in order that they may hang on to their privileges and give nothing to increase the standards of living of the population."[43]

The left was not alone in arguing for enhanced federal power to deal with the Depression. Powerful capitalist forces, such as the Montreal Board of Trade, made a similar pitch,[44] and the Rowell-Sirois Commission seemed to agree. The war years saw the introduction of unemployment insurance and family allowances as a federal responsibility, as well as greater federal control over the whole taxation field. In 1945, the proportion of state revenue passing through the hands of the central government stood at almost 70 per cent,[45] while the immediate post-war period, which saw Canada officially adopting Keynesian monetary and fiscal policies, promised more of the same.

But that was not to be. The provinces, especially Ontario and Quebec, dug in their heels over continued revenue-appropriation by Ottawa. The post-war resource boom got under way – symbolized in Quebec by Ungava, in Ontario by uranium and nickel, in Alberta by Leduc, and in British Columbia by hydro development – and with this boom came enhanced provincial power. Infrastructural developments – highways, ports, pipelines – in part or whole provincially financed came first. Later came increased social spending on education, health and hospitals, welfare, and the like. Increasingly, state growth took place at the provincial rather than federal level, even if the federal government, through transfer and equalization payments, was financing a significant portion of provincial expenditures. By 1979 the ratio between provincial and federal percentages of total state expenditures had been reversed par rapport 1945, with the provinces accounting for 42.8 per cent and the federal government 33 per cent.[46]

The Canadian left, by and large, did not alter its attitude toward federalism in the immediate post-war years. True, a social democratic government came to power in Saskatchewan in 1944 and remained ensconced until 1964, enacting a number of bold reforms, including medicare. This made the national C C F and later N D P a little more forthright in their defence of the federal system (cf. the Winnipeg Manifesto of 1956 and the N D P Declaration of 1961), albeit with a continued proclivity to enhanced federal power. Most provincial governments remained in conservative hands, evoking no greater sympathy from the left than had been the case in the 1930s. A good deal of Canadian politics was still taken up with federal-provincial bickering, and John Porter spoke for many when, in *The Vertical Mosaic*, he castigated the federal system for standing in the way of "creative politics," i.e., a class-based politics.[47]

Pierre Trudeau, in his contribution to the 1961 manifesto of Canadian social democracy, *Social Purpose for Canada*, argued for Canadian socialists adopting a federalist strategy. Their road to power, he argued, seemed far more inviting at the provincial than at the federal level. They should use the opportunity to enact reforms in those provinces where they were strongest, enhancing their credibility as a would-be national force.[48] But Trudeau's commitment was not to socialism, as his leap into federal Liberal politics some years later was to show, nor did his arguments undercut the traditional socialist case for an economically powerful central government.

It was nationalism, the very phenomenon that Trudeau was committed to combat, that made the question of federalism a more serious one for the left after 1960. In that year the Quiet Revolution had begun in Quebec; its long-term consequences were to give a new social and class basis to Québécois nationalism. The traditional concerns of Quebec's governments - language, culture (religiously defined), a laissez-faire approach to the economy - gave way to political and economic interventionism. The Quebec government now asserted its power over a whole series of areas, leading to increased conflict over both jurisdiction and revenue with the federal government. The Quebec left, which began to emerge out of the long night of reaction and obscurantism, was strongly attracted to nationalist politics.

The N D P, at its founding convention in 1961, made some verbal concessions to Quebec's national character: "The New Democratic Party strongly affirms its belief in a federal system which alone insures the united development of the two nations which originally associated to form the Canadian partnership ... Canada's constitution particularly guarantees the national identity of French Canadians and the development of their culture."[49] It stopped well short, however, of accepting actual duality in the political structures of the country, contenting itself with a vague commitment to co-operative federalism. At its 1971 convention, the year after the October Crisis, it turned back a resolution emanating from the radical wing of the party, the Waffle, calling for recognition of Quebec's right to self-determination.

As a result, the N D P never really got off the ground in Quebec in the 1960 and 1970s. Francophone socialists instead gravitated toward the Rassemblement pour l'Indépendance nationale (R I N), the Parti socialiste du Québec, the Parti québécois (P Q), the trade union movement, and more revolutionary, if short-lived, formations like the Front de Libération du Québec (F L Q).[50] The intellectual temper of Quebec's new middle class was hostile to federalism with its implied limitations on the powers of the Quebec state. This was so despite the feverish attempts of the Canadian political élite, beginning with the Royal Commission on Bilingualism and Biculturalism of the mid-1960s and the Official Languages Act of 1969, to redefine Canada on the basis of full equality of language rights for the two founding peoples. As the English-Canadian establishment discovered a new vocation in bi- and multiculturalism, Quebec, especially much of the Québécois left, moved toward an increasingly Jacobin concept of nation.

The English-Canadian left was experiencing its own Jacobin moment in the late 1960s. Intellectuals, students, and political activists in English Canada, coming to recognize the legitimacy of nationalism for Quebec, were no less attracted to it themselves. As the Vietnam War developed, opposition to American policy and to Canada's support thereof grew. The Watkins Report of 1968 raised anew the issue of economic nationalism, and two political movements, the Waffle within the N D P and the Committee for an Independent Canada, placed it on their political agendas. Both neo-Marxist and neo-Innisian nationalists looked to a strong Canadian state – the federal government – to counteract the domination of American multinational corporations. The provinces had but a secondary role to play in any such strategy, all the more since most of them were strongly opposed to economic nationalism. The only reference in the Waffle Manifesto of 1969 to federalism was with regard to Quebec and to the need for socialists in the two nations to ally in fighting American imperialism. Federalism within English Canada was irrelevant to the socialist transformation that the Waffle envisaged for Canada.[51]

Nationalism has experienced its ups and downs in Quebec and in English Canada since 1970. The invocation of the War Measures Act in October of that year against the F L Q spelled a mortal blow to revolutionary forms of nationalism in Quebec. The P Q, however, increased its popular support steadily from that point on, coming to power in November 1976 in an election that rocked the federalist foundations of Canada. Though the P Q was by now committed to holding a referendum before attempting to negotiate a form of sovereignty-association with the rest of Canada, the possibility of an independent Quebec had never loomed larger. The defeat of the P Q's referendum of May 1980 – one in which the federal government was heavily engaged on the other side – by a margin of 60 per cent "no" to 40 per cent "yes" seemed to spell the demise of any such prospect for at least a generation. Despite the P Q's re-election to office in 1981, it was unable to withstand the Trudeau government's constitutional offensive of 1980–1 or to weather a sharp decline in popularity following its roll-back of public-sector wages in 1982–3. The result was a crushing defeat in 1985, and a period of wandering in the wilderness, from which Jacques Parizeau's accession to the leadership is unlikely to rescue it overnight – witness the outcome of Quebec's September 1989 election. Nationalism will remain an important force in Quebec, but it must coexist, for the moment, with a federal framework.

Economic nationalism in English Canada fell on harder times after the oil crisis of 1973 and the nose-dive in the international capitalist economy during the remainder of the decade. The N D P, true to Trudeau's prognostication, did achieve power at the provincial level in Manitoba in 1969, Saskatchewan in 1971 after a seven-year lull, and in British Columbia in 1972 – precisely in western Canada, where protest movements had always been strongest. Whatever the limitations of the powers of provincial governments or the limitations of social democracy itself, a number of significant reforms were carried out. This development served to enhance the appeal of the federal division of powers to sections of the left, all the more since there was little prospect of any major breakthrough at the national level.

By the beginning of the 1980s, the problems of Canadian federalism had taken a new turn. International shifts in the world capitalist economy – to the Pacific and away from the Atlantic region, from First World manufacturing to manufacturing in the newly industrializing countries, to energy- and resource-rich areas – led to a temporary boom in western Canada. Regional capitalist blocs like that of Alberta emerged, grouping the provincial government, multinational oil companies, and number of local resource firms in opposition to eastern capital and federal policies. The federal government responded with the National Energy Program of October 1980, appealing to national self-sufficiency as against regional power. For a short period, from the fall of 1980 to the late winter of 1981, separatism became a political force of some significance in Canada's oil-rich province. Alberta, at least, was passing through a Girondin moment.

In a not-altogether unrelated development, the federal government, following the breakdown of federal-provincial constitutional talks that had been going on all summer, decided to proceed with unilateral patriation of the B N A Act. In the process, Pierre Trudeau, fresh from his victory in the February 1980 federal election and May 1980 Quebec referendum, sought to entrench a number of important provisions, including a Charter of Rights, the Official Languages Act, and an amendment formula that favoured the federal government. Though there was evidence of significant opposition to unilateral action from every region of the country, most especially Quebec and the west, the federal N D P decided to go along with the measure, subject to a few modifications.

More recently still, the period of the Mulroney government has seen two simultaneous developments: weakening of Canadian nationalism vis-à-vis the United States, of which the Canada- U . S . Free Trade Agreement was the symbol, and the Meech Lake Accord, which repaired some of the damage done to Quebec by the 1981 proceedings by recognizing the latter's character as the "distinct society" but simultaneously strengthened the power of all the provinces vis-à-vis the federal government.

For the left, by and large, there is little mileage in increased integration with the United States – at least not with one as wedded to "free enterprise" principles as has been true of recent American administrations like that of Ronald Reagan. Yet the result of the 1988 election, in part reflecting the trend to regional blocs within the world capitalist economy, has been to make the Canada- U . S . Free Trade Agreement a reality.

Meech Lake, not unlike the constitutional package of 1981, poses other problems. In general, the English-Canadian left does not favour a federal state so weakened that it will not be able to act decisively in economic or social matters, for example, by imposing national standards when necessary, as with the Canada Health Act of 1984. Nor does it welcome the type of regionalism and blatantly capitalist province-building associated with premiers such as Peter Lougheed, Grant Devine, or Bill Vander Zalm. Yet, conversely, it had fewer reasons in the late 1980s to believe that centralization was the inevitable accompaniment of a socialist strategy for English Canada or for Canada as a whole. At the same time, unlike the Trudeau faction of the Liberal party, English-Canadian socialists had less reason to deny Quebec's legitimate aspirations to recognition as a distinct nationality within Canada. (It is also true, however, that Québécois must come to better understand English Canada's own desire to remain a distinct society vis-à-vis the United States.)[52]

What would have made sense in 1980-1 and, more recently, with respect to Meech Lake would have been a clear stand by Canadian socialists in favour of democratic procedures in constitution-making. As I have argued in chapter 5, we have had all too much of parliamentary sovereignty in this country, and far too little of popular sovereignty. In the events of 1980-1, socialists had no more reason to side with Trudeau in his exercise in anti-democratic constitution-making than with the provinces. But they did have every reason to advance the alternative of an elected constituent assembly, with ratification of any resulting constitutional text by a majority of the population. Similarly, in 1987, instead of simply endorsing the Meech Lake deal, worked out behind closed doors by elected politicians, as the federal N D P resolved to do, it would have been far better to call for direct popular ratification of any agreement. Questions of the federal-provincial division of powers and of constitutional arrangements generally speak directly to the nature of political institutions and to the rules by which the state *itself* ought to be governed. Who but the people can ultimately determine such matters?

Let me, in conclusion, speak to some of the elements that ought to colour the socialist position on federalism in Canada.

(1) *Democracy.* The argument of size and scale continues to be one for units smaller than the central one in a large territorial entity like Canada. If participation is a key value in political, no less than economic, matters, if we mean by democracy something more than the choice between competing élites to which contemporary liberal theorists such as Schumpeter, Lipset, and Sartori reduce it, then we must be able to envisage some type of face-to-face structures at the base.

This is not necessarily an argument for federalism. As a number of writers have observed, provinces and states can also cover a large extent of territory and their governments provoke as great a feeling of alienation on the part of their inhabitants as any national government. Only reasonably small units, corresponding to the sections of the French Revolution, Jefferson's wards, the soviets of the 1905 and 1917 revolutions, and the Räte of the abortive German revolution would solve this problem.[53]

A grouping of these base units from the bottom up is clearly necessary. While it may be argued that such groupings should be along territorially organized lines, it does not follow that these territories must have distinct powers vis-à-vis the centre. A unitary form of state with participatory democracy at the base, so that all major decisions can be debated and, if necessary, altered by the citizenry, has a good deal more to commend it than an officially federal state with only limited citizen participation.

The key element, from the socialist point of view, must be popular sovereignty. This has been used to justify the concentration of major economic and political decision-making power at the centre from Robespierre to Lenin. It must now become an argument for the dispersal of some of that decision-making power to the citizenry. If federal structures can help the process along, well and good, so long as it is clear that the maximization of democracy is what is being sought.

(2) *Nationalism*. The Jacobin argument militates against excessive regional power in the name of the nation-state. It is a persuasive argument to many regimes born of revolution or, for that matter, of decolonization. One will not lightly dismember a political unity achieved at great cost, often against hostile power(s). Even the United States, federal regime par excellence, fought a bloody civil war to avoid such a fate.

Still, multinational states exist, as do significant regional/geographical units within linguistically unified states. Where there is more than one significant nationality, as in Canada, appropriate power must be given to the minority nationality. Nor would homogeneity among the English-speaking provinces of Canada necessarily be a good idea. Regional economic interests vary, political traditions and cultures vary as well, and the view of the nation is not quite the same from Ontario as from British Columbia. One could argue that there is something artificial about these provincial lines, that had Canada developed differently, it would have been a unitary form of state like Britain or France. But Canada is no Britain or France, rather a thinly populated country sprawling over the northern half of a continent. Jacobin-type centralization, except under crisis conditions, accordingly elicits strong resistance.

(3) *Efficiency*. There are conflicting arguments for assigning power to one level or another. The tendency to monopoly concentration under capitalism has long served socialists as an argument for centralization of economic power in the hands of the state. To this was added a supplementary argument after 1945 stemming from the tremendous power of transnational corporations. As a further eco-

nomic argument against federalism, one can point to the unnecessary duplication of services, as in education, and the balkanization that sets in.

Conversely, one can argue the greater diversification that flows from a decentralized economy. Economic democracy probably has a much better chance to work within smaller regional enterprises than huge national ones. Small-scale economies are not only more human; they may be more innovative and productive. Moreover, communications technology today makes possible a high degree of decentralization. Large is not always efficient or beautiful or democratic, and so this traditional critique of federalism only partly holds.

(4) *Models of socialism*. There is no hard and fast rule as to whether the provincial or the federal level is likely to be more conducive to progressive change. Federal governments in Canada have been responsible for a certain amount of progressive legislation over the years, but a good deal of reactionary legislation as well – for example, price and wage controls. The same has been true of provincial governments.

Socialism in the Western world has generally fared better in unitary states like Britain, France, and Sweden; by comparison, federal states have been more resistant. But is federalism the independent variable here, or is something else? In Australia, with its fairly evenly divided political forces, it may well have blocked the introduction of more radical measures by Labor governments in the late 1940s (the proposed nationalization of banks) or in the early 1970s. But what of Canada or the United States, with their relatively low levels of working-class consciousness in the first place, when compared to older European societies? The real task the left faces is that of making socialism itself a more appealing set of ideas in the rather altered circumstances that face a political economy like Canada's at the end of the twentieth century. As I suggest in chapter 12, we may well need a new formulation of socialism, which places less emphasis on state power and more on radical democratic practice, both in politics and in economics. It is by no means evident that federalism would prove an insurmountable obstacle to moving in the direction of a decentralized and market form of socialism. Indeed, the first halting steps may well occur at the provincial level.

If socialism is to come to Canada, it will clearly entail the use of central, not only provincial, powers. The historical objections to federalism, however, no longer hold. If the fracturing of popular sovereignty that the Jacobins and their successors emphasized remains a danger, there is a still greater danger in the twentieth century of excessively centralized state power. Just as socialist theorists, East and West, should be rethinking some of their criticisms of the separation-of-powers argument of eighteenth-century liberalism, so they can rehabilitate at least part of federalist theory. To be a good socialist does not necessarily mean to be a centralizer. Federalism, like democracy itself, has a worthy place in socialist theory in the late twentieth century.

CHAPTER TWELVE

Democracy, Socialism, and the State

Let me begin by outlining the dilemma facing the three principal variants of twentieth-century left-wing thought with regard to the concepts of democracy, socialism, and the state.

Social democracy, it can be argued, has a theory of democracy – liberal democracy – and a theory of the state – the interventionist welfare state – but can it really be said to have a theory of socialism? Surely not, unless one means by this term little more than the mixed economies, predominantly privately owned, though state-influenced, that characterize the OECD economies, i.e. the Western industrialized states.

Marxism-Leninism, in contrast, has a theory of the state, which it sees as the instrument of dominant classes throughout history. Moreover, it has a theory of socialism, which it equates with collective ownership over the means of production, an incontestable feature of the various state socialist regimes of the contemporary era. But can it really be said to have a theory of democracy, when the logic of democratic centralism and one-party dictatorship has time and time again closed off most forms of direct participation and control from below over decision-making?

Finally, the alternative left – a capsule term for various left/radical theories from revolutionary syndicalism through council communism down to the student movements of the 1960s and the adherents of popular and grass-roots movements in civil society today – has made much of participatory as opposed to representative democracy in its arguments. It has generally not shared social democracy's commitment to incremental reforms or the management of the mixed economy, while in its vision of socialism, to the degree that it has had one, it has placed much greater emphasis on the self-management of the producers than on the dictatorship of/over the proletariat practised by Marxism-Leninism. The alternative left, however, lacked the most important ingredient of all, a theory of the state, though it may well have had important insights into the nature of the political.

My starting position, then, is that none of these three currents has provided a resolution to the relationship among democracy, social-ism, and the state and that a satisfactory theory has to go beyond them in addressing these three components simultaneously. This requires, first, forthright criticism of the failures of each, as well as some understanding of why they developed the way they did. Sec-ond, it requires some attention to the heritage of non-Marxist, as well as Marxist, political theory, in an attempt to build on earlier insights into the problem of the state. Third, it requires projective thinking about concrete conditions in Western and in state socialist societies, which in turn predetermine any possible transformations.

Social democracy is the eldest daughter of the Marxist church, though arguably the one that has strayed most from the parental hearth. Even before the First World War, social democracy à la Bern-stein, Jaurès, and Kautsky reflected the reformist as opposed to revolutionary character of important sections of the European work-ing class. Nationalism was already looming up as more important than internationalism, while most social democratic parties had embarked upon a parliamentary path to which Marx in 1872 and Engels in 1895 had at least opened the door.

Its leaders had come to accept the virtues of liberal democracy, pressing for extension of the franchise, maximization of individual freedoms, and new social and economic rights under a reformed capitalist system. As early as the 1890s, Kautsky had rejected out of hand theories of direct democracy then abroad in the German work-ers' movement,[1] while German social democracy's hostile stance to both the soviets of the 1905 and 1917 revolutions and to the Räte of Germany's own abortive revolution of 1918–19 heralded its funda-mental alignment with the institutions of liberal parliamentarism. In the Weimar period, this stance led the Social Democratic Party (S P D) to an uncritical belief in constitutionalism, even though the forces of the right were clearly unprepared to play by any such rules. Since 1945, the West German and other social democratic par-ties have, in neo-Schumpeterian fashion,[2] accepted the reduction of democracy to the competitive party struggle within the electoral arena. They had little patience for the student movement, with its extra-parliamentary theories, or for the more radical of Greens and continue, despite occasional nods in the direction of greater partici-pation by workers and employees in economic decision-making, to see parliamentary politics as both the focus and essence of a modern theory of democracy.

Where state ownership is concerned, the experience of social democratic parties has varied. The immediate post-war years did see large-scale nationalizations carried out by governments in France and Britain. In the decades since, social democratic parties have shown less of a penchant for socialization of the means of production. Swedish, West German, and Austrian social democracy – the success stories, so to speak – were concerned more with effective management of a still essentially capitalist-controlled economy or with increasing social services ("capitalism with a human face") than with any transition to a socialist economy. The Bad Godesberg Congress of the West German S P D in 1959, where the last of the old Marxist credo was laid to rest, symbolized what was happening elsewhere. At the same time, the alignment of socialist party leaderships and trade unions with the United States during the Cold War years did little to bolster socialist commitment. The late 1960s and the 1970s did see the emergence of left wings of greater or lesser importance in the British, French, West German, and other social democratic parties. But the relative failure of the left program undertaken by the French Socialist government between 1981 and 1983, and the exigencies of an international division of labour in which market imperatives prevail, have much reduced the scope for socialist experimentation in the West and narrowed the range of debate within socialist and social democratic parties.

Social democracy has largely made its peace with the liberal capitalist state. It has pressed for many of the welfare measures recently under attack from the right, while accepting the overall logic of Keynesian economics. Some social democrats, building on an interest-group theory of the state, accept the logic of neo-corporatism; others may press for a larger working-class or new-middle-class share of the pie under the aegis of an economically interventionist state. The institutional structures of the Western state go largely unchallenged, even as social democratic parties have proved staatsfähig (capable of governing) in ways international and domestic capital have usually found quite acceptable. (To be sure, in countries where better alternatives on the centre or right are available, large capital normally prefers these).

In its defence, social democracy's moderation and acceptance of a reformed capitalist system and state do reflect the profound embourgeoisement of large sections of the working class and the new middle class in industrial and post-industrial societies. Social democracy may well represent the outer limits of what is electorally possible in Western-type states.[3] Still, social democratic leaders have been reticent to champion radical forms of equality or redistribution of wealth or to question the exclusively representative theory of democracy that prevails in our societies. They have been agents, not passive victims, of the adaptation to capitalist and liberal values.

Marxism-Leninism is an outgrowth of the displacement of the revolution eastward in ways unforeseen by its founding fathers. It took root in the most backward of European nations, one with only a nascent capitalist mode of production (cf. Gramsci's description of "the revolution against *Capital*"). Seeking to leapfrog stages, the Bolsheviks, unlike the social democrats, showed no indulgence toward private capital, embarking on full-scale nationalization almost at once. The New Economic Policy (NEP) period in the 1920s proved but an interlude on the road to the collectivization of the late 1920s and early 1930s and to centralized state control over the economy.

A socialism with Gulags through the 1930s, 1940s, and 1950s, the Soviet Union had done little to realize significant measures of democracy in the work-place or in broader spheres of life. It has maintained much of the division of labour that characterizes capitalism and most of its underlying logic, for example, faith in growth and in technology and science and wanton disregard for nature. One thing it has engendered is a very powerful state.

Despite Lenin's *State and Revolution*, the transitional stage that precedes the withering away of the state shows no sign of ending in the Soviet Union, while much since the Civil War – elimination of rival parties, a tight rein of the central party apparatus over intra-party matters, the cult of the personality under Stalin and Brezhnev – has served to strengthen central power. The Soviet state may not, from the Marxist point of view, be an instrument of the bourgeoisie, but it has brought an extraordinary degree of repression to bear both on the internal population and on client states. The "politbureaucracy," as Rudolf Bahro once called it,[4] has been a powerful source of domination in its own right, underlining the inadequacy of traditional Marxist explanations of state power in terms of class interest.

If Marxism-Leninism gives rise to an impressive state machine, its main shortcomings lie in the realm of democracy. The problem, as already suggested, goes right back to the Revolution and Civil War period, to the crushing of soviet power, the substitution of a party monopoly, increasing recourse to repression, from the Cheka through forced collectivization and the great purges. Paper declarations about democracy in the Stalin Constitution of 1936 or in the 1977 model are legion: "Soviet citizens are guaranteed freedom of speech, of the press, and of assembly, meeting, street processions

and demonstrations; they have the right to associate in public organizations, the right to freedom of conscience, to protection of the
family and to inviolability of person and home, to privacy of correspondence, telephone conversations and telegraphic communications."[5] Invariably, such rights "must not be used against the Soviet
social system," with the party remaining "the guarantor of the successful progressive development of socialist democracy."[6] The inadequacy of such provisions is apparent to many Western socialists and
Marxists today,[7] and increasingly to reform elements in the new
Soviet leadership under Mikhail Gorbachev. But the road to genuine
democratization promises to be perilous and long.

China, the other major Marxist-Leninist type state and sometime
rival to the Soviet Union, is not without its problems, too. The "hundred flowers" phase of 1957–8 was followed by intensified repression. The Cultural Revolution, for all its seeming mass political
participation, was subject to orchestration from above and to a cult
of personality no less intense than Stalin's. In the years that have
followed, market principles have come to the fore, with socialist self-
sufficiency (and some would argue, socialism) giving way to
increased emulation of the capitalist West. Democratization does not
hold pride of place for the current Chinese leadership (witness the
crushing of the student movement in June 1989), and China's foreign
policy shows much the same mixture of Realpolitik and self-interest
as Soviet.

Though Marxism-Leninism, then, continues to be the ruling ideology for over one and a half billion people, though a number of Third
World states have come to subscribe to it, it is a less attractive model
in today's world than twenty-five or fifty years ago. Its economic
system, despite recent or projected reforms, is unduly centralized
and bureaucratic, while a heavy party hand has until now vitiated
the democratic content so central to the original socialist vision.

The alternative left, for its part, has never had occasion to put its
theories into practice. It reminds one a little of what Polybius, in
discussing ancient constitutions in book v i of The Histories, wrote,
disqualifying Plato's Republic from consideration since it was the
blueprint for an imaginary, rather than real, state. Nor are the different movements that I have earlier cast as constituting the alternative
left necessarily of a single mould. Still, in their various guises, they
do represent a potential intellectual alternative to social democracy
and Marxism-Leninism.

On the score of socialism, adherents of an alternative left have
often stood with Marxist-Leninists in believing in collective (though
not necessarily state) ownership over the means of production as the

cornerstone of an egalitarian society. But unlike these, they have rejected any notion of dictatorship by a party, placing great emphasis on workers' control and direct democracy instead. In their critique of Leninist-type practices, they have insisted like Rosa Luxemburg, that socialist democracy must transcend liberal democracy, while incarnating the best of its individual freedoms alongside new, collectivist ones.

The alternative left has usually been no less critical of social democracy, obsessed as it was with bourgeois parliamentary institutions whose roots were far from democratic. While formal rights loomed large in the constitutional documents of liberal democratic states, tremendous inequality of wealth persisted, with the power of capital extending over social democratic governments themselves. Nor did social democratic governments seem to do enough to empower the very constituencies – workers, women, welfare recipients, the elderly – they were meant to serve.

In retrospect, it is clear that the alternative left, like classical anarchism before it, has lacked a theory of the state and state power. While naïvely postulating loose structures for political and economic participation, it has been unwilling or unable to recognize that a socialist society would have to have elaborate political and economic institutions, with significant delegation of power. Leninism, with its dictatorship of the proletariat exercised by a vanguard party, and social democracy, with its liberal, representative institutions, were more realistic in this regard.

We have reached the end of the 1980s with socialist and Marxist theory in full-blown crisis. As Louis Althusser had the temerity to recognize over a decade ago: "We have to be frank about it: there does not *really* exist any "Marxist theory of the state." Not that Marx and Lenin tried to dodge the question – it lies at the heart of their political thought. But what you find in the classical authors beneath a discussion of the forms of relation between the state on the one hand and the class struggle and class domination on the other ... is only a repeated warning to avoid all bourgeois concepts of the state – a rather negative demarcation line and definition."[8]

We live in the shadow of the state, East, West, and Third World, yet the writings of Marx, Engels, Lenin, and Luxemburg are of little help. True, there are gleanings from their writings – a critique of alienation, "the self-government of the producers" of Paris Commune days, a theory of spontaneity, of revolutions as "festivals of the oppressed" – but the lacunae are more glaring. Marx's focus on political economy in the second part of his life meant that political theory received short shrift. The result is political writings inspired by specific events such as *The 18th Brumaire of Louis Bonaparte* and *The Civil War in France*, rather than mature reflection on the political along the lines of Montesquieu's *The Spirit of the Laws* or Rousseau's *The Social Contract*. A further result is brilliant insight into specifics, but failure to develop an adequate overall theory of the state. One finds denunciation of the bourgeois domination lurking behind the capitalist state, a prophecy of some future withering away of the state in socialist society, and a transitional period of uncertain length dubbed "the dictatorship of the proletariat." No wonder the game of going back to Marx for one's political theory can be so self-defeating.

This is not a matter of castigating Marxism, like the French nou-veaux philosophes of yesteryear, for every crime of twentieth-century state socialism, any more than it is one of uncritically embracing liberal political theory. There is a parallel shortfall in con-temporary liberal theory, where the reconciliation of individual with collective liberties is concerned, and the crimes committed in the names of market freedom and corporate power – the underpinnings of liberal-type societies – are also legion. As Sartre, one of the most lucid of his generation, noted, all ideologists have dirty hands; there are questions of degree and kind. If the angelic moralism of a Camus is, to use Rousseau's term, "for a people of gods, not men," we need, none the less, to devise a socialism more ethical, more democratic, but simultaneously better grounded in the problems and concrete possibilities present in the contemporary world, than what has come before.

Some of the answers to our dilemma may be found by turning to the past, more particularly to classical political theory. Modes of produc-tion may change over time – forms of political domination as well – yet certain ongoing problems regarding power, justice, and equality endure. The famous second chorus in *Antigone* (lines 334–75), which praises human accomplishments in the sciences, arts, and medicine and yet recognizes how much more difficult is progress in the realm of good and evil, has a very contemporary ring. Many are the analo-gies that can be drawn between the inter-imperial rivalry that Thucydides describes and that of our age, while the public sphere of fifth- and fourth-century B C Greece (and sometimes republican Rome) has served as a magnet to which political writers of subse-quent ages have, for good reasons, returned time and time again.

Rousseau is perhaps the most intriguing theorist to have attemp-ted the return: unlike Machiavelli, Montesquieu, and Hegel, he can be seen as a would-be theorist of democracy (cf. chapter 1). A good deal has been written regarding Rousseau's contribution to a theory of participatory democracy,[9] his attempt to reinstate something of the Greek sense of the political, his grounding of sovereignty in a direct expression of the popular will, his critique of representative institutions, and his penchant for small, face-to-face communities and republics over large, centralized states. Clearly, we cannot simply go back to the ancient polis or *res publica* or to the Spartan and Roman models that Rousseau had in mind. But we need something of the Athenian sense of democracy – direct citizen involvement, a feeling for the political, the great public rituals of that city-state's theatre and festivals. And we need Rousseau's concept of sovereignty to oppose to rulers, be they Western-style presidents, prime ministers, and parliaments or Eastern-style politburos and party congresses, that usurp it. The problem is how to give it institutional moorings.

There is not only a democratic tradition to come to terms with – there is the whole legacy of reflections on the state. Thucydides' quite amoral reading of international relations anticipates Hobbes and Clausewitz and must surely give socialists today pause. Is power in the hands of great states – socialist states – exercised any differently? Did the Soviet Union treat Hungary, Czechoslovakia, or Afghanistan with any particular compassion? (To assure equal time to the other important imperialism, one might also recall u s interventions in Latin America or in Vietnam). If not, we have little reason to suppose that socialism, even at the world level, would necessarily eliminate great-power domination or guarantee the rights of smaller nations.

Plato was no doubt a reactionary thinker, bitterly opposed to the spirit of Athenian democracy. Yet the central value he places upon right leadership in a state cannot simply be brushed aside. Socialists need only recall Trotsky's fulsome praise of Lenin's genius in his *History of the Russian Revolution*; or the dominant role of such personalities as Stalin, Mao, Tito, and Castro, for good or evil, in their respective states; or the crucially innovative role now being played by Gorbachev to ask themselves whether a Marxist theory of the state even begins to own up to the importance of this element.

From Plato and Aristotle comes also a sense of the comparative forms of states and the possibility of classifying them. The most famous ranking is that of the one, the few, and the many, divided as between good and bad forms of regime. Could we do any worse in classifying capitalist and socialist regimes according to some such scale, also distinguishing good from bad forms, and even acknowledging, like Ernst Bloch, that the corruption of socialism, as in

Stalinism, can be far worse than the better forms of capitalism, such as liberal democracy?

St Augustine offers another element toward a theory of the state, his famous libido dominandi. Not sharing his theological premises regarding the fall of man or the resolution of this predicament in the City of God, one might be tempted to just shunt him aside. The term *libido*, however, has thrust itself onto our twentieth-century consciousness through quite a different door – the suitably secular Freud. And conditioned as we have become to accept both sexual and economic lusts as central drives in contemporary capitalist society, can we dismiss the lust for power? And is it limited to strictly capitalist society?

From Machiavelli, socialists may be tempted to borrow an emphasis on virtù, in turn based on the earlier Roman republican ideal. More double-edged is the Florentine's realism. Is his Cesare Borgia really the incarnation of the historically progressive forces of the time, as Gramsci saw it, his doctrine fundamentally humanistic, as Merleau-Ponty argued in a striking essay?[10] If so, his art of politics has enduring lessons for us. But this aspect of Machiavellianism comes suspiciously close to the Stalinist justification of the means by the end and can, if stretched far enough, become a defence of any and all acts committed in the name of a historically progressive doctrine by a self-proclaimed vanguard. However, Machiavellian tactics are certainly used by the enemies of socialism – one need but think of the intelligence services of the Western powers or of the destabilizing activities that powerful economic interests can direct against governments of the left (as in Allende's Chile). Can we afford to neglect the role of force and fraud – practised so stealthily by political leaders of all stripes – in human affairs?

From theorists of the absolute state, such as Bodin and Hobbes, come a number of home truths. First, there is "an absolute or perpetual power" called sovereignty which states claim to exercise. Second, this sovereign power comes to be lodged in some individual or assembly who do not easily yield it up again. Third, this Leviathan is the guardian of order, and security, not participation, is what human beings in civil society hanker after.

Subsequent centuries were to see sovereignty vested more explicitly in the people, though the institutional custodians remain an individual or assembly. Is state power any less absolute for all that, save for periods of revolutionary upheaval, which may see one form replaced by another? The theme of order or system-maintenance is dear to the hearts of rulers East and West, North and South, while the demise of the earthly Leviathan seems as far-fetched today as the Messianic tales that foresaw the righteous eating of the flesh of Leviathan and Behemoth at the banquet Jehovah was to ordain at the Last Judgment.[11]

If this is indeed the case, where is socialism to turn for some counter-balance to the absolutist version of the state? Non-democratic or anti-democratic liberal theory of the late seventeenth and eighteenth centuries may offer some answers. It is quite easy to dismiss this theory from Locke to Montesquieu to Diderot or Madison for its obsession with property, for its bourgeois restrictions on citizenship, and for its preoccupation with individual rights at the expense of the collectivity.

The liberty Montesquieu, for example, was most concerned to safeguard was the aristocratic sort of libertas dear to Cicero and other defenders of the mixed constitution in the late Roman Republic. Fear of the lower classes, of their potential invasion of the privileges and properties of their betters, justified the elaborate separation of powers and restrictions on the franchise liberal theorists advanced. There remains, none the less, more than a kernel of truth to their perception that some form of divided sovereignty was a necessary hedge to the abuse of power by such potentates as Louis x i v and Frederick of Prussia.

By focusing on institutional safeguards, liberals saw further into the political "superstructure" than the Marxist founding fathers of the following century. "We need a Montesquieu of socialism,"[12] was the cry of Polish reformers in the early 1980s, arguing for a clearer delineation between central authority, intermediary bodies and ordinary citizens than the fusion of party-state allowed. Montesquieu may have been mistaken in his reading of the English constitution, and American and French revolutionaries may have made too much of a dogma out of the formal separation of powers. However, unless we build some institutional pluralism into the political structures of socialism, we end up with the monolithic unity of Marxism-Leninism. The real loser is democracy.

But what of Marxism itself, regarding a theory both of the state and of democracy? The legacy may be imperfect, patchy, but surely it has its own strengths, compared to liberal, absolutist, medieval, or classical theories. First, and most important, of course, is the materialist reading of history, its attempt to relate political power to the balance of class forces in any particular society, to the mode of production and level of development both internally and internationally. The state is not simply a disembodied abstraction, and there is every reason to talk about the feudal state, the capitalist state, and the socialist one as well, depending on which class exercises dominant power.

Second, there is at least a glimmer of a theory of direct democracy in the writings of Max and some of his successors. The communal structures he describes eulogistically in *The Civil War in France*, what he calls "the self-government of the producers," has echoes of Rousseau and of the Greeks, welded onto the economic structure of a socialist society. Marx's caustic dismissal of the "servile statism" of the Lassalleans in *Critique of the Gotha Programme* seems pointed in a similar direction. Luxemburg, in her defence of revolutionary spontaneity, and Lenin in the most libertarian of his texts, *State and Revolution*, also imply transcendence of the ruler–ruled distinction: "Under socialism *all* will govern in turn and will soon become accustomed to no one governing."[13] That such tenets mix poorly with the theory of the vanguard party or the reality of the dictatorship of the proletariat is not a reason to ignore them.

Third, Marxism contains the seeds of a potentially crucial distinction between politics and the state. Marx, in his discussion of the Paris Commune, points to legitimate as opposed to illegitimate functions that the new communal authorities continued to perform.[14] So it was perhaps only the coercive function of the state that was meant to vanish (or greatly diminish) in a future classless society, while its economic function, for example, persisted. More telling still is the inevitable revalorization of politics in a socialist society, in which all will come to participate more actively than is the case in capitalist ones. In other words, the withering away of the (coercive) function of the state may represent not the end of the political but its new importance in all spheres of civil society. The alternative left's vision of politicization and the classical Marxist one are here the same.

These potentially positive elements in Marxism do not, however, eliminate the blind-spots and shortcomings I hinted at earlier or negate the value of classical political theory. To advance this discussion, let me at last offer definitions of the three key terms we have been looking at, before suggesting what I think the relationship among them ought to be.

(1) *The state*. The state is a network of institutions, centred in, though not limited to, executive, legislative, and judicial branches called government(s). These claim to incarnate the sovereignty formally vested in the people and bring a combination of symbolic, consensual, and coercive powers to bear on their tasks. They further reflect the intrinsic balance of class forces in any particular society

and the underlying mode of production, the level of development, and the international position of a territorially defined entity. Some individual or group of individuals exercises political leadership therein for a specific or unlimited time interval.

(2) *Democracy*. Democracy is participation by all citizens of a certain age in affairs of state, both directly, through appropriate organizations in work-place and community, and indirectly, through the choice of representatives to oversee and fill various state positions. The frequency or infrequency and openness or non-openness of this participation determine how extensive democracy in any particular society really is.

(3) *Socialism*. Socialism is collective rather than private ownership over the principal means of production. This principle has usually entailed a significant, even overwhelming, degree of state ownership, but it can no less plausibly be rooted in more decentralized structures, i.e. some form of collective self-government on the part of the producers and a non-statist version of the public sphere.

Regarding the state, we must cease to regard it as a strictly transitional phenomenon. While the nation-state per se is a relatively recent development, the state form itself (polis, empire, feudal or tribal kingdom) has been around for millennia. There is thus every reason to take it as an empirical given – it is not about to enter Engels's museum of antiquities along with the spinning-wheel and the bronze axe.

Once we do this, we must start taking its institutional structures more seriously. The "state" itself may seem to be an abstraction; there is nothing abstract about the three classical governmental powers and their extensions – the military, state economic enterprises, and institutions of socialization and legitimation. We can, of course, develop typologies of states according to their levels of development, modes of production, and so forth. But we will have to deal with concrete institutions in which leadership comes to be exercised through symbolic, consensual, or coercive means. It makes a good deal of difference which of these means is used, just as it matters enormously how responsive leadership is to the formal subject of most modern states – the citizens or people. Institutional structures thus provide the basis for a properly political form of domination which will persist as long as states continue to exist.

The problem that has preoccupied neo-Marxism in recent decades – the so-called autonomy of the state – has therefore been falsely posed. The state is more than a mirror reflection of antagonistic class forces – it itself engenders the most potent divisions, based on access or non-access to institutional sources of power. In capitalist societies there may be a reasonably high correlation between access to such power and economic domination, though there is no perfect fit, as even Marx, in his discussion of Bonapartism, seemed to recognize. In state socialism, where private ownership over the means of production has largely been abolished, the question of institutional access to power becomes all-important. Membership or non-membership in the communist party – the state party – has until now been the most important criterion, just as in traditional societies hereditary kinship or priestly unction played a determining role.

We have now returned full-scale to an age-old question – the nature of political power. We do so in a context in which activities of the state have grown immensely both in capitalist and in state socialist societies and where the economic functions of the state, even in the West, have rendered obsolete much of the old base–superstructure distinction going back to Marx's *Preface to a Critique of Political Economy*. Organized capitalism, to use Hilferding's term (cf. chapter 8), just like the statism of the East, requires new conceptions.

Our problem, as I see it, is to define for our own times a public sphere in which citizens can find a means of controlling the state and no-less powerful economic forces. If the face-to-face community of the polis is an impossibility in the large nation-state, then some lesser divisions – territorial and economic – offer the best alternative. We must seek to revive that spirit of the collectivity that led Pericles to regard the citizen "who takes no part in [public] duties not as unambitious but as useless."[15] We must do so, moreover, in a manner that preserves the familial and intermediate spheres – that does not simply collapse individuality into a manipulated collectivism.[16]

What we are really confronting is the question of democracy. How can we venture beyond the formal electoral mechanisms of liberal democracy, what Macpherson calls equilibrium democracy,[17] to a more profound type of citizen control? How, in the Western world, do we sunder democratic theory from élitist assumptions or liberal premises of individual private property? How, in the Eastern world, do we sunder it from the vanguard party and the dictatorial state?

The enemies of democracy are all around! The conditions of the 1970s and 1980s saw not only romantic conservatives but hard-nosed liberals pressing for a roll-back from the "radical" demands of the 1960s. The Trilateral Commission's theorists talked about the ungovernability of democracies: "The vitality of democracy in the 1960s produced a substantial increase in governmental activity and a substantial decrease in governmental authority ... What is in short supply in democratic societies today is not consensus on the rules of the game but a sense of purpose as to what one should achieve by playing the game."[18]

The economic crisis made the task of restoring order a lot easier. Trade unions became concerned with defending eroding wages for their members and preserving jobs, even as multinational corporations and finance capital enjoyed a field-day. Neo-conservative governments, riding a wave of taxpayer revolts, attacked the welfare state; at the same time, they proved generally hostile to the political empowerment of new social movements and to any expression of democratic sentiment inimical to undiluted market principles.[19]

Authoritarian-type thinking has not been lacking in the Soviet bloc. The suppression of the Prague Spring of 1968, of worker revolts in Gdańsk and other Baltic cities of Poland in 1970 and 1976, and of the Solidarity movement after 1981, and the arrest, harassment, and expulsion of dissidents in the Soviet Union down to the mid-1980s suggested how narrow the limits of real socialism remained. In language worthy of Creon, Soviet academicians thus defined the duties of the Soviet citizen in 1979: "Citizens of the USSR are obliged to observe the Constitution of the USSR and Soviet laws, comply with the standards of socialist conduct ... preserve and strengthen socialist property, protect the interests of the Soviet state, strengthen its power and prestige."[20] True, the tone at the moment is more promising of change than at any time since the Russian Revolution: "We wish to turn our country into a model of a highly developed state, with a society with the most advanced economy, the broadest democracy, the most humane and lofty ethics. The Politburo considers the perfection of the Soviet election system to be one of the main areas in democratizing our life. Democratization is introducing substantial correction into the relationships between those who criticize and those who are criticized."[21] But there is no guarantee of just how far the process of glasnost is likely to go or that, at a certain point, the party, faced with potential threats to its authority, will not, true to its historical tradition, repress democratic tendencies. (Recent developments throughout eastern Europe, however, suggest that some deeper mutation in the nature of the party-state may finally be under way.)

The struggle for greater democratization remains very much on the agenda for socialists today. We need more realism in this regard than the new left and its precursors showed. The question is not one of unlimited direct democracy, of non-stop participation by members of society in political affairs. That may work in periods of revolutionary insurgency – sections in the early 1790s, soviets in 1905 and 1917, Räte in 1918–19 – rare moments in a people's history. A measure of delegation and representation is inevitable in the modern state.

What is not inevitable is the alienation of political power into the hands of a chosen or self-chosen leadership with only minimal input from the citizenry as a whole. In other words, we need institutions for direct participation at all levels of society, feeding into but not swallowed up by the executive and legislative structures of the central state. Is it really beyond our political imaginations to conceive of a network of basic councils, into which the whole population would be territorially divided, each council meeting perhaps monthly? Citizens, through these councils, would in turn elect district, regional, and national councils, which would have some checking power against the activities of the state, for example, through the ability to initiate referenda. Democratically controlled structures might also come to be constituted in major economic institutions.[22]

There are problems with such a proposal if we simply try to graft it onto existing institutions. Under capitalism, private property and the unequal power flowing from it would void council democracy and worker participation in many of the same ways that corporate power now voids parliamentary-type democracy. In the words of Charles Lindblom, "The large private corporation fits oddly into democratic theory and vision. Indeed, it does not fit."[23] In Soviet-type states, party monopoly has in the past reduced such councils to transmission belts (cf. the experience of the soviets after 1917). Base-level democracy presupposes a form of socialism qualitatively different from the bureaucratic statism that has prevailed.

We thus come up against the question of how we define socialism. Socialism, in Marxist-Leninist societies, has meant overwhelming party-state control over the principal means of production. The consequence has been a near-absence of autonomy for different economic actors, be they collective farms, firms, or trade unions, and, in the process, an erosion of independence in civil society overall. What Feher, Heller, and Markus refer to as the "dictatorship over needs"[24] has come to prevail, with the party/bureaucracy defining the overt interests of the producers and authoritatively determining in what way they will be realized.

It is the coercive, top-down character of Soviet-style planning, the so-called command economy, that has also led to the host of problems such economies face today.[25] It has also earned the system such a negative reputation in the West and played directly into the hands of liberal or conservative critics of socialism, who equate it with statism – the abjuration of political, economic, and individual liberties. And, in truth, state socialism has become synonymous with the dreary collectivism of an unresponsive Leviathan, one from which the humanist ideals historically associated with socialism have long since vanished.

To counter such criticisms effectively, to make of socialism something that can regain its appeal to large currents of society, a major rethinking is called for. Not only is there no need to equate collective ownership over the means of production with state control, but there is every reason to distinguish between the type of control that can be vested in groups of workers and employees acting with a good deal of autonomy within an open and decentralized economy from that exercised over their heads by an authoritative (and authoritarian) state apparatus. Nor need socialism entail collectivization of each and every economic activity, down to small-scale agriculture and commerce. On the contrary, there must be a place for the private sphere – at least where small amounts of capital and small numbers of employees are involved – alongside the larger, co-operatively or collectively owned enterprises. In their relations with one another, moreover, enterprises in a socialist economy will engage in market-type activities. Only market socialism can begin to reconcile real autonomy in economic decision-making with democratic political principles throughout the society.

The state in the modern world, not unlike the giant corporation, lacks legitimacy in a number of important respects. It stands too far removed from the citizens it ostensibly represents. Its ethical appeal – Hegel's Sittlichkeit notwithstanding – has worn thin. It is too much the purveyor of sovereignty, the cold sovereignty of the mailed fist, and too little the embodiment of genuine community.

The tremendous attraction of socialism in the nineteenth and again the twentieth centuries was not linked to the aggrandizement of the state. Rather, it held forth the promise of a society in which solidarity and co-operation would win through over greed, in which the injustice of class oppression would give way to the rule of the immense majority of humankind, in which the yoke of state exactions – the state of aristocrats, warlords, and capitalists – would be permanently broken. It was its millenarian aspirations to a more just social order that imbued socialism and Marxism with a prophetic mission, appealing to the millions who came under its spell.

The experience of the Soviet Union, especially Stalinism, has done much to dim that appeal. Concurrently came the routinization of social democracy, its transformation into a party of social reform within the capitalist system and of a bureaucratically administered welfare state. The utopian dimension of socialism, the ethical-political remaking of society, has largely fallen by the wayside.

The question facing us is whether we can restore that dimension to it. It is not enough simply to hold out for economic transformation – collective ownership over the means of production – important though that principle remains. We must incorporate into socialism an ethical dimension that, in Kantian fashion, sees citizens as ends and not simply as means. In the political realm, this means that participation is not an afterthought but of the very essence to the organization of any future society.

We will still be faced with the state, with the ineluctable reality of political leadership, with the symbolic, consensual, and – for a long time to come – coercive features of political power. Here we are no longer innocents, dreaming of some magical transcendence of political power in terms of democracy versus the state. Rather, we must rethink our theoretical priorities in terms of socialism, democracy, and the state.

We need some of the utopian thinking that characterized the new left at its most generous, some of the energy that went into the student movement of the 1960s, into the women's, environmental, and peace movements of the 1970s and 1980s, and into the trade union movement on questions of workers' control, occupational health, and full employment. We need some of the grass-roots democracy that surfaced in the Prague Spring, in the Solidarity movement in Poland, in the more progressive wing of the Soviet dissident movement. But it is within the interstices of liberal democracy and of state socialism that an ongoing struggle for democratization will have to be waged.

The maximization of democracy is the key to the renewal of socialism's appeal. In the Soviet Union and eastern Europe, the techno-structure, the working class, and the peasantry are well aware of the economic drawbacks of over-centralization – shortages, inefficiencies, the parallel economy. This has certainly created pressure in the direction of greater democratization, to which Gorbachev's perestroïka is testament. Whatever degree of pluralism may be introduced into Soviet-type societies, however, these are not all likely to become liberal democracies in the Western mould. Rather, one may see greater autonomy for intermediary bodies like trade unions and local soviets, more intra-party and increasingly multi-party democracy as in eastern Europe today, and a broadening of individual and collective, for example, national, rights. This will be a process in which the international situation will cast a shadow, and the polit-bureaucracy only reluctantly surrender its privileges. To the degree, however, that Soviet-type societies become more open, more participatory, more market-oriented, without abjuring egalitarian objectives altogether, they cannot but provide a more positive model than has been true of state socialisms hitherto. To this degree at least, they will ease the task of developing Western models of socialism. (To put it another way, they will give Western socialists less to be ashamed of.)

In the West, we begin not with collective ownership of the means of production but with liberal democratic institutions and a more-or-less developed welfare state, albeit one under attack. We do not begin with a favourable bias toward community and collectivity – individualism pervades at the realm of ideas, especially in the English-speaking world. Economic restructuring over the past decade has coincided with the ascendancy of neo-conservative and neo-liberal ideology. Friedman and Hayek provide a less favourable terrain for socialist-type departures than the liberal and left-Keynesian credo that pervaded Western polities between 1945 and 1975.

We need, however, to have a sense of history, a sense of the inevitable alternations that take place between individualistic and collectivist, conservative and radical, moments in social development.[26] And there are good reasons why a more solidaristic set of values may yet follow on the largely egotistical, profit-maximizing ethos of the 1980s. There have been and will be many more losers than winners in the casino-type capitalism of our age. The international debt crisis, ecological catastrophes, industrial restructuring, technological unemployment, and changing demographic patterns all ensure that public-sphere solutions to the problems posed by the operation of the market-place will still be needed. At the same time, the participatory impulses that surfaced in the political movements of the past two decades bespeak a potentially large reservoir of support for greater democratization within Western polities. Greater democratization, if past practice is anything to go by, usually entails a more egalitarian set of values. And to that degree, at least, it provides a potential opening for socialist (or, more concretely, market socialist) ideas and communitarian concerns.

I do not want to gainsay the hurdles that stand in the way of such an evolution – the real staying power that capitalism as an economic credo continues to show in the West and that the party-state as a political phenomenon shows in societies like the Soviet Union or China. Realism must be the order of the day. We can reform the state – liberal democratic or Marxist-Leninist – but we cannot escape it. We can aspire to greater participation and democratic practice, but we cannot forfeit other objectives – functioning political authority, an extensive division of labour, a vibrant familial and private sphere – in the process. We can aspire to a greater measure of collective ownership over the means of production within capitalist societies and to greater equality of condition at the global level, while recognizing that efficiency, incentives, and productivity are not to be neglected and that an all-powerful state is not the only, or even the best, means to achieve egalitarian social ends. The reconciliation of socialism, democracy, and the state remains a burning political issue for the left at the end of the twentieth century.

Notes

INTRODUCTION

1 Cf. Carl Schmitt, *The Concept of the Political*, New Brunswick, N J: Rutgers University Press, 1976.
2 Examples of recent works that attempt such an aproach would include Michael Mann, *The Sources of Social Power* 1, Cambridge: Cambridge University Press, 1986, with two subsequent volumes to follow; Philip Corrigan and Derek Sayer, *The Great Arch: English State Formation as Cultural Revolution*, Basil Blackwell, 1985; and Anthony Giddens, *The Nation-State and Violence*, Cambridge: Polity Press, 1985.
3 Cf. Kenneth Dyson, *The State Tradition in Western Europe: A Study of an Institution and an Idea*, Oxford: Oxford University Press, 1980; Theda Skocpol, *States and Social Revolutions: A Comparative Analysis of France, Russia, and China*, Cambridge: Cambridge University Press, 1979.
4 For example, the Thirteenth World Congress of the International Political Science Association in Paris in 1985, which had as its official theme, "The Changing State and its Interaction with National and International Society."
5 Cf. Ralph Miliband, *The State in Capitalist Society*, London: Weidenfeld and Nicolson, 1969; Nicos Poulantzas, *State, Power, Socialism* London: New Left Books, 1979; Perry Anderson, *Lineages of the Absolutist State* London: New Left Books, 1973; Claus Offe, *Contradictions of the Welfare State*, Cambridge, Mass.: M.I.T. Press, 1985; Bob Jessop, *The Capitalist State: Marxist Theories and Methods* (Oxford: Martin Robertson, 1982).
6 See J.R. Strayer, *On the Medieval Origins of the Modern State*, Princeton: Princeton University Press, 1970; Charles Tilly, ed., *The Formation of National States in Western Europe*, Princeton: Princeton University Press, 1975; Gianfranco Poggi, *The Development of the Modern State*, Stanford: Stanford University Press, 1978; Reinhard Bendix, *Kings or People,*

Berkeley: University of California Press, 1978; Eric Nordlinger, *On the Autonomy of the Democratic State*, Cambridge, Mass.: Harvard University Press, 1981.

7 Cf. the publications of the Institute of Economic Affairs in Britain, of the American Enterprise Institute, or of the Fraser Institute in Canada and, at a more theoretical level, the writings of Friedrich von Hayek, Milton Friedman, James Buchanan, and Robert Nozick.

8 Cf. various of the articles in Ali Kazancigil, ed., *The State in Global Perspective*, Aldershot: Gower/ U N E S C O, 1986.

CHAPTER ONE

1 Plato, *The Republic*, I V– V I.

2 Neal and Ellen Wood, *Class Ideology and Ancient Political Theory: Socrates, Plato and Aristotle in Social Context* Oxford: Blackwell, 1978.

3 Aristotle, *The Politics*, I I I, xvii.

4 Ibid. V I I, ix; V I, iv; V I I– V I I I.

5 Cicero, *De Officii*, I I, xxii, cited in Claude Nicolet, *Les idées politiques à Rome sous la République*, Paris: Armand Colin, 1964, 154.

6 Cicero, *De Republica*, I I, xxiii, xxxiii.

7 "Pour Cicéron, pauvreté est synonyme de méchanceté; il ne recerche en rien les causes possibles de l'appauvrissement des masses." Nicolet, *Les idées*, 52.

8 Machiavelli, *The Discourses*, London: Routledge & Kegan Paul, 1950, I, 37.

9 J.G.A. Pocock, ed., *The Political Works of James Harrington*, Cambridge: Cambridge University Press, 1977, 183.

10 Montesquieu, *De l'esprit des lois*, X I, 6.

11 Louis Bredvold and Ralph Ross, eds., *The Philosophy of Edmund Burke*, Ann Arbor: University of Michigan Press, 1960, 210.

12 Bonald typifies this post-1789 aristocratic bias. "Dans la société politique, il n'y a de force de *conservation* que dans la profession essentiellement *conservatrice*, c'est-à-dire la noblesse." Louis Gabriel Ambroise, vicomte de Bonald, *Oeuvres complètes*, reprinted Geneva: Slatkne, 1982, I I I, 236.

13 Gaetano Mosca, *The Ruling Class*, New York: McGraw-Hill, 1939, 50, 61, 417.

14 Joseph Schumpeter, *Capitalism, Socialism, & Democracy*, 3rd edition, New York: Harper and Row, 1950.

15 Karl Marx, *The Civil War in France*, in Robert Tucker, ed., *The Marx-Engels Reader*, New York: Norton, 1972, 553.

16 Polybius, *The Histories*, I I I, Loeb Classical Library, 1923, V I, 273.

17 Cicero, *De Republica*, Loeb Classical Library, reprinted 1959, I I, xxiii.

18 Polybius, *Histories*, 309-11.

19 Machiavelli, *Discourses*, I, 2.

20 Ibid., III, 8.

21 Ibid., I, 47.

22 Ibid., I, 41.

23 Ibid., I, 44.

24 Ibid., II, 47.

25 Friederich Meinecke, *L'idée de la raison d'état dans l'histoire des temps modernes*, Genève: Librairie Droz, 1973, 36.

26 Cf. J.G.E. Pocock, *The Machiavellian Moment: Florentine Political Thought and the Atlantic Republican Tradition*, Princeton: Princeton University Press, 1975.

27 *The Political Works of Harrington*, 183.

28 Ibid., 257.

29 Montesquieu, *De l'ésprit des lois*, XI, 6.

30 Ibid., XI, 4.

31 Clinton Rossiter, ed., *The Federalist Papers*, New York: Mentor Library, 1961, LI, 323.

32 "The federal and State governments are in fact but different agents and trustees of the people" (ibid., XLVI, 294).

33 Ibid., X, 81.

34 Ibid., LXIII, 387.

35 Ibid., X, 84.

36 Thucydides, *History of the Peloponnesian War*, New York: Modern Library College edition, Crawley translation, 1951, V, 331.

37 Ibid., 333.

38 Ibid., 334.

39 Herbert Deane, "Classical and Christian Political Thought," *Political Theory*, 4 (Nov. 1973), 424.

40 St Augustine, *The City of God*, IV.

41 Machiavelli, *The Prince*, Penguin: Harmondsworth, 1961, VI, 52.

42 Ibid., XV, 91.

43 Ibid., XVII, 96.

44 Ibid., XVIII, 99.

45 Jean Bodin, *Six Books on the Republic*, cited in Henri Baudrillart, *Bodin et son temps*, Paris, 1853, réimpression Aulea, 1964, 235.

46 Bodin, book II. Cf. also the discussion in Dolf Sternberger, "Ancient Features of the Modern State," *History of European Ideas*, 5, no. 3 (1984), 225-35.

47 Bodin, in Baudrillart, *Bodin*, 270ff.

48 "Quand le chef de famille vient à sortie de la maison où il commande pour traiter et négocier avec les autres chefs de famille ... au lieu de seigneur il s'appelle citoyen qui n'est d'autre chose en propres termes,

que le franc subject tenant de la souveraineté d'autruy." I, 6, cited in Baudrillart, *Bodin*, 262.

49 Hobbes, *Leviathan*, ed. C.B. Macpherson, Harmondsworth: Penguin, 1968, chap. 13 et seq.

50 Ibid., chap. 17.

51 Ibid., chap. 18.

52 Ibid., chap. 19.

53 "And by reading of Greek and Latine authors, men from their child-hood have gotten the habit, under a false show of liberty, of favouring tumults, and of licentious controlling the actions of sovereigns ... with the efusion of so much blood, as I think I may truly say that was never any thing so deerly bought as these Western parts have bought the learning of the Greek and Latine tongues." Ibid., chap. 21, 267-8.

54 Ibid., chap. 17.

55 Hegel, *Philosophy of History*, cited in Meinecke, *L'idée*, 329.

56 Hegel, *Philosophy of Right*, trans. T.M. Knox, Oxford: Oxford University Press, 1967, 283.

57 Ibid., 288.

58 Ibid., 210.

59 Meinecke, *L'idée*, 357.

60 I have enormous respect for Charles Taylor's interpretation of Hegel's political philosophy in terms of "expressivism" and the longing to recreate the shattered unity of the *polis* (*Hegel*, Cambridge, 1975), just as I have learned much from Alexandre Kojève's subtle reading of the "master-slave" relationship in Hegel's *Phenomenology of Spirit* (*Introduction à la lecture de Hegel: Leçons sur la Phénomenologie de l'Esprit*, Paris: Gallimard, Bibliothèque des Idées, 1968). Yet their work does not, in my eyes, take away from the strongly statist tone of the later Hegel and from the openings this offers to a philosophy of order.

61 Joseph W. Bendersky, *Carl Schmitt: Theorist for the Reich*, Princeton: Princeton University Press, 1983.

62 Carl Schmitt, *Political Theology: Four Chapters on the Concept of Sovereignty*, Cambridge, Mass.: M.I.T. Press, 1985; *The Crisis of Parliamentary Democracy*, Cambridge, Mass., 1985; *The Concept of the Political*, New Brunswick, NJ, 1976.

63 Schmitt, *La notion de politique*, Paris: Calmann-Lévy, 1971, 107.

64 Schmitt, *Crisis*, 8.

65 Schmitt, *Political Theology*, 5.

66 Schmitt, *Crisis*, 37.

67 John Locke, *Two Treatises on Government*, New York: Hafner Publishing, 1969, Second Treatise, chap. 9, para. 123.

68 Ibid., chap. 13, 154.

69 Ibid., chap. 13, 151.

70 Cf. Martin Seliger, *The Liberal Politics of John Locke*, London: Allen & Unwin, 1968; John Tully, *A Discourse on Property: John Locke and His Adversaries*, Cambridge: Cambridge University Press, 1980; Richard Ashcraft, *Revolutionary Politics and Locke's Two Treatises of Government*, Princeton: Princeton University Press, 1986.

71 Locke, *Second Treatise*, chap. 11, 138.

72 Ibid., chap. 10, 187.

73 Ibid., chap. 16, 196.

74 C.B. Macpherson, *The Political Theory of Possessive Individualism*, Oxford: Oxford University Press, 1962, chap. 5; Neal Wood, *John Locke and Agrarian Capitalism*, Berkeley: University of California Press, 1984; Jeffrey Isaac, "Was John Locke a Bourgeois Theorist? A Critical Appraisal of Macpherson and Tully," *Canadian Journal of Political and Social Theory*, 11 no. 3 (1987), 107–29.

75 *Esprit des lois*, x i, 6.

76 Ibid., x i i, 1.

77 Ibid., x x– x x i i i.

78 Ibid., i i i, 3.

79 "L'esprit de modération est ce qu'on appelle la vertu dans l'aristocratie" (v, 8). "C'est dans la monarchie que l'on verra autour du prince les sujets recevoir ses rayons; c'est là que chacun, tenant, pour ainsi dire, un plus grand espace, peut exercer ces vertus qui donnent à l'âme, non pas de l'indépendance, mais de la grandeur" (v, 12).

80 Bredvold and Ross, eds., *The Philosophy of Edmund Burke*, 43.

81 Cited by Isaac Kramnick, *The Rage of Edmund Burke*, New York: Basic Books, 1977, 159.

82 *Reflections on the Revolution in France*, in Bredvold and Ross, eds., *The Philosophy of Edmund Burke*, 147.

83 *Speech to the Electors of Bristol*, in Bredvold and Ross, eds., *The Philosophy of Edmund Burke*, 147–8.

84 *Works and Correspondence*, cited in Michael Freeman, *Edmund Burke and the Critique of Political Radicalism*, Oxford: Blackwell, 1980, 126.

85 *The Philosophy of Edmund Burke*, 219.

86 *Speech at His Arrival at Bristol* and *Reflections on the Revolution in France*, in *The Philosophy of Edmund Burke*, 64, 198–9.

87 *Federalist Papers*, x, 82.

88 Ibid., x x x v, 215–16.

89 Ibid., x, 84.

90 Ibid., l x x, 423.

91 "The additional securities in republican government, to liberty, and to property, to be derived from the adoption of the plan under consideration" (ibid., l x x x v, 521).

92 Ibid., x l i v, 282.

93 Ibid., L I, 323.

94 Ibid., L X X V I I I, 469.

95 G.W.F. Hegel, *The Philosophy of Right*, no. 189, 126-7.

96 Manfred Reidel, *Between Tradition and Revolution: The Hegelian Transformation of Political Philosophy*, Cambridge: Cambridge University Press, 1984, 148.

97 For a good collection of articles on this, see Z.A. Pelczynski, ed., *The State and Civil Society: Studies in Hegel's Political Philosophy*, Cambridge: Cambridge University Press, 1984. For more recent discussion of this theme, see John Keane, ed., *Civil Society and the State*, London: Verso Press, 1988.

98 Hegel, *Philosophy of Right*, no. 260, 160.

99 Ibid., no. 278, 180. For the reference to Montesquieu, see no. 273, 176-8.

100 Ibid., 294.

101 Ibid., no. 308, 201.

102 Benjamin Constant, "De la liberté des anciens comparée à celle des modernes," in *De la liberté chez les modernes*, Paris: Pluriel, 1980. A very similar argument is made by Jacob Burckhardt some fifty years after Constant: "Human rights in antiquity, there were none"; cited in Sternberger, "Ancient Features of the Modern State," 231.

103 Constant, "De la liberté," 499.

104 Ibid., 512.

105 John Stuart Mill, *Utilitarianism, Liberty, Representative Government*, London: J.M. Dent, reprinted 1972, 107.

106 Ibid., 170.

107 Ibid., 167.

108 *Representative Government*, 226.

109 Ibid., 254.

110 Ibid., 237ff.

111 Ibid., 282.

112 Ibid., 285.

113 J.S. Mill, *Principles of Political Economy*, book V, chap. X I, "On the Grounds or Limits of the Laisser-Faire or Non-Interference Principle," ed. W.J. Ashley, reprinted New York: Augustus Kelley, 1965, 941-79.

114 *Representative Government*, 207. This is the sort of passage that Carole Pateman, *Participation and Democratic Theory*, Cambridge: Cambridge University Press, 1970, 29ff., and C.B. Macpherson, *The Life and Times of Liberal Democracy*, Oxford: Oxford University Press, 1977, 56-64, use in constructing a participatory Mill.

115 Thucydides, *History*, I I, 105.

116 *Protagoras*, in *The Dialogues of Plato*, trans. B. Jowett, 4th ed., Oxford: Clarendon Press, 1953, I, 147-8.

117 Herodotus, *The Histories*, I I I.

118 In its stronger, political sense, Gregory Vlastos has argued (*Platonic Studies*, Princeton: Princeton University Press, 1973, 181), it refers to "equality of access to political office." But I think it is useful in the present discussion to distinguish isonomía from isegoría.

119 J.D. Lewis, "Isegoria at Athens: When Did It Begin?," *Historia*, 20 (1971), 129–40.

120 Claude Massé, "Egalité," in *La démocratie grecque*, Paris, M A Editions, 1986.

121 Ibid.

122 Gerrard Winstanley, *The New Law of Righteousness*, cited in Mulford Q. Sibley, *Political Ideas and Ideologies: A History of Political Thought*, New York: Harper & Row, 1970, 368.

123 Col. Rainborough, speaking at the Putney Debate of 1647, A.S.P. Woodhouse, ed., *Puritanism and Liberty*, Chicago: University of Chicago Press, 1938, 53.

124 Jean-Jacques Rousseau, *Du contrat social*, I I, i, "Que la souveraineté est inaliénable," *Oeuvres complètes*, I I I, Paris: Pléiade, 1964, 368–9.

125 Rousseau, *Discours sur l'origine de l'inégalité*, in *Oeuvres*, 164, 178.

126 *Du contrat social*, I, ix, 367.

127 Ibid., I I I, iv, 405.

128 Ibid., I I I, xv, 430.

129 Ibid., I V, i; I I I, xviii.

130 *Projet de constitution pour la Corse*, in *Oeuvres complètes*, I I I, 901–50.

131 "A l'instant que le Peuple est légitement assemblé en corps Souverain, toute jurisdiction du Gouvernement cesse, la puissance est suspendu, et la personne du dernier Citoyen est aussi sacré et inviolable que celle du premier Magistrat, parce qu'où se trouve le Réprésenté, il n'y a plus de Réprésentants" *Du contrat social*, I I I, xiv. For discussions of the role of the sans-culottes during the French Revolution, cf. Daniel Guérin, *La lutte de classes sous la première république*, (Paris: Gallimard, 1961); Albert Soboul, *Mouvement populaire et gouvernement révolutionnaire en l'an 11: 1793–4*, Paris: Flammarion, 1973.

132 For one bit of evidence, compare the attack that neo-conservatives like Keith Joseph and Jonathan Sumpton mount against Rousseau in their essay *Equality*, London: John Murray, 1979, 8–11, arguing that Rousseau more than Marx is the source of contemporary egalitarian precepts.

133 Karl Marx "Critique of Hegel's Doctrine of the State," in L. Colletti, ed., *Early Writings*, Harmondsworth: Penguin, 1975, 87–8.

134 Ibid., 194. Compare the interesting discussion in Christopher Pierson, *Marxist Theory and Democratic Politics*, Berkeley: University of California Press, 1986, chap. 1.

135 *The Communist Manifesto*, in Tucker, ed., *The Marx-Engels Reader*, New York: Norton, 1972, 353.

136 *The Civil War in France*, in Tucker, *Reader*, 553.

137 Cf. Schumpeter, *Capitalism, Socialism, and Democracy*, chaps. X X I–
X X I I I.

138 G. Sartori, *Democratic Theory*, Detroit: Wayne State University Press,
1962, 77, 88.

139 William Kornhauser, *The Politics of Mass Society*, Glencoe: Free Press,
1959, 43.

140 W.H. Morris-Jones, "In Defence of Apathy: Some Doubts on the Duty
to Vote," *Political Studies*, 2 (1954), 37.

141 Pateman, *Participation*, 43.

142 Macpherson, *Life and Times*, 108.

143 Ibid., 100, 102–6.

144 Benjamin Barber, *Strong Democracy: Participatory Politics for a New Age*,
Berkeley: University of California Press, 1985; David Held, *Models of
Democracy*, Stanford: Stanford University Press, 1987; John Keane, *Pub-
lic Life and Late Capitalism: Towards a Socialist Theory of Democracy*, Cam-
bridge: Cambridge University Press, 1984; Jurgen Habermas, "The
Public Sphere," *New German Critique*, 1, no. 3 (1974); also *Strukturwandel
der Öffentlichkeit: Untersuchung zu einer Kategorie der bürgerliches Gesell-
schaft*, Darmstadt & Neuwield, 1962; Charles Taylor, *Philosophical
Papers*, I I, *Philosophy and the Human Sciences*, Cambridge: Cambridge
University Press, 1985.

145 Habermas, "The Public Sphere," 49.

146 Taylor, *Philosophy and the Human Sciences*, 317.

147 Cf. Andras Hegedus, *The Humanisation of Socialism: Writings of the Budapest School*, London: Allison & Busby, 1976; Vladimir Fisera, *Prague: la
révolution des conseils ouvriers: 1968–9*, Paris: Seghers, 1977; Jacek Kuron,
Solidarnósc: The Missing Link?, London: Bookmarks, 1982.

148 *The 18th Brumaire of Louis Bonaparte*, in Tucker, *The Marx-Engels Reader*,
437.

149 Thucydides, *History*, I I, 121.

CHAPTER TWO

1 W.L. Morton, "The Possibility of a Philosophy of Conservatism," in
Journal of Canadian Studies (Feb. 1970), cited in David Bell and Lorne
Tepperman, *The Roots of Disunity*, Toronto: McClelland and Stewart,
1979, 215.

2 Gad Horowitz, "Conservatism, Liberalism and Socialism in Canada:
An Interpretation," *Canadian Journal of Economics and Political Science*, 32
(May 1966), reprinted in Hugh Thorburn, ed., *Party Politics in Canada*,
Toronto: Prentice-Hall, 1985, 48.

3 Cf., for example, J.A. Corry, *The Growth of Government Activities since Con-*

federation, Study for the Rowell-Sirois Commission, Ottawa, 1940; Harold Innis, *Essays in Canadian Economic History*, Toronto, 1956, 81-2, 195, 234, 384; Hugh Aitken, "Defensive Expansionism: The State and Economic Growth in Canada," in W.T. Easterbrook and M.H. Watkins, eds., *Approaches to Canadian Economic History*, Toronto: Carleton Library, 1967, 183-221; Leo Panitch, ed., *The Canadian State*, Toronto: University of Toronto Press, 1977.

4 Edmund Burke, *Letter to the Comte de Mercy*, Aug. 1793, in *The Philosophy of Edmund Burke*, Ann Arbor: University of Michigan Press, 1960, 219.

5 Cf. the discussion in Daniel Guérin, "La révolution déjacobinisée," *Pour un marxisme libertaire*, Paris: Robert Laffont, 1969, 41-67, and in Stanislaw Ehrlich, "Pluralism and Marxism," in S. Ehrlich and G. Wootton, eds., *Three Faces of Pluralism*, Aldershot: Gower, 1980, 34-45, especially the subsection "In What Sense Were Marx, Engels and the Bolsheviks Jacobins?"

6 Marcos Kaplan, "The Theory of the State and the Third World," in Ali Kazancigil, ed., *The State in Global Perspective*, Aldershot: U N E S C O/ Gower, 1986, 287.

7 M. Arienza and C. Mallmann, "Argentina on the Road to Democracy," *International Social Science Journal*, no. 103, 37, no. 1, 1985, 45.

8 Marc Bouloiseau, *The Jacobin Republic 1792-1794*, Cambridge: Cambridge University Press, 1983, 16.

9 St-Just, *Oeuvres choisies*, Paris: Idées, 1968, 256.

10 Bouloiseau, *Republic*, 16.

11 Albert Soboul, *Mouvement populaire et gouvernement révolutionnaire en l'an 11, 1793-4*, Paris: Flammarion, 1973, 487.

12 Bouloiseau, *Republic*, 230.

13 Edmund Burke, *Reflections on the Revolution in France*, Harmondsworth: Penguin, 1969, 194.

14 Wilhelm I I at Königsberg, 25 Aug. 1910, cited in Franz Neumann, *Behemoth*, New York: Oxford University Press, 1944, 7.

15 Sir John A. Macdonald, "Speech on the Quebec Resolutions," in H.D. Forbes, ed., *Canadian Political Thought*, Toronto, Oxford University Press, 1985, 71, 77.

16 Macdonald, Confederation Debates, cited in Peter J. Smith, "The Ideological Origins of Canadian Confederation," Canadian Political Science Association *Papers*, 1985, 35. A somewhat shortened version of Smith's paper appears in *Canadian Journal of Political Science*, 20, no. 1 (March 1987).

17 Confederation Debates, cited in Smith, "Origins," 37.

18 Cited by Albert Soboul, "De l'ancien régime à la révolution: problème régional et réalités sociales," in Christian Gras and Georges Livet, eds., *Régions et régionalisme en France*, Paris: P U F, 1977, 42.

19 D'Arcy McGee, *Parliamentary Debates on the Subject of the Confederation of the British North American Provinces*, Quebec, 1865, reprinted Ottawa: King's Printer, 1951, 131. See also the discussions in W.L. White et al., *Canadian Confederation: A Decision-Making Analysis*, Toronto: Carleton Library, 1979), 73–81.

20 St-Just, *Oeuvres*, 232.

21 Ibid., 110.

22 Bouloiseau, *Republic*, 229.

23 Robespierre, cited in ibid., 31.

24 Thus P.S. Hamilton of Nova Scotia argued in 1864: "One great object to be obtained by the Union is the complete breaking down of all local prejudices, and a fusion of races, throughout the provinces"; *Union of the Colonies of British North America*, cited in Smith, 'Origins,' 26.

25 Claude Bissell, cited in Raymond Reid, ed., *The Canadian Style*, Toronto: Fitzhenry & Whiteside, 1973, 184.

26 John Strachan, cited in D.F. Wise, "God's Peculiar Peoples," in W.L. Morton, ed., *The Shield of Achilles*, Toronto: McClelland & Stewart, 1968, 54.

27 Joseph Pope, *Memoirs of Sir John A. Macdonald*, London: Edward Arnold, 1894, 335–6.

28 J.H. Coyne, "Memorial to the United Empire Loyalists," in L.F.S. Upton, ed., *The United Empire Loyalists: Men and Myths*, Toronto: Copp Clark, 1967, 138.

29 Conrad Cherry, ed., *God's New Israel: Religious Interpretations of American Destiny*, Englewood Cliffs, N J: 1971.

30 John Strachan, cited in Wise, 'Peoples,' 55.

31 Smith, 'Origins,' 25.

32 John A. Macdonald, Confederation Debates, cited in Robert A. Mackay, *The Unreformed Senate of Canada*, Carleton Library, 1963, 48.

33 Edmund Burke, *Speech on the Repeal of the Marriage Act (1781)*, in *The Philosophy of Edmund Burke*, 139.

34 "People own property primarily in order to live. It is untrue that property can be incompatible with men's subsistance"; Robespierre, cited in Bouloiseau, *Republic*, 34.

35 Bouloiseau, *Republic*, chap. 3.

36 St-Just, *Oeuvres*, 179–80.

37 Alexander Gerschenkron, "Typology of Industrial Development," in *Continuity in History and Other Essays*, Cambridge, Mass.: Belknap Press, 1968, 81.

38 Alexander Gerschenkron, *Economic Backwardness in Historical Perspective*, Cambridge, Mass: Harvard University Press, 1962, 6–7.

39 *Robert Laird Borden: His Memoirs*, I, Toronto: Macmillan, 1938, 484.

40 Ibid., II, 699.

41 *The Rowell-Sirois Report*, book 1, ed. Donald V. Smiley, Toronto: Carleton Library, 1963, 123.

42 Geoffrey K. Fry, *The Growth of Government*, London: Frank Cass, 1979, 193.

43 A.T. Peacock and J. Wiseman, *The Growth of Public Expenditure in the United Kingdom*, Princeton, 1961, 27–34. See also chap. 6 of this volume.

44 Ernest Watkins, *R.B. Bennett*, Toronto: Kingswood House, 1963, 257, 260–1.

45 Leclerc and St-Just, cited in Bouloiseau, *Republic*, 32–3.

46 Macdonald, cited by Stanley Ryerson, *Unequal Union*, Toronto: Progress Books, 1968, 365.

47 Smith, "Origins," 43.

48 Richard M. Bird, *The Growth of Government Spending in Canada*, Toronto: Canadian Tax Foundation, 1970, Appendix C, Tables 1 and 33, 239, 279.

49 Pierre Elliott Trudeau, *Federalism and the French Canadians*, Toronto: Macmillan, 1968, 193.

50 Trudeau, T V interview with Tim Raffe of the C B C on 13 Oct. 1970, cited in John Saywell, ed., *Canadian Annual Review for 1970*, Toronto: University of Toronto Press, 1971, 73.

51 Trudeau, C T V interview of 28 Dec. 1975, in John Saywell, ed., *Canadian Annual Review of Politics and Public Affairs for 1975*, Toronto: University of Toronto Press, 1976, 96–7.

52 Trudeau, House of Commons Debates, 32nd Parl., 1st sess., Vol. 1, 15 April 1980, 32–3.

53 *Globe and Mail*, 28 May 1987, A7.

54 Michael Cross, ed., *The Decline and Fall of a Good Idea: CCF-NDP Manifestoes 1932–1969*, Toronto: Hogtown Press, 1974, 22.

55 "New Party Declaration," in ibid., 39.

56 Cf. the discussion in my essay, *Parliament vs. People*, Vancouver: New Star, 1984, section 2.

57 For a lucid discussion of the extent of industrialism in late-nineteenth-century Canada and some of the long-term implications of the road we travelled down, see Gordon Laxer, "Foreign Ownership and Myths about Canadian Development," *Canadian Review of Sociology and Anthropology*, 22, no. 3 (Aug. 1985), 311–45, and his more recent *Open for Business: The Roots of Foreign Ownership in Canada*, Toronto: Oxford University Press, 1989.

CHAPTER THREE

1 Custel de Foulanges, *La cité antique*, Paris: Flammarion, 1984, 376. Cf. also Victor Ehrenberg, *The Greek State*, London: Methuen, 1969, chap. 2,

"The *polis*," and Claude Nicolet, *Le métier de citoyen dans la Rome républi-caine*, Paris: Gallimard, 1976, e.g. chap. 1, "Civitas, le citoyen et sa cité."

2 Thomas Hobbes, *Leviathan*, Harmondworth: Penguin, 1981, chaps. 4, 5, pp. 106, 116.

3 Donald Creighton, *Dominion of the North*, 2nd ed., Toronto, 1957, 304; "Dominion," *The Encyclopedia of Canada*, 11, Toronto, 1935, 223.

4 Cited by David H. Fulton, House of Commons Debates, 14 Dec., 1951, 1947.

5 See the article "Herrschaft" in *Geschictliche Grundbegriffe*, 111, Stuttgart: Klett-Cotta, 1982, 10 (a multi-volumed German lexicon of political terms, tracing etymology and usage through many centuries of German and European practice).

6 Cited by John S. Ewart, *The Kingdom of Canada*, Toronto, 1908, 28.

7 Ibid., 27.

8 For example, *Report of the Minister of Agriculture for the Dominion of Canada for the Year ended March 31, 1949*, Ottawa, 1949, or the description of the *Canada Yearbook for 1948–9* as "The Official Statistical Annual of the Resources, History, Institutions, and Social and Economic Conditions of the Dominion of Canada," Ottawa, 1949.

9 Adam Shortt and Arthur Doughty, *Canada and Its Provinces*, XXIII, Edinburgh, 1917, Index, 75–8.

10 Sir Robert Borden, *Canada in the Commonwealth*, Oxford, 1929.

11 Robert MacKay, "Dominion of Canada," in "Government," *Encyclopedia of the Social Sciences*, VII, New York: Macmillan, 1932, 27–9.

12 Donald Creighton, *Dominion of the North*, Boston: Houghton Mifflin, 1944; Alexander Brady, *Democracy in the Dominions: A Comparative Study in Institutions*, Toronto: University of Toronto Press, 1947.

13 *Imperial Conference 1911*, London, 5, 19.

14 "Address at Queen's University," 18 Aug. 1938, in *The Public Papers and Addresses of Franklin D. Roosevelt, 1938*, New York: Macmillan, 1941, 493.

15 Cited by Louis St Laurent, House of Commons Debates, 21 Nov. 1951, 1228.

16 Bona Arsenault, House of Commons Debates, 27 Apr. 1948, 3352.

17 Phileas Coté, House of Commons Debates, 14 Feb. 1951, 460.

18 Tellingly, the one francophone Tory MP, Leon Balcer, who spoke up in these debates supported the dropping of the term *dominion* which, quoting Funk and Wagnells, he associated with "obedience, servitude, slavery, subjection, subjugation, submission"; House of Commons Debates, 14 Dec. 1951, 1975.

19 J.H. Blackmore, House of Commons Debates, 25 June 1951, 4662.

20 J.M. Macdonnell, House of Commons Debates, 29 June 1951, 4954.

21 Hansard, 14 Dec. 1951, 1927–47; 6 March 1952, 163–70; 4 July, 9 Aug. 1956.

22 The only fleeting exception I can find is Eugene Forsey, who, in a short entry to *The Canadian Encyclopedia*, 1, Edmonton: Hurtig, 1985, 504, persists in arguing that the term *Dominion* has not been constitutionally abolished and, by implication, still applies to the federal government, Parliament, and to Canada as a whole. But then there are still pretenders to the throne of France.

23 Jean-Charles Bonenfant, "Les cadres politiques," in Guy Sylvestre, ed., *Structures sociales du Canada français*, Quebec: Laval, 1966, 69.

24 J.A. Macdonald, *Parliamentary Debates on the Subject of the Confederation of the British North American Provinces*, Ottawa: King's Printer, reprinted 1951, 25.

25 R.C. Brown and Margaret Prang, eds., *Confederation to 1949: Selected Documents*, Scarborough: Prentice-Hall, 1966, 23.

26 Ibid., 91.

27 Ibid., 154.

28 The text is reproduced in H.D. Forbes, ed., *Canadian Political Thought*, Toronto: Oxford, 1985, 38–42.

29 *Parliamentary Debates on the Subject of Confederation of the British North American Provinces*, Brown, 85; McGee, 143; Scoble, 906.

30 Ibid., Mackenzie, 425.

31 Ibid., Scoble, 907.

32 Ibid., 97, 100.

33 Ibid., 27.

34 "The duties, powers, and functions of the Secretary of State of Canada extend to and include all matters over which the Parliament of Canada has jurisdiction, not by law assigned to any other department, branch or agency of the Government of Canada, relating to: citizenship, elections, State ceremonial, the conduct of State correspondence, and the custody of State records and documents"; *Canada Yearbook, 1967*, Ottawa: Queen's Printer, 1967, 139.

35 This was first attached to the office of the Secretary of State (1909), came under the direct supervision of the prime minister in 1912, and only in the aftermath of the Second World War was given a full-time minister of its own. F.W. Soward, "Canada's Growth in External Status," *Canada Year Book, 1945*, 75.

36 Statutes of Canada, 1890, 68(1).

37 Cited in Douglas Owram, *The Government Generation: Canadian Intellectuals and the State 1900–1945*, Toronto: University of Toronto Press, 1986, 38–9.

38 Alric Barthe, *Laurier on the Platform, 1890*, from *Speeches on the Address (1871), the Quebec Ministerial Crisis of 1871, Dual Representation, Political Liberalism, the Jesuit Estate Bill (1889)*, 90, 86, 15, 16, 76, 523.

39 In Forbes, *Canadian Political Thought*, 184, 186.

40 Cited in Owram, *Generation*, 75–6.
41 House of Commons Debates, 1917, 2438.
42 Ibid., 2558.
43 Cited in Owram, *Generation*, 97.
44 Brig.-Gen. W.A. Griesbach, House of Commons Debates, 8 Sept. 1919, 2nd session, 94.
45 *B.C. Federationist*, 6 June 1919.
46 "The State," *New Democracy*, Hamilton, 10 July 1919.
47 Brown and Prang, *Confederation*, 86.
48 Frank Underhill, cited in Owram, *Generation*, 172–3.
49 Edgar McInnes, cited in ibid., 163.
50 Spry's 1932 comments are cited in, among other places, Ramsay Cook, *Canada, Quebec and the Uses of Nationalism*, Toronto: McClelland & Stewart, 1986, 121.
51 Cf. *Essays in Canadian Economic History*, Toronto: University of Toronto Press, 1956, 84, 306; also *Political Economy in the Modern State*, Toronto, 1946. In Innis's essays, nonetheless, the term *government* is used more frequently than 'state.'
52 Vincent Massey, Introduction to *The Liberal Way*, Toronto, 1933, cited in Owram, *Generation*, 189.
53 *Social Planning for Canada*, Toronto, 1935, chaps. 10, 11, 16, 17.
54 Brown and Prang, *Confederation*, 244. The same broadcasts, however, speak of "Government regulation" and "Government intervention."
55 Cited in Gérard Bergeron, *Pratique de l'état au Québec*, Montreal, Québec/Amérique, 1984, 48.
56 Maximilen Caron, "La province du Québec est-elle un Etat?," *Actualité Economique*, May 1938, 131.
57 "Etat," *Le Robert: Dictionnaire alphabétique et analogique de la langue française*, tome 2, Paris, 1977, 665.
58 Ibid.
59 "State: The Concept," *International Encyclopedia of the Social Sciences*, x v, Macmillan: Free Press, 1968, 150.
60 See Charter of the United Nations in *Yearbook of the United Nations*, 29 (1978), 1096–1109, articles 2, 3, 9, 11, and 32 for uses of 'state'; for more recent examples, see *United Nations Disarmament Yearbook 1985*, 9, 20ff. and 82, for terms such as "member state" and "nuclear-weapons state."
61 House of Commons Debates, 20 March 1945, 29.
62 House of Commons Debates, 1946, 516.
63 House of Commons Debates, 1964, 4326.
64 Compare the statement appearing opposite the opening inside page of all Fraser Institute publications referring to "government control" and "government intervention" – for example, opening inside page, Kristian S. Palda, *Industrial Innovation*, Vancouver: Fraser Institute, 1984.

65 Bonenfant, 'Les cadres,' 68–9.

66 Province de Québec, Commission royale d'enquête sur les problèmes constitutionnels, Annexe 1, 1955–6, 17ff. I thank James Ian Gow of the Université de Montréal for bringing to my attention this and a number of other Quebec documents of the 1950s and early 1960s.

67 *Lesage s'engage*, Montreal: Les Editions politiques du Québec, 1959, 113.

68 Guy Bourassa, "La crainte de l'Etat," in Institut Canadien des Affaires Publiques, *Le rôle de l'État*, Montreal, 1962, 109.

69 Pierre Dansereau, "Conscience de l'État," epilogue, in ibid., 168.

70 Gérard Fortin, "Transformations des structures du pouvoir," in *Le pouvoir dans la société canadienne-française*, Quebec: P . U . L ., 1966.

71 Cited in J.-J. Simard, *La longue marche des technocrates*, Montreal: Albert St. Martin, 179, 32.

72 Hubert Guindon, "Le modernisation du Québec et la légitimité de l'État canadien," *Recherches sociographiques*, 18 no. 3, 1977, 337–66; Louis Maheu, "Pouvoir et société au Québec: le problème de l'état et les appareils d'état," in A C S A L F, *La transformation du pouvoir au Québec*, Montreal: Albert St. Martin, 1980, 17–26; Réjean Pelletier et Gérard Bergeron, *L'état du Québec en devenir*, Montreal, 1980; Nicole Laurin-Frenette, *Production de l'état et formes de la nation*, Montreal: Nouvelle Optique, 1978; P.-A. Linteau et al., *Histoire du Québec contemporain: Le Québec depuis 1930*, Montreal: Boréal, 1986, 430, 431, 439, 625.

73 Bonenfant, "Les cadres," 68–9.

74 Daniel Johnson, *Egalité ou Indépendance*, Montreal, 1965, concluding chapter.

75 *PQ. Le Programme 1975*, cited in André Bernard, *What Does Quebec Want?*, Toronto: Lorimer, 1978, 109–10.

76 Government of Quebec, Editeur Officiel du Québec, *Quebec-Canada: A New Deal*, 1979, 54.

77 Jacques Brossard, *L'accession à la souveraineté et le cas du Québec*, Montreal: Presses Universitaires de Montréal, 1971, part 2, "La succession de l'état," "la succession de l'état sur le plan international," "la succession de l'état sur le plan interne," 387–627.

78 Pierre Elliott Trudeau, *Federalism and the French Canadians*, Toronto: Macmillan, 1968, 191.

79 See, for example, *Advances in Politics*, and *An Appeal for Reason in Politics*, reprinted in Forbes, *Canadian Political Thought*, 326–48, or Trudeau's address of 5 Nov. 1980, cited in David Milne, *Tug of War: Ottawa and the Provinces Under Trudeau and Mulroney*, Toronto: Lorimer, 1986, 40; also in the same source, 35.

80 N A T O, *Facts and Figures*, 3rd ed., Brussels, 1970, Appendix 4; O T A N, *Documentation*, Brussels, 1971, Annexe 4.

81 For example, Pierre Fournier, *Les sociétés d'état et les objectifs économiques*

du Québec; une évaluation préliminaire, Quebec: Editeur Officiel du Québec, Ministère des Communications, 1979; Rapport du comité sur la privatisation des sociétés d'état, *De la révolution tranquille à l'an deux mille*, Présenté à Pierre Fortier, Ministre délégué à la privatisation, Québec, 1986.

82　Alexander Brady, "The State and Economic Life," in George W. Brown, ed., *Canada*, Berkeley: University of California Press, 1950, 353–71; Hugh Aitken, "Defensive Expansionism: The State and Economic Growth in Canada," in W.T. Easterbrook and M.H. Watkins, eds., *Approaches to Canadian Economic History*, Toronto: Carleton Library, 1967, 183–221.

83　For example, R. MacGregor Dawson, *The Government of Canada*, Toronto: University of Toronto Press, 1947, and subsequent editions; John A. Corry and J.E. Hodgetts, *Democratic Government and Politics*, Toronto: University of Toronto Press; John Porter, *The Vertical Mosaic*, Toronto: University of Toronto Press, 1965, with its very frequent references to 'government' and exceedingly rare ones to 'state.'

84　Two recent examples of its uses are Keith Banting, *The Welfare State and Canadian Federalism*, Montreal: McGill-Queen's Press, 1982; A. Moscovitch and G. Drover, "Social Expenditures and the Welfare State: The Canadian Experience in Historical Perspective," in Allan Moscovitch and Jim Albert, eds., *The Benevolent State: The Growth of Welfare in Canada*, Toronto: Garamond Press, 1987, 13–43, though the writings of Tawney or Titmuss had reached Canada long before the 1980s.

85　Cf. the near-absence of the term *state* in Michael Oliver, ed., *Social Purpose for Canada*, Toronto: University of Toronto Press, 1961, e.g. Jack Weldon's essay, "Economics of Social Democracy."

86　Leo Panitch, ed. *The Canadian State: Political Economy and Political Power*, Toronto: University of Toronto Press, 1977.

87　Examples include John Richards and Larry Pratt, *Prairie Capitalism: Power and Influence in the New West*, Toronto: McClelland and Stewart, 1979; Denis Olsen, *The State Elite*, Toronto: McClelland & Stewart, 1980; Allan Tupper and G. Bruce Doern, eds., *Public Corporations and Public Policy in Canada*, Montreal: Institute for Research on Public Policy, 1981, chapters by Tupper and Doern, Pratt, Laux and Molot, Tupper, and Stevenson; J.K. Laux and M.A. Molot, *State Capitalism: Public Enterprise in Canada*, Ithaca, N Y: Cornell University Press, 1987.

88　Tom Traves, *The State and Enterprise: Canadian Manufacturers and the Federal Government, 1917–1931*, Toronto: University of Toronto Press, 1979, no. 1 in the series; Paul Craven, *An Impartial Umpire: Industrial Relations and the Canadian State 1900–1911*, Toronto: University of Toronto Press, 1980, no. 3; Melissa Clark-Jones, *A Staple State: Canadian Industrial Resources in Cold War*, Toronto: University of Toronto Press, 1987, no. 10.

89 H.V. Nelles, *The Politics of Development*, Toronto: Macmillan, 1974, introduction, viii, also chap. 12.

90 Cf. James Eayrs, "The Military Policies of Contemporary Canada: Principles, Policies and Prospects," in Robert Leach, ed., *Contemporary Canada*, Durham, N C: Duke University Press, 1967, 225; Kim Nossal, "Analyzing the Domestic Sources of Canadian Foreign Policy," *International Journal*, 39 (1983–4), 1–22; John Kirton and Blair Dimock, "In Canada ... foreign policy remains the preserve of the state and its constitutionally embedded competitors, Parliament and the provinces, rather than of actors within society itself," cited by Tom Keating, "The State, the Public, and the Making of Canadian Foreign Policy," in Robert Jackson et al., eds., *Contemporary Canadian Politics*, Toronto: Prentice-Hall, 1987, 365.

91 Cf. O.P. Dwivedi, ed., *The Administrative State in Canada: Essays in Honour of J.E. Hodgetts*, Toronto: University of Toronto Press, 1982; Marsha Chandler, "The Politics of Public Enterprise," in J. Robert Prichard, ed., *Crown Corporations in Canada: The Calculus of Instrument Choice*, Toronto: Ontario Economic Council, Butterworths, 1983, subsection, "Explanations of State Behaviour," 186–90; John Langford, "Privatization: A Political Analysis," in W.T. Stanbury and Thomas E. Kierans, eds., *Papers on Privatization*, Montreal: Institute for Research on Public Policy, 1985, 60, 70, 72.

92 Cf. Donald Smiley, "Federal States and Federal Societies with Special Reference to Canada," *International Political Science Review*, 5 (1984), 443–54; Donald Smiley and Ronald Watts, *Intrastate Federalism in Canada*, study for Royal Commission on the Economic Union and Development Prospects for Canada, vol. 39, Toronto: University of Toronto Press, 1986.

93 Stanley G. French, ed., *Philosophers Look at Canadian Confederation*, Canadian Philosophical Association, Montreal, 1979, with contributions such as "Why Do Nations Have to Become States?," "Nation, State, and Consent," "Nation, State, and History," "Nation, State, Society, and Self-Preservation."

94 Douglas V. Verney, *Three Civilizations, Two Cultures, One State: Canada's Political Traditions*, Durham, N C: Duke University Press, 1986, 391–404.

95 Keith Banting, ed., *State and Society in the Modern Era*, studies for Royal Commission on the Economic Union and Development Prospects for Canada, vols. 31–2, Toronto: University of Toronto Press, 1986.

96 Let me list a number of recent references to "state" by other Canadian social scientists or historians: Anthony Scott, "The State Property: Water Rights in Western Canada," in Duncan Cameron, ed., *Explorations in Canadian Economic History*, Ottawa: University of Ottawa Press, 1985; W.T. Stanbury, "Restraining the State: The Role of Deregula-

tion," in Peter Aucoin, ed., *The Politics and Management of Restraint in Government*, Institute for Research on Public Policy, 1981, 145-60; Milne, *Tug of War*, 28, 35, 40, 229, 237; Michael Bliss, "Rich by Nature, Poor by Policy: The State and Economic Life in Canada," in R.K. Carty and W.P. Ward, eds., *Entering the Eighties*, Toronto: Oxford University Press, 1980; Roger Gibbins, *Conflict and Unity: An Introduction to Canadian Political Life*, Methuen, 1985, chap. 7, "Intergovernmental Relations and the Canadian Federal State."

97 *Canada Year Book 1985*, Ottawa: Statistics Canada, 1985, 600, 603.

98 Statutes of Canada, 1984, 615-6, 2(*a-b*).

99 Statutes of Canada, 1984, Articles I, I I(1), I V(2a).

100 *Report of the Royal Commission on the Economic Union and Development Prospects for Canada*, Ottawa, 1985, I, chap. 1; II, chap. 14; III, chap. 23.

101 "[Section 251] asserts that the woman's capacity to reproduce is to be subject not to her own control, but to that of the state ... The state here is endorsing one conscientiously held view at the expense of another ... The view of the fetus supports a permissive approach to abortion in the early stages, where the woman's autonomy would be absolute, and a restrictive approach in the later stages, where the state's interest in protecting the fetus would justify its prescribing conditions"; Mme Justice Bertha Wilson, cited in *Maclean's*, 8 Feb. 1988, 11.

102 I have not attempted to trace this here, but it is my strong suspicion that increased recourse to the term *state* in English Canada from the late 1960s on was, in part, a function of the invocation of 'état,' with its overtones of sovereignty, by Quebec nationalists and indépendantistes.

103 I have sketched such an argument for direct democracy in my essay, *Parliament vs. People*, Vancouver: New Star Books, 1984, chaps. 8-9. Cf. also chapter 5 in this volume.

CHAPTER FOUR

When this chapter appeared in the *Canadian Journal of Political Science*, 20 no. 1 (March 1987), 97-115, it was accompanied by comments by Janet Ajzenstat and Rod Preece as well as a reply by the author (117-29).

1 Montesquieu, *De l'esprit de lois*, X I, 8, in *Oeuvres complètes*, I I, Paris: Pléiade, 1958, 409.

2 Frank Underhill, *In Search of Canadian Liberalism*, Toronto: Macmillan, 1960, 6-7.

3 Gad Horowitz, "Conservatism, Liberalism and Socialism in Canada:

An Interpretation," *Canadian Journal of Economics and Political Science*, 32 (1966), 143–71.

4 Reg Whitaker, "Images of the State in Canada," in Leo Panitch, ed., *The Canadian State*, Toronto: University of Toronto Press, 1977, 28–68, especially 42, 45; Dennis Smith, *Bleeding Hearts ... Bleeding Country*, Edmonton: Hurtig, 1971, especially 84, 88.

5 Rod Preece, "The Political Wisdom of Sir John A. Macdonald," *Canadian Journal of Political Science* (1984), 459–86.

6 This is reflected in the short essay by Charles de Koninck, "La philosophie au Canada de langue française," Royal Commission Studies (Massey Commission), Ottawa, 1951, 135–44.

7 Examples of the Marxist approach include Gilles Bourque and Anne Legaré, *Le Québec: la question nationale*, Paris: F. Maspero, 1979; sections of Denis Monière, *Ideologies in Quebec: The Historical Development*, Toronto: University of Toronto Press, 1981; and many of the articles in Alain G. Gagnon, ed., *Quebec: State and Society*, Toronto: Methuen, 1984.

8 *The Federalist Papers*, New York: Mentor, 1961, No. 47, 301–3.

9 *Les constitutions de la France depuis 1789*, Paris: Garnier-Flammarion, 1970, 35.

10 F.T.H. Fletcher, *Montesquieu and English Politics (1750–1800)*, London: Edward Arnold, 1939, 119–20, 127, 132.

11 M.J.C. Vile, *Constitutionalism and the Separation of Powers*, Oxford: Clarendon Press, 1967, 102.

12 Edmund Burke, *Appeal from the New Whigs to the Old*, cited in C.P. Courtney, *Montesquieu and Burke*, Oxford: Basil Blackwell, 1963, 165.

13 Polybius, *The Histories*, v i. See also Cicero, *De res publica*.

14 "La liberté politique ne se trouve que dans les gouvernements modérés" *De l'esprit des lois*, x i, 4; "moi qui crois que l'excès même de la raison n'est pas toujours désirable, et que les hommes s'accommodent presque toujours mieux des milieux que des extrémités" (ibid., x i, 6).

15 Ibid., x i, 6, 397.

16 Ibid., x i, 6, 400.

17 Ibid., x i, 6, 401.

18 Ibid., x i, 6, 405.

19 Vile, *Constitutionalism*, 80.

20 *De l'esprit des lois*, x i, 6, and again x i x, 27.

21 Isaac Kramnick, *The Rage of Edmund Burke*, New York: Basic Books, 1977: "Tocqueville's fears and that of latter-day critics of mass society were already expressed by Burke in his lament that "all the indirect restraints which mitigate despotism are removed." The intellectual source for Burke and Tocqueville, and for these modern writers as well, is, of course, Montesquieu" (201, n 77).

22 Vile, *Constitutionalism*, 96.

23 *De l'esprit des lois*, x1, 6, 401.

24 Ibid., v111, 3, 352.

25 Cf. Harold Innis, *Essays in Canadian Economic History*, Toronto: University of Toronto Press, 1956, 383-5; Seymour Martin Lipset, "Revolution and Counterrevolution: The United States and Canada," in *Revolution and Counterrevolution* New York: Anchor Books, 1968, 37-75.

26 Kaspar Naegele, "Canadian Society: Some Reflections," cited in Lipset, "Revolution and Counterrevolution," 43.

27 John Farthing, *Freedom Wears a Crown*, Toronto: Kingswood House, 1957; Donald Creighton, "Preserving the Peaceable Kingdom," in *The Passionate Observer: Selected Writings*, Toronto: McClelland and Stewart, 1980: "Our Canadian traditions, which we derive from Great Britain, are unique on the continents of North and South America. We have stood for historical continuity rather than revolution, for monarchy rather than republicanism" (42).

28 G.E. Carter, Confederation Debates, as cited in Robert A. Mackay, *The Unreformed Senate of Canada*, Ottawa: Carleton Library, 1963, 47.

29 D'Arcy McGee, Confederation Debates, as cited in ibid., 49.

30 John A. Macdonald, Confederation Debates, cited in ibid., 48.

31 Letter from Macdonald to Lord Knutsford, 1889, cited in Joseph Pope, *Memoirs of the Right Honourable Sir John A. Macdonald*, London: Edward Arnold, 1894, 236.

32 Ibid., 247.

33 Pope's *Documents*, cited in Mackay, *The Unreformed Senate*, 47-8.

34 Norman Ward, *The Canadian House of Commons: Representation*, Toronto: University of Toronto Press, 1950, 212.

35 Ibid., 216.

36 Blackstone writes: "To exclude such persons as are in so mean a situation that they are esteemed to have no will of their own"; *Commentaries on the Laws of England*, cited in Robert Shackleton, *Montesquieu: A Critical Biography*, Oxford: Oxford University Press, 1961, 290, n1.

37 James Bryce, *Modern Democracies*, 1, London: Macmillan, 1921, 501-2, cited in Lipset, "Revolution and Counterrevolution," 46.

38 Pope, *Memoirs of Sir John A. Macdonald*, 241.

39 Ibid., 242.

40 L.J. Lemieux, *The Governors General of Canada 1608-1931*, London: Lake and Bell, n.d.

41 Alpheus Todd, *Parliamentary Government in the British Colonies*, Boston: Little, Brown, 1880, 583.

42 Pope, *Memoirs of Sir John A. Macdonald*, 237.

43 Ibid., 236.

44 Arno Mayer, *The Persistence of the Old Regime*, New York: Pantheon Books, 1981.
45 See, for example, Frank R. Scott, *Essays on the Constitution: Aspects of Canadian Law and Politics*, Toronto: University of Toronto Press, 1977, for a critique of the Judicial Committee's decentralizing role, and Alan Cairns, "The Judicial Committee and Its Critics," *Canadian Journal of Political Science*, 4 (1971), 301-45, for a defence.
46 Mackay, *The Unreformed Senate of Canada*, 95. Mackay adds that such bills constituted 2.4 per cent of all government bills brought up during this period.
47 Ibid., 138.
48 Ibid., 124-5.
49 Ibid., 135-6.
50 *De l'esprit des lois*, x1, 6, 401.
51 Mackay, *The Unreformed Senate*, 62.
52 *De l'esprit des lois*, x1, 6, 400.
53 Ibid., x1, 4, 395.
54 Cartier, Confederation Debates, cited in Mackay, *The Unreformed Senate*, 48.
55 *The Federalist Papers*, x, l1.
56 Farthing, *Freedom Wears a Crown*, 49, 159.
57 Pierre E. Trudeau, *Federalism and the French Canadians*, Toronto: Macmillan, 1968, 197.
58 Report of the Royal Commission on the Economic Union and Development Prospects for Canada (Macdonald Report), 1, Ottawa, 1985, 20.
59 British Columbia Law Reports, 64, Re b.c. Government Employees' Union, 27 June 1985, Chief Justice N. Nemetz, 117.
60 "Nous avons choisi de proposer aux Québécois un régime de type présidentiel ... A notre avis, il serait donc souhaitable de revenir plutôt au régime présidentiel "classique," où l'on élit séparément un chef de l'Etat qui est en même temps responsable du pouvoir exécutif et une Assemblée Nationale libre de toute attache ministérielle dans l'exercice de ses fonctions législatives et budgétaires" (Parti québécois, *Quand nous serons vraiment chez nous* [1972], 29-30).
61 Macdonald Report, 111, Ottawa, 1985, 87-95.

CHAPTER FIVE

1 John A. Macdonald, *Parliamentary Debates on the Subject of the Confederation of the British North American Provinces*, Ottawa: King's Printer, reprinted 1951, 1004, 1007.
2 R.C. Henders, "Presidential Address to the Manitoba Grain Growers Association, 1911," cited in David Laycock, "Populism and Democratic

Thought in the Canadian Prairies, 1919-1945," P H D thesis, University of Toronto, 1985, 90.

3 *Speech to the Electors of Bristol,* in *The Philosophy of Edmund Burke,* Ann Arbor: University of Michigan Press, 1960, 147-8.

4 Issac Kramnick, *The Rage of Edmund Burke,* New York: Basic Books, 1977, 123-4.

5 Jean-Jacques Rousseau, *Du contrat social,* I I I, 15, in *Oeuvres complètes,* I I I, 1964, 429-30, Cranston translation, *The Social Contract,* Harmondsworth: Penguin, 1968.

6 Michael Freeman, *Edmund Burke and the Critique of Political Radicalism,* Chicago: University of Chicago Press, 1980, 216.

7 Though writers like Jacob Talmon, *The Origins of Totalitarian Democracy,* New York, 1960, thinking of Robespierre and the Jacobins, have stressed the potentially dictatorial strains in Rousseau's vision, I sympathize with James Miller's attempt to link Rousseau "with the modern tradition of direct democratic action" – *Rousseau: Dreamer of Democracy,* New Haven: Yale University Press, 1984, 203ff. and 257 n10.

8 Edmund Burke, *Works and Correspondence,* v I, London: Rivington, 1852, cited in Freeman, *Edmund Burke,* 108.

9 Ibid., I I I, cited in Freeman, *Burke,* 127.

10 Ibid., I, cited in Freeman, *Burke,* 126.

11 Rousseau, *The Social Contract,* I I I, 14.

12 Ibid., I I I, 18.

13 For some examples, see Margaret Canovan, *Populism,* New York: Harcourt, Brace & Jovanovich, 1981, chap. 5, "Populist Democracy in Theory and Practice"; Laura Tallian, *Direct Democracy: An Historical Analysis of the Initiative, Referendum & Recall Process,* Los Angeles, 1977; David Butler and Austin Ranney, eds., *Referendums: A Comparative Study of Practice and Theory,* Washington: American Enterprise, 1978; Hans Huber, *How Switzerland Is Governed,* 3rd ed., Zurich, 1974.

14 Frank H. Underhill, "Some Reflections on the Liberal Tradition in Canada," reprinted in H.D. Forbes, *Canadian Political Thought,* Toronto: Oxford University Press, 1985, 234.

15 Alexander Brady, *Democracy in the Dominions,* Toronto: University of Toronto Press, 1952, 67.

16 Alex Campbell and Alexander Morris, *Parliamentary Debates on the Subject of Confederation,* 293, 440-1.

17 Ibid., 77.

18 Ibid., 914.

19 Macdonald Papers, 8 Oct. 1866, cited in Chester Martin, *Foundations of Canadian Nationhood,* Toronto: University of Toronto Press, 1955, 255.

20 Henri Taschereau, *Parliamentary Debates,* 874.

21 M.C. Cameron, ibid., 975.

22 *Parliamentary Debates*, 39.

23 Ibid., 59, 62.

24 Ibid., 146.

25 League for Social Reconstruction, *Social Planning for Canada*, Toronto, 1935, 502–3.

26 His Honour A.E. Richards, Appeal Court of Manitoba, 1916, cited in W.L. Morton, "Direct Legislation and the Origins of the Progressive Movement," *Canadian Historical Review*, 25 (Sept. 1944), 287.

27 *Parliamentary Debates*, 1005.

28 Ulric Barthe, *Laurier on the Platform 1871–1890*, 1890, "On Political Liberalism," 59.

29 Joseph Schumpeter, *Capitalism, Socialism and Democracy*, New York: Harper and Row, 1950. For good recent discussions of the competitive-élite model, see C.B. Macpherson, *The Life and Times of Liberal Democracy*, Oxford: Oxford University Press, chap. 4, and David Held, *Models of Democracy*, Palo Alto: Stanford University Press, 1987, chap. 5.

30 Mackenzie King's version of the "Constitutional Crisis," reprinted from *Maclean's*, 1 Sept. 1926, in R.C. Brown and Margaret Prang, eds., *Confederation to 1949*, Toronto: Prentice-Hall, 1966, 198.

31 Ibid., 199.

32 Walter Young, *The Anatomy of a Party: The National CCF*, Toronto: University of Toronto Press, 1969, 235.

33 P.E. Trudeau, "Advances in Politics," an article dating from 1958, in Forbes, *Canadian Political Thought*, 327.

34 Trudeau's television address of 16 Oct. 1970, following the proclamation of the War Measures Act, cited in Dennis Smith, *Bleeding Hearts ... Bleeding Country*, Edmonton: Hurtig, 1971, 87. Smith writes, regarding Trudeau: "Political authority, for the Prime Minister, is granted essentially through the electoral system ... Any possible acts the government might undertake were ... justified in advance by the party's victory in the general election" (ibid., 87).

35 See Brown and Prang, *Confederation to 1949*, 175.

36 W.F. Cockshutt, House of Commons Debates, Ottawa, 1917, 2601.

37 Ibid., A.C. MacDonell, 2849.

38 Ibid., Hon. C.J. Doherty, Minister of Justice, 3030.

39 Cited in Doug Owram, *The Government Generation: Canadian Intellectuals and the State 1900–45*, Toronto: University of Toronto Press, 1986, 44.

40 "The Phantom Public," *Canadian Forum*, April 1926, cited in ibid., 121.

41 R. MacGregor Dawson, *The Government of Canada*, Toronto: University of Toronto Press, 1947, and subsequent editions, chap. 1, "Representative and Responsible Government"; J.A. Corry and J.E. Hodgetts, *Democratic Government and Politics*, Toronto: University of Toronto Press; J.R. Mallory, *The Structure of Canadian Government*, Toronto: Macmillan, 1971,

chaps. 1, 6, 7; Robert Jackson et al., *Politics in Canada: Culture, Institutions, Behaviour and Public Policy*, Toronto: Prentice-Hall, 1986.

42 André Bernard, *La politique au Canada et au Québec*, Sillery: Presses de l'Université du Québec, 1982, 428.

43 A.O. Hirschman, *Shifting Involvements: Private Interest and Public Action*, Princeton, NJ: Princeton University Press, 1982, 112, 117.

44 Hans Kelsen, *General Theory of Law and the State*, cited in L. Colletti, *From Rousseau to Lenin*, London: New Left Books, 1972.

45 Rousseau, *The Social Contract*, III, 15.

46 See some of the references cited in note 13 above, as well as Jane Mansbridge, *Beyond Adversary Democracy*, New York: Basic Books, 1980.

47 Paul F. Sharp, *The Agrarian Revolt in Western Canada: A Survey Showing American Parallels*, Minneapolis: University of Minnesota Press, 1948, 20.

48 Ibid., 55.

49 Laycock, *Populism*, 191.

50 John L. Kennedy, addressing the 1909 convention of the Manitoba Grain Growers, cited in Morton, op. cit., 284.

51 Morton, "Direct Legislation," 285.

52 Henry Wise Wood, "In Defence of Group Politics," *Canadian Forum*, Dec. 1922, reprinted in J.L. Granatstein and Peter Stevens, eds., *Forum: 1920-1970*, Toronto, 1975, 20.

53 William Irvine, *The Farmer in Politics*, 152, 156, 161, cited in Laycock, *Populism*, 188-9.

54 While C.B. Macpherson, in the concluding chapter to his *Democracy in Alberta*, Toronto: University of Toronto Press, 1953, tends to play down such Rousseauean notions of equality as "petit bourgeois," I see something more positive in a theory that argues that "the social state is advantageous to men [and women] only when all have something and none too much"; *The Social Contract*, I, 9, fn 1. It remains a fairly radical precept, even for advanced capitalist societies like our own.

55 Laycock, however, suggests that the technocratic element tended to prevail in the CCF and provides an acute analysis of the reasons: "Combining decisive state action in the business of social transformation with methods of popular control over such state action has posed a challenge to all egalitarians since Rousseau ... Most socialists in power have resorted to reliance upon technocratic methods to reduce the power of those opposed to social change ... Such moves are not self-consciously undertaken to undermine the power of the popular movement vis-à-vis the state ... However, this is often an unintended effect"; *Populism*, 362.

56 Norman Priestly, "Cooperative Institutions," cited in ibid., 347.

57 Carlyle King, "Socialism and Cooperatives," cited in ibid., 349.

58 André Siegfried, *The Race Question in Canada*, Toronto: Carleton Library, 1966, 137–8.

59 Laycock, *Populism*, 1, 527.

60 Reproduced in Forbes, *Canadian Political Thought*, 21.

61 For example, François-Xavier Tessier, a doctor and patriote elected to the Assembly in 1833, of whom the *Dictionnaire biographique du Canada*, v i, *1821–1835*, Quebec: P U L, 1987, 843, notes: "Tessier admirait Jean-Jacques Rousseau et croyait à la bonté de l'homme ... Comme plusieurs représentants patriotes, il semblait admirer la république voisine, guidée par 'la génie de la liberté.' "

62 Cf. Léon Dion, *Quebec: The Unfinished Revolution*, Montreal: McGill-Queen's, 1976, chap. 5.

63 Cited in Brady, *Democracy*, 98.

64 "Les étudiants montrent la voie de la véritable démocratie," *L'Action*, 3 April 1965.

65 Cited in Edouard Cloutier, "Le régime politique au Québec: qui est souverain?," in Daniel Latouche, ed., *Premier mandat: une prospective à court terme du gouvernement péquiste*, 1 1, Montreal: L'Aurore, 1977, 148. Cloutier's own essay is a call for greater popular sovereignty in a post-independence Quebec.

66 Québec, *Débats de l'Assemblée nationale*, 5 April 1978, 708.

67 Ibid., 4 March 1980, 4962.

68 See Michel Roy, "Coup de théâtre de Trudeau: le front des huits s'effondre," *Le Devoir*, 5 Nov. 1981, 3, for an account of the "developing Quebec-Canada alliance" between Lévesque and Trudeau on submitting the patriated constitution and charter to a referendum and on the opposition to such a proposal from the majority of English-speaking provinces.

69 Réjean Pelletier, "Un référendum sur le libre-échange," *Le Devoir*, 6, Nov. 1987, 11.

70 Stéphane Dion, "Le libre-échange: pour un référendum," *Le Devoir*, 16 Dec. 1987, 9.

71 *Our Generation*, 6 no. 4 (June 1969), editorial, "Towards an Extra-Parliamentary Opposition," 16.

72 *Parti pris*, 3 no. 7 (Feb. 1966), editorial 4.

73 Michel Crozier et al., *The Crisis of Democracy*, New York, 1975.

74 *Le Québec Statistique 1985–6*, Quebec, 1985, 331, 352–3.

75 See Michael Clague, *Reforming Human Services: The Experience of the Community Resource Boards in B.C.*, Vancouver: U B C Press, 1984.

76 Jacques Godbout, *La démocratie des usagers*, Montreal: Boréal, 1987, 30. See also his earlier *La participation contre la démocratie*, Montreal, 1983, and Frédéric Lestmann, *Du pain et des services*, Montreal: St. Martin, 1981.

77 Philip Resnick, *Parliament vs. People: An Essay on Democracy and Canadian
    Political Culture*, Vancouver: New Star Books, 1984.
78 For a Canadian example of this, I might cite various essays in Warren
    Magnusson et al., eds., *After Bennett: A New Politics for British Columbia*,
    Vancouver: New Star, 1986. The larger Western literature would
    include the writings of Claus Offe, John Keane, André Gorz, Samuel
    Bowles, and Carole Pateman.
79 For one recent example, see John Faustman, "When Workers Turn
    Bosses," *Globe and Mail Report on Business Magazine* (March 1988), dis-
    cussing workers' buy-out of Lamford Cedar in New Westminster, B C.
    A twenty-seven-year-old tallyman, Danny Rackett, is quoted: "A lot of
    my friends I talk to would love to work here because a majority makes
    decisions"; ibid., 47. For further discussion of industrial democracy in
    a Canadian context, see John Richards, "Industrial Democracy," in
    Magnusson, *After Bennett*, 96–114; Gilbert Tarab and Pierre D'Argan,
    "Participation in Business: Is It Viable? Under What Circumstances?,"
    in Robert Stern and Sharon McCarthy, eds., *International Yearbook of
    Organizational Democracy*, I I I, Chichester: John Wiley & Sons, 1986,
    217–30; Donald V. Nightingale, *Workplace Democracy: An Inquiry into
    Employee Participation in Canadian Work Organizations*, Toronto: Univer-
    sity of Toronto Press, 1982.
80 Blackstone, *Commentaries on the Laws of England*, I, 60, cited in John V.
    Jesierski, "Parliament or People: James Wilson and Blackstone on the
    Nature and Location of Sovereignty," *Journal of the History of Ideas*, 32
    (Jan.–March 1971), 96.
81 J.G.A. Pocock, *The Ancient Constitution and the Feudal Law*, Cambridge:
    Cambridge University Press, republished 1987, 234.
82 Letter to Samuel Kercheval, 5 Sept. 1816, *The Works of Thomas Jefferson*,
    X I I, New York: Federal Edition, 1905, 15.

CHAPTER SIX

1 J.P. Nettl, "The State as a Conceptual Variable," *World Politics*, 20 no. 4
   (1968), 559.
2 Here I must take issue with C.B. Macpherson's "Do We Need a Theory
   of the State?" *European Journal of Sociology*, 18 (1977), 223–44, where he
   asserts that only Marxism and social democracy need such a theory.
   On the contrary, conservative, liberal, and fascist theorists have shown
   no less interest in this question, as some of the references below will
   suggest.
3 See, for example, the article "Stateless Society," *Encyclopedia of the
   Social Sciences*, X V, 157–68, with its extensive bibliographical references. See also Pierre Clastres, *La société contre l'état*, Paris, 1974, and the

intelligent critique thereof in Jean-William Lapierre, *Vivre sans état?*, Paris, 1977.

4 Cf. Gramsci's discussion of the role of religion and the national press in "State and Civil Society" in *Selections from the Prison Notebooks*, London: Lawrence & Wishart, 1971, and Althusser's concept of state ideological apparatuses in "Idéologie et appareils idéologiques d'état," in *Positions*, Paris: Editions Sociales, 1976.

5 N. Poulantzas, *L'état, le pouvoir, le socialisme*, Paris: P U F, 1978, 180, maintains that our knowledge concerning the current economic functions and certain aspects of monopoly capitalism is to be attributed exclusively to Marxist theory.

6 The most extensive discussion of Wagner's law is contained in Herbert Timm, "Das Gesetz der Wachsenden Staatsausgaben," *Finanzarchiv*, Tübingen, 21 (1961), 201–47. The biographical article on Wagner in the *Staatslexikon*, V I I I, Freiburg, 1963, sketches his relationship to the so-called socialists of the chair (Kathedersozialisten). A.T. Peacock and J. Wiseman, *The Growth of Public Expenditures in the United Kingdom*, Princeton: Princeton University Press, 1961, 18–24, provides a useful summary.

7 For a brilliant discussion of this intellectual climate, see Michael Lowy, *Pour une sociologie des intellectuels révolutionnaires*, Paris, 1976, chapter 1.

8 Solomon Fabricant, *The Trend of Government Activity in the United States*, New York, 1952; Peacock and Wiseman, *Growth*; Suphan Andic and Jindrich Veverka, "The Growth of Government Expenditure in Germany," *Finanzarchiv*, 23 (1964), 169–277; R.M. Bird, *The Growth of Government-Spending in Canada*, Toronto: Canadian Tax Foundation, 1970; C. André, R. Delorme, and G. Terny, "Les dépenses publiques françaises depuis un siècle," *Economie et statistique*, March 1973, 3–14.

9 Richard M. Titmuss, *Essays on 'The Welfare State*," London: Allen & Unwin, 1959, 86.

10 Pitrim A. Sorokin, *Man and Society in Calamity*, New York: Greenwood Press, 1942.

11 Ibid., 120, 122.

12 Andic and Veverka, "Growth," 193 and table 1, p. 183.

13 André, Delorme, and Terny, "Les dépenses," graph 1, table 3.

14 Cf. O E C D, *National Accounts Statistics*, Paris, 1976.

15 Paul Boccara et al., *Le capitalisme monopoliste d'état*, 2 vols., Paris: Editions sociales, 1976.

16 Cf. H. Claude, *La concentration capitaliste: Pouvoir économique et pouvoir gaulliste*, Paris: Editions sociales, 1965.

17 Rudolf Hilferding, *Le capital financier*, Paris, 1970, 451.

18 Cf. the introductory article in H.A. Winkler, ed., *Organisierter Kapitalismus*, Göttingen, 1974.

19 Cf. Jürgen Kocka, *Klassengesellschaft im Krieg 1914–18*, Göttingen, 1973; Charles S. Maier, *Recasting Bourgeois Europe*, Princeton: Princeton University Press, 1975.

20 Cited in Winkler, *Organisierter*, 9.

21 Jürgen Kocka, "Organisierter Kapitalismus oder Staatsmonopolistischer Kapitalismus?" in ibid., 25.

22 To cite but some of the literature on corporatism: J.T. Winkler, "Corporatism," *Archives européennes de sociologie*, 17 no. 1, 1976, 100–36; Philippe Schmitter and Gerhard Lehmbruch, eds., *Trends towards Corporatist Intermediation*, London: Sage Publications, 1979; J.M. Malloy, ed., *Authoritarianism and Corporatism in Latin America*, Pittsburgh and London: University of Pittsburgh, 1977; Leo Panitch, "Recent Theorizations of Corporatism: Reflections on a Growth Industry," *British Journal of Sociology*, 31 no. 2, (June 1980), 159–87.

23 John Holloway and Sol Picciotto, "Capital, Crisis and the State," *Capital and Class*, no. 2 (1977), 76–101; Joachim Hirsch, *Staatsapparat und Reproduktion des Kapitals*, Frankfurt, 1974.

24 Louis Fontvielle, "Evolution et croissance de l'état français," *Economies et sociétés*, 10 nos. 9–12, 1976.

25 E. Altvater, *Rahmenbedingungen und Schranken staatlichen Handelns. Zehn Thesen*, Frankfurt, 1976.

26 P. Baran and P. Sweezy, *Monopoly Capital*, New York, 1966; Michael Kidron, *Western Capitalism since the War*, London, 1968.

27 James O'Connor, *The Fiscal Crisis of the State*, New York: St. Martin's Press, 1973.

28 R. Carré de Malberg, *Contribution à la théorie générale de l'état*, Paris, 1920, reprinted 1962, 7.

29 Gyoergy Antalffy, *Basic Problems of State and Society*, Budapest, 1974, 116, 120.

30 Werner Sombart, *Das Wirtschaftsleben im Zeitalter des Hochkapitalismus*, Munich and Leipzig, 1928, chap. 6.

31 Charles Eisenmann, "Les fonctions de l'état," in *Encyclopédie française*, x, *L'état*, 1964, 311.

32 Bertrand de Jouvenel, *Les débuts de l'état moderne*, Paris, 1976, 156–7.

33 Poulantzas, *L'état*, 162.

34 Cf. the interesting contrast between Marx's inadequate theorizing of political events in France 1848–50 and his far superior ad hoc political analysis of the same events: Martin E. Spencer, "Marx on the State: The Events in France betwen 1848–1850," *Theory and Society*, 17 nos. 1 and 2 (Jan.–March 1979), 167–98.

35 The term *libido dominandi* derives from St Augustine's *De civitate dei*. Henri Lefebvre makes use of the concept in his treatise *De l'état*, espe-

cially vol. I, *L'état dans le monde moderne*, and vol. III, *Le mode de production étatique*, Paris, 1976-7.

36 Carl Schmitt, *La notion de politique*, Paris, 1972, contains a translation of his most important essay of the early 1930s, as well as a much later piece on the theory of the partisan; in English, *The Concept of the Political*, New Brunswick, N J: Rutgers University Press, 1976.

37 Julien Freund, *L'essence du politique*, Paris, 1965, 1.

38 Michel Maffesoli, *Logique de la domination*, Paris: P U F, 1976, 158-9.

39 Ibid., 188.

40 Victor Ehrenberg, *The Greek State*, London: Methuen, 1969, 74-7.

41 Cicero, *De republica*, I, 7, cited in Helmut Kuhn, "Der Staat als Herrschaftsform," *Zeitschrift für Politik*, 14 (1967), 229.

42 S. Verba, "The Kennedy Assassination and the Nature of Political Commitment," in B.S. Greenberg and E.B. Parker, eds., *The Kennedy Assassination and the American Public*, Palo Alto, 1965; Edward Shils and Michael Young, "The Meaning of the Coronation," *Sociological Review*, 1 (1953).

43 Georges Burdeau, *Traité de science politique*, vol. II, *L'état*, Paris, 1967.

44 Rudi Supek, "La 'main visible' et la dégradation de l'individu," in Alain Touraine et al., *Au-delà de la crise*, Paris: Seuil, 1976.

45 Andras Hegedus, *Socialism and Bureaucracy*, London, 1976; F. Feher, A. Heller, and G. Markus, *Dictatorship over Needs*, Oxford: Basil Blackwell, 1983.

46 Lefebvre, *De l'état*, vol. I V, *Le mode de production étatique*, Paris, 1977, 248.

47 Lefebvre's analysis was heavily influenced here by the French translation of Kari Levitt, *Silent Surrender*, Toronto: Macmillan, 1970; cf. vol. II of *De l'etat: Les contradictions de l'état moderne*, 190-3.

48 Claus Offe, "Political Authority and Class Structure," in Paul Connerton, ed., *Critical Sociology*, London, 1976, 393, 395-6.

49 Jürgen Habermas, *Legitimationsprobleme im Spätkapitalismus*, Frankfurt, 1973, 105, 128, 130.

50 Max Weber, *Economy and Society*, III, New York, 1968, 954.

51 Raymond Polin, "Analyse philosophique de l'idée de légitimité," in Polin, *L'idée de légitimité*, Paris: Annales de philosophie politique, 1967.

52 Racine, *Théâtre complet, Thébaïde*, Paris: Garnier, 1960, 21.

53 Cited in Polin, "Analyses," 23.

54 Cf. articles by Norberto Bobbio and Sergio Cotta in Polin, *L'idée*.

55 Ibid., 23.

56 Cf. Habermas's discussion of economic, rationality, legitimation, and motivation crises in *Legitimation Crisis*, Boston: Beacon Press, 1975.

57 O'Connor, *Fiscal Crisis*, chap. 1, 4, and 5.

58 Ralph Miliband, *The State in Capitalist Society*, London: Weidenfeld & Nicolson, 1969, chap. 7-8; Habermas, *Crisis*.

59 Gramsci, *Selections*; Phil Slater, *Origin and Significance of the Frankfurt School*, London: Routledge & Kegan Paul, 1977.

60 Michel Droit, *Homme du destin*, III, *Le Retour*, 365.

61 Cited in Peter Wiles, "War and Economic Systems," *Science et conscience de la société, mélanges en l'honneur de Raymond Aron*, II, Paris, 1971, 286.

62 Cited in Alain Peyrefitte, *Le mal français*, Paris: Plon, 1976, 96.

63 Theda Skocpol, *States and Social Revolutions*, Cambridge: Cambridge University Press, 1979, 31.

64 Fontvielle, "Evolution," 1705.

65 André Piettre, *Les grands problèmes de l'économie contemporaine*, I, Paris: Cujas, 1976, 16.

66 Pierre Chaunu, "L'état," in Fernand Braudel and Ernest Labrousse series editors, *Histoire économique et sociale de la France*, vol. I, *1450-1660*, Paris: P U F, 1970, 223.

67 For example, Ezra Suleiman, *Les hauts fonctionnaires et la politique*, Paris, 1976; J. Siwek-Pouydesseau, "French Ministerial Staffs," in Mattei Dogan, ed., *The Mandarins of Western Europe*, New York: Wiley, 1975; Pierre Birnbaum, *Les sommets de l'état*, Paris: Points, 1977.

68 *Pour nationaliser l'état, réflexions d'un groupe d'études*, Paris, 1968, 31.

69 Henri Lefebvre, *Le temps des méprises*, Paris, 1975, 229.

70 W.O. Henderson, *The Rise of German Industrial Power 1834-1914*, Berkeley and London: University of California Press, 1976; W.F. Bruck, *Social and Economic History of Germany from Wilhelm II to Hitler, 1880-1938*, London, 1940.

71 Peter-Christian Witt, "Finanzpolitik und Sozialer Wandel," in H.V. Wehler, ed., *Sozialgeschichte Heute*, Göttingen, 1974, 565-74; Walter Rathenau, "German Organization at the Beginning of the War," in J.M. Clark, W.H. Hamilton, and H.G. Moulton, *Readings in the Economics of War*, New York, 1918.

72 Maier, *Recasting Bourgeois Europe*.

73 Among the better analyses of the Nazi state, one may cite Franz Neumann, *Behemoth*, New York: Oxford University Press, 1944, and A. Schweitzer, *Big Business in the Third Reich*, Bloomington: Indiana University Press, 1964.

74 Andic and Veverka, "Growth of Government Expenditure," 283. To be fair, however, spending on social security would have accounted for a much larger share of total state expenditure in 1958 than in 1938.

75 Willy Brandt, Bruno Kreisky, and Olof Palme, *La sociale démocratie et l'avenir*, Paris, 1976, 27-8.

76 Tom Nairn, "The Twilight of the British State," *New Left Review*, nos. 101-2 (1977), 6.

77 Nettl, "The State," 570.

78 De Jouvenel, *Les débuts*, 69.

79 Nairn, "Twilight," 16. "State power was appropriated by a self-regulating elite group which established powerful conventions of autonomy: that is of forms of self-organization and voluntary action independent of state action."

80 As is suggested in the essay by Christopher Hewitt in Philip Stanworth and Anthony Giddens, eds., *Elites and Power in British Society*, Cambridge: Cambridge University Press, 1974.

81 O E C D, *National Accounts 1961–1972*, Paris, 1974; O E C D, *Expenditure Trends in OECD Countries 1960–1980*, Paris, 1972.

82 *Statistical Abstracts of the United States*, various years, cited in Piettre, *Les grands problèmes*, Annexe 7, 53.

83 *United States Monthly Labor Review*, May 1975, 80.

84 David Vogel, "Why Businessmen Distrust Their State: The Political Consciousness of American Corporate Executives," *British Journal of Political Science*, 8 (Jan. 1978), 45, 78.

85 Antalffy, *Basic Problems*, 157.

86 J.A. Tikhominov, *Pouvoir et administration dans la société socialiste*, Paris: C N R S, 1973, 62.

87 Antalffy, *Basic Problems*, 186.

88 Ibid., 100.

89 Jean Elleinstein, *Histoire du phénomène stalinien*, Paris, 1975.

90 Gramsci, *Selections from the Prison Notebooks*, London: Lawrence & Wishart, 1971, 238.

91 According to Pierre Clastre, *La société contre l'état*, Paris: Seuil, 1974, 12, it is not obvious that coercion and subordination constitute everywhere and always the essence of political power. Though Clastre's account focuses on primitive societies, is it too much to suggest that, not unlike Rousseau, he is reading prescriptive qualities into his anthropology?

92 Alain Touraine, *Production de la société*, Paris: Seuil, 1973, 259.

CHAPTER SEVEN

1 Alan Cairns and Cynthia Williams, "Constitutionalism, Citizenship and Society in Canada: An Overview," in Alan Cairns and Cynthia Williams, eds., *Constitutionalism, Citizenship and Society in Canada*, Royal Commission Research Studies, vol. 33, Toronto: University of Toronto Press for Supply and Services Canada, 1985, 2.

2 Report of the Royal Commission on the Economic Union and Development Prospects for Canada (Macdonald Report), 1, Ottawa: Minister of Supply and Services, 1985, 11.

3 Ibid., 12.

4 Ibid., 65.

5 Thus, the term *state* appears on 7, 11, 26-7, 31, and 39 of vol. I of the Report and the term *government* on 24-5, 28, 35, and 38.

6 Bertrand Badie and Pierre Birnbaum, *The Sociology of the State*, Chicago: University of Chicago Press, 1983, part 3.

7 Thomas Mann, *Reflections of a Non-Political Man*, New York: Frederick Ungar, 1983, 178.

8 Compare Claude Nicolet, *L'idée républicaine en France (1789-1924)*, Paris: Gallimard, 1982.

9 Macdonald Report, I, 41, 43, 65.

10 Ibid., 65.

11 Alan Cairns, "The Embedded State: State-Society Relations in Canada," in Keith Banting, ed., *State and Society: Canada in Comparative Perspective*, Royal Commission Research Studies, vol. 31, Toronto: University of Toronto Press for Supply and Services Canada, 1986, 55.

12 Ibid., 57.

13 Ibid., 68, 71, 82.

14 Benjamin Constant, I I, *De la liberté des anciens comparée à celle des modernes*, in *Cours de politique constitutionnelle*, Paris: Guillaumin, 1872, 539-60. An English translation appears in B. Fontana, ed., *Benjamin Constant: Political Writings*, Cambridge: Cambridge University Press, 1988, 307-28.

15 Report, I, 20.

16 Cairns, "The Embedded State," 83.

17 Michel Crozier, Samuel P. Huntington, and Joji Watanaki, *The Crisis of Democracy*, The Trilateral Commission, New York University Press, 1975.

18 Cairns and Williams, "Constitutionalism, Citizenship and Society in Canada," 44.

19 The same process is at work in the federalism section of the research studies with Daniel Latouche's passionately nationalist essay (vol. 70), encompassed within a sea of more conventional federalist discourse.

20 Bruce Doern, "The Politics of Canadian Economic Policy: An Overview," in Bruce Doern, ed., *The Politics of Economic Policy*, Royal Commission Research Studies, vol. 40, Toronto: University of Toronto Press for Supply and Services Canada, 1985, 6.

21 Louis Althusser, "Les appareils idéologiques d'État," in *Positions*, Paris: Éditions sociales, 1976, 67-125.

22 Doern, "The Politics of Canadian Economic Policy," 1.

23 Ibid., 6-7.

24 David Laidler, "Economic Ideas and Social Issues: An Overview," in David Laidler, ed., *Approaches to Economic Well-Being*, Royal Commission Research Studies, vol. 26, Toronto: University of Toronto Press for Supply and Services Canada, 1985, 5.

25 Ibid., 9.

26 Ibid., 21.

27 Keith Banting, "Images of the Modern State: An Introduction," in Banting, ed., *State and Society*, 1.

28 Ibid., 17.

29 James Rice, "Politics of Income Security: Historical Developments and Limits to Future Change," in Doern, ed., *The Politics of Economic Policy*, 247.

30 David R. Cameron, "The Growth of Government Spending: The Canadian Experience in Comparative Perspective," in Banting, ed., *State and Society*, 21-51.

31 Walter Korpi, *The Democratic Class Struggle*, London: Routledge and Kegan Paul, 1983.

32 A.T. Peacock and J. Wiseman, *The Growth of Public Expenditure in the United Kingdom*, Princeton: Princeton University Press, 1961.

33 James Buchanan and Richard E. Wagner, *Democracy in Deficit: The Political Legacy of Lord Keynes*, New York: Academic Press, 1977; Class Offe, *Contradictions of the Welfare State*, Boston: M.I.T. Press, 1984; James O'Connor, *The Fiscal Crisis of the State*, New York: St. Martin's Press, 1973.

34 Andrew Martin, "The Politics of Employment and Welfare: National Policies and International Interdependence," in Keith Banting, ed., *The State and Economic Interests*, Royal Commission Research Studies, vol. 32, Toronto: University of Toronto Press for Supply and Services Canada, 1986, 157-241, 158.

35 Ibid., 158-9 (my emphasis).

36 Ibid., 229.

37 A.G. Blomqvist, "Political Economy of the Canadian Welfare State," in Laidler, ed., *Approaches to Economic Well-Being*, 102.

38 Laidler, "Economic Ideas and Social Issues," 30, 31.

39 Ibid., 38.

40 Blomqvist, "Political Economy of the Canadian Welfare State," 103-4.

41 Keith Banting, "The State and Economic Interests: An Introduction," in Banting, ed., *The State and Economic Interests*, 1-33.

42 William D. Coleman, "Canadian Business and the State," in ibid., 249.

43 Ibid., 251, 252.

44 Leo Panitch, "The Tripartite Experience," in Banting, ed., *The State and Economic Interests*, 37-119.

45 Ibid., 113.

46 Ibid., 112.

47 K.D. McRae, "Linguistic Diversity and Economic Decision-Making: Three European Case Studies," in Banting, ed., *The State and Economic Interests*, 152.

48 Pierre Fournier, "Consensus Building in Canada: Case Studies and Prospects," in Banting, ed., *The State and Economic Interests*, 291-335.
49 Ibid., 294.
50 David Wolfe, "The Politics of the Deficit," in Doern, ed., *The Politics of Economic Policy*, 133.
51 Ibid., 137, 138.
52 Robin Broadway and Neil Bruce, "Theoretical Issues in Tax Reform," in Laidler, ed., *Approaches to Economic Well-Being*, 137-93.
53 Wolfe, "The Politics of the Deficit," 154.
54 Ibid., 141.
55 Doern, "The Politics of Canadian Economic Policy," 16.
56 Ibid.
57 Anthony H. Birch, "Political Authority and Crisis in Comparative Perspective," in Banting, *State and Society*, 87-130.
58 Richard Rose and Guy Peters, *Can Government Go Bankrupt?*, New York: Basic Books, 1978.
59 Birch, "Political Authority and Crisis," 120.
60 Cairns, "The Embedded State," 54.
61 Carl Schmitt, *The Concept of the Political*, New Brunswick, N J: Rutgers University Press, 1976; *Political Theology: Four Chapters on the Concept of Sovereignty*, Boston: M.I.T. Press, 1985.
62 Birch, "Political Authority and Crisis," 90.
63 Cairns and Williams, "Constitutionalism, Citizenship and Society in Canada," 41.
64 Cynthia Williams, "The Changing Nature of Citizen Rights," in Cairns and Williams, eds., *Constitutionalism, Citizenship and Society in Canada*, 99-131.
65 Cairns and Williams, "Constitutionalism, Citizenship and Society in Canada," 31.
66 Ibid., 34., See also Macdonald Report, I, 20.
67 Cairns and Williams, "Constitutionalism, Citizenship and Society in Canada," 38.
68 Rainer Knopff and F.L. Morton, "Nation-Building and the Canadian Charter of Rights and Freedoms," in Cairns and Williams, eds., *Constitutionalism, Citizenship and Society in Canada*, 133-82.
69 Ibid., 145.
70 Macdonald Report, I, 70.
71 Ibid., 69.
72 Charles Taylor, "Alternative Futures: Legitimacy, Identity and Alienation in Late Twentieth Century Canada," in Cairns and Williams, eds., *Constitutionalism, Citizenship and Society in Canada*, 183-229.
73 Ibid., 212, 213.
74 Ibid., 198.

75 Ibid., 211.

76 For examples of such economic and political alternatives one might cite Alec Nove, *The Economics of Feasible Socialism*, London: George Allen and Unwin, 1983; Geoff Hodgson, *The Democratic Economy*, London: Pelican, 1984; Benjamin Barber, *Strong Democracy: Participatory Politics for a New Age*, Berkeley: University of California Press, 1984; and Robert Dahl, *A Preface to Economic Democracy*, Berkeley: University of California Press, 1985. This whole literature is clearly foreign to this commission.

77 "Western societies appear to be condemned to long periods of privatization during which they live through an impoverishing "atrophy of public meanings" followed by spasmodic outbursts of "publicness" that are hardly likely to be constructive. What is to be done about this atrophy and subsequent spasm? How do we reintroduce more steady concern with public affairs as well as "genuine public celebrations" into our everyday lives?" Albert O. Hischman, *Shifting Involvements: Private Interest and Public Action*, Princeton: Princeton University Press, 1982, 132.

CHAPTER EIGHT

1 The best discussion of Wagner's law is Herbert Timm, "Das Gesetz der Wachsenden Staatsausgaben," *Finanzarchiv*, Tubingen, 21, 1961, 201-47. A.T. Peacock and J. Wiseman, *The Growth of Public Expenditures in the United Kingdom*, Princeton: Princeton University Press, 1961, 18-24, contains a good summary, as does R.M. Bird, *The Growth of Government Spending in Canada*, Toronto: Canadian Tax Foundation, 1970, chap. 4. Bird is the Canadian fiscal historian whose work has been most influenced by Wagner.

2 John L. Howard and W.T. Stanbury, "Measuring Leviathan: The Size, Scope, and Growth of Governments in Canada," in George Lermer, ed., *Probing Leviathan*, Vancouver: Fraser Institute, 1984.

3 J.A. Corry, *The Growth of Government Activities since Confederation*, Study for the Royal Commission on Dominion-Provincial Relations, Ottawa, 1939, 4.

4 Alan Cairns, "The Embedded State: State-Society Relations in Canada," in Keith Banting, ed., *State and Society: Canada in Comparative Perspective*, Royal Commission Research Studies, vol. 31, Toronto: University of Toronto Press, 1986. For my critique of Cairns and of the Macdonald Commission's argument, see chap. 7.

5 Hugh Aitken, "Defensive Expansionism: The State and Economic Growth in Canada," in W.T. Easterbrook and Mel Watkins, eds., *Approaches to Canadian Economic History*, Toronto: Carleton Library, 1967, 183-221.

6 Harold Innis, *Essays in Canadian Economic History*, Toronto: University of Toronto Press, 1956, and other writings.

7 Herschel Hardin, *A Nation Unaware: The Canadian Economic Culture*, Vancouver: J.J. Douglas, 1974.

8 Leo Panitch, ed., *The Canadian State: Political Economy and Political Power*, Toronto: University of Toronto Press, 1977.

9 Rudolf Hilferding, *Finance Capital: A Study of the Latest Phase of Capitalist Development*, with an introduction by Tom Bottomore, London: Routledge and Kegan Paul, 1981.

10 Ibid., 334.

11 Rudolf Hilferding, "The Organized Economy," in Tom Bottomore and Patrick Goode, eds., *Readings in Marxist Sociology*, Oxford: Oxford University Press, 1983, 247.

12 Ibid., 249.

13 Ibid., 251.

14 Corry, *Growth*, 4.

15 Cf. Alfred Dubuc, "The Decline of Confederation and the New Nationalism," in Peter Russell, ed., *Nationalism in Canada*, Toronto: McGraw-Hill, 1966, 112–32; R.T. Naylor, "The Rise and Fall of the Third Commercial Empire of the St. Lawrence," in Gary Teeple, ed., *Capitalism and the National Question in Canada*, Toronto: University of Toronto Press, 1972, 1–41.

16 Cf. G.T. Kelley, *Early Canadian Industrialization: A Case Study of Relative Backwardness*, P H D thesis, Clark University, 1971, University Microfilm 72–9747. Kelley, in turn, is influenced by Alexander Gerschenkron, *Economic Backwardness in Historical Perspective*, Cambridge, Mass.: Harvard University Press, 1962.

17 *Financial Capital*, 322. Hilferding argues that export capital feels most comfortable when its own state is in control of such territories, but he also notes that "so long as there exists a state power (in these countries) which is capable of maintaining some kind of order, direct rules over these areas is less important," something particularly true where "relatively advanced white or yellow peoples" were concerned (321). This would seem to encompass the Canadian case.

18 Kelley, *Industrialization*, 266.

19 Alexander Brady, "The State and Economic Life," in George W. Brown, ed., *Canada*, Berkeley: University of California Press, 1950, 353–71.

20 R.T. Naylor, *A History of Canadian Business*, I I, Toronto: Lorimer, 1975, 280–1.

21 Abram Epp, "Cooperation among Capitalists: The Canadian Merger Movement 1909–13," P H D thesis, Johns Hopkins University, 1973.

22 Gustavus Myers, *History of Canadian Wealth*, reprinted Argosy Antiquarian, 1968, i–iii.

23 There is a good discussion in Epp, "Cooperation": "Canadian Finance Capitalism," 175ff.

24 Hilferding, *Finance Capital*, chap. 22, "The Export of Capital and the Struggle for Economic Territory."

25 Cf. H.V. Nelles, *The Politics of Development: Forests, Mines and Hydro-Electric Power in Ontario, 1849–1941*, Toronto: Macmillan, 1974.

26 Cf. Paul Craven, *An Impartial Umpire: Industrial Relations and the Canadian State, 1900–1911*, Toronto: University of Toronto Press, 1980.

27 Allan Moscovitch and Glenn Drover, "The Growth of the Welfare State in the 20th Century," in A. Moscovitch and J. Albert, eds., *The Benevolent State: The Growth of Welfare in Canada*, Toronto: Garamond Press, 1987, 20.

28 My figures are taken from Bird, *Growth*, table 25, Total Government Expenditures Selected Years 1867–1967, 266. My figures for Germany come from Peter-Christian Witt, "Finanzpolitik und Sozialerwandel," in H.U. Wehler, ed., *Sozialgeschichte Heute*, Göttingen, 1974, table 1, 568.

29 Cf. Hans Rosenberg, *Bureaucracy, Aristocracy and Autocracy: The Prussian Experience 1660–1815*, Cambridge, Mass.: Harvard University Press, 1958.

30 My figure is drawn from Witt, "Finanzpolitik." The exact figure given for 1914–18 is 57.7 per cent of G N P. For an excellent study of Germany during the First World War, see Jurgen Kocka, *Facing Total War*, London: Berg Publishers, 1984.

31 Leslie Hannah, *The Rise of the Corporate Economy*, London: Methuen, 1976, 29–30.

32 Michael Bliss, *A Canadian Millionaire: The Life and Business Times of Sir Joseph Flavelle 1858–1939*, Toronto: Macmillan, 1978, 318.

33 Cf. R.T. Naylor, "The Canadian State, the Accumulation of Capital, and the Great War," in *Dominion of Debt*, Montreal: Black Rose Books, 61–107.

34 Peacock and Wiseman, *Growth of Public Expenditures*, xxiv.

35 Bird, *Growth*, 266.

36 Stephen Leacock, cited in Doug Owram, *The Government Generation: Canadian Intellectuals and the State 1900–1945*, Toronto: University of Toronto Press, 1986, 89.

37 *The Rowell-Sirois Report*, book 1, ed. Donald V. Smiley, Toronto: Carleton Library, 1963, 136.

38 Edward S. Herman, *Corporate Control, Corporate Power*, Cambridge: Cambridge University Press, 1981, 240–1.

39 The house journal of Sperlings, cited in Hannah, *Rise*, 40–1.

40 Report of the Royal Commission on Price Spreads, Ottawa, 1937, 21.

41 Edgar McInnes, *Canadian Forum*, Nov. 1930, cited by Owram, *The Government Generation*, 163.

42 Francis Hankin and T.W.L. McDermot, *Recovery by Control*, Toronto: J.M. Dent, 1933, 21.

43 Owram, *The Government Generation*, chap. 7 and 8.

44 Alvin Finkel, *Business and Social Reform in the Thirties*, Toronto: Lorimer, 1979, 94.

45 Cited in John H. Thompson with Allen Seager, *Canada 1922–1939: Decades of Discord*, Toronto: McClelland and Stewart, 1985, 261.

46 For a list of prominent businessmen supporting Bennett's radio addresses see Finkel, *Business and Social Reform*, 37.

47 D.G. Creighton, "Federal Relations in Canada," in *Canada in Peace and War*, Oxford: Oxford University Press, 1941, 215.

48 *Canada in World War II: Post War Possibilities*, Montreal: William Boas and Co., 1945, 31.

49 Bird, *Growth*, Figure 4, 16, for the 50 per cent of gross national expenditure figure; civil service employment figures are given by Owram, *The Government Generation*, 256, citing *Canada Year Book* for 1946.

50 Jean-Marie Nadeau, *Horizons d'après guerre; essais de politique économique canadienne*, Montreal, 1944, 114, my translation.

51 *Canada in World War II*, 30–1.

52 Robert M. Campbell, *Grand Illusions: The Politics of the Keynesian Experience in Canada 1945–75*, Peterborough: Broadview Press, 1987, 65.

53 Bird, *Growth*, 266.

54 Campbell, *Grand Illusions*, 32–8.

55 J.L. Granatstein, *The Ottawa Men: The Civil Service Mandarins 1935–1957*, Toronto: Oxford University Press, 1982, 168.

56 Cited in ibid., 167.

57 Keith Banting, "Images of the Modern State: An Introduction," in K. Banting, ed., *State and Society*, Royal Commission Studies, vol. 31, Toronto: University of Toronto Press, 1986, 1.

58 Hugh Armstrong, "The Labour Force and State Workers in Canada," in Panitch, *The Canadian State*, table 6, 302.

59 The figures are drawn from Aidan Vining and Robert Botterell, "An Overview of the Origins, Growth, Size and Function of Provincial Crown Corporations," 303–67, and John W. Langford and Kenneth Huffman, "The Uncharted Universe of Federal Public Corporations," 219–301, both in J.R.S. Prichard, ed., *Crown Corporations: The Calculus of Choice*, Toronto: Butterworths, 1983.

60 Howard and Stanbury, "Measuring Leviathan," 94.

61 Howard Gamble, "The Road to Tomorrow," *Canadian Business*, Jan. 1954, cited in Lloyd Musolf, "The Boundaries of Public Enterprise," in K.J. Rea and J.T. McLeod, eds., *Business and Government in Canada: Selected Readings*, Toronto: Methuen, 1969, 176.

62 Cf. Leo Panitch, "The Role and Nature of the Canadian State," in

Panitch, *The Canadian State*, 3-27, or Moscovitch and Drover, "Social Expenditures and the Welfare State," in Moscovitch and Albert, *The Benevolent State*, 13-43, both of which make use of James O'Connor's construct in *The Fiscal Crisis of the State*, New York: St. Martin's, 1973.

63 Herman, *Corporate Control, Corporate Power*, 300.

64 Andrew Shonfield, *Modern Capitalism: The Changing Balance of Public and Private Power*, Oxford: Oxford University Press, 1965, 377.

65 John Kenneth Galbraith, *The New Industrial State*, Boston: Houghton Mifflin, 1967, 32.

66 John Porter, *The Vertical Mosaic*, Toronto: University of Toronto Press, 1965, 240.

67 Wallace Clement, *The Canadian Corporate Elite*, Toronto, McClelland & Stewart, 1975; "The Changing Structure of the Canadian Economy," in *Class, Power and Property*, Toronto: Methuen, 1983, 1-25.

68 Andrew Shonfield's *Modern Capitalism* remains the best single study of this phenomenon, and many of the tendencies he discerns, such as the increased influence of public authorities, preoccupation with social welfare, taming of the violence of the market in the private sector are ones I would include in the term *organized capitalism*. The major difference between Shonfield's formulation and Hilferding's, which I prefer, is that the latter places greater emphasis on transformations in the nature of finance and industrial capital in explaining the emergence of a more interventionist/dirigiste type of political economy in which large corporations predominate.

69 Jean Fourastié, *Les trente glorieuses*, Paris: Fayard, 1979.

70 David Wolfe, "The Rise and Demise of the Keynesian Era in Canada: Economic Policy, 1930-1982," in Michael Cross and Gregory Kealey, eds., *Modern Canada: 1930-1980*, Toronto: McClelland & Stewart, 1984, 46-78.

71 Alan Noël, "L'après-guerre au Canada: politiques keynésiennes ou nouvelles formes de regulation," in G. Boismenu and G. Dostaler, eds., "La 'Théorie générale' et le keynésianisme," Montreal: Politique et Economie, 6, 1987, 91-107.

72 Campbell, *Grand Illusions*, 214.

73 Louis St Laurent cited in Maurice Lamontagne, "The Role of Government" (1954), in Rea and McLeod, *Business and Government*, 68-70.

74 Ibid., 70.

75 Paolo Sylos Labini, "The General Theory: Critical Reflections Suggested by Some Important Problems of Our Time," in Fausto Vicarelli, ed., *Keynes' Relevance Today*, London: Macmillan/University of Pennsylvania Press, 1985, 149.

76 Leo Panitch and Donald Swartz, *From Consent to Coercion: The Assault on Trade Union Freedoms*, Toronto: Garamond Press, 1985.

77 The figures are drawn from O E C D, *Social Expenditures 1960–90* and are cited by Richard Langlois, "La politique sociale canadienne et le libre echange," in *Interventions économiques*, no. 18 (1987), 93–118, table 2, 96. Regarding the rate of increase, Moscovitch and Drover note: "By 1978 G N P had increased fourfold over 1946, while total government expenditures increased sixfold and social expenditures eighteenfold," in Moscovitch and Albert, *The Benevolent State*, 31.

78 Cf. Banting, "Images."

79 Thus, Peter Flora and Arnold Heidenheimer write: "Using [Durkheim's] perspective, the welfare state may be understood as an attempt to create a new kind of solidarity in highly differentiated societies, and as an attempt to respond to problems in the division of labour"; "The Historical Core and Changing Boundaries of the Welfare State," in Peter Flora and Arnold Heidenheimer, *The Development of Welfare States in Europe and America*, New Brunswick, N J: Transaction Books, 1981, 24.

80 Cf. Asa Briggs, "The Welfare State in Historical Perspective," *Archives européennes de Sociologie*, 2 (1961), 221–58; Richard M. Titmuss, *Essays on the Welfare State*, London: Allen & Unwin, 1959; Leonard Marsh et al., *Report on Social Security for Canada*, Ottawa, 1943.

81 Pierre Elliott Trudeau, C T V interview of 28 Dec. 1975, in John Saywell, ed., *Canadian Annual Review of Politics and Public Affairs*, Toronto: University of Toronto Press, 1976, 96–7.

82 Langlois, "La politique sociale," 97.

83 Thus Claude Ryan, Quebec's minister of education, is quoted in *Le Devoir* of 27 Oct. 1987, p. 10, as acknowledging the interest of the federal government in higher education because of its general responsibility for economic development. What goes for the federal government, needless to say, also goes for provincial ones.

84 Harold Innis, *Political Economy in the Modern State*, Toronto: University of Toronto Press, 1946. The complete sentence reads, "The descent of the university into the market place is the lie at the heart of modern society."

85 David Strangway, president, University of British Columbia, *Engine of Recovery*, President's Office, U B C, 1986.

86 William Cochrane, vice-president, Guaranty Trust, "Make Professors Pay Their Way," *Globe and Mail*, 3 Nov. 1986, A7.

87 Galbraith, *New Industrial State*, 20.

88 Walter Light, Northern Telecom, cited favourably by Brian Mulroney, "Where I Stand: A Conservative Perspective," in K.J. Rea and Nelson Wiseman, eds., *Government and Enterprise in Canada*, Toronto: Methuen, 1983, 53–4.

89 Harold Wilson won the 1964 British general election in part on the

promise of leading Britain into a new scientific revolution. Mulroney, before his election to office, spoke of the need for a strong government role in research and development and a further increase of its share in our G N P by 1 per cent ("Where I Stand," 54).

90 Cf. Stephen Cohen, *Modern Capitalist Planning: The French Model*, Cambridge, Mass.: Harvard University Press, 1969; John Zysman, *Political Strategies for Industrial Order: State, Market and Industry in France*, Berkeley: University of California Press, 1971; Ira Magaziner and Thomas Hout, *Japanese Industrial Policy*, Berkeley: University of California Press, 1981.

91 Cf. Marsha A. Chandler, "The State and Industrial Decline: A Survey," in Andre Blais, ed., *Industrial Policy*, Royal Commission Studies, vol. 44, Toronto: University of Toronto Press, 1986, 171-218.

92 Cited by Andrew Gollner, "The Effects of Business-Government Relations on Industrial Policy," in Blais, *Industrial Policy*, 299.

93 Andre Blais, *A Political Sociology of Public Aid to Industry*, Royal Commission Studies, Toronto, 1986, vol. 45, Toronto: University of Toronto Press, 29.

94 Paul Davenport et al., "Industrial Policy in Ontario and Quebec," in Rea and Wiseman, *Government and Enterprise*, 85-100.

95 Thomas d'Aquino, president, Business Council on National Issues, "1984 and Beyond," in Rea and Wiseman, *Government and Enterprise*, 36-7.

96 Peter F. Bartha, Imperial Oil, "Incorporating Public Affairs in Business Management: Problems and Opportunities," in V.V. Murray, ed., *Theories of Business-Government Relations*, Toronto: Trans-Canada Press, 1985, 364.

97 Mulroney, "Where I Stand," 55-6.

98 Melissa Clark-Jones, *A Staple State: Canadian Industrial Resources in Cold War*, Toronto: University of Toronto Press, 1987.

99 Cf. the author's *The Land of Cain: Class and Nationalism in English Canada*, Vancouver: New Star Books, 1977, chap. 5.

100 Canada, Department of External Affairs, *The Canada-United States Trade Agreement in Brief*, 1987, 1.

101 François Houle, "Reflexions sur la restructuration de l'état au Canada," in *Interventions économiques*, no. 18 (1987), 72.

102 Jean Lesage, 3 June 1961, cited in Rejean Pelletier, "Les partis politiques et l'état," in Gerard Bergeron et Rejean Pelletier, eds., *L'état du Québec en devenir*, Montreal: Boreal Express, 1980, 245.

103 Howard and Stanbury, "Measuring Leviathan," 93.

104 Cited in "L'état en transition," *Interventions économiques*, no. 18 (1987), 48.

105 These terms are taken from P Q programs of the early 1970s and are

cited by Richard French, "Governing without Business: The P Q in Power," in Murray, *Theories of Business-Government*, 159–80.

106 Cf. my article, "La vengeance des huguenots: sur l'héritage de la révolution tranquille," in Robert Comeau, ed., *Jean Lesage et l'éveil d'une nation*, Sillery, Presses de l'Université du Québec, 1989, 322–9.

107 House of Commons Debates, Bud Cullen, 30 Oct. 1980, 4271.

108 Throne Speech, House of Commons Debates, 14 April 1980, 60; *The National Energy Program*, 103, cited in Larry Pratt, "Energy and the National Policy," *Studies in Political Economy*, no. 7, 1982, 41.

109 Vining and Botterell, "An Overview,"

110 Langford and Huffman, "The Uncharted Universe."

111 See the author's "The Maturing of Canadian Capitalism," *Our Generation*, 15, no. 3, 1982, 11–24, for relevant figures.

112 Lynn K. Mytelka, "The State and Foreign Capital in the Advanced Industrial Capitalist Countries," in A. Blais, *Industrial Policy*, table 4–1, 122.

113 Ibid., table 4–6, 131.

114 Richard Barnet, *The Lean Years*, New York: Simon and Shuster, 1980, 241, notes that 68 of the top 156 companies in the world by asset size in 1976 were American, compared to 111 in 1959. For a more recent analysis of American economic decline, see Bertrand Bellon and Jorge Niosi, *L'industrie américaine: fin de siècle*, Montreal: Boréal, 1987.

115 Cf. Leo Panitch's sweeping overview of European corporatism in Keith Banting, ed., *The State and Economic Interests*, Royal Commission Studies, vol. 32, Toronto: University of Toronto Press, 1986, 37–119. An argument can be made, however, regarding the existence in Canada of a so-called meso-corporatism, confined to particular industrial sectors. Cf. Michael Atkinson and William Coleman, "Corporatism and Industrial Policy," in Alan Cawson, ed., *Organized Interests and the State: Studies in Meso-Corporatism*, Beverly Hills: Sage, 1985, 22–44.

116 Cf. Warren Magnusson et al., eds., *The New Reality*, Vancouver: New Star Books, 1984; Don Blake, "The Electoral Significance of Public Sector Bashing," *BC Studies*, no. 62 (1984), 29–43; and the author's "Neo-Conservatism on the Periphery: The Lessons from B C," *BC Studies*, no. 77 (1987), 3–23.

117 Two recent studies, from opposite sides of the political spectrum, make this argument. John Crispo, ed., *Free Trade: The Real Story*, Toronto: Gage, 1988; John Warnock, *Free Trade and the New Right Agenda*, Vancouver: New Star, 1988.

118 Claus Offe, *Disorganized Capitalism: Contemporary Transformations of Work and Politics*, Cambridge, Mass.: M . I . T . Press, 1985. Cf. also Scott Lash

and John Urry, *The End of Organized Capitalism*, Cambridge: Polity Press, 1987.

CHAPTER NINE

1 Cf. Kari Levitt, *Silent Surrender*, Toronto: Macmillan, 1970; John Hutcheson, *Dominance and Dependency: Liberalism and National Policies in the North Atlantic Triangle*, Toronto: McClelland & Stewart, 1978; Wallace Clement, *Class, Power and Property: Essays on Canadian Society*, Toronto: Methuen, 1983; Daniel Drache, "The Crisis of Canadian Political Economy: Dependency Theory vs. the New Orthodoxy," *Canadian Journal of Political and Social Theory*, fall 1983, 25–49.

2 Cf. Steve Moore and Debbi Wells, *Imperialism and the National Question in Canada*, Toronto: New Hogtown Press, 1975, and to a certain degree David McNally, "Staple Theory as Commodity Fetishism: Marx, Innis and Canadian Political Economy," *Studies in Political Economy*, no. 6 (autumn 1981), 35–63.

3 See Gordon Laxer, "Foreign Ownership and Myths about Canadian Development," *Canadian Review of Sociology and Anthropology*, Aug. 1985, 333; and his more recent *Open for Business: The Roots of Foreign Ownership in Canada*, Toronto: Oxford University Press, 1989.

4 Cf. Wallace Clement, "Debates and Directions: A Political Economy of Resources," in Wallace Clement and Glen Williams, eds., *The New Canadian Political Economy*, Montreal: McGill-Queen's University Press, 1989, 36–53; also Philip Ehrensaft and Warwick Armstrong, 'The Formation of Dominion Capitalism: Economic Truncation and Class Structure," in A. Moscovitch and G. Drover, eds., *Inequality: Essays on the Political Economy of Social Welfare*, Toronto: University of Toronto Press, 1981, 99–155.

5 Cf. this author's, "The Maturing of Canadian Capitalism," *Our Generation*, 15 no. 2 (fall 1982), 11–24.

6 On the decline in American hegemony, see among others, Richard Barnet, *The Lean Years*, New York, 1980: Bertrand Bellon and Jorge Niosi, *L'industrie américaine: fin de siècle*, Montreal: Boréal, 1987; David Calleo, *Beyond American Hegemony: The Future of the Western Alliance*, New York: Basic Books, 1987; and the works by Robert Keohane and Robert Gilpin referred to below.

7 Immanuel Wallerstein, *The Modern World System*, 1, New York: Academic Press, 1974.

8 Without rejecting the heuristic value of the larger enterprise, I share some of the criticisms directed against Wallerstein's formulation by Theda Skocpol, "Wallerstein's World Capitalist System: A Theoretical and Historical Critique," *American Journal of Sociology*, 82 (March 1977), 1075–90, and Peter Gurevitch, "The International System and Regime

Formation: A Critical Review of Anderson and Wallerstein," *Comparative Politics*, 10 (April 1978), 419–38.

9 Wallerstein, *System*, 102–3, 349.

10 Immanuel Wallerstein, *The Modern World System*, I I, New York: Academic Press, 1980, 38.

11 Ibid., I, 302.

12 Ibid., I, 102–3.

13 Ibid., I, 349.

14 Ibid., I, 107; I I, 179.

15 Cf. the latter chapter in vol. I I and also Wallerstein, "The Rise and Future Demise of the World Capitalist System: Concepts for Comparative Analysis," *Comparative Studies in Society and History*, 16 no. 4 (Sept. 1974), 408, where Russia and Japan are cited as semi-peripheries for the nineteenth century.

16 Peter Lange, "Semiperiphery and Core in the European Context: Reflections on the Postwar Italian Experience," in Giovanni Arrighi, ed., *Semiperipheral Development: The Politics of Southern Europe in the Twentieth Century*, Beverly Hills: Sage, 1985, 183–5.

17 Cf. Mel Watkins, "A Staple Theory of Economic Growth," reprinted in W.T. Easterbrook and M.H. Watkins, eds., *Approaches to Canadian Economic History*, Toronto:Carleton Library, 1967, where the notion of a "staples trap" is first introduced. (Watkins, in this article, does not suggest that Canada is necessarily caught within such a trap.) Cf. also Pierre Bourgault, *Innovation and the Structure of Canadian Industry*, Ottawa: Science Council of Canada, 1972, and J. Britton and J. Gilmour, *The Weakest Link: A Technological Perspective on Canadian Industrial Underdevelopment*, Background Study 43, Ottawa: Science Council of Canada, 1978.

18 Glen Williams, *Not for Export: Toward a Political Economy of Canada's Arrested Industrialization*, Toronto: McClelland & Steward, 1983, table 1, 8.

19 Cf. Levitt, *Silent Surrender*; Hutcheson, *Dominance and Dependency*.

20 Cf. Mel Watkins, "The Political Economy of Growth," in Clement and Williams, *The New Canadian Political Economy*, 31: "The economy is staples-based, the industrial structure is truncated and dependent; the Canadian bourgeoisie is continentalist, to the core." For the term *advanced resource capitalism*, see D. Drache, "Staple-ization: A Theory of Canadian Capitalist Development," in Craig Heron, ed., *Imperialism, Nationalism and Canada*, Toronto: New Hogtown Press, 1977, 15–33. For examples of the singling out of the importance of resources within Canadian capitalism, compare the chapter by Clement in Clement and Williams, *Political Economy*.

21 Cf., for example, Abram Epp, "Cooperation among Capitalists: The

Canadian Merger Movement, 1909-1913," P H D thesis, Johns Hopkins University, 1973, and, though he emphasizes the commercial character of indigenous Canadian capitalism in this period, Tom Naylor, *A History of Canadian Business*, I I, Toronto: Lorimer, 1973, with numerous examples of industry in Canada.

22 Tom Kemp, *Historical Patterns of Industrialization*, London: Longman, 1978, 164.

23 Jean-Charles Asselin, *Histoire économique: De la révolution industrielle à la première guerre mondiale*, Paris: Presses de la Fondation Nationale des Sciences Politiques, 1985, 254.

24 Ibid., 247, 270.

25 Laxer, "Foreign ownership," 312.

26 Michael Edelstein, *Overseas Investment in the Age of High Imperialism: The United Kingdom, 1850-1914*, New York: Columbia University Press, 1986, table 9.4, 206-7.

27 Simon Kuznets, *Economic Growth of Nations*, Cambridge, Mass.: Harvard University Press, 1971, table 1, 11-14.

28 Michael Mulhall, *Industries and Wealth of Nations*, London: Longmans, 1896, cited in ibid., 24.

29 A. Maddison, *Economic Growth in the West: Comparative Experience in Europe and North America*, New York: Twentieth Century Fund, 1964, cited in Nicole Bosquet, "From Hegemony to Competition: Cycles of the Core," in T. Hopkins and I. Wallerstein, eds., *Processes of the World System*, Beverly Hills: Sage, 1980, 71.

30 Edelstein, *Overseas Investment*, 285-6.

31 Mira Wilkins, *The Emergence of Multinational Enterprise: American Business Abroad from the Colonial Era to 1914*, Cambridge, Mass.: Harvard University Press, 1970, chap. 7, also p. 202.

32 Edelstein, for example, observes: "British owners seem to have exerted much more control over their Argentinian railway investments than in the Canadian case. Hence, the higher percentage of portfolio investment in the Canadian case represents a substantive, rather than merely a definitional, difference in the degree of activism and control"; *Overseas Investment*, 36.

33 Otto Hintze, "Military Organization and the Organization of the State," in *The Historical Essays of Otto Hintze*, Princeton: Princeton University Press, 1975.

34 Cf. Anthony Giddens, *The Nation-State and Violence*, Cambridge: Polity Press, 1985, chap. 4, 9.

35 Gautam Sen, *The Military Organization of Industrialization and International Trade Rivalry*, London: Frances Pinter, 1984, 249.

36 Gordon Laxer, "The Political Economy of Aborted Development: The

Canadian Case," in Robert Brym, ed., *The Structure of Canadian Capitalism*, Toronto: Garamond, 1986, 80.

37 Cf. C.P. Stacey, *Canada and the Age of Conflict*, 2 vols., Toronto: University of Toronto Press, 1981, 1984.

38 Cf. Peter B. Evans, D. Rueschemeyer, and T. Skocpol, eds., *Bringing the State back in*, Cambridge: Cambridge University Press, 1985. See also Wallerstein, *The Modern World System*, 11, 284: "A state is strong to the extent that those who govern can make their will prevail against the will of others outside or inside the realm ... The truly strong state seldom has need to show its iron fist."

39 Hans-Dieter Evers and T. Schiel, "Exchange, Trade and the State," *Review*, 10 no. 3 (winter 1987), 467–9.

40 Malcolm Alexander, "The Political Economy of Semi-Industrialized Capitalism: A Comparative Study of Argentina, Australia, and Canada 1950–70," P H D thesis, McGill University, 1979, 10.

41 Leo Panitch, "Dependency and Class in Canadian Political Economy," *Studies in Political Economy*, no. 6 (autumn 1981), 23.

42 Melissa Clark-Jones, *A Staple State: Canadian Industrial Resources in Cold War*, Toronto: University of Toronto Press, 1987.

43 Jorge Niosi, *Canadian Multinationals*, Toronto: Between the Lines, 1985, table 1, 37.

44 Cf. John Porter, *The Vertical Mosaic*, Toronto: University of Toronto Press, 1965; Wallace Clement, *The Canadian Corporate Elite*, Toronto: McClelland and Stewart, 1975.

45 For the roots of this inflow, see H.F. Marshall, F. Southard, and K. Taylor, *Canadian-American Industry*, Toronto: Carleton Library, reprinted 1976; for rates of growth of U S direct investment in Canada see William Carroll, *Corporate Power and Canadian Capitalism*, Vancouver: U B C Press, 1986, table 8–1, 203.

46 See the author's *The Land of Cain*, Vancouver: New Star Books, 1977, chap. 5, for a further discussion.

47 Statistics Canada, *Companies and Labour Unions Returns Act, 1979*, vol. 1, Ottawa, 1981, 43, 45.

48 Jeanne Laux and Maureen Molot, *State Capitalism: Public Enterprise in Canada*, Ithaca: Cornell University Press, 1987, 59.

49 Cf. Niosi, *Canadian Multinationals*, table 13, 57.

50 *Fortune*, 4 Aug. 1986, 207–8.

51 U N Centre on Transnational Corporations, *Salient Features and Trends in Foreign Direct Investment*, New York, 1983.

52 Rowland Frazee, cited by Andrew Malcolm, "More Than Ready for the Big Leagues," *Canadian Business*, June 1985, 249.

53 Leo Panitch, "Class and Power in Canada," *Monthly Review*, April 1985, 16.

54 Michael Clow, "Canadian Political Economy and the International Underdevelopment and Dependency Debate," Canadian Political Science Association Papers, Ottawa, June 1982, 47.

55 *Globe and Mail Report on Business Magazine*, July 1986, 28.

56 Malcolm, "More Than Ready," 249.

57 Statistics Canada, *Quarterly Estimates of the Canadian Balance of International Payments* and *Canada's International Investment Position*, cited by Alan Rugman, "Canada in the United States: Foreign Direct Investment Flow Reversed," *Multinational Business*, E C U (spring 1987), table 1. See also O C D E, *Investissement international et entreprises multinationales: tendances récentes des investissements directs internationaux*, Paris, 1987, 21, 98–104, 193, for tables that confirm this pattern.

58 William Carroll, *Corporate Power*, table 8.1, 203.

59 Ibid., 211.

60 Bellon and Niosi, *L'industrie américaine*, 176.

61 Paul Kellogg, "Canada as a Principal Economy," Canadian Political Science Association Papers, McMaster 1987, 14.

62 See the author's "The Maturing."

63 See the excellent article by Duncan Cameron, "The Dealers: Who's behind the Free Trade Deal?" *This Magazine*, 21 (Feb. 1988), 18–23.

64 Alexander Gerschenkron, *Economic Backwardness in Historical Perspective*, Cambridge: Harvard University Press, 1962.

65 Cf. M. Fennema, *International Networks of Banks and Industry*, The Hague: Martinus Nijhoff, 1982, table 3.1, 80.

66 John M. Stopford, John Dunning, and Klaus Haberich, *The World Directory of Multinational Enterprises*, 1, London: Macmillan, 1980, table 2, xv.

67 Wallace Clement, *Continental Corporate Power*, Toronto: McClelland & Stewart, 1977.

68 Robert Keohane, *After Hegemony: Cooperation and Discord in the World Political Economy*, Princeton: Princeton University Press, 1984, 32.

69 O E C D, *Economic Outlook*, July 1982, puts the U S share of the O E C D's total G D P in 1980 at 34.6 per cent.

70 Bellon and Niosi, *L'industrie américaine*, table 4, 32.

71 Bernard Slade and Raj Mohindra, *Winning the Productivity Race*, Lexington, Mass.: Lexington Books, 1985, 41.

72 Lawrence G. Franko, "Multinationals and the end of U.S. dominance," *Harvard Business Review*, Nov.–Dec. 1978, 96.

73 *Fortune*, 4 Aug. 1986, 207–8.

74 Cf. Bellon and Niosi, *L'industrie américaine*, chap. 1, 2.

75 Robert Gilpin, *The Political Economy of International Relations*, Princeton: Princeton University Press, 1987, 336.

76 Ibid., 5–6.

77 Ibid., 355, 358.

78 As Kees van de Pjil has argued, at least with respect to the Atlantic world, in his *The Making of an Atlantic Ruling Class*, London: Verso, 1984.

79 Wallerstein, *The Modern World System*, 1, 67.

80 Peter F. Drucker, "The Changed World Economy," *Foreign Affairs*, spring 1986, 791.

81 Leonard Silk, "The U.S. and the World Economy," *Foreign Affairs*, 63, no. 3 (1987), 467.

82 Immanuel Wallerstein, *The Politics of the World Economy*, Cambridge: Cambridge University Press, 1984, 7.

83 Giovanni Arrighi and Jessica Drangel, "Stratification of the World Economy: An Exploration of the Semiperipheral Zone," *Review*, Summer 1986, 11.

84 Niosi, *Canadian Multinationals*, 178. Also Williams, *Not for Export*.

85 Williams, *Not for Export*, chap. 1.

86 *Salient Features and Trends in Direct Foreign Investment*, table 3, 35.

87 Carroll, *Corporate Power*, 204, 206.

88 Charles Adams et al., "Potential Output in Major Industrial Countries," *Staff Studies for the World Economic Outlook*, Washington, DC: International Monetary Fund, Aug. 1987, table 1, p. 3.

89 Ibid., table 8, 24.

90 Cited in Kellogg, "Canada as a Principal Economy," 13, using figures from OECD, *Historical Statistics, 1960–1983*, Paris, 1983, 45.

91 Adams et al., *Potential Output*, table 4, 92.

92 Ibid., table 4, "Structure of Civilian Employment by Sector," 11.

93 Economic Council of Canada, *The Bottom Line*, 1983, 90.

94 "Aide Mémoire de la Vie Economique," *Faits et Chiffres*, Paris, 1985, 190–1.

95 OECD, *Historical Statistics, 1960–1985*, Paris 1987, "Social Policy Transfers as a Percentage of Gross Domestic Product," 63.

96 CALURA reports for 1983 and 1970.

97 *Mike: The Memoirs of the Right Honourable Lester B. Pearson*, II, *1948–57*, Toronto: University of Toronto Press, 1972, 31, cited in R.D. Cuff and J.L. Granatstein, *American Dollars and Canadian Prosperity*, Toronto: Samuel-Stevens, 1978, 183.

98 For a favourable assessment of this development, see Cuff and Granatstein, *American Dollars*. For the opposite view, see Clark-Jones, *A Staple State*.

99 Cf. John Holmes, *The Shaping of Peace: Canada and the Search for World Order 1943–1957* II, Toronto: University of Toronto Press, 1982.

100 Lester Pearson, Address to Kiwanis International, Los Angeles, *Statements and Speeches*, 8 June 1948, cited in Ian Lumsden, ed., *Close the 49th Parallel, Etc.*, Toronto: University of Toronto Press, 1970, 96.

101 Cf. James Eayrs, *In Defence of Canada: Indochina, Roots of Complicity*,

Toronto: University of Toronto Press, 1983, and Ramesh Thakur, *Peace-keeping in Vietnam: Canada, India, Poland and the International Commission*, Edmonton: University of Alberta Press, 1984. Douglas Ross, *In the Interests of Peace: Canada and Vietnam 1954–1973*, Toronto: University of Toronto Press, 1984, offers a defence of the Canadian role that I find unconvincing.

102 Keohane, *After Hegemony*, 45.
103 James Eayrs, cited in Kim Richard Nossal, *The Politics of Canadian Foreign Policy*, Toronto: Prentice-Hall, 1985, 14.
104 P. Lyon and B. Tomlin, cited in ibid., 14.
105 David Dewitt and John Kirton, *Canada as a Principal Power*, Toronto: John Wiley & Sons, 1983, 40.
106 Cf. Wallerstein's treatment of Holland as a hegemonic power in seventeenth-century Europe, despite its military insignificance: *The Modern World System*, I. Cf. also the comment by Arrighi and Drangel, "Stratification," 15: "We shall use the term 'semiperiphery' exclusively to refer to a position in relation to the world division of labour and never to refer to a position in the interstate system."
107 Jean Bodin, *Six Books on the Republic*; Thomas Hobbes, *Leviathan*. For a useful modern summary, see F.H. Hinsley, *Sovereignty*, 2nd ed., Cambridge, 1986.
108 J.J. Rousseau, *The Social Contract*; Bertrand de Jouvenel, *Les débuts de l'état moderne*, Paris, 1976, 156–7.
109 B. Rowthorn, "Imperialism in the 1970s – Unity or Rivalry," in Hugo Radice, ed., *International Firms and Modern Imperialism*, Harmondsworth: Penguin, 1975, cited in Carroll, *Corporate Power*, 198.
110 Cf. Peter Hall, *Governing the Economy: The Politics of State Intervention in Britain and France*, Cambridge: Polity Press, 1986; Alain Liepietz, *L'enlisement ou l'audace: sur les politiques économiques de la gauche*, Paris: La Découverte, 1984.
111 Massimo Salvadori, *Karl Kautsky and the Socialist Revolution 1880–1938*, London: New Left Books, 1979, chap. VI, section 1, "The Hypothesis of 'Ultra-Imperialism.'"

CHAPTER TEN

1 André Siegfried, *The Race Question in Canada*, Toronto: Carleton Library, 1966, 22.
2 H.McD. Clokie, *Canadian Government and Politics*, Toronto: Longmans, 1944, 8.
3 J.A. Corry, *The Growth of Government Activities since Confederation*, Study for the Royal Commission on Dominion-Provincial Relations, Ottawa, 1939, especially 1–18; H.G.J. Aitken, "Defensive Expansionism: The

State and Economic Growth in Canada," in W.T. Easterbrook and M.H. Watkins, eds., *Approaches to Canadian Economic History*, Toronto: Carleton Library, 1967, 183–221; George Grant, *Lament for a Nation*, Toronto: Carleton Library, 1970, 70–1.

4 Donald V. Smiley, "Federalism, Nationalism and the Scope of Political Activity in Canada," in Peter Russell, ed., *Nationalism in Canada*, Toronto: McGraw-Hill, 1966, 100.

5 John. A. Macdonald, 1861 speech to the Legislative Assembly, cited in Chester Martin, *Foundations of Canadian Nationhood*, Toronto: University of Toronto Press, 1955, 319.

6 Immanuel Wallerstein, *The Politics of the World-Economy: Essays*, Cambridge: Cambridge University Press, 1984: "The states are defined by and constrained by their membership in an interstate system," 134.

7 John S. Ewart, *The Kingdom of Canada*, Toronto: Morang, 1908, 6.

8 John A. Macdonald, "Confederation Debates 1865," cited by Stanley Ryerson, *Unequal Union*, Toronto: Progress Books, 1968, 365.

9 *Parliamentary Debates on the Subject of the Confederation of the British North American Provinces*, Quebec, 1865; Ottawa: King's Printer, reprinted 1951, 293.

10 Ibid., 440–1.

11 See the Preamble to the B N A Act.

12 Joseph Pope, *Memoirs of the Right Honourable Sir John A. Macdonald*, I I, London: Edward Arnold, 1894, 334.

13 Cited by Terence Ranger, "The Invention of Tradition in Colonial Africa," in Eric Hobsbawm and Terence Ranger, eds., *The Invention of Tradition*, Cambridge: Cambridge University Press, 1983, 216.

14 *The Program of the Nationalist League* in H.D. Forbes, ed., *Canadian Political Thought*, Oxford: Oxford University Press, 1985, 184.

15 Siegfried, *The Race Question*, 85.

16 Alexander O. Potter, *Canada as a Political Entity*, Toronto: Longmans, 1923, 9.

17 Clokie, *Canadian Government*, 7–8.

18 Ranger and Hobsbawm, *Invention*.

19 On individualism in American political culture, see James O'Connor, *Accumulation Crisis*, Oxford: Blackwell, 1984, chap. 1.

20 House of Commons Debates, 32nd Parl. 1st Sess., 15 April 1980, vol. I, 33.

21 *Tocqueville au Bas-Canada*, cited by Gérard Bergeron, *Pratique de l'état au Québec*, Montreal: Québec/Amérique, 1984, 23 n3.

22 Wallerstein, *Politics*, 134.

23 André Laurendeau, "The Nigger-King Hypothesis," in *André Laurendeau: Witness for Quebec*, ed. Philip Stratford, Toronto: Macmillan, 1973, 177–9.

24 Paul-André Linteau, René Durocher, Jean-Claude Robert, *Histoire du Québec contemporain*, Montreal: Boréal-Express, 1979, 258, 263.

25 Kenneth Buckley, *Capital Formation in Canada, 1896–1930*, Toronto: University of Toronto Press, 1955, 57.

26 Bergeron, *Pratique*, 48.

27 Cited in ibid.

28 Albert Faucher and Maurice Lamontagne, "History of Industrial Development," in Marcel Rioux and Yves Martin, eds., *French-Canadian Society*, Toronto: Carleton Library, 1964, 269.

29 Cf. Everett Hughes, *French Canada in Transition*, Chicago: Phoenix Edition, 1963, 203–7; Jacques Dofny and Marcel Rioux, "Social Class in French Canada," in Rioux and Martin, *French-Canadian Society*, 313–15, for statistical evidence.

30 Chubby Powers, *Memoirs*, Toronto: Macmillan, 1966, 374.

31 Cited by Albert Faucher, *Histoire économique et unité canadienne*, Montreal: Fides, 1970, 171.

32 For the "new middle class" thesis see Hubert Guindon, "Two Cultures: An Essay on Nationalism, Class and Ethnic Tension," in Richard H. Leach, ed., *Contemporary Canada*, Durham, N C: Duke University Press, 1967, 33–59; Jacques Brazeau, "Les nouvelles classes moyennes," in Fernand Dumont and Jean-Paul Montminy, *Le pouvoir dans la société canadienne-française*, Quebec: Laval, 1966, 151–63; Charles Taylor, "Nationalism and the Political Intelligentsia: A Case Study," *Queen's Quarterly*, 72 (spring 1965), 150–68.

33 Teodor Shanin, *Russia as a Developing Society*, London: Macmillan, 1985, 130–1.

34 Cf. Jorge Niosi, *Canadian Capitalism*, Toronto: Lorimer, 1981, chap. 3, "The New French Canadian Bourgeoisie," See also my article, "La vengeance des huguenots: sur l'héritage de la révolution tranquille," in Robert Comeau, ed., *Jean Lesage et l'éveil d'une nation*, Sillery: Presses de l'Université du Québec, 1989, 322–9.

35 Linteau et al., *Histoire*, 234.

36 Siegfried, *The Race Question*, 35.

37 Ibid., 22.

38 Jean Hamelin, cited in Linteau et al., *Histoire*, 525.

39 Fernand Dumont, "Transformation within the Religious Culture of Francophone Quebec," in *Religion/Culture*, Comparative Canadian Studies, Association for Canadian Studies, V I I, 1985, 25.

40 Siegfried, *The Race Question*, 48.

41 See, for example, "The Programme Catholique," in Forbes, *Canadian Political Thought*, 93–95.

42 David Kwavnick, ed., *The Tremblay Report*, Toronto: Carleton Library, 1973, 50, 70, 71.

43 Pierre Elliott Trudeau, "Quebec on the Eve of the Asbestos Strike," in Trudeau, ed., *The Asbestos Strike*, Toronto: Lorimer, 1974.

44 Lionel Groulx, "If Dollard Were Alive Today," in Ramsay Cook, ed., *French Canadian Nationalism*, Toronto: Macmillan, 1971, 192, 201.

45 Jean Drapeau, Letter to Jean Lesage, 20 July 1960, cited in Gérard Bergeron, *Notre miroir à deux faces*, Montreal: Québec/Amérique, 1985, 23.

46 Jean Lesage, 3 June 1961, cited in Réjean Pelletier, "Les partis politiques et l'état," in Gérard Bergeron and Réjean Pelletier, eds., *L'état du Québec en devenir*, Montreal: Boréal-Express, 1980, 245.

47 René Lévesque, interview in *Le Devoir*, 5 July 1963, cited in Bergeron, *Notre miroir à deux faces*, 52.

48 Daniel Johnson, *Egalité ou Indépendance*, Montreal: Editions de l'Homme, 1965, 23.

49 André Blais and Kenneth McRoberts, "Dynamique et contraintes des finances publiques au Quebec," *Politique*, no. 3 (hiver 1983), table 1, 29.

50 John Breuilly, *Nationalism and the State*, Manchester: Manchester University Press, 1982, 352.

51 Ibid., 374.

CHAPTER ELEVEN

1 P.J. Proudhon, *The Principle of Federalism*, Toronto: University of Toronto Press, 1979, 68–9.

2 Rosa Luxemburg, *The National Question: Selected Writings*, ed. Horace B. Davis, New York: Monthly Review Press, 1976, 194.

3 Reference might also be made to the original tribes of Israel, but unified monarchy came to be the characteristic state form there.

4 Cf. W. den Boer, "The Dutch Republic and Antiquity," in J.C. Boogman and G.M. van der Plaat, eds., *Federalism: History and Current Significance of a Form of Government*, The Hague: Martinus Nijhoff, 1980, 47–64, and references to the Greek Confederation in *The Federalist Papers*.

5 "Any republican state, no matter how oligarchic, could call itself a democracy"; J.A.O. Lassen, *Representative Government in Greek and Roman History*, cited by den Boer, "The Dutch Republic," 55.

6 J.C. Boogman, "The Union of Utrecht: Its Genesis and Consequences," in Boogman and van der Plaat, *Federalism*, 18.

7 Ibid., 33.

8 Jean-Jacques Rousseau, *Sur le gouvernment de la Pologne*, in *Oeuvres complètes*, III, Paris: Bibliothèque de la Pléiade, 1966, 971.

9 Cf. the Declaration of the National Convention of 25 Sept. 1792, which first used this term; *Les constitutions de la France depuis 1789*, ed. Jacques Godechot, Paris: Garnier-Flammarion, 1970, 79.

10 Proudhon, *Principle*, 59.

11 Alexis de Tocqueville, *Democracy in America*, I, cited by Franz Neumann, "On the Theory of the Federal State," in *The Democratic and the Authoritarian State*, New York: Free Press, 1957, 226.

12 St-Just, *Oeuvres choisies*, Paris: Idées, 1968, "Essai de Constitution," 124.

13 Cited by Albert Soboul, "De l'ancien régime à la révolution: problème régionale et réalités sociales," in Christan Gras and Georges Livet, ed., *Régions et régionalisme en France*, Paris: P U F, 1977, 42.

14 Ibid., 37.

15 St-Just, *Oeuvres*, 66, 256.

16 See Daniel Guérin, *La lutte de classes sous la 1ère république*, Paris: Gallimard, 1968, I, Introduction; II, chap. XI.

17 Cited by Luxemburg, *The National Question*, 125.

18 Ibid., 119.

19 Geoffrey Sawer, *Modern Federalism*, London: Watts, 1969, 25.

20 Proudhon, *Principle*, 72–3.

21 Bakounine, *La liberté: choix de textes*, Paris: J.J. Pauvert, 1965, 272.

22 Marx and Engels, *Selected Works*, London: Lawrence and Wishart, 1968, 292.

23 Otto Bauer, *Social Democracy and the National Question*, excerpts in Georges Haupt, Michael Lowy, and Claude Weill, *Les Marxistes et la question nationale*, Paris: Maspero, 1974, 242.

24 Ibid., 267.

25 Lenin, *Questions of National Policy and Proletarian Internationalism*, Moscow, 1964, 113.

26 Cited in Z.R. Dittrich, "Der russische Vielvölkerstaat zwischen Zentralismus und Föderation," in Boogman and van der Plaat, *Federalism*, 301.

27 *Constitution (Fundamental Law) of the Union of Soviet Socialist Republics*, Moscow, 1977.

28 Fritz W. Hondius, *The Yugoslav Community of Nations*, The Hague: Mouton, 1968, 148.

29 Ibid., 194.

30 "The preoccupation with the issue of federalization explains why Slovakia accounted for only five per cent of the total number of [workers] councils; federalization made it possible to get rid of the political left of Bohemia-Moravia in a roundabout way"; Vladimir Fisera, *Workers' Control in Czechoslovakia, 1968-9*, London, 1979, 13.

31 "The nation state is the form of state which corresponds most closely to modern economic relations, the one which allows it best to realize the tasks which fall to it. But each state is not destined to achieve this form. Just as modern relations of production preserve numerous economic activities inherited from the feudal period ... so vestiges of a period when the state could be made up of the most heterogeneous

national elements subsist"; in Haupt, Lowy, and Weill, *Les Marxistes*, 140.

32 K.C. Wheare, *Federal Government*, Oxford: Oxford University Press, 1946, 255–6.

33 Cited by V.C. Ramachandran, "Aspects of Federalism," in S.P. Aiyar and V. Mehta, eds, *Essays on Federalism*, Bombay: Allied Publishers, 1965, 65.

34 Sawer, *Modern Federalism*, 183.

35 Cited by Stanley Ryerson, *Unequal Union*, Toronto: Progress Books, 1968, 355.

36 Ibid., 365.

37 Confderation Debates, cited by Frank R. Scott, *Essays on the Constitution*, Toronto: University of Toronto Press, 1977, 18.

38 E.A. Partridge, prominent agrarian reformer of the beginning of the century, cited by John Richards in "Partridge of Sintaluta," a text that appears under another title in Larry Pratt and Garth Stevenson, eds., *Western Separation*, Edmonton: Hurtig, 1981.

39 Michael Cross, ed., *The Decline and Fall of a Good Idea: CCF-NDP Manifestoes 1932 to 1969*, Toronto: New Hogtown Press, 1974, 22.

40 League for Social Reconstruction, *Social Planning for Canada*, Toronto, 1935, 507.

41 Tim Buck, *Our Fight for Canada*, Toronto, 1959, 112.

42 Ibid, 114.

43 Leslie Morris, *Look on Canada Now*, Toronto: Progress Books, 1970, 24.

44 Alvin Finkel, *Business and Social Reform in the Thirties*, Toronto: Lorimer, 1979, 138–9.

45 Canada, Department of Finance, *Economic Review*, 1980, Reference Table 78, "Allocations of Revenue after Transfer, by Levels of Government 1945–1979," 243.

46 Ibid.

47 John Porter, *The Vertical Mosiac*, Toronto: University of Toronto Press, 1965, 369 ff.

48 Pierre Elliott Trudeau, "The Practice and Theory of Federalism," in Michael Oliver, ed., *Social Purpose for Canada*, Toronto: University of Toronto Press, 1961, 371–93.

49 Cross, *CCF-NDP Manifestoes*, 39.

50 For a good discussion of these developments, see Roch Denis, *Luttes de classes et question nationale au Québec, 1948–1968*, Montreal: Presses Socialistes Internationales, 1979.

51 Cross, *CCF-NDP Manifestoes*, 44.

52 In a recently published essay, *Letters to a Québécois Friend*, Montreal: McGill-Queen's, 1990, I have further developed my thoughts on Meech Lake, free trade, and so on. In it, I take a more critical view of recent

Quebec nationalism than I tend to do in this chapter which, despite some revision, dates from the early 1980s.

53 Cf. my essay, *Parliament vs. People*. Vancouver: New Star books, 1984, sections 8-9, for a model of something I call base-level democracy.

CHAPTER TWELVE

This chapter is a substantially revised version of a paper originally presented at a 1980 session of the Political Economy section of the Canadian Political Science Association meetings in honour of C.B. Macpherson.

1 Karl Kautsky, *Parlamentarismus und Demokratie*, 2nd ed., Stuttgart, 1911.

2 Joseph Schumpeter, *Capitalism, Socialism and Democracy*, 3rd ed., New York: Harper & Row, 1950, 269.

3 Cf. Adam Przeworski, *Capitalism and Social Democracy*, Cambridge: Cambridge University Press 1985; Adam Przeworski and John Sprague, *Paper Stones: A History of Electoral Socialism*, Chicago: University of Chicago Press, 1986.

4 Rudolf Bahro, *The Alternative in Eastern Europe*, London: New Left Books, 1978.

5 *Soviet Democracy in the Period of Developed Socialism*, Moscow: Progress Books, 1979, 16-17.

6 Ibid., 17.

7 Cf., for example, Frank Cunningham, *Democratic Theory and Socialism*, Cambridge: Cambridge University Press, 1987, and Christopher Pierson, *Marxist Theory and Democratic Politics*, Berkeley: University of California Press, 1986.

8 Louis Althusser, "The Crisis of Marxism," in *Power and Opposition in Post-revolutionary Societies*, London, 1979, 234.

9 Carole Pateman, *Participation and Democratic Theory*, Cambridge: Cambridge University Press, 1970, and *The Problem of Political Obligation*, Berkeley: University of California Press, 1985; Lucio Colletti, *From Rousseau to Lenin*, New York: Monthly Review Press, 1972; James Miller, *Rousseau: Dreamer of Democracy*, New Haven: Yale University Press, 1984.

10 Antonio Gramsci, *Selections from the Prison Notebooks*, London: Lawrence & Wishart, 1971, 141; Maurice Merleau-Ponty, "Note sur Machiavel," *Signes*, Paris, 1960.

11 Cf. Raphael Patai, *The Messiah Texts*, New York, 1979, "The Banquet," 235-46.

12 Cited in Bernard Guetta's article on Poland in *Le Monde hebdomodaire*, 14-20 Feb. 1980.

13 V.I. Lenin, *State and Revolution*, in *Selected Works*, London: Lawrence and

Wishart, 1969, 348.

14 Karl Marx, *The Civil War in France*, in Marx and Engels, *Selected Works*, London: Lawrence and Wishart, 1968: "While the merely repressive organs of the old governmental power were to be amputated, its legitimate functions were to be wrested from an authority usurping pre-eminence over society itself, and restored to the responsible agents of society," (292).

15 Thucydides, *The Peloponnesian Wars*, London: Everyman's Library, 1952, 94.

16 This is the problem that Benjamin Constant first posed in his 1819 text, *De la liberté des anciens comparée à celle des modernes*, reprinted in B. Constant, *De la liberté chez les modernes*, Paris: Pluriel, 1980.

17 C.B. Macpherson, *The Life and Times of Liberal Democracy*, Oxford: Oxford University Press, 1977, chap. 4.

18 M. Crozier, S.P. Huntington, and J. Watanaki, *The Crisis of Democracy: Report on the Governability of Democracies to the Trilateral Commission*, New York, 1975, 64, 159.

19 Stuart Hall and Martin Jacques, *The Politics of Thatcherism*, London: Lawrence & Wishart, 1986; Joel Krieger, *Reagan, Thatcher and the Politics of Decline*, New York: Oxford University Press, 1986; Warren Magnusson et al., *The New Reality: The Politics of Restraint in British Columbia*, Vancouver: New Star Books, 1984.

20 *Soviet Democracy in the Period of Developed Socialism*, 17–18.

21 M. Gorbachev, Speech to the Central Committe of the Communist Party of the Soviet Union, *New York Times*, 27 Jan. 1987, A8; *Perestroïka: New Thinking for Our Country and the World*, New York: Harper & Row, 1987, 78.

22 I have developed the outline of such a model in my essay, *Parliament vs. People*, Vancouver: New Star Books, 1984, sections 8–10.

23 Charles Lindblom. *Politics and Markets: The World's Political Economic Systems*, New York: Basic Books, 1977, 356.

24 F. Feher, A. Heller, and G. Markus, *Dictatorship over Needs*, Oxford: Basil Blackwell, 1983.

25 For a lucid discussion of the failures of Soviet-type economics by an author sympathetic to socialism, see Alec Nove, *The Economics of Feasible Socialism*, London: Allen & Unwin, 1983, chap. 2–3.

26 Cf. A.O. Hirschman, *Shifting Involvements: Private Interests and Public Actions*, Princeton: Princeton University Press, 1982.

Index

aboriginal, 148
absolutism, 21, 24, 116, 128, 130, 201, 223, 225, 253, 254
academic, 136
accumulation, 38, 113, 115, 116, 121, 129, 130, 134, 143, 153, 158, 186, 189
accumulation function, 166
Achaean League, 222
Action nationale, 217
administration, 32, 90, 124, 133, 138, 160, 186, 216, 223, 224, 226, 228, 230, 232, 240, 260
Aetolian League, 222
Afghanistan, 252
Africa, 126
agrarian, 14, 23, 32, 90, 96, 105, 128, 216, 223, 225, 234, 254
agrarian democracy, 32
agrarian law, 14, 15, 30
agriculture, 157, 164, 171, 176, 183, 187, 260
Agriculture Canada, 172
Air Canada, 38, 174, 177, 211
Aitken, Hugh, 153, 208
Alberta, 55, 58, 59, 61, 97, 189, 212, 232, 236, 240
Alberta Heritage Founda-' tion, 176

alienation, 32, 105, 135, 147, 150, 241, 250, 259
Allende, Salvador, 253
alternative left, 8, 245, 246, 249–50, 255
Althusser, Louis, 110, 138, 250
altruism, 142
American Revolution, 54, 76, 89, 200, 224, 225
Amin, Idi, 117
Amin, Samir, 116
amorality, 20
Anabaptists, 31
anarchism, 221, 228, 250
anarchy, 113, 154
ancien régime, 67, 74, 99
Ancien Regime and the Coming of the French Revolution, The, 41
Anderson, Perry, 4
Andic, S., and J. Veverka, 111, 112
André, C., R. Delorme, and G. Terry, 111
anglophone, 58, 69, 94
anthem, national, 49, 210
anthropology, 109, 130
anti-democratic, 5, 41, 92, 223, 241, 254
anti-élitist, 89
anti-federalist, 227
Antigone, 115, 251
Anti-Inflation Board, 168,

170, 171
anti-nuclear, 34
anti-statist, 98
anti-terrorist, 126
apathy, 34, 149
Approaches to Economic Well-Being, 133
archein kai archeisthai, 29, 33
Argentina, 40, 184, 232
aristocracy/aristocratic, 6, 13–17, 18, 24, 27, 28, 30, 31, 36, 43, 45, 74, 75, 77, 80, 82, 85, 86, 87, 88, 89, 90, 97, 222, 223, 254, 260
Aristotle, 14, 29, 65, 72, 117, 131, 252
Armenia, 230
army, 45, 110, 185
Arrighi, G., and J. Drangel, 195
Articles of Confederation, 225
artisans, 31
ASEAN, 194
assassination, 119
Asselin, J.C., 183
assembly, 27, 29, 30, 31, 32, 41, 74, 89, 90, 92, 96, 99, 222, 248, 253
assimilation, 218
Athens, 18, 19, 29, 30, 33, 222, 252
Atlantic Development

Board, 170
Atomic Energy of Canada, 38
atomism, 31, 150
Attica, 30
Attlee, Clement, 57
Australian Labour party, 232, 243
Austro-Hungary, 15, 42, 229
Austro-Marxism, 7, 154
authoritarian/ism, 27, 40, 114, 125, 186, 232, 258, 260
authority, 15, 20, 21, 22, 23, 29, 41, 44, 46, 49, 50, 63, 72, 74, 76, 82, 90, 92, 100, 121, 133, 134, 136, 139, 147, 157, 200, 222, 224, 226, 229, 230, 254, 255, 257, 258, 262
autocracy, 97
autonomy, 3, 63, 114, 117, 118, 124, 125, 127, 130, 137, 139, 143, 146, 149, 151, 159, 181, 182, 197, 210, 218, 229, 231, 234, 256, 259, 260

Babeuf, Gracchus, 33, 227
Babylon, 20
Bad Godesberg Congress, 247
Badie, B., and P. Birnbaum, 135
Bagehot, Walter, 78
Bahro, Rudolf, 24
Bakunin, Michael, 221 228
balance of payments, 202
balance of trade, 193
Balcer, Leon, 276 n 18
Baltic, 230, 258
Bank of Canada, 162, 174, 186
Bank of Commerce, 159
Bank of Montreal, 215
bankers, 28
banks, 104, 154, 155, 158,

159, 184, 187, 189, 190, 191, 192, 193, 243
Banting, Keith, 139, 140, 143, 144
Barber, Benjamin, 35
Barber, Clarence, and John McCallum, 143
Baring Brothers, 233
base, 115, 121, 122, 130, 132, 257
base-level democracy, 103-4, 259
Basque, 42, 226
Bastille, 43, 234
Bauer, Otto, 229
BBC, 127
B.C., Electric, 176
behavioural, 132
Behemoth, vii, 136, 254
Belgium, 144
Bendix, Reinhard, 4
Bennett, R.B., 46, 48, 62, 162, 163, 234
Bergeron, Gérard, 72, 215
Bernard, André, 95
Bernstein, Eduard, 246
Beveridge, William, 142
Beveridge Plan, 163
biculturalism, 238
big business, 125, 126, 128, 161, 165, 166, 169, 177, 212
big government, 149, 166
big state, 133
Bill 101, 174, 175, 220
Bill 178, 220
bill of rights, 83, 84, 92, 148, 211
bi-national, 43
Birch, Anthony, 147-8
Bird, Robert, 111
Bismarck, Otto von, 125, 142
Bissell, Claude, 43
Blackstone, William, 56, 73, 78, 81, 86
Blais, André, 173
Blanqui, Auguste, 227
Bloc populaire, 217
Bloch, Ernst, 252

Blomqvist, Ake, 140, 142-3
Bodin, Jean, 19, 21, 110, 136, 253
Boer War, 159
Bolingbroke, Lord, 75, 76, 86
Bolshevik, 118, 130, 248
Bombardier, 175
Bonald, 15
Bonapartism, 224, 257
Bonenfant, Charles, 59
Borden, Robert, 46, 57
Borgia, Cesare, 253
Bourassa, Henri, 61
Bourassa, Robert, 220
bourgeois/bourgeoisie, 23, 26, 34, 43, 80, 90, 116, 118, 121, 123, 124, 125, 127, 132, 181, 189, 216, 221, 223, 229, 250, 251, 254
Brady, Alexander, 57, 91
branch plant, 157, 158, 185, 187, 188, 190, 196
Brandt, Willy, 126
Bretton Woods, 173
Breuilly, John, 220
Brezhnev, Leonid, 248
Brezhnev doctrine, 201
Bristol, 89
British Columbia, 103, 104, 148, 170, 177, 212, 236, 239, 242
British constitution, 52, 71, 73, 77, 78, 79, 80, 86, 210
British Empire, 44, 55, 57, 60, 79, 210, 214
British North America, 44, 45, 59, 77, 157, 184, 214, 233
British North America Act, 41, 47, 49, 55, 56, 59, 66, 69, 72, 76, 77, 80, 82, 83, 91, 92, 234, 235, 240
broadcasting, 49, 62, 139, 171, 212
Brossard, Jacques, 66
Brown, George, 60
Bryce, James, 78, 228

Buchanan, James, and
  Richard Wagner, 141
Buchenwald-Belsen, 137
budget, 141, 145, 146, 165,
  177
Bukharin, N., 113
Buonarroti, 227
bureaucracy/bureaucratic,
  68, 113, 119, 120, 123,
  126, 138, 143, 150, 155,
  186, 249, 259, 260
Burns, Robert, 100
business, 143, 144, 145, 146,
  155, 159, 160, 161, 162,
  163, 166, 173, 194, 215
Business Council on
  National Issues, 172, 173,
  191
business cycle, 170

cabinet, 73, 82, 105, 106,
  138, 169
Cairns, Alan, 132, 136, 137,
  138, 146, 147, 148, 153
Caisse de Dépôts, 174, 216
caisse populaire, 105
calamity, 112
Cameron, David, 140, 141,
  145
Campbell, Alexander, 209
Campbell, Robert, 164,
  168
Camus, Albert, 251
Canada/Canadian, 5, 6, 7,
  8, 9, 25, 38-53, 55-70,
  71-87, 88-106, 112, 124,
  133-52, 153-78, 179-204,
  207-20, 222, 224, 231, 232,
  233-44
Canada and Its Provinces, 56
Canada Assistance Plan,
  141
Canada Council, 211
Canada Day, 56, 58
Canada First, 212
Canada Health Act, 240
Canada Pension Plan, 141,
  169, 170
Canada-US Auto Pact, 196
Canada-US Free Trade
  Agreement, 52, 101, 173,

179, 194, 240
Canada Year Book, 56, 69
Canadian Bankers' Associ-
  ation, 158
Canadian Broadcasting
  Corporation, 38, 139,
  174, 211
Canadian Cement, 162
Canadian Citizenship Act,
  57, 63, 148, 211
Canadian Development
  Corporation (CDC), 52,
  175, 176, 188
Canadian Labour Con-
  gress, 143, 169
Canadian Manufacturers'
  Association, 191
Canadian National Rail-
  ways, 38, 161, 166, 174,
  186, 211
Canadian Northern Rail-
  way, 159
Canadian Pacific Railway,
  38, 159, 162, 215
Canadian Security Intelligence Act, 69
Canadian State, The, 68
Canadian Wheat Board,
  162, 174, 186
Canadianization, 176, 191
Canberra, 232
Cancun Conference, 199
canton, 222, 223
capital, 45, 47, 53, 105, 111,
  113, 114, 115, 125, 129,
  130, 135, 143, 153, 156,
  157, 158, 160, 166, 171,
  173, 176, 179-204, 215,
  216, 225, 227, 235, 239,
  247, 248, 250, 260
Capital, 33, 115, 248
capitalism/capitalist, 3, 7,
  23, 31, 33, 35, 36, 46, 47,
  52, 53, 62, 67, 68, 72,
  109-31, 133, 137, 138, 142,
  144, 145, 150, 151, 152,
  153-78, 179-204, 211, 212,
  215, 216, 222, 226, 227,
  229, 231, 233, 234, 235,
  236, 239, 240, 242, 245-63
capitalist world economy,

7, 154, 173, 179-204, 239,
  240
Caribbean, 158
Caron, Maximilien, 63
Carroll, William, 191, 195
cartel, 155, 158, 160, 165,
  172
Cartier, George-Etienne,
  39, 74, 76, 82, 86, 92,
  99
casino capitalism, 262
Castro, Fidel, 252
catastrophe, 178, 262
Catholic, 119, 218
Caucasus, 230
Central America, 199
centralized/centralization,
  5, 39, 40, 41, 42, 43, 45,
  47, 48, 51, 52, 53, 63, 65,
  98, 105, 114, 115, 122, 124,
  130, 156, 158, 160, 161,
  167, 208, 211, 221, 224,
  225, 227, 228, 229, 230,
  231, 232, 233, 240, 242,
  244, 249, 261
centre, 132, 247
centre-periphery, 68
Centres locaux de ser-
  vices communautaires
  (CLSC), 103
certification, 163, 169
chancellor, 126
charisma, 16, 36, 120, 123
Charter of Rights and
  Freedoms, 50, 83, 84, 94,
  101, 104, 138, 148, 149,
  150, 220, 240
Chateaubriand, duc de, 15
checks and balances, 19,
  75, 82, 84, 85, 123
Cheka, 248
Christian Democrats, 168
Christianity, 19, 20, 43
church, 66, 119, 139,
  216-17, 218
Churchill, Winston, 127
Cicero, 14, 15, 17, 29, 74,
  119, 254
citizen/ship, 19, 21, 23, 25,
  26, 27, 28, 29, 30, 31, 32,
  34, 35, 36, 37, 54, 61, 66,

76, 89, 90, 91, 92, 93, 94,
96, 98, 100, 101, 102, 104,
117, 129, 130, 132, 133,
134, 135, 136, 137, 147,
148, 149, 150, 209, 222,
223, 224, 226, 242, 248,
252, 254, 256, 257, 258,
259, 260, 261
citizen initiative, 90, 96,
97, 104, 105, 234
city, 137, 222, 227
City of God, The, 20
city-state, 29, 118, 252
civic holiday, 210, 213
civic religion, 79, 119
civil disobedience, 102, 147
civil liberties, 49, 117
civil rights, 193
civil service, 122, 124, 162,
163, 165, 213
Civil Service Commission,
161
civil society, 4, 8, 21, 22,
24, 26, 33, 68, 90, 102,
110, 120, 130, 133, 134,
136, 138, 139, 147, 149,
151, 152, 154, 216, 220,
245, 253, 255, 259
civil war, 22, 31, 42, 55, 227,
228, 242, 248
Civil War in France, The, 17,
33, 123, 221, 251, 255
civilization, 137, 149, 228
civitas, 54
Clark, Michael, 61
class(es), 17, 25, 28, 29, 33,
39, 44, 67, 77, 81, 96, 98,
102, 110, 113, 114, 116,
117, 118, 119, 120, 121,
122, 124, 127, 129, 144,
146, 153, 170, 178, 181,
194, 213, 226, 229, 233,
234, 237, 245, 248, 250,
254, 255, 256, 260
classification of regimes,
252
Clastre, Pierre, 295 n 91
Clausewitz, Karl von, 252
Clement, Wallace, 68, 167,
192, 308 n 20
Clive, Robert, 126

Clokie, H.McD., 207
Clow, Michael, 189
coercion, 5, 115, 136, 155,
161, 255, 256, 259, 261
Cold War, 128, 173, 188,
191, 192, 198, 247
Coldwell, M.J., 93
Coleman, William, 143, 144
collective/collectivist, 37,
48, 95, 101, 112, 139, 149,
150, 161, 164, 203, 204,
212, 233, 250, 251, 257,
260, 261, 262, 263
collective bargaining, 62,
144, 169
collective ownership, 245,
249
collectivity, 224, 254, 257,
262
collectivization, 248, 260
colonial, 39, 44, 71, 74, 91,
92, 155, 182, 187, 200,
215, 234
colony, 60, 64, 70, 77, 79,
82, 157, 183, 201, 209,
213, 231
Combines Investigation
Act, 61
command economy, 259
commerce, 23, 24, 27, 32,
52, 110, 154, 210, 222, 225,
234, 260
Committee for an Inde-
pendent Canada, 212,
238
Committee of Public
Safety, 43, 229
Commons, 73, 75, 76, 78,
80, 85, 86, 106
commonwealth, 17, 18, 21,
23
Commonwealth, 57, 188,
199, 211
commune, 33, 34, 105, 112,
228, 229, 255
communism, 14, 33, 129,
198, 230
Communist Manifesto, The,
33, 123, 227
communist party, 113, 122,
235, 236, 257

communitarian, 36, 37, 98
community, 30, 32, 35, 37,
62, 69, 89, 90, 94, 98,
103, 104, 105, 115, 120,
134, 137, 147, 148, 150,
152, 154, 162, 166, 209,
224, 229, 252, 257, 260,
262
competition, 113, 114, 116,
154, 155, 156, 159, 166,
174, 178, 193, 194
comprador bourgeoisie,
116
concentration, 166, 172,
177, 178, 227, 231, 233,
242
concentration effect, 111
Concept of the Political, The,
22
Condorcet, 227
Confederacy, 42
confederation, 223, 229
Confederation, 55, 60, 65,
66, 76, 77, 79, 82, 91, 99,
157, 180, 184, 203, 208,
209, 214, 217, 219, 234
Confederation Debates,
47, 59, 60, 76, 80, 234
congress, 25, 73, 89, 225
Congress Party, 232
conquest, 110
conscription, 46, 48, 61,
94, 210, 217
consent, 5, 23, 31, 90, 144,
256, 261
conservative/conserva-
tism, 15, 16, 26, 34, 38,
39, 41, 42, 44, 92, 99, 110,
130, 139, 162, 222, 227,
228, 234, 237, 257, 259,
262
Conservative, 46, 47, 48,
58, 60, 77, 78, 93, 94, 97,
159, 162, 173, 177
*Considerations on the Gov-
ernment of Poland*, 224
Constant, Benjamin, 23,
27–8, 121, 137
constituency, 78, 81, 85,
100
constituent assembly, 100,

224, 241
constituents, 88, 89, 93, 94
constitution, 24, 25, 26, 27,
    32, 33, 36, 41, 43, 50, 52,
    55, 57, 60, 62, 63, 64, 66,
    71–87, 88–106, 133, 138,
    148, 149, 163, 209, 210,
    222, 224, 225, 226, 228,
    230, 235, 237, 239, 240,
    241, 246, 249, 250, 258
constitutional monarchy,
    76
constitutional patriation,
    53, 58, 94, 101, 211, 240
consuls, 17, 74
consumer, 98, 165, 168
continentalism, 175, 188,
    191
contract, 110, 150
Convention, 40, 47
co-operative, 98, 99, 105
co-operative common-
    wealth, 98
Co-operative Common-
    wealth Federation (CCF),
    51, 93, 97, 162, 168, 235,
    236, 237
co-operative federalism,
    238
Copernican revolution,
    122
core, 7, 52, 68, 156, 164,
    180, 181, 183, 184, 186,
    187, 188, 191, 192, 194,
    195, 196, 197, 200, 202,
    203
coronation, 119
corporate/corporation, 50,
    68, 83, 97, 105, 128, 135,
    136, 138, 145, 151, 152,
    156, 159, 160, 161, 162,
    165, 166, 167, 168, 170,
    171, 173, 174, 176, 187,
    188, 192, 251, 259, 260
corporatism, 114, 143, 165,
    169, 173, 176, 292 n 22
Corry, J.A., 153, 208
Corsica, 32, 89
Coulanges, Fustel de, 54
council, 29, 35, 97, 105, 129,
    222, 231, 259

council communism, 245
counter-culture, 100
counter-revolution/ary,
    39, 40, 42, 43, 47, 56, 76,
    92, 99, 106
county, 106, 226
court(s), 6, 66, 73, 84, 105,
    138, 150
covetousness, 20–2
Coyne, J.H., 44
credit union, 105
Creighton, Donald, 57, 68,
    163, 284 n 27
creole Leviathan, 40
Crimean War, 201
Criminal Code, 69, 80
criminality, 126
crisis, 47, 48, 62, 69, 112,
    121, 123, 132, 134, 145,
    146, 202, 210, 231, 235,
    239, 242, 250, 258, 262
Crisis of Parliamentary
    Democracy, The, 22
Critique of the Gotha Pro-
    gramme, 33, 229, 255
Croatia, 231
crown, 27, 38, 41, 44, 47, 55,
    67, 77, 91, 209
crown corporation, 38, 48,
    67, 139, 162, 163, 164,
    166, 167, 174, 176, 177,
    211
cult of personality, 248,
    249
Cult of Supreme Reason,
    39
Cultural Revolution, 249
culture, 21, 51, 52, 53, 68,
    83, 110, 121, 122, 129, 131,
    156, 181, 192, 200, 201,
    207, 211, 216, 219, 220,
    229, 230, 237

daily life, 118, 119
debt, 161, 165, 202, 225,
    226, 262
decentralization, 5, 35, 47,
    99, 103, 104, 124, 126,
    208, 226, 228, 230, 232,
    233, 235, 243, 260
Declaration of the Rights

of Man and the Citizen,
    73, 81, 89
decolonization, 242
defence, 111, 198, 209, 211,
    223
defensive expansionism,
    38, 153, 177, 208
deference, 90, 92, 99, 128,
    153, 198, 222
deference to authority, 78
deficit, 140, 145, 146, 165,
    170
definition(s), 54, 138, 139,
    255–6
deflation, 141
de Gaulle, Charles, 35, 113,
    117, 121, 122, 135, 201, 227
deindustrialization, 188,
    196
Delbez, 63
delegate, 35, 81, 88, 89, 93,
    224, 234
democracy/democratic, 6,
    8, 13–37, 39, 40, 42, 43,
    54, 67, 71–87, 88–106,
    113, 114, 119, 126, 133,
    135, 137, 144, 147, 148,
    149, 150, 151, 152, 198,
    221–44, 245–63; defini-
    tion, 256
Democracy in the Domin-
    ions, 57
democratic centralism, 16,
    34, 230, 245
Democratic party, 232
democratization, 65, 101,
    121, 151, 249, 258, 261,
    262
demos, 28, 44
Denmark, 101
Department of Munitions
    and Supplies, 163
Department of Regional
    and Economic Expan-
    sion, 170
departments, 40, 224, 226
dependence, 156, 182, 192,
    203, 213
dependency, 179, 182, 185,
    187, 195
Depression, 53, 112, 127,

140, 141, 156, 163, 165, 170, 209, 236
deputies, 33
deregulation, 177
derived industrialization, 45
despotism, 24, 27, 28, 75, 76, 80, 225, 226
despotism of liberty, 39
development, 154, 156, 157, 170, 172, 179, 180, 181, 184, 198, 201, 209, 214, 215, 231, 254, 256
Devine, Grant, 240
Dewitt, D., and J. Kirton, 199
Dicey, 228
dictatorship, 40, 41, 43, 44, 245, 250, 257
dictatorship of the proletariat, 33, 129, 229, 245, 250, 251, 255
dictatorship over needs, 259
Diderot, Denis, 254
Diefenbaker, John, 58, 83
Diet, 81, 223
Diggers, 31
Dion, Léon, 72
Dion, Stéphane, 101
diplomacy, 180, 185, 187, 197, 198, 199, 201, 202
direct action, 102
direct democracy, 35, 36, 43, 74, 95, 102, 129, 246, 250, 254, 258, 286 n 7
direct investment, 189, 190, 191, 192, 193
direct legislation, 97, 98
dirigisme, 152, 168, 173
Discourses, The, 15, 21
disorganized capitalism, 154, 177
displacement effect, 46, 111, 140, 161
dissent, 117, 126, 147, 202
dissident, 117, 258, 261
distinct society, 240, 241
distribution, 139, 143
divine right of kings, 106
division of labour, 52, 98,

105, 110, 117, 133, 135, 159, 165, 170, 181, 193, 202, 215, 220, 235, 247, 248, 262
Doern, Bruce, 138, 140, 146
Dollard, 218
domestic, 135, 141, 154
domination, 3, 72, 116, 117-20, 123, 124, 127, 129, 130, 131, 132, 134, 154, 178, 197, 245, 248, 250, 251, 252, 256, 257
dominion, 6, 46, 51, 52, 54-70, 71, 73, 77, 79, 106, 126, 157, 163, 183, 185, 213, 215, 221, 235
Dominion Bureau of Statistics, 56, 58
Dominion Day, 56
Dominion Election Act, 56, 58
Dominion Land Act, 56
Dominion of the North, 57
dominium, 56
Dorion, A.A., 42
Doughty, Arthur, 56
Drache, Daniel, 308 n 20
Drew, George, 58
Droit publique, 63
dualism, duality, 52, 144, 217, 237
Dumont, Fernand, 217
Duplessis, Maurice, 51, 99, 214, 217, 236
Durham Report, 48

East-West relations, 199, 203
Eayrs, James, 199
ecclesia, 29, 30
ecology, 117, 262
economic, 7, 23, 26, 38, 41, 45, 52, 53, 63, 65, 66, 67, 69, 70, 96, 98, 99, 104, 109-31, 132-52, 153-78, 179-203, 209, 210, 211, 212, 213, 215, 217, 218, 221-44, 246, 249, 250, 253, 255, 257, 258, 259, 260, 262
Economic and Philosophical

Manuscripts, 33
Economic Council of Canada, 173
economic democracy, 35, 104, 151, 243, 299 n 76
economic function of the state, 109, 110-15
economic history, 110
economic nationalism, 173, 177, 188, 199, 238, 239
economic summit, 144, 193, 199
economics, 67, 114, 119, 126, 133, 139, 142, 150, 234, 247
economist(s), 138, 142, 145, 146, 151, 165, 168
economy, 34, 68, 96, 112, 121, 125, 127, 133, 135, 139, 141, 143, 145, 155, 156, 160, 162, 168, 170, 172, 173, 174, 175, 176, 177, 179-204, 216, 231, 235, 237, 243, 245, 247, 248, 259, 261
Edelstein, Michael, 183, 309 n 32
Eden, Anthony, 127
education, 14, 121, 139, 143, 165, 166, 167, 171-2, 196, 212, 217, 229, 232, 236, 243
efficiency, 242-3, 263
E.G. Eddy, 162
Egypt, 112
Ehrenberg, Victor, 54
Eighteenth Brumaire of Louis Bonaparte, The, 123, 251
Eisenmann, Charles, 116
election(s), 31, 34, 88, 94, 102, 103, 149, 165, 173, 210, 220, 239, 240
elector, 100, 105
electoral, 93, 100, 102, 246, 247, 257
electorate, 78, 94, 96, 224, 234
electricity, 182, 186, 189
élite, élitism, 16, 25, 34, 35, 38, 50, 68, 79, 89, 93, 95, 99, 102, 157, 159, 188,

198, 211, 213, 238, 241, 257
Elizabeth I, Queen, 79, 126
embedded liberalism, 193
embedded state, 133, 136-7, 150, 151, 153
embourgeoisement, 247
emergency powers/situation, 23, 45, 48, 49, 163, 209
empire, 44, 45, 79, 159, 160, 184, 185, 197, 210, 212, 217, 256
empiricism, 132
employees, 103, 246, 260
employer, 28
employment, 128, 133, 141, 142, 164, 165, 196
Employment and Social Insurance Act, 46
Encyclopedia of the Social Sciences, 57
energy, 170, 182, 239
Engels, Friedrich, 3, 33, 110, 125, 130, 227, 246, 250, 256
English Canada, 7, 8, 47, 53, 56, 61, 64, 67, 69, 71, 72, 83, 95, 99, 101, 159, 174, 207-20, 222, 238-42
English-Canadian nationalism, 47, 56, 99, 207-14, 219, 220, 238-42
English constitution, 6, 25, 72, 73, 83, 254
English-French conflict/ division, 208, 210, 214, 215, 217, 220
English-speaking, 64, 77, 109, 126, 127, 146, 168, 215, 262
Enlightenment, 89
entrepreneur, 158, 173, 195
environment, 102, 132, 232
Epp, Abram, 158
equality, 28, 29-35, 36, 37, 39, 43, 65, 76, 89, 90, 98, 139, 142, 209, 236, 248, 250, 251, 261, 262, 263, 271 n 132, 288 n 54
equality of condition, 26,

31, 36, 263
equilibrium democracy, 257
essence of politics, 118, 119
establishment, 102
estates, 17, 23, 27, 54, 74, 222
état, 41, 55, 59, 63, 64, 65, 66, 67, 109, 120, 122, 137, 215
ethics, 251, 260, 261
ethnic, 102, 132, 232
European Community, 101, 125, 127, 194, 201
executive (branch of government) 18, 23, 55, 73, 75, 76, 82, 84, 85, 86, 90, 91, 104, 125, 127, 128, 138, 139, 223, 224, 225, 259
Expo '67, 24
export(s), 173, 182, 193, 195, 196, 197
External Affairs, 60, 173, 185

Fabian, 235
Fabricant, Solomon, 111
faction, 44
factory, 35, 158, 160
Factory Act, 126
Falklands/Malvinas, 127, 202
falling rate of profit, 115
family, 15, 21, 26, 218, 249, 257, 262
family allowance, 48, 140, 163, 169, 211, 236
famine, 112, 178
farmers, 95, 97, 98, 159, 161, 162, 165, 236
fascism, 16, 109, 113, 114, 119, 121
Fathers of Confederation, 53, 55, 56, 78, 92, 105, 209, 235
federal, 19, 26, 36, 38, 48, 49, 50, 55, 59, 63, 64, 65, 66, 67, 69, 77, 82, 84, 85, 94, 99, 126, 128, 133, 145, 146, 162, 163, 165, 166,

169, 170, 173, 174, 175, 177, 188, 200, 207, 209, 210, 211, 214, 217, 218, 219, 220, 221-44
federalism, 5, 8, 40, 42, 47, 50, 51, 68, 71, 82, 84, 128, 138, 144, 163, 168, 221-44
Federalist Papers, The, 18, 73, 82, 225, 233
federation, 40, 66, 82, 220, 221, 223, 226, 228, 230, 232
Feher, F., A. Heller, and G. Markus, 259
feminism, 34
fetishism of commodities, 33
feudal(ism), 32, 89, 129, 225, 231, 254, 256
Fichte, 125
Fifth Republic, 113, 125, 141
finance/financial, 24, 51, 105, 113, 135, 145, 154, 158, 160, 162, 167, 170, 171, 173, 174, 179, 188, 191, 233, 235
finance capital, 113, 114, 154-5, 157, 158, 192, 258
Finance Capital, 113, 154
finance ministers, 193, 199
financier, 79, 236
Finkel, Alvin, 162
firm, 155, 158, 160, 161, 167, 175, 182, 191, 259
First World, 231, 239
First World War, 45, 48, 55, 60, 61, 83, 96, 111, 112, 124, 125, 127, 155, 159, 160, 163, 177, 182, 185, 209, 210, 211, 213, 214
fiscal crisis, 145
fiscal policy, 141, 146, 147, 162, 165, 168, 170, 194, 236
Fisera, V., 317 n 30
Fisheries Canada, 172
flag, 49, 58, 64, 210, 211
Flavelle, Joseph, 160, 161
Fletcher, F.T.H., 73
Flora, P., and A. Heiden-

heimer, 304 n 79
force, 20, 121, 136, 253
forced labour, 181
forces of production, 119
foreign affairs/policy, 60,
  68, 79, 116, 182, 185, 186,
  188, 198, 199, 209, 211,
  220, 231, 249
foreign control/ownership,
  165, 175, 176, 179, 182,
  185, 186, 189, 196-7
foreign investment, 176,
  184, 190
Foreign Investment
  Review Agency (FIRA),
  52, 175, 188
foreman, 28
forestry, 182
Forsey, Eugene, 277 n 22
Fortin, Gérard, 65
Fortune, 189
forward development of
  capitalism, 167, 171-4
Fourastié, J., 168
Fournier, Pierre, 144-5
franchise (electoral), 28,
  75, 78, 246, 254
francophone, 58, 65, 69,
  210, 216, 238
francophonie, la, 199
Frank, André Gunder, 116
Frankfurt School, 121
fraternity, 43
Frederick II, 254
free enterprise, 164, 172,
  240
free trade, 52, 101, 142, 151,
  177, 191, 192, 195, 197,
  201, 220
freedom, 28, 75, 90, 150,
  154, 229, 246, 250, 251
French Canada/Canadian,
  47, 48, 49, 53, 56, 61, 65,
  72, 100, 174, 175, 207,
  214-20, 237
French Revolution, 6, 15,
  32, 52, 54, 67, 76, 89, 105,
  124, 125, 200, 222, 224,
  227, 241
French Socialist party,
  144, 227, 247

Freud, Sigmund, 117, 253
Freund, Julien, 118, 119
Friedman, Milton, 139,
  262
friend-enemy distinction,
  3, 22, 37, 118, 119, 130
Front de libération du
  Québec (FLQ), 238
full employment, 141, 145,
  147, 164, 261
Fulton, Davie, 58
Fulton-Favreau formula,
  100
functions of the state, 7,
  62, 90, 109-31, 134, 135,
  140, 146, 178, 231, 232,
  255, 257
fur trade, 160, 182

Galbraith, John Kenneth,
  114, 166
GATT, 173
Gdańsk, 258
gender, 148
general will, 32, 40, 89, 91,
  150, 224, 226, 234
Geneva, 89, 223
gentleman, 31
gentry, 15, 18, 74, 85
geography, 52, 63, 122, 128,
  225, 242
geopolitics, 199
Gerschenkron, Alexander,
  45, 191
Geschictliche Grundbegriffe,
  56
Gilpin, Robert, 193, 198
Girondins, 39, 40, 47, 226,
  227, 232, 240
glasnost, 258
global debt, 193
globe/global, 117, 128, 130,
  155, 156, 157, 172, 173,
  178, 203, 221, 263
god(s), 20, 22, 41, 43, 119
Gorbachev, Mikhail, 230,
  249, 252, 261
Gouin, Lomer, 99, 215
governed, 32, 117, 135, 148
government, 6, 18, 19, 23,
  25, 26, 27, 28, 29, 31, 32,

33, 36, 38-53, 54-70,
  71-87, 90, 92, 93, 94, 96,
  97, 99, 102, 104, 106, 111,
  112, 116, 121, 124, 126,
  127, 128, 132-52, 153-78,
  183, 185, 186, 208, 209,
  212, 213, 214, 215, 217,
  219, 220, 221-44, 247,
  253, 256, 257, 258
government-centred, 166
governor-general, 57, 77,
  78, 79, 83, 211, 233
governors, 32, 117, 135, 148
Gramsci, Antonio, 110,
  121, 123, 248, 253
Granatstein, J.L., 164
Grand Trunk Railway, 38,
  159, 215
Grant, George, 208
grass roots, 98, 102, 212,
  234, 245, 261
Greece, 29, 54, 118, 119, 251
greed, 260
Greek(s), 22, 24, 29, 30, 33,
  119, 252, 255
Green, Howard, 58
Greens, 34, 102, 246
gross national product
  (GNP), 48, 111, 112, 124,
  125, 126, 128, 139, 140,
  153, 159, 160, 161, 163,
  164, 166, 169, 171, 173,
  180, 181, 182, 183, 192,
  193, 195, 196
Groulx, Lionel, 62, 63, 215
group government, 97-8
Gulag, 137, 248

Habermas, Jurgen, 35, 120,
  121
Halifax, Marquis of, 75
Hamelin, Jean, 217
Hamilton, Alexander,
  25-6, 47, 72, 84
Hannah, Leslie, 160
Hansard, 56, 59
Hapsburgs, 222
hard frontier, 153
Hardin, Herschel, 153
Harrington, James, 15, 18
Hartz, Louis, 72

Hauriou, 63, 66
Hayek, Friedrich von, 262
Heagerty Report, 163
health, 103, 111, 142, 143, 165, 166, 196, 212, 232, 236, 261
health insurance, 163, 169
Heath, Edward, 127
Hegel, G.W.F., 13, 19, 22, 23, 26-7, 33, 41, 87, 109, 119, 123, 125, 136, 251, 260, 268 n 60
hegemony, 93, 121, 142, 179, 180, 181, 187, 188, 191, 192, 195, 197, 198, 201, 211
Held, David, 35
Hellenistic, 31
Henders, R.C., 88
Hepburn, Mitchell, 51, 236
hereditary (principle), 25, 31, 81, 90
Herman, Edward, 166
Hermes, 29
Herodotus, 30
Hewart, Lord, 80
hewers of wood, 182
hierarchy/hierarchical, 44, 76, 139
Hilferding, Rudolf, 7, 113-14, 130, 154-6, 157, 158, 165, 172, 178, 257, 300 n 17, 303 n 68
Hirschman, A.O., 95-6, 299 n 77
historians, 38, 64, 68, 76, 91, 114, 125, 208, 227
Histories, The, 249
history/historical, 38, 56, 65, 74, 92, 101, 109, 112, 118, 122, 127, 129, 130, 131, 143, 152, 158, 160, 219, 225, 228, 230, 234, 245, 257, 258, 262
History of Canadian Wealth, 158
History of Florence, 20
History of the Peloponnesian War, 19
History of the Russian Revolution, 252

Hitler, Adolf, 22, 117, 125, 126
Hobbes, Thomas, 19, 21, 22, 23, 36, 37, 54, 72, 73, 87, 110, 117, 118, 136, 252, 253
Hobsbawm, Eric, and Terence Ranger, 211
Holy Grail, 109
Holy Roman Emperor, 56
home rule, 60
honour, 75, 76, 78, 79
Horowitz, Gad, 72
hospital insurance, 142, 169
Houle, François, 173-4
House of Commons, 25, 56, 81, 95
Howe, C.D., 164
Hughes, Sam, 61
human nature, 20, 21, 22, 37, 44, 90, 118, 142
Human Resource Boards, 103
humanism, 260
Hydro Québec, 166, 174, 216

ideal type, 13, 154, 177
identity, 106, 137, 149, 211, 214
ideology/ideological, 5, 38, 39, 42, 47, 48, 53, 65, 95, 96, 109, 114, 115, 119, 121, 126, 127, 128, 130, 132, 136, 144, 146, 149, 162, 168, 189, 198, 201, 202, 212, 249, 251, 262
illegitimate, 96, 106, 255
illness, 140
image of the state, 133, 134
IMF, 193, 195, 200
immigration, 157
Impartial Umpire, An, 68
impeach(ment), 75
imperial, 52, 55, 56, 57, 60, 63, 79, 80, 112, 128, 158, 185, 198, 201, 211, 214, 234
imperial conference, 57
Imperial Munitions Board,

160
Imperial Oil, 162
imperialism/imperialist, 30, 39, 48, 114, 116, 129, 183, 210, 227, 238
imperium, 54
import control, 170
import substitution, 181, 182
income policy, 144
income tax, 46, 160
independence, 56, 63, 66, 92, 96, 127, 154, 182, 198, 199, 207, 211, 212, 213, 217, 219, 223, 228, 229, 231, 239, 259
indigenous, 53, 165, 181, 187
individual/individualism, 21, 27, 29, 40, 62, 83, 92, 97, 98, 112, 120, 126, 134, 135, 137, 139, 142, 148, 149, 150, 162, 200, 212, 226, 232, 233, 246, 250, 251, 253, 254, 257, 261, 262
individual rights, 26, 37, 84
industrial/industrialization, 45, 46, 51, 53, 80, 126, 137, 157, 158, 160, 161, 164, 177, 179, 180, 182, 183, 185, 187, 189, 190, 195, 196, 200, 201, 202, 216, 224, 228, 235, 245, 247
industrial capital, 114
Industrial Disputes Investigation Act, 160
industrial policy, 52, 167, 172-3
industrial relations, 140, 169, 186
industrial sector, 182
industrialist, 79, 125, 236
industry, 154, 155, 158, 160, 165, 172, 173, 183, 184, 193, 196, 215, 227
inequality, 32, 35, 98, 111, 127, 144, 230, 250
inflation, 141, 147

infrastructure, 45, 47, 156,
    157, 165, 173, 180, 186,
    212, 236
injunction, 169
injustice, 260
Inland Revenue Act, 56
Innis, Harold, 62, 68, 153,
    171, 182
inspection effect, 111
Institut Canadien des
    Affaires Publiques, 65
institution(al), 54, 69, 71,
    72, 74, 78, 81, 83, 85, 86,
    90, 91, 96, 99, 103, 105,
    112, 116, 121, 122, 127,
    133, 135, 138, 139, 145,
    150, 151, 166, 174, 209,
    226, 231, 247, 250, 252,
    254, 256
intellectual, 6, 62, 71, 72,
    74, 75, 162, 210, 215, 238,
    249
intelligence service, 117,
    253
Intercolonial Act, 56
interdependence, 136, 137,
    178
interest groups, 138, 143,
    148, 165
intergovernmental rela-
    tions, 64
international affairs/rela-
    tions, 4, 19, 49, 68, 179,
    199, 201, 252
International Control
    Commission, 198, 312
    n 101
*International Encyclopedia of
    the Social Sciences*, 63
international law, 57, 63
international political
    economy, 133, 141, 142,
    156, 187
international politics, 200
international system, 116,
    119, 135
internationalism, 116, 229,
    246
internationalization, 155,
    192
interstate, 68

intervention/intervention-
    ist, 45, 53, 68, 112, 113,
    132, 133, 134, 141, 156,
    161, 162, 163, 168, 170,
    174, 175, 177, 207, 212,
    217, 219, 234, 237, 245,
    247
intrastate, 68, 214
invention of tradition, 211,
    217
investment, 144, 145, 155,
    157, 165, 167, 172, 176,
    184, 189, 191, 194, 197,
    215
investor, 157, 158
Irvine, William, 97, 99
isegoría, 30, 33, 34
isomoiría, 30, 34
isonomía, 30, 34

Jacobin, 6, 8, 25, 38–53,
    122, 208, 222, 224, 226–7,
    230, 232, 233, 238, 242,
    243
Jaenicke, F.E., 63
Jaurès, Jean, 227, 229, 246
Jefferson, Thomas, 32, 72,
    92, 97, 106, 224, 225,
    241
Jeffersonian democracy,
    92, 106
Jerusalem, 37, 92
Jessop, Bob, 4
job creation, 196
Johnson, Daniel, 66, 100,
    219
Jouvenel, Bertrand de, 65,
    116
judicature, 21, 82
judicial, 18, 55, 73, 76, 82,
    85, 86, 128, 138, 148, 225
Judicial Committee of the
    Privy Council, 57, 80,
    82, 83, 97, 163, 211, 234
judiciary, 19, 26, 84
junior partner, 49, 159,
    180, 188, 197, 198, 211
Junker, 40
juridical, 63, 66, 110, 127,
    149
jurist, 64, 115

justice, 14, 19, 20, 26, 61,
    126, 132, 251

Kantian, 261
Kautsky, Karl, 202, 229,
    231, 246, 317 n 31
Keane, John, 35
Kellogg, Paul, 191
Kelsen, Hans, 96
Kemp, Tom, 183
Keohane, Robert, 192, 198
Keynes/Keynesian, 48,
    114, 132, 138, 141, 143,
    145, 152, 164, 165, 167,
    168–9, 174, 177, 178, 193,
    211, 236, 247, 262
Kiel, 113, 155
king, 39, 61, 73, 75, 76, 106
King/Queen-in-Parlia-
    ment, 81, 82, 88, 90
King, Carlyle, 98
King, William Lyon Mac-
    kenzie, 48, 49, 61, 63, 93,
    94, 95
kingdom, 20, 55, 124, 217,
    250
kingship, 83
kinship, 257
knight/knighthood, 79
Knopff, R., and F.L. Mor-
    ton, 148–9
knowledge, 114, 155
Kojève, A., 268 n 60
Koninck, Charles de, 65
Korpi, Walter, 140, 145
Kosovo, 231
Kramnick, Isaac, 75, 89,
    283 n 21
Kuznets, S., 183

labour, 31 44, 62, 80, 141,
    142, 143, 144, 155, 159,
    162, 168, 169, 171, 173,
    177, 181, 235
Labour/Le Travail, 68
labour force, 111, 139, 162,
    166
Labour party, 51, 127, 141,
    144
labourer, 28, 161
Lachine Canal, 38

Laidler, David, 139, 140, 142, 145
landowners, 25, 33
Lange, Peter, 181
laissez-faire, 28, 45, 46, 128, 154, 161, 162, 201, 234, 237
language, 47, 52, 53, 68, 109, 118, 144, 148, 175, 209, 210, 213, 216, 219, 220, 230, 232, 233, 237, 238, 242
language rights, 84
Lassalle, F., 255
Last Judgment, 254
late developer, 157, 182, 191
Latin, 22
Latouche, Daniel, 296 n 19
Laurendeau, André, 214
Laurier, Wilfrid, 48, 59, 61, 93, 94
Laux, J., and M. Molot, 189
Laval University, 65, 100
Lavalin, 175
law, 27, 30, 32, 54, 62, 63, 66, 74, 89, 92, 100, 133, 147, 150, 233
law and order, 44, 147
law lords, 80
law of increasing state expenditure, 110, 153
law of nature, 20
lawgiver, 36
Laws, The, 14
Laxer, Gordon, 185
Laycock, David, 97, 99, 288 n 55
leader(ship), 36, 61, 89, 100, 105, 117, 123, 124, 127, 158, 170, 246, 249, 252, 256, 259, 261
League for Public Broadcasting, 212
League for Social Reconstruction, 51, 62
League of Nations, 57, 62, 185, 201, 209, 211
Lefebvre, Henri, 120, 122
left, 5, 8, 51, 68, 104, 122,

125, 132, 140, 144, 146, 156, 204, 221, 232, 234, 236, 237, 238, 239, 240, 243, 245, 247, 263
legal, 134, 139, 148, 149, 151
legal rights, 31, 76
legality, 121, 136, 147
legislation, 21, 28, 126, 159, 169, 220, 223, 224, 233, 235
legislative, 18, 23, 55, 73, 74, 75, 76, 82, 84, 85, 86, 90, 91, 94, 96, 99, 101, 126, 128, 138, 200, 225, 259
legislative union, 41, 233
legislator, 25, 93, 94, 96
legislature, 41, 94, 97, 100, 104, 208, 233
legitimate/legitimacy, 7, 33, 39, 41, 65, 67, 81, 85, 88, 90, 91, 92, 94, 95, 96, 99, 100, 102, 105, 106, 120–2, 124, 125, 126, 127, 128, 129, 130, 133, 134, 138, 139, 146, 147, 151, 152, 159, 174, 187, 217, 219, 238, 241, 255, 260
legitimation, 110, 115, 120–2, 144, 153, 166, 256
Lenin, Vladimir, 16, 23, 40, 113, 123, 230, 242, 248, 250, 252, 255
Leninism, 16, 40, 119, 250
Lesage, Jean, 65, 100, 219
Letter on Toleration, 24
Letters from the Mountain, 223
Levellers, 31, 92
Lévesque, René, 100, 101, 219
Leviathan, vii, 4, 125, 136, 139, 153, 253, 254, 260
Leviathan, 21
Levitt, Kari, 68, 184
liberal(ism), 6, 13, 22, 23–9, 34, 36, 37, 42, 45, 53, 62, 71, 84, 86, 99, 117, 118, 121, 122, 123, 132, 137, 146, 164, 189, 193, 223, 224, 227, 244, 246, 247,

248, 250, 251, 254, 257, 259, 262
Liberal, 47, 48, 53, 58, 60, 61, 62, 72, 74, 94, 162, 165, 168, 173, 209, 228, 232, 237, 241
liberal democracy, 119, 125, 178, 201, 202, 245, 246, 250, 253, 257, 261, 262
liberalization, 141
libertas, 15, 254
liberty, 17, 18, 19, 21, 23, 24, 25, 26, 28, 29, 36, 37, 41, 42, 43, 44, 54, 72, 75, 82, 83, 91, 93, 96, 106, 113, 137, 149, 150, 151, 225, 226, 233, 251, 254, 259
libido, 253
libido dominandi, 20, 37, 117, 253
Lindblom, Charles, 259
linkage, 182
Lipset, Seymour Martin, 241
local, 104, 105
Local Prohibition case, 234
Locke, John, 23–4, 72, 73, 86, 110, 254
Lolme, de, 73
London, 121, 191, 200, 233, 234
lords, 73, 75, 76, 77, 80, 81, 86, 106
lot, 29, 103
Lougheed, Peter, 59, 240
Louis XIV, 41, 122, 254
Lower Canada, 47, 99, 209, 214, 233
lower class, 126, 223, 254
lower house, 85
Loyalist, 77, 95
Luxemburg, Rosa, 113, 123, 221, 229, 250, 255
luxury, 24, 28, 32, 89
Lyon, P., and B. Tomlin, 199

McCracken Report, 145
McCraney, George, 61

Macdonald, John A., 6, 39, 41, 43, 47, 49, 55, 59, 60, 72, 74, 77, 78, 79, 82, 86, 88, 92, 93, 209, 210, 233
Macdonald Commission, 7, 68, 69, 84, 85, 132–52, 153, 173
McGee, D'Arcy, 76, 82, 86
McIver, Robert, 95
Mackay, Robert, 57, 81
Mackenzie, Alexander, 157
Mackenzie, William Lyon, 60
Mackintosh, W.A., 164
Macmillan, Harold, 127
Mapherson, C.B., v, 35, 257, 288 n 54, 290 n 2, 319
McRae, Kenneth, 144
Macedonia, 222
Machiavelli, 13, 15, 17, 19, 20, 21, 22, 87, 251, 253
Madison, James, 18–19, 23, 25–6, 82, 84, 233, 254
Maffesoli, Michel, 118–19, 130
magistracy, 25
Maistre, Joseph de, 15
majesty, 79, 136
Malberg, Carré de, 115
Malcolm, Andrew, 190
mandate, 89, 96
Manifesto of the Equals, 33
Manitoba, 62, 97, 144, 217, 239
Manitoba Grain Growers Association, 99
Mann, Thomas, 136
manners, 32
manpower training, 167, 171
manufactures/manufacturing, 24, 28, 157, 161, 167, 179, 180, 188, 193, 195, 196, 197, 211, 234, 239
Mao, 123, 252
Marat, 39
Marcuse, Herbert, 118
Maréchal, Sylvain, 32
Maritimes, 234

market, 50, 70, 105, 122, 123, 132, 134, 135, 136, 139, 149, 151, 152, 154, 155, 158, 161, 162, 164, 165, 166, 167, 171, 177, 181, 192, 193, 212, 247, 249, 251, 258, 260, 261, 262
market socialism, 5, 243, 260, 262
marketeer, 133, 140, 152
Marsh, Leonard, 142
Marsh Report, 163, 164
Martin, Andrew, 141–2
Marx, Karl, 3, 17, 31, 33–4, 35, 37, 39, 110, 112, 115, 117, 125, 130, 221, 227, 228, 229, 246, 250, 251, 255, 257
Marxism, 14, 16, 34, 39, 67, 68, 72, 87, 109, 110, 112, 114, 115, 116, 117, 118, 119, 120, 121, 122–4, 127, 130, 150, 152, 156, 189, 221, 245–51, 254–5, 260
Marxism-Leninism, 8, 35, 113, 130, 156, 221, 245, 246, 248–50, 254, 259, 262
mass consumption, 202
mass media, 121, 138, 200
mass society, 75
Massey, Vincent, 62
masters in our own home, 49, 174
material(ist), 38, 127, 254
Mathiez, 227
mature capitalism, 179, 187, 191
May 1968, 102, 117, 125
Mayer, Arno, 80
means of production, 130, 245, 247, 249, 257, 259, 260, 261, 262, 263
mechanics, 26
medicare, 52, 140, 141, 169, 170, 237
medieval, 112, 120, 217, 254
Meech Lake Accord, 51, 53, 94, 240, 241, 318 n 52
mega-project, 172
Meighen, Arthur, 59, 62,

93
Meinecke, Friedrich, 18, 22
Melian dialogue, 19
member of Parliament, 81, 88, 89, 93, 104
mercantilism, 200, 233
merchants, 25, 28, 222
Mercier, Honoré, 53, 234
merger, 156, 158, 167, 176, 191
meritocracy, 14, 16
Merleau-Ponty, M., 253
metropolitan, 179, 182, 183
Michelet, 227
Michels, Robert, 16
Middle Ages, 31, 54
Middle East, 198
Miliband, Ralph, 4, 116, 121, 127
military, 25, 43, 45, 51, 52, 75, 114, 116, 117, 121, 128, 133, 134, 135, 136, 138, 143, 146, 150, 151, 155, 179, 180, 184, 185, 186, 188, 192, 199, 201, 202, 203, 210, 225, 256
Mill, John Stuart, 23, 28–9, 37, 72, 137
mining, 176, 182, 188, 197
minister(s), 21, 49, 75, 100
Ministry of Munitions, 160
minority rights, 226
mixed constitution, 6, 17, 21, 24, 74–82, 85–7, 222, 223, 254
mixed economy, 166, 202, 245
mob, 27, 82, 92
mode of production, 115, 119, 120, 122, 124, 131, 248, 251, 254, 256
moderation, 74, 75, 76, 82, 85, 86, 87
Modern World System, The, 180
modernity, 149–50
Moellendorff, von, 113
monarch/y, 6, 15, 21, 24, 27, 31, 44, 55, 60, 67, 74–87,

91, 127, 200, 222, 225, 227, 233
monetarism, 127, 202
monetary policy, 162, 165, 168, 170, 194, 236
monoculture, 181
monopoly, 97, 98, 113, 114, 125, 155, 234, 242, 248, 259
monopoly clause, 45
Montesquieu, 6, 8, 13, 15, 18, 23, 27, 71–87, 223, 225, 251, 254, 283 n 21
Montreal, 158
Montreal Board of Trade, 236
morality, 19, 20, 44, 129
Morris, Alexander, 209
Mosca, Gaetano, 16
Moscovitch, Allan, and Glen Drover, 159
Moscow, 200
movement(s), 34, 53, 100, 102, 121, 147, 148, 212, 225, 239, 245, 246, 258, 261, 262
Mowat, Oliver, 53, 234
Mulroney, Brian, 64, 85, 172, 240
multiculturalism, 238
multinational corporation, 33, 50, 104, 120, 135, 165, 174, 176, 192, 193, 201, 238, 242, 258
multinational state, 229, 230, 242
municipal, 105, 127, 166, 226
mutualism, 228
Myers, Gustavus, 158

Nairn, Tom, 126, 295 n 79
Napoleon, 21, 201, 227
nation, 7, 8, 25, 27, 29, 54, 62, 66, 68, 70, 89, 93, 99, 100, 116, 159, 174, 207–20, 226, 227, 228, 238, 242, 252, 261
Nation Unaware, A, 153
National Assembly, 32, 66, 100, 101

National Energy Program (NEP), 50, 145, 172, 173, 174, 176, 189, 239
national interest, 50
national liberation, 116
National Policy, 38, 53, 157, 209, 213
national question, 221, 229, 233
National Research Council, 161, 172
nationalism/t, 5, 7, 42, 47, 49, 52, 53, 56, 61, 62, 65, 67, 84, 96, 99–102, 123, 147, 173, 174, 175, 177, 188, 199, 200, 207–20, 227, 229, 230, 231, 232, 233, 237–42, 246
Nationalist League, 61, 210
nationality, 47, 71, 209, 210, 211, 229, 233, 241, 242
nationalization, 124, 127, 174, 189, 243, 247, 248
nation-building, 50, 148, 167, 174–6, 189, 211, 232
nation-state, 30, 37, 54, 67, 68, 89, 105, 128, 135, 201, 202, 210, 211, 224, 225, 227, 231, 242, 256, 257
native groups, 102
NATO, 67, 188, 200
nature, 248
Naylor, Tom, 68, 158, 233
Nazi, 3, 22, 117, 125, 126
Negro-king, 214
neighbourhood, 35, 102
Nelles, H.V., 68
neo-colonial, 181, 187
neo-conservatism/ive, 4, 5, 64, 133, 138, 139, 141, 144, 150, 153, 167, 177, 202, 258, 262, 271 n 132
neo-Keynesian, 152
neo-liberal, 126, 133, 138, 152, 262
neo-Marxism/t, 4, 5, 7, 67, 110, 114, 119, 120, 132,

138, 139, 141, 152, 153, 166, 256
Nettl, J., 109
New Brunswick, 42, 55, 77
New Deal, 46, 62, 163, 235
New Democratic Party (NDP), 51, 93, 103, 104, 144, 176, 235, 237, 238, 239, 240, 241
New Economic Program, 248
New England, 96
new left, 102, 258
new middle class, 212, 216, 238, 247, 315 n 32
New York, 191
New York Times, 190
Nicolet, Claude, 54
Nietzsche, Friedrich, 16
Nigeria, 231
night-watchman state, 178
Niosi, Jorge, 191, 195
nobles/nobility, 15, 18, 74, 75, 78, 81, 99
non-democratic, 254
non-governmental organization, 201
non-interventionist, 232
non-Marxist, 246
Noël, Alan, 168
NORAD, 198
Nordlinger, Eric, 4
North Atlantic triangle, 170, 188
North-South relations, 193, 199, 203
notables, 215
nouveaux philosophes, 251
Nova Scotia, 42, 55, 77
nuclear deterrent, 202

Oath of the Tennis Court, 234
obedience, 22, 90
obligation, 62, 132, 149

Oceana, 15, 18
O'Connor, James, 115, 116, 121, 129, 141
October Crisis, 49, 53, 72, 117, 238
Offe, Claus, 4, 120, 141, 177
Office de la Langue française, 64
Official Languages Act, 238, 240
Official Secrets Act, 60
old age pensions, 52, 80, 140, 163, 169, 196, 211
oligarchy, 30, 33, 78, 81, 223, 233
oligopoly, 158
Olson, Mancur, 142
Ontario, 58, 59, 61, 64, 68, 144, 159, 217, 234, 236, 242
Ontario Hydro, 159, 166, 174, 186
OPEC, 49
order, 25, 37, 253
Ordre Jacques-Cartier, 217
organic, 38, 39, 83, 111, 121, 139
Organization for Economic Co-operation and Development (OECD), 112, 128, 139, 140, 145, 147, 169, 172, 182, 193, 194, 195, 196, 199, 200, 245
organized capitalism, 7, 8, 105, 113, 114, 115, 125, 130, 153-78, 186, 257
Orsberg, Lars, 140
Ottawa, 51, 65, 175, 207, 217, 220, 232, 236
overload, 133, 137, 138, 147

Pacific, 193, 239
Panitch, Leo, 143-4, 153, 189
Papineau, Louis-Joseph, 99
Pareto, Vilfredo, 16
Paris, 33, 40, 96, 200, 228
Paris Commune, 33, 119, 125, 227, 228, 250, 255

parish, 216, 218
parish relief, 28
Parizeau, Jacques, 175, 239
Parliament/ary, 23, 25, 28, 32, 33, 34, 41, 42, 56, 57, 61, 67, 71, 72, 73, 83, 84, 88-106, 122, 125, 138, 148, 156, 177, 200, 209, 213, 235, 246, 247, 250, 252, 259
parliamentarism, 84, 102, 127, 246
Parliamentary Army, 92
parliamentary sovereignty, 6, 72, 81, 88-106, 234, 235, 241
Parti québécois, 53, 66, 84, 100, 175, 238, 239, 285 n 60
Parti socialiste du Québec, 238
participation/participatory, 17, 27, 29-37, 89, 91, 96-105, 129, 135, 141, 148-50, 223, 232, 233, 241, 242, 245, 246, 249, 250, 253, 258, 259, 261, 262
participatory democracy, 35, 37, 94, 96, 97, 99, 102, 103, 150, 224, 242, 252
party (political), 34, 35, 40, 85, 91, 93, 100, 101, 104, 113, 117, 119, 127, 129, 138, 140, 143, 144, 147, 156, 165, 168, 170, 224, 227, 245, 246, 247, 248, 250, 258, 259
party congress, 252
Pateman, Carole, 35
patriarchal, 24
Patriotes, 99
patriotism, 42, 43, 44, 47, 61, 210, 213, 220, 225
PC 1003, 48, 163
peace, 20, 21, 27, 82, 102, 111, 126, 147, 163, 164, 201, 225, 261
"Peace, Order and Good Government," 49, 72
Peacock, A.T., and J. Wise-

man, 111-12, 140, 161
Pearson, Lester, 49, 64, 197
peasant(ry), 32, 121, 222, 261
Pelletier, Réjean, 101
people (popular), 15, 17, 18, 19, 23, 24, 26, 32, 33, 40, 42, 43, 44, 45, 53, 54, 56, 62, 74, 75, 77, 78, 80, 81, 82, 83, 85, 88-106, 109, 116, 121, 124, 126, 129, 213, 224, 225, 226, 227, 230, 233, 234, 236, 241, 245, 256, 258
perestroika, 36
Pericles, 29, 36, 257
perimeter of the core, 8, 177, 179-204
periphery, 7, 45, 52, 68, 116, 157, 180, 181, 182, 183, 186, 187, 196, 203, 213
Persian Wars, 30
personality, 123
Peterloo Massacre, 126
Petro-Canada, 38, 50, 52, 166, 174, 176, 189
petty bourgeoisie, 215, 288 n 54
philosopher-king, 14, 17, 123
philosophy/er, 22, 64, 68, 71, 72, 91, 119, 120, 131, 140, 152, 170, 200
Philosophy of History, 22
philosophy of order, 6, 13, 19-23, 36, 37, 200, 253
Philosophy of Right, 22
Pinochet, A., 117
plague, 112
planning, 51, 114, 115, 118, 122, 154, 155, 156, 160, 162, 164, 165, 166, 167, 168, 172, 174, 235, 259
Plato, 13-14, 29, 123, 252
plebs, 15, 17
pluralism, 3, 67, 98, 126, 129, 138, 254, 261
Pocock, John, 18, 106
Poggi, Gianfranco, 4

police, 26, 110, 117, 126
polis, 30, 54, 69, 119, 150,
    252, 256, 257
politbureaucracy, 248
politburo, 252, 258
political culture, 25, 47, 76,
    104, 106, 127, 170, 200,
    242
political discourse, 5, 54,
    55, 56, 59, 61, 64, 99
political economy, 5, 26,
    39, 48, 67, 68, 104, 107,
    110, 118, 120, 122, 131,
    133, 146, 166, 179, 189,
    191, 203, 212, 221, 233,
    243, 250
political man/woman, 137
political philosophy, 54,
    89, 132
political science, 4, 9, 67,
    68, 69, 95, 109, 132, 134,
    140, 151
political sociology, 5, 107
Political Theology, 22
political theory, 5, 6, 11, 17,
    22, 31, 35, 72, 87, 110, 118,
    119, 123, 131, 179, 246,
    250, 251, 255
politics, 5, 118, 119, 124,
    125, 133, 137, 138, 140,
    142, 148, 150, 151, 200,
    219, 237, 243, 253, 255
Politics, The, 14, 131
polity, 208, 210, 262
Polybius, 17, 74, 222, 223,
    249
polycentrism, 187, 194, 231
Pompidou, Georges, 122
poor, 29, 32, 78, 81, 102,
    139
popular culture, 202
popular sovereignty, 7, 17,
    29, 32, 36, 39, 40, 41, 43,
    55, 72, 82, 88–106, 116,
    149, 200, 223, 224, 226,
    233, 234, 241, 242, 243,
    252, 253
populism, 96, 97, 98, 99,
    225, 234
*Populism and Democratic
    Thought in the Canadian*

Prairies, 97, 99, 288 n 55
Port Huron statement, 102
Porter, John, 167, 237
possessive individualism,
    23
post-industrial, 105, 180,
    196, 247
Potash Corporation of
    Saskatchewan, 176
Potter, Alexander, 210
Poulantzas, Nicos, 4, 110,
    116, 117
poverty, 15, 46, 203
power, 3, 19, 20, 31, 42, 44,
    45, 49, 50, 51, 60, 74, 75,
    76, 85, 88, 89, 92, 93, 99,
    100, 102, 103, 105, 109,
    110, 115, 117, 118, 119,
    123, 124, 127, 128, 129,
    130, 132, 135, 136, 144,
    149, 154, 179, 180, 185,
    186, 187, 192, 198, 200,
    201, 202, 207, 210, 211,
    214, 220, 223, 225, 228,
    229, 230, 232, 234, 236,
    237, 242, 248, 250, 251,
    253, 254, 256, 257, 259
Power Corp., 175
powerlessness, 135
Prague Spring, 231, 258,
    261
prairie(s), 98, 99, 234
Preece, Rod, 72
*Preface to a Critique of Politi-
    cal Economy*, 257
premier, 94, 101, 176, 217
prescription, 15
president/cy, 19, 73, 83,
    119, 128, 225, 231, 252
press, 138, 217, 248
Priestly, Norman, 98
primary commmodities,
    182, 196, 197
primary sector, 171, 180,
    181, 188
prime minister, 51, 79, 83,
    93, 94, 119, 252
prince, 17, 20, 95, 121
Prince, The, 20
*Principles of Political Econ-
    omy*, 28

privacy, 249
private enterprise/owner-
    ship, 153, 157, 162, 166,
    174, 176, 220, 257
private goods, 137
private liberty, 137, 149,
    151
private sector, 143, 164,
    165, 170, 171, 172, 176,
    177, 189
private sphere, 134, 151,
    262
privatization, 127, 177
privilege, 81
producer, 98, 102
production, 119, 160, 163
productivity, 104, 118, 142,
    155, 174, 180, 193, 195,
    263
profession/al, 25, 28, 103,
    165
progressive, 253, 261
Progressives, 97
proletarian, 33, 54, 123, 144
property, 14, 15, 19, 21, 23,
    24, 25, 26, 28, 32, 33, 44,
    45, 61, 62, 77, 78, 80, 81,
    90, 159, 160, 225, 226,
    233, 254, 257, 259
proportional representa-
    tion, 85, 97
prosperity, 168, 169
Protagoras, 29
protection, 45
protest, 147, 148, 202, 239
Protestant Reformation, 31
Proteus/protean vii, 5, 9,
    110, 124, 178
Proudhon, P.J., 221, 224,
    228
province, 33, 44, 50, 51,
    54–70, 77, 78, 85, 92, 103,
    104, 159, 170, 176, 218,
    221–44
province-building, 50, 53,
    59, 167, 174–6, 212, 215,
    240
provincial, 38, 40, 47, 50,
    80, 82, 84, 99, 104, 159,
    165, 166, 173, 174, 177,
    186, 188, 211, 213–18,

234–43
Prussia, 15, 22, 41, 42, 160, 181, 226
Psalm 72, 55
psychology, 119
public choice, 142
public enterprise/ownership, 52, 98, 125, 153, 174, 176, 220
public finance, 111
public liberty(ies), 106, 137, 148, 149, 151
public opinion, 35, 47, 83, 96, 121, 128, 213
public policy, 68, 144, 165
public sector, 64, 112, 139, 170, 174, 177
public sphere, 6, 26, 30, 35, 36, 134, 152, 159, 251, 257, 262
purges, 248

Quebec, 7, 8, 48, 49, 50, 53, 54–70, 72, 77, 83, 84, 94, 96, 99–102, 103, 104, 144, 147, 159, 170, 174, 175, 176, 189, 207–20, 222, 232, 234, 236, 237–41
Quebec City, 217
Quebec nationalism, 49, 51, 65, 96, 99–102, 175, 207–8, 214–20, 237–9, 241, 242
Quebec Pension Plan, 169, 170
Quebec Resolutions, 41
Québécois, 64, 72, 95, 161, 174
Queen's University, 95
Queensland, 232
Quiet Revolution, 53, 59, 64, 84, 99, 215, 216, 237

race, 102, 207, 210, 218, 235
Racine, J., 121
radical/ism, 52, 82, 89, 95, 97, 102, 106, 117, 123, 124, 133, 222, 245, 248, 257, 262
radical democracy, 5, 97,

98, 243
railway construction, 45, 53, 157, 159, 182, 186, 209, 234
Rankin, Arthur, 91
Rao, Subba, Mr. Justice, 232
Rassemblement pour l'Indépendance nationale (RIN), 238
Räte, 241, 246, 258
Rathenau, W., 113
ratification, 92, 241
rationalization movement, 161
raw materials, 180
Reagan, Ronald, 128, 240
real socialism, 115, 258
Realpolitik, 19, 249
reason of state, 21, 23
Rebellions of 1837, 91, 92, 216, 233
recall, 90, 97, 98, 234
Reciprocity Treaty, 42
red scare, 80
red Tory, 208
redistribution, 164, 166, 248
referendum, 50, 66, 84, 91, 94, 95, 96, 97, 100, 101, 102, 104, 207, 213, 220, 227, 234, 239, 240, 259
Reflections of a Non-political Man, 136
Reflections on the Revolution in France, 24
Reform Bill, 74
regime, 121, 125, 130, 147
Regina Manifesto, the, 51, 235
region/alism, 40, 50, 51, 53, 59, 96, 148, 150, 159, 165, 168, 170, 172, 174, 212, 213, 225, 226, 227, 231, 232, 234, 239, 240, 242, 243
regulation, 112, 139, 143, 164, 166, 170
Reich, 22, 125
relations of production, 121, 123, 124, 129

relative autonomy, 114, 117, 133, 184
religion, 23, 25, 26, 37, 44, 47, 54, 60, 99, 118, 119, 121, 122, 127, 137, 207, 209, 216, 218, 220, 232, 233, 235
representation/ive, 6, 8, 23, 24, 25, 26, 27, 28, 32, 33, 34, 37, 73, 74, 77, 78, 81, 88–92, 95, 96, 98, 101, 103, 104, 106, 145, 147, 169, 171, 222, 223, 226, 230, 245, 248, 250, 252, 259
repression, 117, 130, 169, 248, 249
republic, 14, 15, 18, 40, 42, 43, 52, 55, 72, 74, 106, 128, 136, 150, 153, 222, 223, 224, 225, 226, 230, 231, 234, 252, 253, 254
Republic, The, 14, 17, 249
republican/ism, 6, 13, 14, 17–19, 21, 24, 25, 26, 39, 54, 55, 60, 76, 79, 82, 83, 85, 86, 97, 106, 110, 223, 227, 251
Republican party, 232
res publica, 30, 54, 252
research, 161, 167, 172, 174
residents' association, 102
Resistance, 121
resources, 50, 68, 125, 128, 157, 160, 172, 173, 179, 187, 188, 195, 211, 212, 214, 232, 239
responsible government, 93
restructuring, 135, 178, 196, 262
retrenchment, 141
revenue, 25
revolution, 16, 18, 26, 33, 41, 42, 43, 52, 96, 112, 144, 213, 224, 225, 226, 227, 233, 241, 242, 246, 248, 258
revolutionary, 39, 40, 44, 45, 54, 71, 72, 112, 125, 147, 246, 253, 254

revolutionary syndicalism, 245
Ricardo, David, 26
Rice, James, 140
rich, 32, 78
Richelieu, Cardinal, 21
Riel, Louis, 217
right, 69, 122, 132, 144, 145, 146, 246, 247
rights, 54, 94, 96, 132, 137, 148, 149, 150, 261
rights of man, 39, 226
riot, 217
Rioux, Marcel, 72
Robertson, Gideon, 62
Robespierre, Maximilien, 37, 39, 226, 242
Roblin, Rodmond, 97
Rocher, Guy, 72
Roland, 227
Roman Empire, 31, 54
Rome, 14, 15, 17, 30, 54, 74, 112, 120, 222, 223, 251, 252, 253, 254
Roosevelt, F.D., 46, 57
Rose, R., and G. Peters, 147
Ross, John, 91
Rousseau, Jean-Jacques, 6, 27, 31–3, 34, 37, 40, 87, 88–91, 93, 95–106, 110, 118, 119, 149, 150, 200, 223–4, 251, 252, 255, 286 n 7, 288 n 54
Rowthorn, Bob, 202
Royal Bank of Canada, 189
Royal Commission on Bilingualism and Biculturalism, 238
Royal Commission on Dominion-Provincial Relations (Rowell-Sirois) 56, 153, 163, 208, 235, 236
Royal Commission on the Economic Union and Development Prospects for Canada. See Macdonald Commission
ruling class, 3, 16, 33, 44, 115, 116, 194

Russia, 15, 16, 41, 112, 130, 157, 181, 184, 201, 208, 216, 229
Russian Revolution, 34, 227, 230, 248, 258

sacred, 78
safety net, 169
St Augustine, 19, 20, 253
St-Just, 39, 40, 226
St Laurent, Louis, 49
San Francisco, 63
sans-culottes, 32, 37, 40, 92, 227
Sartori, G., 241
Sartre, Jean-Paul, 251
Saskatchewan, 103, 104, 176, 189, 237, 239
Sawer, Geoffrey, 232
Say, 26
Schmidt, Helmut, 117
Schmitt, Carl, 3, 19, 22, 37, 117–18, 119, 130, 147
Schumpeter, Joseph, 16, 93, 148, 241, 246
science, 114, 155, 156, 161, 167, 171, 200, 202, 248, 251
secession, 40, 147, 230
second chamber, 85
Second World War, 6, 48, 53, 56, 57, 63, 83, 112, 113, 121, 126, 127, 163–4, 177, 179, 187, 209, 211, 213, 214, 232
secondary sector, 171, 188
Secretary of State, Department of, 60
sectional democracy, 32, 92, 227
sections (Paris), 40, 241, 258
self-determination, 100, 116, 229, 238
self-government, 57, 97, 102, 183, 213
self-government of the producers, 33, 34, 228, 229, 245, 250, 255
self-interest, 142, 143
self-management, 35, 230

semi-industrial, 187
semi-periphery, 7, 39, 154, 157, 164, 179–204, 209, 211, 213, 234
Sen, G., 185
senate, 18, 19, 74, 78, 80, 81, 83, 85, 151, 233
Senate, Roman, 14, 17
Seneca, 29
separation of powers, 18, 24, 36, 73–4, 76, 82–3, 86–7, 128, 223, 225, 228, 244, 254
separatism, 49, 229, 240
serfdom, 133
servants, 23
service sector, 180, 183, 196
settler society, 71, 156
sexuality, 118, 253
Shaftesbury, 86
Shonfield, Andrew, 114, 166, 303 n 68
Shortt, Adam, 56
Siegfried, André, 207, 210, 216, 217, 218
Skelton, O.D., 95
Skocpol, Theda, 124
slave(ry), 23, 30, 32, 45, 181, 228
small business, 165, 177
Smith, Adam, 24, 26, 193
Smith, Dennis, 72, 287 n 34
Smith, Peter, 47
social contract, 4, 26
Social Contract, The, 32, 119, 224, 251
Social Credit, 97, 103
Social Darwinism, 16, 118
social democracy, 8, 51, 67, 98, 99, 114, 128, 132, 143, 144, 146, 152, 168, 221, 229, 234, 237, 239, 245, 246–8, 260
social force, 4, 121, 131, 159, 212
Social Planning for Canada, 51, 62
social policy, 134, 186, 214
Social Purpose for Canada,

237
social science(s), 3, 38, 56,
  65, 67, 109, 120, 123, 132,
  154
social scientists, 38, 64, 68,
  76, 91, 134, 208
social security, 128, 140,
  163, 165, 169, 177, 212,
  218, 232
social services, 103, 141,
  145, 147, 153, 168, 177,
  247
social spending, 53, 115,
  121, 129, 140, 141, 142,
  143, 146, 151, 159, 162,
  164, 168, 169, 171, 174,
  177, 192, 236
socialism, 5, 8, 26, 48, 51,
  53, 62, 98, 104, 113, 115,
  117, 119, 123, 125, 128,
  129, 131, 133, 144, 152,
  164, 221-44, 245-63; definition, 256
socialization, 51, 139, 164,
  247, 256
société d'état, 67
Société générale de
  financement, 174
Société St-Jean Baptiste,
  218
society/social, 3, 4, 26, 31,
  32, 33, 34, 36, 38, 40, 45,
  49, 52, 54, 72, 91, 99, 102,
  103, 105, 106, 109, 110,
  112, 123, 127, 129, 132,
  133, 134, 135, 137, 139,
  143, 146, 147, 148, 150,
  151, 155, 162, 169, 170,
  174, 178, 180, 196, 201,
  209, 216, 217, 218, 226,
  227, 230, 231, 235, 237,
  240, 250, 254, 257, 259,
  260, 261, 263
society-centred, 135
sociology, 3, 67, 74, 75, 110,
  115, 120, 219
Socrates, 29
soldiers, 31, 45
solidarity, 142, 170, 260,
  262
Solidarity, 148, 258,

261
Solon, 30
Sombart, Werner, 115
Sophocles, 115
Sorel, Georges, 23
Sorokin, Pitrim, 112
sovereign/sovereignty, 7,
  19, 21, 23, 27, 32, 36, 41,
  42, 53, 54, 55, 56, 60, 62,
  63, 64, 66, 68, 69, 79, 81,
  88-106, 110, 115-17, 123,
  124, 125, 126, 127, 129,
  130, 133, 135, 136, 139,
  147, 149, 151, 152, 179,
  180, 185, 186, 188, 200-3,
  208, 209, 213, 214, 219,
  220, 224, 225, 228, 230,
  233, 252, 253, 260. See
  also parliamentary sov-
  ereignty; popular sovereignty
sovereignty-association,
  50, 100, 207, 220
soviet(s), 34, 241, 246, 248,
  258, 259, 261
Soviet, 34, 36, 113, 129, 201,
  230, 231, 248, 249, 258,
  259
Sozialistische Partei
  Deutschlands (SPD), 113,
  155, 232, 246, 247
Sparta, 19, 222, 252
Spartacus, 23
speech, 24, 28, 134, 217,
  248
Spencer, Herbert,
  110
Spirit of the Laws, The, 16,
  72, 73, 223, 251
spontaneity, 250, 255
Spry, Graham, 62
Staat, 109
stabilization, 156, 164,
  167-71, 172
Stalin, Joseph, 36, 117, 230,
  248, 249, 252
Stalinism, 119, 129, 253
Stände, 54
staples, 38, 39, 157, 168,
  181, 182, 183, 184, 195,
  215

state, 1-37, 38-53, 54-70,
  72, 74, 75, 80, 86, 90, 93,
  97, 98, 99, 105, 106,
  109-31, 132-52, 153-78,
  179, 180, 181, 183, 184,
  185, 187, 189, 200, 201,
  202, 203, 204, 207-20,
  221, 222, 223, 228, 229,
  230, 231, 232, 236, 238,
  241, 242, 243, 245-63;
  definition, 255-6
State and Revolution, 248,
  255
state capitalism, 68
state enterprise, 50, 68,
  127, 157, 159, 186, 189,
  256
state expenditures, 46,
  110, 111, 112, 115, 124-8,
  133, 139, 140, 141, 145,
  147, 153, 159, 161, 164,
  165, 169, 173, 219, 236
state ideological appara-
  tus, 138
State in Peace and War, The,
  61
state monopoly capital-
  ism, 113, 114, 156
state of nature, 21, 37
state ownership, 247
state rights, 41, 225,
  228
state sector, 55, 137, 216
state socialism, 4, 123, 245,
  246, 251, 257, 259, 261,
  262
State and Society in the Modern Era, 133
state-building, 6, 52, 67,
  68, 234
state-centred, 135, 208
statecraft, 20, 23, 202
state-society relations,
  133, 135, 136-7, 148, 154
statism, 26, 104, 115, 120,
  122, 126, 145, 168, 173,
  231, 255, 257, 259
Statistics Canada, 56, 176,
  191
status, 80
Statute of Westminster,

57, 185, 209
Strachan, Bishop John, 43,
  44
stratification, 111
Strayer, J.R., 4
strong state, 136, 186
student(s), 34, 100, 102,
  117, 121, 238, 245, 249
Students for a Democratic
  Society, 102
Studies in Political Economy,
  68
Suez, 127
suffrage, 33, 73, 97, 228
Supek, Rudi, 119
superstructure, 115, 121,
  122, 132, 254, 257
Supreme Court, 69, 79, 83,
  84, 148, 220, 225, 232
Supreme Soviet, 230
survivance, la, 215
symbolism, 49, 59, 91, 118,
  119, 133, 136, 148, 185,
  193, 208, 209, 210, 211,
  213, 247, 256, 261

tariff, 154, 157, 158, 182,
  183, 186, 201
Taschereau, Alexandre,
  99, 215
Task Force on Canadian
  Unity, 85
tax/taxation, 45, 46, 61, 66,
  139, 140, 145, 146, 160,
  165, 167, 173, 236
Taylor, Charles, 35, 149–50,
  152, 268 n 60
technocratic, 98
technology, 52, 155, 156,
  165, 166, 171, 172, 178,
  182, 183, 185, 192, 195,
  200, 202, 243, 248, 262
technostructure, 261
territory, 47, 115, 124, 147,
  156, 160, 200, 223, 226,
  230, 233, 241, 242
terror, 43
tertiary sector, 188
Thatcher, Margaret, 127,
  199
Thebes, 222

theories of the state,
  13–37, 99, 109, 130, 131,
  246, 247, 250, 251, 253,
  254, 290 n 2
thin concept of citizen-
  ship, 148, 151
third estate, 226
Third International, 113,
  133
third option, 199
Third Republic, 201
Third World, 116, 175, 178,
  182, 198, 208, 216, 231,
  249, 250, 257
Thomism, 72
Throne Speech, 58, 79
Thucydides, 19, 29, 36, 251
Tilley, Leonard, 55, 59, 92
Tilly, Charles, 4
Tirpitz, Admiral von, 122
Titmuss, Richard, 111, 142
Tito, 231, 252
Tocqueville, Alexis de, 41,
  75, 137, 214, 226, 283 n 21
Todd, Alpheus, 79
Toronto, 158
Tory(ism), 38, 39, 40, 42,
  43, 44, 45, 47, 49, 52, 77,
  83, 208, 209
Tory Jacobinism, 39, 40, 44
totalitarianism, 112, 133
Toulon, 42
trade, 141, 155, 160, 165,
  168, 170, 173, 181, 184,
  186, 187, 188, 192, 194,
  197, 211, 227
trade unions, 48, 50, 62,
  80, 100, 125, 140, 144,
  145, 156, 159, 163, 165,
  192, 211, 238, 247, 258,
  259, 261
trading regime, 193
tradition, 41, 44, 95, 120,
  121, 122, 124, 126, 153,
  214, 217, 218, 233, 242,
  257, 258
Trans-Canada Pipeline,
  173
Treaty of Versailles, 62, 125
treaty-making power, 182,
  185

Treitschke, 41
Tremblay Commission, 65
tribal nationalism, 49
tribes, 29, 74, 256
tribunes, 15, 17, 74
Trilateral Commission,
  102, 137, 138, 257
tripartism, 133, 143, 144,
  146
Trotsky, Leon, 39, 252
Trudeau, Pierre Elliott,
  49–51, 64, 67, 83, 84,
  93–4, 101, 117, 145, 148,
  173, 213, 218, 224, 235,
  237, 239, 240, 241
trusts, 155, 156, 158, 165,
  234
tsar/ist, 15, 16, 201
Two Treatises on Government,
  23, 24
tyranny, 17, 25, 29, 90, 105,
  137, 226

ultramontanism, 77, 95,
  99, 218
Underhill, Frank, 71, 91
UN Centre/Report on
  Transnational Corpora-
  tions, 189, 190, 195
UN Declaration of Human
  Rights, 148
uneven development,
  130
unemployment, 140, 141,
  144, 162, 196, 262
unemployment insurance,
  48, 52, 140, 141, 144, 155,
  162, 196, 262
ungovernability, 257
Union government, 60
Union Jack, 43
Union nationale, 65
Union of Soviet Socialist
  Republics, 230, 258
Union of Utrecht, 222
unitary state, 242, 243
United Empire Loyalists,
  38, 44
United Farmers of
  Alberta, 97
United Nations, 57, 63,

188, 194, 197, 200, 201,
211
universal suffrage, 33, 77,
85, 92
universality, 143
university, 171, 172, 218
University of Toronto, 68,
95, 134
Upper Canada, 60
upper house, 81, 85
utopia(n), 123, 260, 261

Valmy, 43, 46
Vancouver, 103
Vander Zalm, Bill, 240
vanguard party, 16, 34,
250, 253, 255, 257
Vendée, la, 42
Verney, Douglas, 68
Vertical Mosaic, The, 237
veto, 75, 97
viceroy, 79
Victoria, Queen, 79
Vietnam War, 128, 141, 193,
238, 252
Vile, M.J.C., 73
violence, 147
virtù, 254
virtue, 17, 24, 30, 32, 44, 75,
76, 90, 223
vote, 92, 93, 95, 96
voter, 34

Waffle, 238
wage(s), 155, 169, 181, 182,
183, 239, 258
wage and price controls,
49–50, 145, 163, 167, 170,
176, 243
Wagner, Adolph, 110–11,
130, 153
Wagner Act, 163
Wallerstein, Immanuel, 7,
116, 180, 181, 194, 199,
209, 214, 307 n 8, 310
n 38, 313 n 106
war, 21, 22, 27, 39, 41, 44,
45, 46, 48, 51, 52, 61, 94,
111, 112, 113, 123, 128,
132, 134, 140, 141, 156,

159, 160, 161, 164, 168,
174, 178, 184, 185, 186,
200, 201, 211, 231, 236
War Measures Act, 46, 238
War of 1812, 42
War Supply Board, 163
ward, 35, 106, 224, 241
warlord, 260
Wartime Price and Trade
Board, 163
Washington, 173, 200
Watkins, Frederick, 63
Watkins, Mel, 68, 308 n 17,
n 20
Watkins Report, 238
Watson, John, 61
weak state, 186–7, 214
wealth, 24, 30, 31, 32, 46,
75, 78, 88, 90, 145, 158,
203, 248, 250
Weber, Max, 13, 110, 118,
120, 123, 130
Weimar Republic, 3, 121,
147, 155, 156, 231, 246
welfare, 28, 111, 133, 139,
140, 141, 142, 148, 159,
167, 170, 202, 236, 247,
250
welfare state, 4, 48, 51, 67,
132, 133, 139, 140, 141,
142, 152, 156, 163,
169–70, 171, 196, 211,
245, 258, 260, 262, 304
n 79
western Canada, 45, 53, 77,
96–9, 161, 234, 239, 240
Westminster, 50, 92
What Is to Be Done?, 16
Wheare, K.C., 232
Whig, 83
Whitaker, Reg, 72
White Paper on Employ-
ment and Income,
164–5, 168, 170
White Paper on Sover-
eignty-Association, 66
White Russia, 230
white settler dominion, 71,
183, 185
Whitehall, 127

Wilhelm, Kaiser, 125
Wilkins, Mira, 184
Williams, Cynthia, 132,
137, 148
Williams, Glen, 195
Wilson, Bertha, Mme Jus-
tice, 69
Wilson, Harold, 172
Wilson, Michael, 177
Winnipeg General Strike,
62, 72
Winnipeg Manifesto, 237
withering away of the
state, 33, 123, 125, 129,
130, 229, 248, 251, 255
Wolfe, David, 145–6
women, 30, 97, 102, 161,
250, 261
Wood, H.W., 97
Woodsworth, J.S., 93
work, 26, 229
work camps, 46
worker(s), 80, 90, 102, 104,
105, 117, 137, 166, 246,
250, 258, 259
worker control, 34, 102,
104, 105, 151, 231, 250,
260, 261, 290 n 79
working class, 16, 28, 62,
113, 121, 125, 155, 156,
212, 221, 229, 233, 235,
243, 246, 247, 261
Workman's Compensation
Act, 159
World Bank, 193, 200
world (capitalist) system,
8, 125, 129
world economy, 164, 166,
181, 187, 193, 194, 239,
240
world-spirit, 19, 22
written constitution, 83

Young, Walter, 93
youth, 102
Ypres, 46

Zeus, 29
Zurich, 223
Zwangsökonomie, 112, 160